METROPOLITAN COLLEGE OF NY
LIBRARY, 12TH FLOOR
431 CANAL STREET
NEW YORK, NY 10013

PLAINS HISTORIES

John R. Wunder
Series Editor

Editorial Board
Durwood Ball
Peter Boag
Pekka Hämäläinen
Jorge Iber
Todd M. Kerstetter
Clara Sue Kidwell
Patricia Nelson Limerick
Victoria Smith
Donald E. Worster

Also in Plains Histories

America's 100th Meridian: A Plains Journey, *by Monte Hartman*

American Outback: The Oklahoma Panhandle in the Twentieth Century, *by Richard Lowitt*

As a Farm Woman Thinks: Life and Land on the Texas High Plains, 1890–1960, *by Nellie Witt Spikes; edited by Geoff Cunfer*

Children of the Dust, *by Betty Grant Henshaw; edited by Sandra Scofield*

The Death of Raymond Yellow Thunder: And Other True Stories from the Nebraska–Pine Ridge Border Towns, *by Stew Magnuson*

From Syria to Seminole: Memoir of a High Plains Merchant, *by Ed Aryain; edited by J'Nell Pate*

"I Do Not Apologize for the Length of This Letter": The Mari Sandoz Letters on Native American Rights, 1940–1965, *edited by Kimberli A. Lee*

Indigenous Albuquerque, *by Myla Vicenti Carpio*

Nikkei Farmer on the Nebraska Plains: A Memoir, *by The Reverend Hisanori Kano; edited by Tai Kreidler*

The Notorious Dr. Flippin: Abortion and Consequence in the Early Twentieth Century, *by Jamie Q. Tallman*

Oysters, Macaroni, and Beer: Thurber, Texas, and the Company Store, *by Gene Rhea Tucker*

Railwayman's Son: A Plains Family Memoir, *by Hugh Hawkins*

Rights in the Balance: Free Press, Fair Trial, and *Nebraska Press Association v. Stuart*, *by Mark R. Scherer*

Ruling Pine Ridge: Oglala Lakota Politics from the IRA to Wounded Knee, *by Akim D. Reinhardt*

Where the West Begins: Debating Texas Identity, *by Glen Sample Ely*

Women on the North American Plains, *edited by Renee M. Laegreid and Sandra K. Mathews*

FREE RADICAL

METROPOLITAN COLLEGE OF NY
LIBRARY, 12TH FLOOR
431 CANAL STREET
NEW YORK, NY 10013

F 670.4
.C53
A75
2012

FREE RADICAL

Ernest Chambers, Black Power, and the Politics of Race

Tekla Agbala Ali Johnson

Foreword by Quintard Taylor

Texas Tech University Press

METROPOLITAN COLLEGE OF NY
LIBRARY, 12TH FLOOR
431 CANAL STREET
NEW YORK, NY 10013

Copyright © 2012 by Tekla Agbala Ali Johnson

All rights reserved. No portion of this book may be reproduced in any form or by any means, including electronic storage and retrieval systems, except by explicit prior written permission of the publisher. Brief passages excerpted for review and critical purposes are excepted.

This book is typeset in Scala. The paper used in this book meets the minimum requirements of ANSI/NISO Z39.48–1992 (R1997). ∞

Designed by Kasey McBeath
Cover photographs reprinted by permission of the *Lincoln Journal Star* and the *Omaha World-Herald*

Library of Congress Cataloging-in-Publication Data
Ali Johnson, Tekla Agbala, 1965–
 Ernest Chambers, Black Power, and the politics of race / Tekla Agbala Ali Johnson ; foreword by Quintard Taylor.
  p. cm. — (Plains histories)
 Includes bibliographical references and index.
 Summary: "A political biography of Nebraska state senator Ernest (Ernie) Chambers, investigating the tumultuous local and national political climate for African Americans from the late twentieth century to today"—Provided by publisher.
 ISBN 978-0-89672-729-8 (hardcover : alk. paper) — ISBN 978-0-89672-761-8 (e-book)
 1. Chambers, Ernest William, 1937– 2. Black power—Nebraska—History. 3. Nebraska—Politics and government. 4. African Americans—Nebraska—Omaha—Politics and government. 5. African Americans—Politics and government. 6. Legislators—Nebraska—Biography. 7. African American legislators—Nebraska—Biography. 8. Nebraska. Legislature. Senate—Biography. I. Title.
 F670.4.C53A75 2012
 328.73'092—dc23
 [B]   2012023334

Printed in the United States of America
12 13 14 15 16 17 18 19 20 / 9 8 7 6 5 4 3 2 1

Texas Tech University Press
Box 41037 | Lubbock, Texas 79409–1037 USA
800.832.4042 | ttup@ttu.edu | www.ttupress.org

For Great Grandmother Jane Witherspoon, who purchased land in Arkansas after the American Civil War during the aftermath of slavery, Grandmother Enora Witherspoon, who held the land for us, and for Grandma Hazel May Grant Mead

Free radical: (noun)

"An especially reactive atom or group of atoms that has one or more unpaired electrons."

Merriam-Webster Dictionary

"An atom or group of atoms containing at least one unpaired electron and existing for a brief period of time before reacting to produce a stable molecule."

World English Dictionary

"Because of their odd electrons, free radicals are usually highly reactive. Certain free radicals are stabilized by their peculiar structure; they exist for appreciable lengths of time, given the right conditions. Most free radicals . . . are capable of only the most fleeting independent existence."

Encyclopedia Britannica

CONTENTS

Illustrations xiii
Plainsword xv
Prologue xxi

Introduction 3

1 Education of a "Radical" 7

2 Man of the People 41

3 Grounded Politician 65

4 The Power of One 97

5 Statecraft 127

6 "Defender of the Downtrodden" 155

7 "Dean" 185

Afterword 221
Acknowledgments 223
Notes 227
Index 269

ILLUSTRATIONS, following p. 154

Map of Legislative District 11 in Omaha

Funeral of Vivian Strong at Greater Bethlehem Temple in Omaha

Aerial view of North 24th Street in Omaha during the uprising that followed Vivian Strong's death

Chambers arrested by Omaha police

Dan Goodwin's Spencer Street Barbershop

Chambers's victory celebration after he was elected to the Nebraska state legislature

"Happy Birthday Senator Chambers"

Chambers and fellow Senator Terry Carpenter

Senators Chambers and John DeCamp survey a Nebraska farm

Chambers and son David in the Nebraska Statehouse

Barbara Kelley and Chambers lead a protest

Lincolnites register to vote

Chambers takes the oath of office again

Anti-apartheid speech at the University of Nebraska

Chambers and Mel Beckman look at "electric chair"

Chambers wearing a "Reagan Hood: from the needy to the greedy" T-shirt

Demonstration by North Omahans on the steps of the Douglas County Courthouse

Cartoon by Paul Fell

Chambers and two new friends at the Million Man March in Washington, D.C.

Mock funeral in North Omaha

Cynthia Grandberry and Nicole

Chambers speaking at the United Nations

PLAINSWORD

Ernie Chambers and the Struggle for Racial Justice in Nebraska

For thirty-eight years Senator Ernie Chambers represented the Eleventh Legislative District in Omaha in Nebraska's unicameral legislature. This was the area where Malcolm X was born in 1925. The two men met briefly when Malcolm visited Omaha in 1964. That district in North Omaha was in many ways a classic ghetto before, during, and after Chambers's many years in office. Chambers recognized and fought against its ghetto-like conditions that stemmed from unemployment, poverty, and crime, but he also saw North Omaha as the home of 34,431 African Americans who comprised ten percent of Omaha's population and two percent of Nebraska's people in 1970, the year he was first elected. Tekla Ali Johnson's *Free Radical: Ernest Chambers, Black Power, and the Politics of Race* explores the world and the worldview of Ernie Chambers.

Chambers's North Omaha was over a century old when he was elected. Its evolution into Nebraska's only sizeable African American community began around the time the state entered the Union in 1867. That year St. John's African Methodist Episcopal (AME) Church was organized, followed by the African Baptist Church in 1874. Zion Baptist, which dates to 1884, became the city's largest African American church by the first decade of the twentieth century. By 1890 Omaha's black community had a Colored Women's Club and the state's first black-owned hotel. On July 3–4, 1894, Omaha's African Americans organized the nation's first Afro-American fair, featuring exhibits mounted by Nebraska's urban and rural black residents.

In 1900, most of Omaha's 3,443 blacks worked as janitors, maids, and porters, but some held jobs in railroad construction, the city's stockyards, and the meatpacking industry. Major firms used African American workers as part of the "reserve army" of strikebreakers. The Union Pacific, for example, introduced black strikebreakers into the region during the 1877 railroad strike. Seventeen years later the major packing companies, Swift, Hammond, Cudahy, and Omaha, used blacks to break a strike. Not all African Americans were anti-union, however. Black Omaha barbers, for example, organized the first African American labor union in the city in 1887 and went on strike because they deemed it "unprofessional" to work beside white competitors. In a city where race and ethnicity defined worker solidarity as much as class, such a development is not surprising.

Omaha's African Americans were politically active even before Nebraska's admission to the Union. In January 1867, the U.S. Congress passed the Territorial Suffrage Act, giving African American males the right to vote. Blacks in Nebraska Territory, Colorado Territory, and other western territories were guaranteed suffrage months before similar rights were extended to African Americans in the southern states and three years before ratification of the Fifteenth Amendment ensured similar rights for African American males in northern and western states.

Political leadership in the city fell to recently arrived southern-born migrants such as Cyrus D. Bell, a newspaper employee, and E. R. Overall, a postal worker, until Dr. Moses O. Ricketts spoke for the community as president of the Colored Republican organization. In 1884, Ricketts became the first African American to graduate from the University of Nebraska College of Medicine. Eight years later, in 1892, he entered the Nebraska state legislature, where he served two terms. Ricketts was elected seventy-eight years before Ernie Chambers took his seat in that same legislature.

Active in the unicameral legislature, Senator Ricketts, a noted orator, introduced bills to legalize interracial marriages and prohibit racial discrimination in public services. The second measure was designed to strengthen Nebraska's 1885 civil rights law.

Ricketts in the 1890s and Chambers nearly a century later were part of a movement by western African Americans to use their votes in defense of their rights. That determination was evident as early as 1866 when African American men meeting in Lawrence, Kansas, 160 miles south of Omaha, let their political views be known in a statewide convention that challenged the then widely held idea that black voting was a privilege that the white male electorate could embrace or reject at its pleasure. The 1866 convention declared it would be a "constant trouble" in Kansas until equal justice became standard. Those words of warning could very well have been issued by black Omaha's most famous native-born resident, Malcolm X, or by Ernie Chambers, who through his ideas, ideals, and actions, became that "constant trouble" in the late twentieth century.

Many nineteenth- and early twentieth-century city residents recall an Omaha where the black community was more residentially dispersed than in the post–World War I period. Josie McCulloch, who grew up in the city in the 1870s and 1880s, recalled the "Swedish, Bohemian, Italian, Irish and Negro children" who played together and "contributed to the process of Americanization." Residential integration, however, did not eliminate racial antipathy or violence. In 1891, a black man, Joe Coe, was accused of assaulting a five-year-old white child, Lizzie Yates. After hearing an erroneous report that the Yates girl had died, a mob of several hundred people overwhelmed the police force at the county jail, seized Coe, and beat him as they dragged him through the streets. Coe was probably already dead when his body was hung from an electric trolley wire in downtown Omaha. Mayor Richard C. Cushing condemned the lynching as "the most deplorable thing that has ever occurred in the history of the county"—but no members of the mob were brought to trial.

Twenty-eight years later one of the most horrific scenes of racial violence anywhere on the North American continent occurred during the Omaha Courthouse Riot. This infamous incident was part of the wave of racial and labor violence that swept the United States during the "Red Summer" of 1919. As in the nation at large, it was a turning point in the history of Omaha's black community.

During the late summer of 1919, Omaha daily newspapers carried lurid, sensational accounts of attacks by African American males on white women, without similar coverage of assaults on African American women by either black or white males. After one particularly provocative story in September 1919, Will Brown, an African American man, was arrested and held in the Douglas County Courthouse. Largely due to the newspaper story, a mob gathered. Omaha Mayor Edward P. Smith was nearly lynched himself when he unsuccessfully attempted to disperse the crowd. Then the mob, estimated at well over 4,000, broke into the recently constructed courthouse, dragged Brown out and hanged him on a nearby lamppost, riddled his body with bullets, and then burned the corpse. In its fury the mob destroyed the Douglas County Courthouse.

Although some of the leaders of the lynching were placed on trial, most received suspended sentences, or were convicted of minor offenses such as destruction of public property. One of the thousands of witnesses to the lynching was a young Henry Fonda, who vowed from that point to work for equal rights and against racial intolerance.

The Courthouse Riot and the doubling of the black population in the city over the previous decade led to greater residential segregation. Redlining and race-restrictive covenants squeezed newcomers and old residents into a denser North Omaha. In the early years of this segregation, the Near Northside developed a thriving business community with over one hundred black-owned businesses as well as physicians, dentists, attorneys, and other professionals who provided services to thousands of African American meatpackers. White and black labor leaders in that industry created the racially integrated Meatpacking Workers of America, which, in turn, joined forces with organizations like the De Porres Club to support the desegregation of public facilities through the 1950s and 1960s. Racial segregation also created a vibrant African American musical and entertainment culture symbolized by the Dreamland Ballroom, which opened in 1923, eventually hosting Duke Ellington, Count Basie, Louis Armstrong, and Lionel Hampton.

This was the black Omaha of Ernie Chambers's youth. The African American Omaha of his adult life, including the decades he would serve as the only black member of the legislature, was a community in decline. By the late 1960s the meatpacking industry and the railroads, historically two of the largest employers of black labor, began to shed workers. North Omaha was devastated by these changes as the loss of jobs meant rising long-term unemployment, family disintegration, rising crime, and acute poverty. When Ernie Chambers entered the legislature in 1970, black Omaha had already been racked by the riots of the 1960s, which in hindsight were a response to economic decline rather than a cause as many observers then incorrectly concluded. When Chambers left office in 2008, black Omaha had the fifth highest black poverty rate in the nation. One-third of Omahans lived below the poverty line, including nearly sixty percent of its children.

Ernie Chambers and most of his constituents were not aware of the subtle yet profound economic changes affecting North Omaha. With the possible exception of Omaha resident Warren Buffett, those who orchestrated the changes lived far from Nebraska. It is doubtful that any individual state senator or even state legislature could have prevented this process. Chambers instead focused on what he thought was possible, relief and justice for his constituency, the poor of North Omaha. As Tekla Agbala Ali Johnson describes, he did so as a firm believer in Black Nationalism and Black Power, which set him apart, especially by the 1980s, from virtually every African American political figure in the nation. For Chambers, defending the Nation of Islam and the Black Panther Party from police harassment, demanding that district elections replace at-large elections (which had historically prevented black politicians from rising to power), and persuading the Nebraska legislature to be the first in the nation to endorse the divestment of state funds from corporations that did business in South Africa were acts of faith to his constituents who responded by reelecting him a record eighteen times.

As Ali Johnson captures so well in *Free Radical,* Ernie Chambers was an enigma. He held a law degree from Creighton University but never practiced and never joined the Nebraska Bar Association. Instead he continued to work as a barber in his Near Northside shop for most of his adult life. While his speeches throughout his career were laced with militant and at times violent rhetoric (he said in 1966, "Someone will have to blow up downtown Omaha to convince the white power structure that we mean business"), Chambers rejected all justifications for violence including those for war, except in self-defense. In fact he became a national leader in the campaign against capital punishment. He even opposed the whipping of children and fought to ban corporal punishment in schools. Chambers prided himself on support from and defense of radical groups such as the Black Panther Party. Yet he rejected Marxism and never joined or supported revolutionary groups. Instead Chambers often perceived himself as the last hope for reforming the political and economic system.

Through it all, Ernie Chambers placed his loyalty to his North Omaha constituents and his desire to address their particular problems above all else—including lobbyists who could have made him a wealthy man, the Democratic Party which could have supported his higher political aspirations, and middle-class and corporate supporters who would have easily bankrolled his numerous political campaigns. Chambers paid an enormous personal and political price for that unwavering loyalty as "defender of the downtrodden" as he would describe himself. Yet, because he willingly accepted and at times welcomed the consequences of his stand, he became Nebraska's most significant twentieth-century profile in political courage.

Quintard Taylor
Scott and Dorothy Bullitt Professor of American History
University of Washington

PROLOGUE

On April 15, 2006, the *New York Times* ran a story by Sam Dillon entitled "Law to Segregate Omaha Schools Divides Nebraska." It was true, a school reorganization bill had polarized the city of Omaha and divided the African American community internally, as well as expanded fractures in the politics of the larger white population. The pandemonium began with a simple act: Senator Ernie Chambers attached an amendment to a school district reorganization bill (LB 1024), sponsored by his colleague Ron Raikes. Raikes hoped to restructure the large Omaha Public School (OPS) District in order to make it more manageable and to improve overall student performance. The bill drew Chambers's eye because he had long wanted to change OPS, which was stricken with notoriously low success rates for low-income and African American students, and about which critics alluded to as serving more as a feeder for the city's gangs or life among the urban poor than as a stepping-stone to higher education. Chambers's amendment would divide the district into three smaller units. But it was the provision in his one-and-a-half page amendment to add district elections for school board members in each of the new divisions that created the uproar. One of Chambers's oldest friends called the measure a "disaster" and wondered whether the senator had lost his bearings with age.

Triggered by opposition from a few wealthy Omahans, the local press had a field day with the amendment. Encouraged by the new president of the Omaha NAACP and OPS administrators (who fought the bill tooth and nail), the national NAACP filed a lawsuit against Chambers for trying to segregate Omaha's public schools. Overnight, Chambers became known to the nation as an inverse racist—an African American "segregationist."

If there was any logic to Chambers's actions, it was lost on a few vocal members of the African American middle class, influential personas among Omaha's educated black elite. Strangely, Chambers's base, the African American working class in Omaha's Near Northside, stood stalwart, trusting that he was acting in their best interest and refusing to desert their senator and spokesman of three decades.

FREE RADICAL

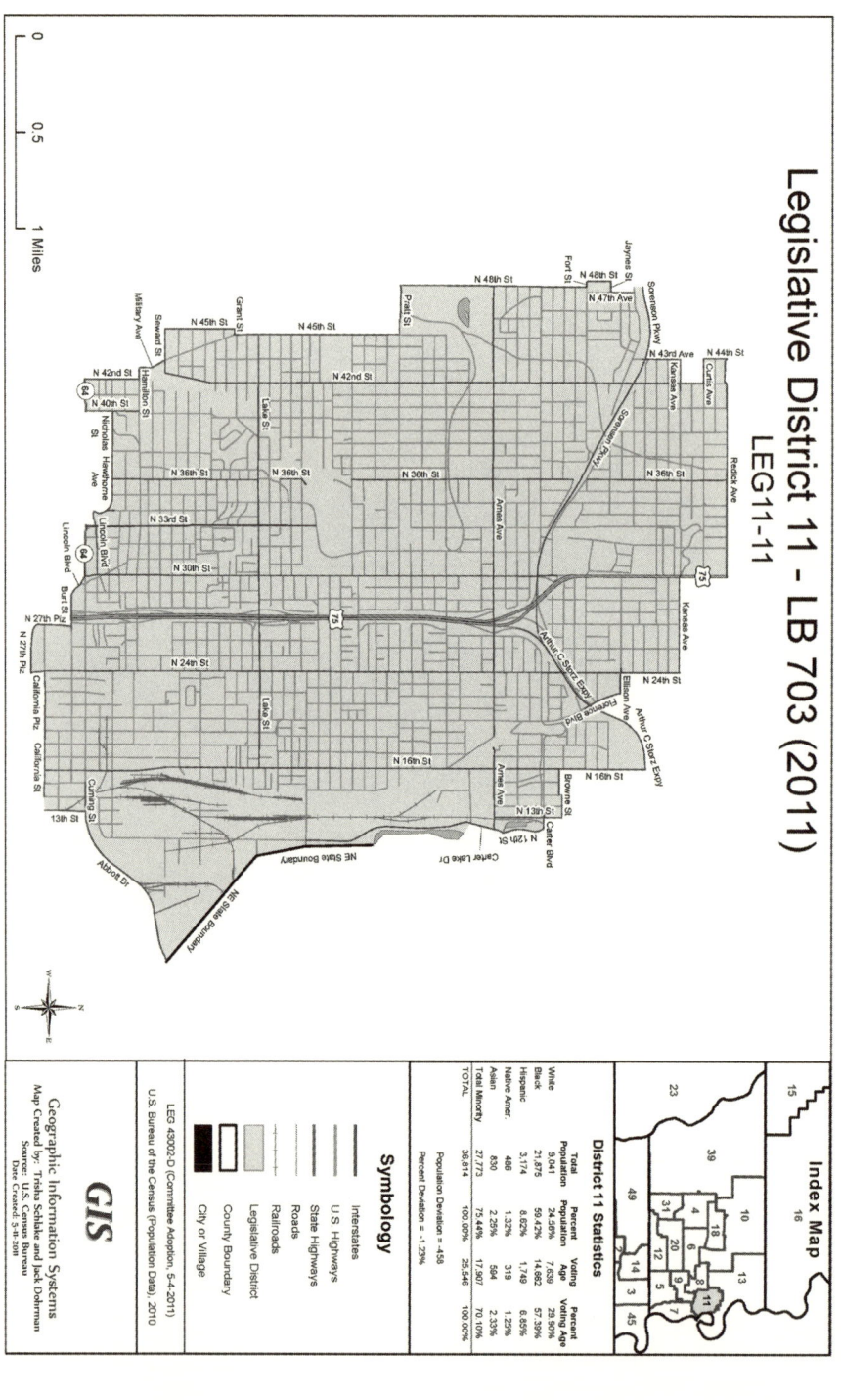

A map of Legislative District 11 as it exists today. Courtesy of the Nebraska State Legislature.

INTRODUCTION

New scholars of the Civil Rights Era have critiqued the tendency of researchers to privilege the images of high-profile leaders while missing the larger picture of freedom work carried out by whole communities. In such cases, struggles are reduced to "personality." Ernest Chambers's Machiavellian mind, "melodious" voice, rhetorical style, wide-ranging interests, battles, defeats, and significant successes easily place him within the "great person" paradigm. On the other hand, the limitation of such studies at finding meaningful implications for ongoing resistance and for liberation demands a wider lens.[1]

Free Radical is informed by the revisionist approach to the study of the Civil Rights and Black Power Movements as organic efforts by communities with multiple independent and (paradoxically) interdependent nuclei, proposed by John Dittmer in *Local People* (1994). Chambers's biography profits from the examples of others on how to write with the new foci, as supplied by Jeanne Theoharis and Komozi Woodard in their edited volume *Ground Work: Local Black Freedom Movements in America* (2005). These revisionists affirm Chambers's response to comparisons of his ideas with those of Malcolm X (El Hajj Malik El Shabazz). Chambers simply reminds those who were not present or active in those years that the struggle for freedom was being waged in local communities simultaneously with other more well-known centers of the movement.

Moreover, the black power struggle in Omaha, Nebraska, started before the Civil Rights and Black Power Movements drew nationwide attention. The struggle in Omaha was, similarly, maintained long after the majority population shifted their attention to other issues. Put another way, "Black Power was local as well as national, tactical as well as ideological, and garnered numerous local successes."[2] Yet, movement activists in Nebraska, including Chambers, made conscious attempts to draw out links that would attach their efforts to larger national human rights events. Activists in Omaha functioned strategically in order to forge solidarity, but more specifically to nurture relationships that would enhance their ability to leverage power at the local level. And even the present project could be said to fit within that generalized tendency.[3]

Still, it is fair to argue that the range of experiences of African American communities across the United States in the late twentieth and early twenty-first centuries are marked by many similarities. The upswing in black electoral politics in the early 1970s brought hundreds of legitimate community leaders into state and national political arenas for the first time since Reconstruction. At that moment the potential for black people to engage in mainstream politics and effect change seemed unlimited. Gradually special interest groups and political machines would curb the influence and stymie the careers of some aspiring African American "grassroots" politicians. Within a decade many African American communities underwent integration and then "urban renewal," subsequently suffering losses in their geographical and political bases. Most African American community leaders with political leanings joined the Democratic or Republican Party, while a handful remained independent. *Free Radical* is the story of one of those freethinkers. This first published biography of Chambers's career documents an intellectual's struggle to stimulate, within African Americans in his hometown, faith in their own latent political power.

Chambers's influence on the state of Nebraska and leadership of the African American community of Omaha spanned four decades. This study of Chambers's "reign" uncovers his sense of humor, his righteous indignation, his genius, and above all his fiercely courageous personality as an intellectual who grapples with—and finds extraordinary means for dealing with—an uneven power relationship between his constituency and white middle-class America. Chambers's political lean to the left and paradoxical reliance on the nation's founding documents, combined with his unusual intelligence and dynamic personality, would thrust the statesman into the leading political debates of the day. Over the course of his long career, Chambers would meet with Malcolm X, who visited Omaha one year before his 1965 assassination; defend at least one member of the Nation of Islam from local police; and demand fair trials for members of the Black Panther Party.

Chambers's political savvy would ultimately allow Nebraska to lead the nation in the passage of the first legislative resolution calling for divestment from apartheid South Africa.

This political biography of Ernest Chambers and the community of North Omaha recounts the history of an African American intellectual from his activist days as a young man through his career as a seasoned state senator. It is also a critical exploration of cultural space in a specific geographical place. The book's perspective emanates from the Near Northside, the sociopolitical terrain where the majority of African Americans in the state of Nebraska resided throughout the twentieth century, referred to alternatively as "North O." The only African American state senator of forty-nine legislators in the conservative midwestern Nebraskan Unicameral, Chambers waged a daily struggle to have the needs of his constituency recognized, just as working-class and very poor urban African Americans utilized Chambers, among other strategies, to express their frustrations, anger, and needs to a system that was designed to silence them. Drastically outnumbered in the electorate (African Americans made up less than two percent of Nebraska's population), Chambers tested innovative methods for winning political battles, victories which he also used to justify his power in the community. These same feats, along with his thoroughness and his reputation for being indomitable, would allow him to manage and ultimately control the Nebraska Unicameral.

Free Radical also, admittedly, tells the story of an exceptional man, but I argue that this is the result of his unusualness rather than in observance of any historical genre. A few examples might prove instructive. Ernest Chambers's oration took the art of the filibuster to new heights. In the course of debate on the statehouse floor, Chambers could wax eloquent over the simplicity of the life of prairie dogs by quoting from Walt Whitman or Henry David Thoreau, or paraphrase passages from the Bible. Later in the day, the senator might accuse his colleagues of having been bought and paid for by lobbyists, call them cold-hearted racists, or "fat" and complacent men (and women) who could not empathize with the suffering of the poor. As a result of his all-out aggressiveness in debate, Chambers was hated in the extreme and loved in the extreme both by people who scarcely knew him and by colleagues who saw him every day.

Children across the state were drawn to Chambers because of his forthrightness; he captivated them with his stories and parables. Chambers put his gift with language to work in politics, and nurtured a genius for reading and interpreting the potential impact and ramifications of proposed legislative bills. His self-assessment of his abilities gave him a uniquely elevated level of confidence; he was willing and able to challenge his colleagues on anything, and he was respected by his fellow senators for his skill at preventing the passage of legislation. After his first years in office, other senators developed the habit of checking with Chambers on bills that they were proposing to see whether they could win his promise not to stop the measures. In the end, his fellow solons paid Chambers tribute by informally giving him the title of "Dean of the Legislature." By his final term in office, Chambers had become the most powerful senator ever to serve in the Nebraska Statehouse.

Throughout his long career, Chambers never forgot that his power came primarily from his working-class constituents, whom he both led and followed. Year in and year out, when he was not on the floor of the Nebraska State Legislature, Chambers responded to calls for assistance from North Omaha. He heard, recorded, and verbalized the political, legal, and financial needs of his constituents on a daily basis. And, although he became a powerful politician, he remained intently, even painfully, aware of what his most impoverished and disenfranchised constituents faced. Chambers kept the nexus of his struggle at the local level precisely because he maintained a constant dialogue with regular community folk. While he did not join or help to build an organization, Chambers was both a beacon for and the voice of the African American freedom movement in Nebraska.[4]

1—Education of a Radical

> *I'm just a Barber, that's all. I'm just a person who lives and works down here in the ghetto, and everyday I see people who are hurting. I see children who don't have what they need in the way of clothing and food and educational opportunities. . . . Our people are just too concerned about getting the necessities to stay alive. They can't be dreamers or poets.*
>
> —"Ernie Chambers," *Black and White: Six Stories from a Troubled Time*

A visitor named Theopholis X was standing on a street corner in downtown Omaha one March afternoon. He was wearing a business suit and tie and selling issues of the Nation of Islam's newspaper, *Muhammad Speaks*. Mr. X was questioned about his work and ultimately beaten by two police officers and by white bystanders, and taken to jail. Before nightfall, "Ernie" Chambers, a young barber-activist was downtown at the Detective Bureau demanding to know why Mr. X had been arrested. He learned that no charges had been filed, although Mr. X was continuing to be held. Chambers told Mayor A. V. Sorensen that Mr. X was a victim of police misconduct. The mayor said that one officer had suffered minor injuries. Chambers said that, if so, he might have hurt himself in his haste to draw his pistol from its holster. Selling papers is not a crime, Chambers told the mayor; the officers exceeded their authority when they grabbed the man. "How predictable," he wrote, "that the police chose the first warm day to renew hostilities against the African community. If there is a trial on this matter, be prepared to defend every act of the police along with the failure to charge Theopholis X with any violation justifying arrest." Chambers's two years in law *school were paying off. He knew how the law worked and was able to make it clear to the County Attorney that if charges were filed against Mr. X, the city would have to contend with him.*[1]

Rural communities speckle an otherwise agricultural landscape, separating prairie grasses that swoon in summer and autumn under a gusty midwestern breeze. Almost anyone born in the state can distinguish Nebraska blindfolded: its icy winters; in warm weather, its sure-welcoming earth under bare feet, the scent of sweet grass, the shaking tassels of corn before a mid-summer's storm; and on hot sunny days, its sea of dark green stalks under a stark blue sky. The expansiveness of the countryside, unbroken by trees or hills, is so vast that it gives one a sense of timelessness. Townsfolk in Fremont, Norfolk, Grand Island, Hastings, Kearney, North Platte, Bellevue, Lincoln, and Omaha are able to experience the beauty of the Great Plains along with the comforts of the city. Whatever one's vantage point in Nebraska, it is impossible to miss the vitality of the region, blessed by Mother Nature with fertility and grace. But, to African Americans who venture here, the white inhabitants (and the stoic countenances many of them turn toward anyone who is not of Northern European extraction), seem out of place. No matter how hard African Americans confined to segregated North Omaha might have tried to imagine European immigrants as natural to the environs, as a group, white people's racialized approach to life failed to match the serenity and calm of the natural scenes.

For as far back as Ernest Chambers could remember, black people in the urban Midwest had experienced hostility from whites. Nebraska had been a free state in the years leading up to the American Civil War and a harbor for Africans fleeing from slavery. But the state's majority population was conflicted about how to engage with free African Americans. Lynching occurred in several of the state's largest cities and towns. A KKK convention drawing 25,000 participants was held in Lincoln around the time the Chambers family came to Nebraska. Chambers's grandparents had migrated from West Point, Mississippi, during the second decade of the twentieth century. The fourth child of Malcolm Chambers of Omaha, and Lillian (Swift) Chambers of Rayville, Louisiana, he was christened Ernest William Chambers at his birth on July 10, 1937. Malcolm, a packinghouse worker who also preached the gospel, and Lillian, a homemaker, eventually became the parents of seven children—three girls (Nettye, Alyce, and JoAnn) and four boys (Ernest, Robert, Eddie, and Gilbert).

Whatever their ethnic or racial background, most immigrant populations in Nebraska describe themselves as possessing a certain uniqueness of character resulting from the experiences of their ancestors, black or white, on the "frontier." It is widely held among Nebraskans that they are a hardworking, pragmatic people. That Nebraskans share some ideals which set them apart from people in other regions of the county is not entirely fanciful. They differ from east coast and west coast Americans in ways that can be quantified by examining their priorities and preferences as exemplified through their voting records. For example, for more than a decade Nebraskans have approved state budgets that spend a third less per capita on public education, a full three-fourths less on intergovernmental agencies, and more than one-fifth less on public welfare than approved by the majority populations of other states. However, they spend significantly more on highways and somewhat more on postsecondary education. They also show a preference for small government. But this is revealed in curious ways, like the fact that Nebraska's state senators enjoy one of the lowest salaries for state legislators in the nation, and are paid about $12,000 in annual wages. It might be safely argued that the citizens of Nebraska have the most in common politically with the populations of other agricultural states.[2]

That his community was separated from the predominately white sections of the city was a fact of life that Chambers learned along with other basic instruction that African American children living in urban Omaha in the 1940s received at home. Later, he discovered that his neighborhood terrified whites, whose fears of blacks bordered on paranoia. These feelings were derived from the homogeneity of their neighborhoods and a phobia of the unknown. The Near Northside, as Chambers's community was often called, also suffered because of bad relations with the local police force. Although domestic servants, members of the clergy, and other elite blacks were sometimes exceptions, as a group African Americans were socially ostracized by most of the state's ninety-plus percent of the population. Chambers was an extremely shy and quiet boy. No one guessed that he would grow up to be the defender and undisputed leader of Nebraska's African American population, and the most powerful legislator the state had ever seen.

As hard as the Great Depression was on white communities, it was even more devastating to North Omaha, a community of about 14,000 (about one-tenth the population of Omaha proper). Chambers's family felt the strain of limited capital and, like most everyone else, responded with increased resourcefulness. Some families' straits were ameliorated by President Franklin D. Roosevelt's New Deal, which provided public works jobs for the unemployed. On the whole, though, African Americans' financial problems were lessened only with the outbreak of the Second World War. The war provided an unprecedented number of black men and black women jobs in the armaments industry.

Meanwhile, with the exception of his all-white teachers and his white classmates, Chambers's world was largely segregated. For more than twenty years, one Catholic priest, Father John Markoe of Creighton University, challenged Omaha's discriminatory customs. Markoe helped to organize the De Porres Club, a group of African American pastors, community leaders, and young people who advocated for equal rights. The members also formed the Citizens Coordinating Committee for Civil Liberties (4CL) to hold watch at city council meetings and record the proceedings. The group condemned segregation in Catholic schools and demonstrated against the Coca-Cola Bottling plant, the Greyhound bus station, Eppley Airfield, and local hotels, all of which refused to employ or to provide service to African Americans. As early as 1948, Omahans demonstrated publicly against housing and job discrimination. The St. Martin De Porres Center would for decades remain a hub of local activism and the site of a chapter of the Congress of Racial Equality (CORE).[3]

North Omaha had its own culture and economy with black-owned businesses and others that belonged to Russian and Jewish immigrants. There were numerous storefront churches. National Urban League chapters in Lincoln and Omaha, Nebraska's largest cities, held adult education and self-help seminars and sponsored health, recreation, and job programs. Many of the programs open to black youth during Chambers's childhood were organized by the NAACP, the Omaha Urban League, and the Culture Center in South Omaha, which provided a separate facility for blacks to supplement the segregated Social Settlement House. (The Culture Center later became known as Woodson Center.[4]) The Urban League tried to negotiate with city leaders to provide African Americans use of a swimming pool in Florence, the neighborhood just to the north, but was refused. It also took on housing discrimination, which turned out to be a battle that would continue for another generation.[5]

Excluded from white clubs and restaurants, African Americans developed their own high society and night life in Omaha. A favorite event of many of Chambers's age mates by late adolescence was the Coronation Ball, held each year at Cecilia and James Jewells' Dreamland Hall on North 24th Street. There the crowds celebrated the crowning of King Borealis and Queen Aurora. This was likely a transformation of traditional African forms of socio-political organization, which emerged in many segregated communities of diasporic Africans. For technical musical training, African American youngsters attended Florence Pinkston's School of Music. Anyone in need of cab service could phone the Sunset Taxicab Company owned by community member Frank James. Later the Ritz and United Cab Companies replaced Sunset as black-owned taxis. When demand for rides increased and white taxi companies refused to service the area, jitney services provided by men driving their own cars out of a jitney stand became popular in Omaha. The community also boasted six black-run grocery stores, two pharmacies, furniture and music stores, eight barbershops, three real-estate offices, eight restaurants, and seven bars. Carpentry, contracting, and plumbing were lucrative ventures for African American business owners—with nearly exclusively African American clientele—and Shipman Brothers Road Building Company was especially successful. Proud of African people's progress, local historian H. J. Pinkett said that African Americans had been nearly 100 percent illiterate in 1865, but by the 1930s there was only four percent illiteracy in the segregated section of the city. Some North Omahans sent their children to be educated at Howard University and other well-known schools. However, most community members worked as unskilled or semi-skilled laborers or in trades. During this era, barbershops were the political and intellectual equivalents of Irish pubs or the soapboxes on Boston Common. There, men gathered and debated relevant topics of the day while youngsters learned about things they did not hear much about at home. Prominent barbers in Omaha in the 1930s and 1940s were R. C. Price, E. W. Killingworth, C. B. Mayo, Richard Taylor, P. M. Harris, C. H. Rucker, and W. H. Taylor. Chambers later recalled going to C. B. Mayo's place as a boy. Mayo, he said, was a grouchy old man who used to cut his hair in a bowl shape before such cuts were in style.[6]

Price was president of the Omaha NAACP for "several terms," and he also served as the chairman of the organization's grievance committee.[7] The activism of barbers and the strategic position of their shops as information hubs is a phenomenon common to many African American communities, and would feature prominently in Chambers's future. P. M. Harris, another barber, was a South Omaha businessman and minister, who, "along with Loretta Busch, helped found the Cultural Center that became the Woodson Center on the Southside" of Omaha.[8] When Chambers was growing up, aside from the African American population that settled around the South Omaha stockyards, African Americans lived "largely in the area bounded by Cuming Street on the South, 18th Street on the East, Wirt Street on the North and 30th Street on the West" in an area not exceeding four square miles. The northern boundary would reach Ames Avenue by the 1960s and then move with each generation farther north until the area doubled in size over the next half century.[9] One historian argues that 12,000 of Omaha's 14,000 blacks lived in this area, "a city within a city."[10]

A Life in the Community, 1937–1970

At home, Chambers had lived with six brothers and sisters, "three of each gender with [himself] in the middle."[11] His birth order helped form his role in the family. Chambers recalled that being the middle child caused him to gain certain communications skills, which he took with him into politics. These skills also caused him to see himself primarily as a justice seeker "sort of like an ombudsman."[12] Chambers's motivation to fight for social justice as an adult was rooted in things that happened to him in childhood. He would recall having observed people in his church who told children not to do certain things, but broke the rules themselves. Chambers became so accustomed to trying to decide what was just and fair in his household and community that it soon seemed natural to him. He once described his work on behalf of the community as seeming to flow from the natural order of things "like running water."[13]

Despite the growth of African American businesses, North Omaha would look increasingly run down to outsiders since "public officials neglect the section [of town]; it has poorer public facilities than any other sections; it is without playgrounds, it is poorly lighted, and it suffers from crowding."[14] In addition, there were only three schools where African American children were allowed to attend and all of them refused to hire black teachers. Pinkett argued that the hiring of fifty African American teachers would help the area more than anything else. Pinkett, in fact, forecasted Chambers's sponsorship of legislation for district elections for the Omaha School Board, when he wrote in 1937, the year of Chambers's birth: "perhaps, a Board of Education will someday be elected which will . . . include Negroes as citizens who should participate fully in community life."[15] Pinkett, an African American attorney with one of the oldest law practices in North Omaha, popularized the concept of "racial and community contribution."[16] Racial "uplift" and personal sacrifice remained important community "bywords" throughout the 1940s and 1950s.[17]

When Chambers was a youngster, there were nine African American attorneys in Omaha; among them were grandfather, John Adams, Sr.; father, John Adams, Jr.; and son, Ralph Adams. John Adams, Sr., and Jr., would each serve as members of the Nebraska state legislature. Chambers went to school with Ralph Adams, Jr., and remembers spending time at the Adams place. In addition to political posts, there were a number of politico-social orders in African American Omaha. Masonic fraternities had existed on Omaha's Northside for over fifty years before Chambers was born. Shunned by city officials, North Omahans formed a Civil Council around 1930 and appointed a "Negro mayor."[18] The duty of the "mayor" was to work in the interests of "constituents," representing North Omaha in dealings with the city. John Owens served as "mayor" for several years and also was a clerk in the Douglas County Register of Deeds Office. He later became a member of the Nebraska state legislature. Unlike Chambers, however, Owens felt that he could not "do anything which may cause criticism or embarrassment" to other county or state officials. His impact on the legislature was miniscule.[19]

In *The Gate City: A History of Omaha* (1997), Lawrence H. Larsen and Barbara J. Cottrell argue that Omaha's political machine helped to fuel "ethnic, racial, and vice problems" in the first half of the twentieth century. That argument, however, could also be made about the subsequent fifty years.[20] Lines were drawn between Omaha's majority, who were of Northern European extraction, and others. Greeks, like African Americans, experienced prejudice and persecution. Many lived in South Omaha in an area called "Indian Hill" or "Greek Town."[21] Headlines helped foment feelings against the Greek community. For example, "Ed Lowery, South Omaha policeman, is shot and killed by Greek," one headline read around the turn of the twentieth century.[22] Lowery had gone to arrest John Masourides on suspicion that he was living with a young "white" woman from Grand Island. A mob met in "Greek Town" and nativist whites rioted, beating Greeks and burning buildings. An "exodus" of Greeks from South Omaha resulted. Pinkett analyzed the causes of the affair in a letter to an Omaha newspaper: "It is too bad that we have to admit that our civilization is so veneered and that men cannot see that the real crime is committed by the men higher up who foster and encourage [ethnic animosity]."[23] Pinkett was also present during the 1919 Omaha race riot that culminated in the lynching of William Brown. Pinkett talked to Brown in his jail cell at the Douglas County Courthouse before the mob took Brown from the jail. During his visit, Pinkett found out that Brown had rheumatism and had a hard time walking. Pinkett was convinced that the police had the wrong man.[24]

Chambers as a Young Man

When Chambers was thirteen years old, the *Lincoln Star* estimated that over half of the homes inhabited by blacks in Nebraska were substandard.[25] In spite of the poverty around him, Chambers grew up with confidence and with a sense of acceptance as child of the community. His understanding that he lived in the "ghetto" would develop later. During those early years African Americans teachers were not allowed to teach in the Omaha Public Schools (OPS) even though blacks were graduating from Nebraska's medical college and dentistry and law schools. The NAACP made employment of African American teachers a priority during the 1940s and 1950s in the hopes of getting jobs for black college-educated teachers and providing black teachers for children. In response to NAACP pressure, OPS hired three African Americans in 1940, who would only be allowed to teach the primary grades and who were assigned to the entirely African American Long School in North Omaha. However, instead of giving the new teachers regular employee status, African American educators were designated permanent substitutes and, therefore, did not receive contracts or benefits. As a result of OPS policies, Chambers found himself in predominantly white classes taught by Euro-American teachers. It would be 1965, when Chambers was twenty-eight-years old, before OPS made its first assignment of an African American teacher to an Omaha secondary school.[26]

The U.S. Supreme Court's *Brown v. Board of Education* decision (May 17, 1954) was the domino leading to the dismantling of overt school segregation across the nation.[27] The decision came too late to impact Chambers directly, and the ridicule that he experienced as a child in white classrooms had left its mark. Chambers remembers practicing his speech as a child, so that he self-consciously spoke perfect English to whites. He spent his entire childhood alternating between being isolated in white classrooms and living in segregated circumstances, a dichotomy of which he would increasingly become aware.[28]

During childhood, Chambers focused on growing up. He made average marks at Technical High School from 1951–1955. However, by the time of his high school graduation, Chambers had developed a thirst for knowledge and immediately enrolled in Creighton University. He had begun to question the organization of society, speaking out in church when he disagreed with the interpretation elders offered about a scripture. Gradually, Chambers grew confident enough in his own thoughts to begin discussing politics, religion, and other topics wherever he went. While still a young man,

Chambers's ability for rational analysis caught the attention of his elders. Saxophonist Preston Love, Omaha's renowned jazz musician, approved of Chambers's outspoken style and the two eventually become close friends. Love had performed with the biggest bands in the country, including Count Basie's Orchestra, Charlie Parker, Duke Ellington, Louis Armstrong, and Dizzy Gillespie, many of whom played in North Omaha's then-thriving nightlife at the Dreamland Ballroom.[29]

1950s and Early 1960s African American Leadership

By the time he was a college man, Chambers began dialoging with a few older activists, expressing his growing political awareness of the situation in Omaha. On top of the cadre of African Americans in positions of authority in Omaha was Charlie Washington, a writer and editor with the *Omaha Star*, who was also a civil rights advocate. Washington's advocacy included pressuring the University of Nebraska to recruit talented African American athletes. It was said among North Omahans that anyone who wanted to get something done would eventually have to consult with Washington. Chambers was friends with Washington from the 1960s onward.[30]

As Chambers was coming of age, the old guard of civil rights leadership watched him develop his own voice as an advocate for human rights. They also noted his exasperation. Whatever work seasoned activists had done, it appeared to Chambers's generation that they had not done enough. African people were still ruthlessly oppressed in Omaha, and young men like Chambers harshly critiqued the old guard for soft-pedaling the needs of the community.[31] At twenty-one, Chambers took stock of the political, economic, and racial climate in his hometown and, in the fall of 1958, published an appraisal in the local paper's opinion page.

> America is a land of paradoxes. Negroes, discriminated against on every hand, include some of the most vociferous upholders of the American way. It seems ironic that it should be left to them to make clear what this nation stands for; strange that the "inferior" should be constantly admonishing the "superior" to honor his own Constitution and obey his own laws.[32]

This first publication of Chambers's views contained his core philosophy on political and social injustice. As a young man just entering adulthood, Chambers faced the more personal quests for independence and for an education. He attended Creighton University from September 1955 through June 1959, when he earned his bachelor's degree in history. His parents had not been able to finance a college education and Chambers knew that it was his responsibility to make his own way.[33]

Chambers joined the army under the Ready Reserves program that required six months of active duty, basic and advanced basic infantry training, plus a commitment of several years in the Reserves. Chambers spent weeks in basic training at Fort Leonard Wood, Missouri, and then attended advanced basic training at Fort Ord, California. Meanwhile, back home the local desegregation movement intensified. Since the early 1940s black Omahans had fought caste laws in various ways, and numerous activists, including community organizer and artist Dorothy Eure and African American State Senator Edward Danner, protested the inequality that went along with segregated facilities. Northsiders watched the progress of the civil rights marches across the country from the late 1950s onward with keen interest. Father Markoe helped to organize a combined civil rights march by North and South Omaha residents in 1963. That year Lawrence W. M. McVoy, president of the local NAACP chapter, received directives from the Office of Field Secretary to organize three new committees. He quickly followed up, and in a memo to his membership announced a new Direct Action Committee, chaired by John Butler and Dale Anders; a new Washington Conference Committee, chaired by Leo Elmore; and a Nebraska and Congressional District Legislation Conference Committee, chaired by himself and Leola Bullock of Lincoln, Nebraska. McVoy and Bullock organized a Bi-Congressional District Conference that would provide ground support for a civil rights agenda. An early outcome of their efforts was a 1965 civil rights march down Omaha's 24th Street. The event drew hundreds of participants. African American photographer Rudy Smith observed law enforcement officers responding to the marchers with hostility and reported that a National Guardsman had threatened to kill him.[34]

With an honorable discharge from the army under his belt, Chambers began attending barbering school at 12th and Farnam Streets in July 1963. The training ran from May until October. That winter, Chambers secured a job with the U.S. Postal Service. He was also hired by Dan Goodwin, owner of Spencer Street Barbershop. Chambers had been barbering only a short time before he was asked to serve as chair of the Near Northside Police Community Relations Council. On behalf of the council, he argued that the police department failed to review the complaints of African American citizens, and therefore did not know what was actually going on between the police and neighborhood citizens. In the fall of 1963, Chambers began writing more regularly to the local newspaper and appeared occasionally on the news speaking about the need for fair employment practices in Omaha. Chambers's artistic and intellectual ability was known to many while he was still in his early twenties. His oratorical skills "made other persons around him feel inferior."[35] Chambers continued writing occasional letters to the *Omaha World Herald*'s "Public Pulse" section throughout the early 1960s. Sometimes his commentary related to international politics: "Why do such men as Senator Goldwater insist that oppressive colonialism (under whites) is better for Africans than Independence?"[36]

Chambers's vision of the world was evolving and he began looking even more critically at his hometown. North Omaha landlords were frequently absentees who charged high rates for units badly in need of repair. The African American population had expanded again and overcrowding worsened. At the same time, the neglect of rental properties by white landlords reduced the value of neighboring black-owned North Omaha homes. Thus, when the state legislature considered an open housing bill in 1965, Mayor A. V. Sorensen, in response to criticism by activists like Chambers and Danner, asked Omaha realtors to support the legislation. Most real estate brokers refused, arguing infamously that property rights were more precious than civil rights. The debate was made public, and news of pervasive white support for long-standing racist policies and customs increased tension between the African community and the white police who patrolled its neighborhoods. Police community relations plummeted further in the mid 1960s over the treatment of African American teenagers, many of whom socialized in the white-owned Safeway grocery store parking lot on 30th and Ames Avenues when the weather was nice, but who were threatened with arrest and violence by officers for gathering there.[37]

By the summer of 1964, some white Omahans had begun to believe that the tension between African American youth and city police pointed to problems regarding the way that services were distributed in Omaha and that job discrimination had created a ghetto. As a result, several projects were initiated to improve Omaha race relations. New members were added to Omaha Human Relations Board. The religious community formed the Nebraska Conference on Race and Religion, and Omaha Mayor James Dworak organized an interethnic committee to address strategies for confronting discrimination in schools, industry, and housing. From September 1963 to May

1964, the Mayor's Employment Subcommittee, working out of the Omaha Urban League, registered more than 1,000 African Americans who were looking for work. This move gave hope to workers who were displaced during the decline of the packinghouses. At least seven hundred of these job seekers were sent to companies with referrals from the mayor's subcommittee, but only 166 ever were hired.[38]

During the same period, twenty African American teachers were employed by OPS to serve throughout the city, and the school district initiated an "open school" policy so that students could apply to attend schools outside of their neighborhoods. Mayor Dworak said that in industry: "We need more than an open hiring policy. . . . We will have to ask employers to hire Negroes wherever possible."[39] A handful of other whites in Omaha took active roles in challenging racist practices. Marvin Oberg, vice president of Northwestern Bell Telephone Company, chaired the Mayor's Employment Subcommittee and to that end he worked with the Omaha Urban League at finding job placements for black people. Although his efforts made few inroads at other white establishments, many African women were hired as operators at the telephone company.[40]

Despite these fair employment practices by a few whites, the majority of Euro-Nebraskan employers were accustomed to African Americans working only in blue-collar or domestic service positions. Paradoxically, during the era of segregation, North Omaha enjoyed scores of independent black-owned businesses. There was a vibrant marketplace and black-owned business owners were able to absorb some community members as workers. Appreciation for black culture was evident in the nightlife, as well as in outdoor flea markets held on Saturday afternoons along North 24th Street between Grant and Lake, where hot plates of fried fish, black-eyed peas, sweet potatoes, cornbread, and other traditional cuisine could be purchased. The *Omaha Star* was the longest-running African American–owned and operated weekly newspaper in Nebraska. The paper had been founded by Mildred Brown-Gilbert in July 1938 and was based upon the principle of economic cooperation; local shop owners advertized in the *Star* and their businesses were patronized by community members. When she published the very first issue, Brown-Gilbert wrote, "we give to you this day a paper of the people." In those days Brown-Gilbert was an activist and used the paper to condemn segregation in the "Gate City." She later joined Bertha Calloway, Denny Holland, Raymond Metoyer, Wilbur Phillips, Donny Butler, Herb Patton, Claude Organ, and an integrated slate of Creighton University students and community activists in the St. Martin De Porres Club under the leadership of Father Markoe. The De Porres Club, which actively protested segregation and inequality from 1948 through the end of the twentieth century, sponsored integrated rallies and led boycotts against segregated businesses. Club members condemned the June 17, 1948, incident at the Morton Park swimming pool where two young African American boys tried to swim, were denied entry to the pool, and then were beaten by a gang of white males. The club organized campaigns to challenge discriminatory hiring practices at Reid's Ice Cream, the local Coca-Cola Bottling Company, Cross-Town Skating Rink, and Safeway Cab Company. Denny Holland reported at one De Porres Club meeting that even after Yellow and Checker Cabs began hiring a token number of black drivers, Safeway refused. Safeway administrators told their customers they would always get a white driver. Popular black-owned businesses in the 1970s and 1980s included Sones Real Estate, Hardy Meeks Shoe Repair, Ritz Cab, and Carter's Restaurant. The restaurant, which was famous for its excellent soul food cuisine, was owned and operated by Lucy Carter. Her daughter, Bertha (Carter) Calloway, the first African American women employed by an Omaha television station, worked in the Public Affairs Department of WOWTV. Concerned about the city's youth during the late 1960s, Calloway, in collaboration with her church, created teen programs to keep youngsters occupied in the late afternoon hours and during the summer months. She later expanded her efforts, holding cultural ceremonies, a Miss Black Nebraska Pageant, and an annual Stone Soul Picnic. In 1976, she founded the Great Plains Black Museum.

Organizing any event in North Omaha could be most effectively done by going through a house of worship. In 1973, there were at least fifty-five black churches in the city, including seven African Methodist Episcopal (AME), twenty-three Baptist, two Catholic, one Christian Methodist Episcopal (CME), thirteen Holiness, and one or two each of Seventh-Day Adventist, Presbyterian, Jehovah's Witness, Mennonite, and United Methodist. Churches that lent themselves to activist causes and whose congregations could generally be counted on to support social justice campaigns included St. Benedict's Church at 2423 Grant (sponsor of the De Porres Center); Clair Memorial United Methodist Church at 2443 Evans (which eventually provided the citizens' defense committee for jailed Black Panther Party members with a meeting room); Wesley United Methodist Church at 2010 N. 34th; and Cleaves Temple (CME) at 25th and Decatur (whose pastors supported the De Porres Club's desegregation initiatives). Mt. Moriah Baptist at 2602 N. 24th, Allen Chapel at 2842 Monroe, and St. John's AME at 2402

North 22nd Street were heavily attended by individuals who also held membership in Masonic lodges. These congregations, while relatively conservative in style, were influential politically as their responses to events were often mirrored across the community. Though fifty miles apart, church denomination, family relations, and lodge membership united members of Lincoln's African American community with North Omaha. For example, James Calloway (of Omaha), McKinley Tarpley (Lincoln), J. R. Kelley (Omaha and Lincoln), and Fred Nevels, Elmer Gant, and Felix Polk (all of Lincoln) were joined together through membership in Iroquois Lodge Number 92. Though their political organizing was carried out behind closed doors, the Masons and other voluntary associations were powerful forces helping to unite African American opinion behind key issues. Unconscious of almost every aspect of African American life in Omaha, Peter Kiewit, owner of Kiewit and Sons, and Daniel Monen, vice president of the Omaha National Bank and the Mayor's Housing Subcommittee chair, suggested certain options in lieu of a fair housing ordinance in response to African American demands for housing relief. Kiewit and Monen preferred encouraging construction of public housing, stiffening standards for rental properties, and a "neighborhood cleanup within the Negro Ghetto."[41] African Americans on the subcommittee argued that white citizens and realtors who discriminated against clients should be prosecuted. Realtors, on the other hand, objected. As the beneficiaries of segregationist policies, they did not want to lose the high rates they could charge African American homeowners whose potential residences were bounded by an invisible line to the west around 50th Street and to the east by the Missouri River. Charles Peters, president of the Omaha Real Estate Board, promised that his organization would fight a fair housing ordinance if one were enacted.[42]

Omaha's resistance to integration was similar to the reaction of whites in other parts of the country. Chambers accepted an invitation to speak at the President's National Commission on Civil Disorders in 1967 where he would make this point. His address to the Kerner Commission on Civil Disorders was to be delivered in Washington D.C. Chairman Otto Kerner introduced Chambers by saying, "Mr. Chambers has been in the forefront of the militant civil rights demonstrations in Omaha."[43] Chambers then gave what would become one of the orator's standard talks on the black experience in America and the hypocrisy of American institutions. He argued that the "founding fathers" had fought the British for liberty and Americans made heroes of those who turned against the "mother" country, yet their descendants used police departments to threaten blacks who spoke publicly and openly about the oppression.[44] Schools were utilized to psychologically damage black youth, Chambers argued, making it unlikely that they would look critically at the social order and identify the source of their problems.

In a style reminiscent of Frederick Douglass, Chambers told the commission:

> You teach us that these colonies were not wrong when they spoke against George III and then Patrick Henry came out specifically against him. . . . Somebody said "treason." And he said, "if this is treason, make the most of it." . . . Then I look at what you're trying to do to Rap Brown and Stokely Carmichael—calling it sedition and treason.[45]

To Chambers, the unrest in major American cities in the late 1960s stemmed from police assaults on black communities. "It's a funny thing that in all these so-called 'riots,' the police and National Guard kill far more people than the so-called 'rioters'."[46] Paraphrasing Machiavelli, Chambers told the commission, "When the government itself violates the law, it brings the whole law into contempt."[47]

The Commission on Civil Disorders report on the causes and nature of the riots that occurred in many urban cities in the 1960s agreed that police actions had ignited the riots. The final report conceded that from 1963–1964, most urban riots had been the result of violent attacks by white mobs or the police on peaceful demonstrations by African Americans, and that blacks had fought back. *Ebony* magazine reported that Chambers's speech helped the commission reach their conclusions. The activist had referred to Malcolm X (El Hajj Malik El Shabazz) a number of times in his talk, and inferred that in 1965, after Malcolm's assassination, African Americans had begun forming defensive organizations when police failed to protect them from white civilian attacks, and when necessary from police officers. On August 11, 1965, the Watts, Los Angeles, riot began with a police stop of an African American youth. Reinforcements were called and one officer struck a bystander. Other bystanders were assaulted by police; some fought back. Eventually 4,000 people were arrested. In Chicago, Nashville, and other cities, riots erupted after an encounter between police and a member of the African American community where onlookers witnessed excessive use of force by lawmen.[48] The commission found that almost every post-1964 riot started with an incident between a community resident and the police. In fact, the commission's recommendations were very much like what Chambers had been asking for as chair of the Near Northside Police Community Relations Council: that officers with poor service records be taken out of African American neighborhoods, and that police misconduct, whether verbal, physical, or simple discourtesy, be stopped.[49] In its report, the commission admonished the police, stating, "It is inconsistent with the basic responsibility and function of a police force in a democracy."[50] Chambers's rhetoric was consistent whether speaking before the commission, or back home:

> If something happens to me there are other people who will come up. They killed Malcolm X and produced Stokely and Rap. You kill Rap: he will multiply. . . . If you get me off the scene, I'll multiply, because each time you handle one of us in this way, you show us what you are.[51]

The attention that Chambers brought to problems in Omaha inspired many of his constituents to believe that things might get better. Chambers's refusal to back down and his sharp socio-political analysis earned him the respect of a large segment of North Omahans, but at the same time he was becoming unpopular with Omaha's city authorities. Arrested for disturbing the peace and interfering with an officer in May 1965, Chambers stood with his attorney, Wilbur L. Phillips, before Douglas County Municipal Court Judge Eugene Leahy. Phillips and his partner, Thomas D. Carey, were confidantes of the newly elected African American state senator Edward Danner, and they were men whom Danner trusted to be supportive in civil rights issues.[52]

The circumstances surrounding Chambers's arrest were dubious. Testifying for the state, police officer Frank Podhaisky said that he was parked in front of the barbershop at 3122 North 24th Street and that his partner was in the fish take-out place next door buying sandwiches. An elderly woman approached the cruiser and asked if the bus would stop on that corner and Podhaisky had said "yes."[53] Podhaisky said that a man came out of the barbershop and spoke to the woman and then reentered the shop. Chambers appeared next with a pad and pencil in hand. Podhaisky said he felt that Chambers was writing notes about him and his squad car. "He had a piece of paper and pencil in his hand and pointed to the cruiser in an investigating manner."[54] Generally, Podhaisky said, he thought Chambers seemed "obnoxious and smart."[55]

Despite the best efforts of prosecuting attorney Richard L. Dunning,

Podhaisky's explanation of the events leading to Chambers's arrest was too weak to convince the judge that Chambers had committed a crime. "I got out of the cruiser and I asked what was going on. . . . I asked him for his identification and he refused to give it to me," Podhaisky said.[56] The officer told Chambers that he was going downtown, but as they were driving, Chambers asked if he was under arrest. When the officer said no, Chambers demanded to be returned to the barbershop. Podhaisky then arrested Chambers for disturbing the peace. Chambers's defense attorney argued that since the officers were apparently on lunch break just prior to the incident, Chambers could not have been interfering with police business. The case was dismissed. The episode lent credence to the belief of community members that Omaha Police Department members felt that blacks should act "humbly" and that not doing so was a sufficient excuse to arrest them.[57]

By now Chambers was in demand and speaking requests poured in from Omaha and around the country. FBI agents later reported that when Chambers spoke at the Teamsters Auditorium in St. Louis, Missouri, he criticized African American ministers and black professionals like Omaha native Bob Gibson, pitcher for St. Louis Cardinals, for lacking in commitment to the black power struggle. Not everyone in North Omaha agreed with Chambers's depiction of African American athletes as having forgotten their responsibility to the community. An editorial in *Everybody Magazine* the following year pointed out that athletes from the Northside like Bob Boozer, Bob Gibson, Roger and Gayle Sayers, and Rick Davis had invested in neighborhood businesses. and Boozer and Gibson owned the Time Out Restaurant on North 30th Street. But other community folk retorted that the Time Out was not really black-owned, and that it merely served as a front for Schwan Foods. Before the year ended, Chambers's speaking engagements also took him to Iowa, Pennsylvania, and Colorado.[58]

In February 1967, *Life Magazine* published a review of *A Time for Burning*, a documentary film in which Chambers appeared. A project of Lutheran Film Associates, the film's purpose was to show how the Civil Rights Movement had impacted one church, Augustana Lutheran in Omaha. Filmmakers taped Pastor William Youngdahl as he tried to get his congregation to participate in an exchange of visits between ten white couples at Augustana Lutheran and ten African American couples from a Lutheran Church only blocks away. In preparation, Youngdahl, visited businesses and individuals in the African American community to explain his plans. When the young white pastor entered Goodwin's Spencer Street Barbershop with the film crew, Chambers told Youngdahl, "as far as we're concerned. . . . Your Jesus is contaminated just like everything else you've tried to force upon us...."[59] In a *Life Magazine* editorial about the film, feature writer José Ferrer called Chambers "an astonishingly articulate Black Nationalist."[60] The documentary was rejected by the major television networks but was shown on National Educational Television. Youngdahl was eventually removed from his position as pastor of Augustana for his role in the project. Chambers's comments about the entrenchment of racism within the city's religious life seemed to have proven true. With no sign that racism and oppression were waning, and with a rise in the number of violent encounters between African American youth and the police, Chambers resolved that African Americans had a duty to fight their oppressors physically, in addition to other forms of resistance. "We are being forced by police misconduct to get together [and] fight the police.... We are going to fight you people like you fight us."[61] Chambers was pictured in *Ebony* magazine with African American police officers Pitmon Foxall and Marvin McClarty from Omaha's Police Community Relations Office. During this period, Chambers served as co-chair of the Police Community Relations Board in North Omaha and in this capacity sent a list of complaints to the police department about officer misconduct—but got no response. He watched while seventeen African American police officers, including McClarty, resigned from the police union (AFL-CIO) when a representative of the police union who was also a member of the Nebraska state legislature, voted against open housing. Chambers reminded police administrators of the multiple attacks that African people in Omaha had sustained from the Omaha police force.[62]

> The police murdered a boy named Eugene Nesbitt a year ago. He was against a fence... shot him in the back with a shotgun. Before the boy's body was cold, the safety director came out with a public statement and said the shooting was 'regrettable' but justified.... There was no inquest. There was no autopsy. The cop was not relieved of duty pending an investigation. Nothing.[63]

Chambers believed that America's treatment of its minority population during slavery had made it into a violent nation and that the majority could "never understand the activities of a meek, mild-mannered, gentle, humble man like Dr. Martin Luther King, Jr."[64] In his statements, Chambers vacillated between respect for King and, at other times, derision of the pacifist's strategy for obtaining civil rights. Although he respected King's humane ideals, Chambers did not believe that nonviolent demonstrations were adequate to meet the oppressive conditions that African Americas faced.[65]

A student of national politics, Chambers observed as a coalition of white and black Mississippians formed a "multiracial Democratic Party" and tried in vain to replace the racist Mississippi Democratic Party.[66] At the 1964 Atlantic City Democratic National Convention, instead of seating the party's leadership headed by Aaron Henry and Fannie Lou Hamer, "Lyndon B. Johnson and Hubert Humphrey, part of the cadre of National Democratic Leadership, seated the racist group as the 'regulars.'"[67] Afterward, some Mississippi Freedom Movement Party members would question the legitimacy of nonviolence as a tool for social change. Chambers said such maneuvering by those in power meant that when you beat them at their own game, they changed the rules. To Chambers, part of the problem was the nation's leadership. He wrote that Johnson would not enforce civil rights laws, and that the president's real feelings about non-whites were apparent in his foreign policy. "He is waging what amounts to a de facto total war in Vietnam . . . killing hundreds of thousands of people without a declaration of war by Congress, which is what the constitution says is necessary."[68] Chambers also complained that when heavyweight prize fighter Muhammad Ali resisted the draft and requested conscientious objector status, he was denied. The federal government refused to give Ali, a Muslim minister in the Nation of Islam, the same consideration that it had extended to scores of white college students. Here is a government, Chambers said, that at the very time when it should have been atoning for past abuses and launching a concerted effort aimed at defending African Americans' rights, instead allowed federal and local police to break the law by practicing fraud as they infiltrated black organizations and framed African American activists.[69]

As tough as Chambers's rhetoric could be to listen to for most whites, his speeches were every bit as poignant for black people whose complex set of experiences were verbalized by Chambers in a manner that seemed affirming. Chambers felt that African Americans were economically exploited by white businesses owners. Nothing was done about grocers in African American communities who sold spoiled food and overcharged "ghetto" residents, he observed. Meanwhile, the blacks who faced inferior schools, unqualified teachers, discrimination, and poor living conditions also faced abusive policemen and a skewed justice system.[70]

Chambers was soon recognized by many as the leader of the human rights movement in Nebraska.[71] Historians Larsen and Cottrell note that after having become accustomed to working with Urban League and NAACP officials, whites were shocked by the new black leadership style typified by Chambers. When Chambers met with the mayor of Omaha, he relayed that the community's biggest concern was the city's failure to address "minority complaints against policemen."[72] Unwilling or unable to focus on the content of Chambers's message, Mayor Sorensen expressed anger after the meeting, complaining that Chambers had offended him. Sorensen said he respected mild-mannered men like local NAACP President McVoy, but that Chambers had "criticized him relentlessly."[73] Still, according to Larsen and Cottrell, until the first Omaha riot, whites believed that most African Americans "were reasonable" and that most black people rejected militants like Chambers.[74]

The civil rights struggle had captured Chambers's attention, intellectually and emotionally. He was still a young man and desired companionship and the comfort of a family. During the summer of 1961, part of which he spent at the Army Reserves camp at Fort Jackson, South Carolina, Chambers met and married Jacklyn Lee, a young woman from the community. Their matrimonial bliss was challenged later that year by a threat to Chambers's job security at the post office. In July, a postal supervisor requested a Federal Bureau of Investigation review of Chambers, telling authorities he suspected Chambers might belong to the Nation of Islam. Meanwhile, Chambers entered Creighton University School of Law. His course load during his first semester included contract law, torts, property, and criminal law. He attended law school at Creighton for two and a half years. By now the growing intellectual had developed his views more solidly. One of his instructors said, "Chambers is the type who stimulates good conversation and requires an instructor to know his subject well."[75] During these years, Chambers served as an officer in the Junior NAACP, a position that allowed him a fresh venue for voicing his opinions on race relations. One associate of Chambers remarked that the activist had an unusual intellectual ability and "could be a power for tremendous good or evil."[76]

FBI

The FBI investigative report on Chambers, written in 1961, noted that none of the persons interviewed believed that Chambers sympathized with foreign countries or "supported anti-white organizations."[77] Some interviewees had commented, however, that Chambers was highly intellectual, "cocky," and "emotional about racism."[78] One insightful law professor said that Chambers's real emotions were hard to decipher as he "talked for effect" much of the time.[79] Chambers was not overly concerned with others' perceptions of him. He was busy shouldering the weight of law school, and using his intellectual power to advocate for his community. During his first year in law school, Chambers wrote an essay about Omaha's segregated schools.

> If the school officials will not institute a policy of free transfer throughout the city, then they ought to provide equal facilities for white and black so that the segregated pattern of education will not disadvantage the black child so much. There are Negro teachers, ministers, doctors, lawyers, and businessmen who should make their voices heard . . . if they have voices. This program of huts for Negro children and new or improved schools for white is unjust by any standards. If the Negro community accepts this latest slap in the face, they are sacrificing their children's chances for a good education to the god of discrimination.[80]

Law school administrators became aware of Chambers's involvement in movement politics, and he was reprimanded by the dean for missing classes. Eventually, a hold was placed on Chambers's registration, effectively barring him from further studies. Asked later why he had quit law school, Chambers replied that he had not but was kept from registering. The school administration said Chambers was spending too much time doing "other things," though Chambers had been on the dean's list and had never failed an exam.[81] "They said it was because of absences, but there were white students who had also exceeded the number of cuts, and they are now practicing lawyers in the community." Chambers later recalled, "They simply did not like the image that I projected."[82]

As a young person, Chambers believed the idea that the Constitution protected Americans' right to free speech. He did not know that the government had him under surveillance and had made repeated inquiries about him during this period. Around the time the government began to scrutinize Chambers, his utterances and essays intensified tenfold. In response to an article asking why blacks felt demonstrations were necessary before giving the government a chance to act, Chambers wrote that the question should be reversed: "Why did the government refuse to act until after Negroes had organized demonstrations?" He further questioned why the federal government failed to intervene in the majority group's repression of African Americans generally.[83] All of the four law instructors interviewed by the FBI about Chambers answered that they did not think that he was a communist. But when the agents interviewed four members of his Army

Reserve unit, two said they did not know if Chambers was a loyal American based on his comments and two said he was absolutely loyal. Pushed out of law school, Chambers had more time on his hands. He now focused his intellectual energy on human rights work, demanding a fair housing ordinance in a speech before the Omaha City Council, condemning discrimination in labor unions, and insisting that the book *Little Black Sambo* be removed from elementary schools.

In an October 1961 memo to the Civil Service Commission Bureau of Personnel Investigations, J. Edgar Hoover wrote that Chambers was disloyal or at least had disloyal tendencies. Moreover, Hoover mailed copies of his findings to the assistant chief of staff for intelligence of the army and the assistant attorney of internal security. The U.S. attorney general also received a copy of Chambers's file along with directions to study it to see whether Chambers had violated any federal laws. Apparently, the FBI wanted to make sure that Chambers's influence on other troops, as well as his access to information, was minimal.[84] The Civil Service gave the post office the green light to fire Chambers, which they did, only after baiting the activist into an argument by talking to him derogatorily. In the end, his supervisors claimed that Chambers's termination was for insubordination. As a result, in 1966, when urban unrest erupted in Omaha, Chambers was a full-time barber, in addition to being a husband and father. He had written fewer articles during this period and stayed closer to home while his two youngest children were born. Although his career focus had changed, he was still a rising member of the city's avant-garde African American intellectual leadership.[85]

The Civil Rights Movement had reached a crescendo by the mid-1960s and was transforming into a decentralized but more revolutionary movement for black power. Chambers had followed news of the sit-ins and voter registration drives across the American South. Now he thought deeply about strategies for African American liberation. Chambers understood why Malcolm X's initial response to the Civil Rights Movement was anger that whites had been allowed to subsidize King so "Reverend Martin Luther King can continue to teach the Negroes to be defenseless."[86] Chambers's ideology aligned with Malcolm's. He expressed contempt for many members of the older generation who, like King, relied on Christianity as the basis of their liberation theology when the very same religion was used to justify the persecution, enslavement, and continued oppression of African Americans. Chambers once said, "Martin Luther King's philosophy of non-violence is out-dated. I think he was beginning to realize it, too. His statements were becoming tougher and his actions were becoming more realistic. . . . He stopped talking about pricking the conscience of America."[87]

Black Militancy

Chambers saw the momentum of the movement ripple across the country like a ship on an uncharted course. African American activists in the Midwest were in step with their counterparts in the rest of the nation. They were open about their resentment at demeaning racial laws. In the summer of 1963, Reverend Everett Reynolds of Omaha joined with Leola Bullock of the Lincoln Branch of the NAACP to lead 150 people on a march in downtown Lincoln, protesting the slaying of Medgar Evers in Mississippi. The group marched from the University of Nebraska at 14th and R Streets to the State Capitol building in a show of solidarity with civil rights activists everywhere. There is no record of Chambers having attended the march, and he would have been disinclined to join an NAACP- or SCLC-led protest because participants were required to respond nonviolently to assaults from white hecklers. Chambers believed in self-defense. By the mid-1960s, demonstrations were being held in Nebraska with increasing frequency. Rights proponents from across the city marched down Omaha's North 24th Street in 1965. Chambers did not march. He did give public addresses about racism. On one occasion he explained the motivation for his work. "If my kids were adults and could judge me, what would be their verdict. That's why I'm concerned about schools, about everything."[88] At the time Chambers and his family lived on North 27th Street in Omaha from which it was a quick walk to work at the barbershop. A guardedly optimistic man in his late twenties, Chambers felt that the movement would net at least some positive results for African Americans. Paradoxically, he was increasingly seen by outsiders as a "troublemaker" and by community members as a rising star.[89]

In 1961 Chambers had no arrest record. But as the decade wore on, he was arrested four times and had his own identification number at the Omaha Police Department—a fact federal agents recorded in their "succinct resume of activities" on Chambers.[90] Although Hoover's basic assumptions about Chambers were warped because of his racist view of the world, the FBI agents trailing Chambers were correct about one thing: he did grow increasingly militant in his statements after 1963. Chambers was arrested in 1962 and again in 1965 for misdemeanors. While Chambers maintains that he was arrested for asking questions of the police in August 1962, police records claim he was arrested for interfering with a police officer. In April

1965, Chambers was arrested for interfering with a police officer and for "disturbing the peace." This time, Chambers recalled, a white supremacist had harassed Dan Goodwin and himself at the barbershop and then turned to the police for support. Earlier Chambers and Goodwin had tried to file a complaint against Raymond Stoops, an Omaha fireman, but the city attorney would not accept the complaint. Chambers charged that his constitutional rights had been violated by the city attorney since he had been subject to arbitrary abuse of power and racism. Chambers demanded a reply from the U.S. attorney.[91]

The FBI would soon realize that while they scrutinized Chambers's activities, he was making his own study of human rights violations by Nebraska lawmen. Hoover responded to two letters from a special agent in charge at Omaha in which Chambers argued that his constitutional rights were violated when a city prosecutor threatened to serve him with an arrest warrant if he testified on behalf of Goodwin. Chambers had written:

> Mr. Fryzek threatened me with arrest if I appeared as a witness on behalf of Mr. Daniel Goodwin against Raymond Stoops, May 5, 1965. I did appear and testify. . . . True to his threat, Mr. Fryzek appeared with his warrant. There was an attempt by a uniformed policeman to serve me with the warrant in the courtroom. Prosecutor Carey and Judge Leahy would not permit it. No finding was made against Mr. Goodwin.[92]

Chambers then filed a complaint against the Omaha city attorney with the U.S. attorney for Nebraska on May 3, 1965, and on May 10, 1965. The district attorney forwarded the complaints to the FBI on May 11. Three days later the bureau decided that in the matter of "Ernest William Chambers. . . . In view of the nature of the complaint made, no further investigation is being made by the Omaha Division."[93] Hoover was not impressed. He wrote that not only were Chambers's claims without merit but that he wanted Chambers's local records checked again to see if his status as an internal security risk had increased.[94]

In spite of FBI culture, which was heavily influenced by Hoover's racism, Chambers continued to press for his rights through the Office of the U.S. Attorney. Chambers urged that the U.S. attorney get involved before a situation developed that "neither you or I can handle."[95] Although Chambers's words could have been taken as a threat, he was also encouraging the federal government to make the local police and city prosecutor act in accordance with the law where the minority population of Omaha was concerned. He demanded they confront Omaha's extralegal, anything-goes dealings with citizens from the segregated portion of the city. Chambers was betting on the desire of the local government to keep Omaha free of urban disruptions. Whatever the odds, he wanted it made clear that black people would not march docilely while suffering abuse. Although this tactic was dangerous because it raised the possibility of mounting police power and unified white support, Chambers was being honest. The community's ability to destroy a large section of the city, especially businesses, was one bargaining chip that the people had.[96]

In March 1968, community members protested George Wallace's campaigning in Omaha, and were beaten up by police and a white mob during the Alabama governor's speech. The demonstrators later reported that they had "been led into a trap."[97] Allowed inside the city auditorium where Wallace was speaking, supporters and demonstrators recalled him asking the police to clear the walkways, which was where the protesters were standing. Eyewitnesses said that white people began throwing folding chairs at the demonstrators and that the police responded by beating the protesters with their nightsticks. "Some of the audience jumped in with fists and boots."[98] Fighting broke out outside of the hall, and the rioting was carried into North Omaha. During the next few days, African American students protested in their school study halls, repeating the slogan "Black Power." Instead of condemning police actions at the auditorium, city administrators provided Omaha policemen with shotguns and shells to better deal with protesters. Officers entered the community during the night following the mob action, ready to squelch—not white marauders—but any sign of resistance or protest from African Americans. Tragically, sixteen-year-old Howard Stevenson was standing outside a North Omaha business when he was shot to death by off-duty police officer James Abbott. Black people had not killed any whites, yet historians Larsen and Cottrell argue that "fear swept through the white community."[99] Chambers understood what white analysts would not—that African American people were also afraid. He demanded in vain that Abbott be fired from the police force. Although the city refused to discipline Abbott, Chambers's courage and defiance of the city officials was respected by many in the community.[100]

Chambers's sphere of influence continued to broaden. That fall his itinerary included multiple speaking engagements outside of North Omaha. One October evening in 1967, Chambers spoke at the West Omaha Unitarian Church. He told a crowd of whites that African Americans had exhausted every other means of redress and that violence was the "only tool left at our disposal."[101] Chambers said that black people would like to see "you [whites] alarmed, your men without jobs, your children hungry."[102] It was his most critical speech to date and would damn him in the eyes of Hoover, as well as many white Nebraskans, as a proponent of violence.

Chambers suspected that Euro-Americans who were unable to empathize with African people's plight could be reached through fear. What they wished most of all to avoid, it seemed to him, was the disruption of their economic system through riots. They dreaded any scenario in which the city was unable to protect white-owned property. Chambers tried to make black violence a bargaining chip with whites. He demanded tighter scrutiny of police action and city services, and job programs for neglected neighborhoods. The inferior school system on Omaha's Northside, Chambers told a crowd, was intended by whites to create slaves but instead had made revolutionaries. "The cracker cops are your servants and our masters. . . . The vestiges of slavery remain."[103] Although he had long believed that violence might be needed to stop racial oppression, in 1966 Chambers stepped up his rhetorical approach in part out of his genius for gauging the frame of mind of his audiences. Many people were in a revolutionary mood. Chambers used his extensive skills to drive home his points. "When violence breaks out," Chambers said, "all the police and National Guardsmen in Nebraska won't be able to save you."[104] Chambers's reputation as an effective speaker and as a "militant" spread. He began to receive invitations to speak before federal commissions on the causes behind the urban uprisings. In the fall of 1967, the *Washington Post* reprinted Chambers's statements to the President's Commission on Civil Disorders. Reporters Drew Pearson and Jack Anderson said Chambers's speech was "must reading for whites who are trying to understand how the black militants feel and what they think."[105]

> You can understand why Jews who were burned by the Nazis hate Germans, but you can't understand why Black people who have been systematically murdered by the government and its agents—by private citizens, by the police departments—you can't understand why they hate white people.[106]

Chambers said that black people going about daily, lawful activities were "attacked by the police and the police are praised for it. And you talk about giving the police more money and more power."[107]

Chambers designed his talks primarily to clarify the political situation for other African Americans, but he also made an effort to point out to Euro-Americans that fear of black people was as much a part of their cultural training as was their practice of dehumanizing the African personality. Both features of European colonialism were acted out by white police officers who did not care to distinguish between lawful and unlawful acts by African American people. All blacks were treated as criminals and white society praised its agents in the ghetto for keeping the "natives" in line. It was a colonizers' mentality, and Chambers's exquisite combination of metaphors, along with his knowledge of the law and history, made him especially able to express the political nature of African American encounters with the police.[108]

In May 1967, Chambers attended a National Conference on Racial Problems in New York, and in September he spoke before the National Advisory Commission on Civil Rights. The FBI reported to Hoover that Chambers advocated the use of violence on both occasions. For a short while, Chambers held a seat on the board of a local antipoverty agency—but he was removed as a board member from Greater Omaha Community Action for failure to attend meetings. David Rice, an acquaintance of Chambers who was also under surveillance by the federal government, was fired by the same agency during this period and it is possible that the FBI played a role in both dismissals.[109]

The federal agents assigned to keep up with Chambers did their best to monitor the community advocate's many activities, especially after the bureau's headquarters in Washington ordered that his investigation be ongoing. From the perspective of the internal security agency, Chambers's views on international affairs were part of his problem. One informant told the FBI that Chambers had said that white missionaries should leave Africans to their own religion and that if he could go to Africa he would try to raise an army against the United States. He would raise non-Christians as he himself did not believe in the white version of God or in the American version of Christianity.[110]

Although his days were filled with thoughts about politics and acting on behalf of African people, many of Chambers's evenings were spent doing the more personal work of parenting his young family. With children in the primary grades—three of his children attended Lothrup Elementary School in 1966—Chambers's focus on education in Northside schools intensified. He continued his fight to end discriminatory treatment of African American children in public schools. He complained that the physical conditions at white schools were kept up-to-date while the schools in the African American neighborhoods had outdated textbooks and their buildings were in constant need of repairs. The black schools were also staffed, it seemed to Chambers, with the worst teachers. When his daughter was in kindergarten, Chambers recalled, he had complained to the Omaha superintendent that there was insufficient heat in the classroom at his child's school and that the children had been forced to wear their coats for the entire day. He pointed out that the church annex, which had been sold to the school district by whites who wished to escape the "darkening... neighborhood," was drafty and that its stairs were unsafe due to weak floorboards.[111] Chambers was incensed that his little girl had a cold one day and could not take the "customary kindergarten nap because the floor was too cold, even with mats, and the teacher was afraid to have the children lie down."[112]

Chambers recalled how in an effort to discourage his complaints and suggestions for improving Lothrup, Principal Charles Krumme invited him to come before the Executive Board of the PTA in order to ask that he be added to the agenda for the following meeting. On February 7, 1967, Chambers attended the meeting and arose to introduce his concerns and to request a spot on the upcoming agenda. When he began talking, the group became hostile. In a follow-up letter to Krumme, Chambers described what happened. "You were at that meeting. You saw and heard how rudely and discourteously I was treated. . . . You saw the President suddenly stand and tell me that I could not talk."[113]

A PTA spokesman said that the board's agenda was full for the next two years. A school representative added that they did not want to hear Chambers's complaints and that they already knew that the toilets needed work. Chambers told Krumme that other parents had been driven away by similar treatment. Now he would go outside of the PTA to handle his concerns. Before he left the meeting, one of the board members told him that the body might listen if 1,200 parents came before them. Chambers replied that one should have been enough.[114]

Chambers had experienced protesting alone. He had, after all, stood alone with his placard outside of the post office, one man battling against unfair treatment. True, he had been fired, but he had not backed down. If necessary, he would wage a private battle against the neglect of North Omaha schools. The earlier fights had toughened him; the older he got the more impervious to other's criticism he became. He would use the strength of these experiences, where under the weight of public criticism he stuck to his convictions, to stand alone on many occasions in the future. Another episode occurred with the public schools that further influenced Chambers's opinion of them. His daughter, at the time a second grader, had been slapped by a retired substitute teacher. Chambers rushed to the school when his wife told him what had happened. When he got there, Chambers found an old woman who could not manage the classroom due to her senility. "I forgot my anger at her and became incensed that school officials would place such a person in a classroom with over twenty-five young children."[115] Chambers was told that the school had run out of substitutes and had to call teachers out of retirement. Chambers wrote a complaint to the superintendent of schools and sent copies to Dr. Claude H. Organ, attorney John Miller, and the *Omaha Star*. Chambers kept his child out of school until the regular teacher returned because he would not compel her to sit in a room with a person who had struck her.[116]

By the winter of 1969, conditions had not improved at Lothrup School. A new principal, Warren Taylor, had been hired. On the very day that Chambers met with him to discuss needed changes at the school and assert that his children were not to receive corporal punishment, he saw a teacher standing near the lunch line slap a young boy twice across the month. "Coming between them, I told her to keep her hands off him and that if it were my child, I would slap the fire out of her."[117] The teacher turned out to be another substitute.[118] He threatened to patrol the hallways of the school himself if the corporal abuse of children continued. Chambers's experiences at Lothrup as a child, along with the mistreatment of children he observed as a young parent, stayed in his mind as he entered state politics. All of his letter writing, which he mainly did at this juncture from home at 32nd and Erskine Streets, helped Chambers refine his voice. He used his oratory—now, as an instrument in full support of the local Black Power Movement. Chambers wrote a letter to Mayor Sorensen in the fall of 1965 following what was supposed to be a police community relations meeting but which Chambers saw as a session filled with threats and attempted intimidation of community members by the city's Public Safety director. Chambers told Sorensen that "as the commander-in-chief of the Police and Public Safety Departments, it was the mayor's job to stop lawmen from trampling over the rights of citizens."[119]

Far from the intellectual but reclusive student that he once had been, Chambers openly expressed his anger at the injustices all around him. He did so with an agile and highly analytical mind trained on the goal of liberation to the benefit of his community and the exasperation of his foes. Back in the spring of 1966, Chambers's solution to the constant oppression of the community and their travail with militarized police was quoted in the

Dundee Sun, a small northwest Omaha publication. "Someone will have to blow up downtown Omaha to convince the white power structure that we mean business."[120] Although Chambers wrote a rebuttal correcting the *Dundee* feature—arguing that the reporter had tried to paint a picture of him as a mad-raving militant and used curse words to enliven the copy—the meat of the article was correct and Chambers would not retreat from his major premises. As for police brutality, Chambers affirmed that "there is physical head-whipping and other rough handling by Omaha police."[121] Worse, there were no means of redress from any authorities, federal or local. "Since there is no redress, we must view the police as armed, dangerous occupation troopers intent on enforcing white supremacy by violence."[122] Chambers's comments were again recorded by FBI agents sent to monitor his talk.

Until the end of the decade, Chambers used the cant of violence in his speeches, but he nearly always pointed out that he had hoped for a peaceful solution to the problems in North Omaha. Unfortunately, he argued, the determination on the part of the mayor, chief of police, public safety director, and city council to use the police to intimidate blacks into silence showed that peace was probably not an option. Besides, he was hopelessly at odds with members of the status quo because his vision for Omaha—for America—included a radical restructuring of society. His overall philosophy included a belief in humanism, a component of which was to provide humane treatment to all groups of people. On the other hand, he once said that blacks should administer all agencies dealing with the public since the abuse that African Americans had suffered created more compassion among them than the apparently "sadistic" white culture produced in its men and women.[123]

Ultimately, the local police stepped up their harassment of Chambers, arresting him in October 1967 for assault. In this case, as previously, Chambers plead not guilty and the charges were eventually dismissed. Four months later, in January 1968, Chambers spoke at a symposium on violence at Northwestern University in Evanston, Illinois. There he repeated his warning that no alternatives were being left to African Americans other than to defend themselves physically from oppressive acts. Two months later on March 9, at 5 a.m., a shotgun was fired into a window of Goodwin's Spencer Street Barbershop where Chambers worked. Chambers told the press that the attack may have been made by Omaha policemen since an unmarked police cruiser was seen in the area shortly before the blast. An unnamed member of the FBI wrote a brief follow-up report on the incident.

"In as much as it does not appear that the incident 3-9-68 was intended to infringe on anyone's civil rights, no federal violation appears to be present. It is recommended that no further action be taken in this matter."[124] Apparently, Chambers's and Goodwin's safety and civil rights were of less concern to federal authorities than Chambers's utterances and his political persuasion.

The two years Chambers spent in law school helped him to formulate his views on government, which were relatively conservative compared to other Black Nationalists of his time. Chambers differed from many other leading intellectuals in the Black Power Movement because he felt that the American system of government was structurally adequate for the development of an equitable society. Chambers's belief that people in the American system kept the nation from functioning fairly makes it difficult to characterize him as a revolutionary in the traditional sense. On the other hand, Wilson Jeremiah Moses points out in his *Golden Age of Black Nationalism* that many Nationalists have had conservative leanings. Moreover, Chambers's own idiosyncrasies, especially his tendency to work independently, may have helped him to escape annihilation by the FBI and local police when those agencies collaborated to stamp out Nationalist and revolutionary activity. A teenager during the Communist purges of the 1950s, Chambers repeatedly said that capitalism and communism or socialism were equally bad or good. It was the unethical and unconstitutional repression of African people that he opposed.[125]

> Systems are not anything one way or the other in or of themselves are no better or worse than the people who make them up.... We have a problem of survival in this country. They're shooting down Black Panthers all over.... In Chicago they want to talk about a shootout where they went in and caught a man in his bed and blasted him.[126]

The problem, as Chambers saw it, was that those in leadership did not uphold the laws of the land or the U.S. Constitution. Determined to make a difference, Chambers ran for the Omaha School Board in 1968, but since the election was at-large, and white voters, for whom he had little appeal, outnumbered his constituents by at least ten to one, he was easily defeated. He ran for the Omaha City Council in the spring of 1969 and again received relatively few votes in the citywide election. In April, Chambers shared the platform with Andrew Young, executive director of the Southern Christian

Leadership Conference, during a forum held at Grinnell College in Iowa. Chambers told the midwestern college students that whites would not do anything to stop the problems they had created. The next month, Chambers spoke in Malcolm X Park (officially named Kountze Park by the city) at a "remember Brother Malcolm X Rally." Raleigh House and Eddie Bolden of the Black Panther Party shared the stage with Chambers, discussing the school system and other problems in the city.[127]

Although Chambers's oratorical and intellectual abilities made him especially conspicuous, his was not a lone voice crying out for change in middle America. A number of civil rights workers, black Christian nationalists, and Black Power advocates engaged in the struggle against racism and toward social change in Omaha. Vietnam War protesters sometimes lent members to the civil rights and black power struggles, and vice-versa. Collectively, the groups helped to inch the pendulum toward the left. Thus, it came to be in vogue for civil rights proponents to remain a part of the freedom movements even though they had defiantly switched from nonviolence in the months after the King and Malcolm X assassinations. Reverend Velton Randall of Quinn Chapel AME Church in Lincoln published an article in the Lincoln press asking whether "anyone in white society [was] listening to 'What the Young Negro is Saying.'"[128]

In Omaha, Chambers's distrust of the mayor had been well earned. Sorensen dismissed Chambers as a militant loudmouth, and he along with the rest of the establishment in Nebraska, including some state legislators, were working aggressively to stifle dissent in an effort to regain what they saw as order. Sorensen condemned the report of the President's Commission on Civil Disorders for its finding that urban unrest in the United States resulted from impoverishment and a lack of jobs, and that the recent waves of rioting had emerged following conflicts between the African American community and the police. A local paper reported Sorensen's comments that the "militant Negro" was the cause of racial tensions in his city. Sorensen also criticized an Omaha Human Relations Department report on the riots for failing to lay blame for "racial tensions on the very militant Negro."[129]

By the summer of 1968, Omaha-based FBI agents stepped up their surveillance of Chambers and other African American activists. The agents began working with and through an intelligence unit of the OPD to set up a "sting" operation in Omaha designed to ensnare black radicals. Their efforts were aimed at fulfilling part of Hoover's agenda to isolate and remove movement leadership. To this end, special agents were directed to keep up with

Chambers's publications in addition to his activities. One of Chambers's essays appeared in the *Buffalo Chip*, a locally published newsletter the FBI considered a "hippie-type underground anonymous publication.... Protesting the war in Vietnam and sympathizing with those advocating racial violence."[130] FBI agents also monitored the comments of those attending protest events, and they recorded pieces of Chambers's speeches. On August 24, special agents observed a rally at Fontenelle Park in Omaha where they saw "Ernest Chambers, a militant Omaha Negro barber, speak at the Peace and Freedom Party Convention."[131] The open-air conference was hosted by white youths. Chambers, always aware of his audience, focused his presentation on condemnation of the Vietnam War, making analogies between imperialism abroad and racism in the United States. Eldridge Cleaver from the national Black Panther Party for Self-Defense headquarters in California also spoke. Cleaver's excessive use of profanity and lack of understanding of local issues led conference organizers to exclaim that Chambers's speech had salvaged the event. Later in the day, a petition was circulated to add the Peace and Freedom Party to the Nebraska ballot. Eddie Bolden, head of the recently formed Omaha branch of the Black Panther Party also spoke. FBI agents recorded statements that were probably delivered by Bolden but attributed them to Chambers. Some of the quotes sounded more like party rhetoric than the typical Chambers's oratory. One agent reported that Chambers said, "to me, Black power is a loaded gun in the hand of the man who knows who his enemy really is."[132] On the other hand, Chambers was becoming increasingly radicalized and revolutionary in his thinking. He associated with a number of Black Panther Party members, including Frank and William Peak, Raleigh and Gary House, Robert Cecil, Ed Brightman, Lewis Davis, as well as Ed Poindexter and David Rice. And, while he cooperated with the Black Panther leadership at political events, he judiciously declined invitations to join their ranks.[133]

2—Man of the People

The civil rights and black power struggles began unfolding in the United States contemporaneously with anticolonial organizing in Africa, and by the mid-1940s they had become chrysalises of the full-blown movements. By some accounts these efforts reinforced each other, as news of valor and boldness in liberation work traveled from west to east and from east to west across the Atlantic, symbiotically infusing confidence into activists and warriors. Africanists, like Chambers, considered the various locations where the black freedom struggle took root merely as alternate theaters in the same war. To understand what Chambers did to help break the reign of repression in Africa's most notorious colonial regime, one must go back to the early days when Chambers was fresh out of the army and still a very young man. His pan-Africanist perspective was published in a 1961 letter he sent to the *Omaha World Herald* when he was in his early twenties.

> Under the Administration of Westerners, whites have grabbed control of much of the natural resources of Africa, bans have been placed on education of Natives, racial discrimination rivals the American tradition, natives are forcibly kept from political participation, many are exiled . . . for refusing to accept a subservient role.[1]

Despite his youth, Chambers was a fervent scholar. He had read a great deal of African history and would have been drawn to explore the life and work of W.E.B. Du Bois. Du Bois led black intellectuals toward an understanding of the international character of the black freedom struggle. He helped found the African National Congress in South Africa (1912), while insisting on political and social equality for black people in the United States. Chambers would also likely have read works from intellectuals like Kwame Nkrumah, George Padmore, and others who demanded that colonialism and segregation end on both sides of the Atlantic.[2]

As a teenager Chambers learned about McCarthyism and noted the public hysteria over communism. Paul Robeson, who was called on to defend himself before the House Committee on Un-American Activities, created a contradiction for young black Americans. Robeson's alleged un-Americanness related to his confrontation with racism in America and colonialism in Africa. Robeson's works, published by the Council on African Affairs, pointed to America's "pro-imperialist" support for the establishment of European trusteeships over African states, and criticized U.S. compromises over racist rule in South Africa. Chambers spoke in support of Robeson while a student at Creighton, and his early writings on racism alluded to these issues. Robeson's message, "Can we oppose white Supremacy in South Carolina and not oppose that same vicious system in South Africa", resonated with Chambers.[3]

For Chambers comparisons between racist regimes in Africa and America were not theoretical but lucid and real. He had personally witnessed two major uprisings in the late 1960s in Omaha. The first incident occurred in the summer of 1966. It began at a grocery store parking lot where community youths were socializing. Police officers arrived and warned the teenagers present to disperse. When the young people argued that they were not doing anything wrong, police used what community members described as excessive force. In return, the youths pelted the officers with rocks and bottles. In the end sixty young people were arrested. Later that night, a few store windows were broken in protest. Police administrators sent multiple units into North Omaha to contain the community folk who walked in the streets demonstrating against the arrests.[4] In spite of an apparent invasion of the community by armed men, the people refused to give over the streets to police. On the third night, the governor brought in 150 National Guardsmen to quell the "milling and rock throwing crowd,"[5] which according to local white historians "ended the first wave of racial trouble in Omaha."[6]

For African Americans, this incident was not the first wave of racial trouble, nor was it the first racial riot the community had endured. Racial trouble defined many aspects of community members' relations with white Omaha. African Americans considered the massive influx of police officers for searches, and violent white marauders, as well as a lynching that had occurred within living memory as race riots. The latest event differed only because it was the first time African Americans had gotten the better of policemen and the white businessmen whose interests the officers protected. Back then, twenty-nine-year-old Ernest Chambers led a community group that "attacked the police response," arguing that the white majority failed to see the enormity of the problems against which African Americans were protesting.[7] Chambers met with Mayor Sorensen. The mayor told the press that the spokesperson gave "no specific reason [for the burning of businesses] beyond suggesting that arrests on the first two nights inflamed the crowd."[8] Sorensen noted that Chambers had mentioned unemployment as a problem in the community, but that constituted nothing new, and was no reason for an outpouring of anger, as far as he could tell. Sorensen suspected that "outside agitators" were behind the upheaval. The new governor, Frank Morrison, who was out of town at the time, was interviewed by phone and answered reporters' questions frankly. Morrison said that much of North Omaha was "an environment that is unfit for human habitation," and so how did they expect people would act living under such trying circumstances?[9]

What were the underlying reasons for such wealth disparities? Historian John Cell's comparison of segregation in the United States after 1890 and apartheid in South Africa at the time of its union in 1910, believes that in both societies, segregation was a solution to maintain labor stratification in modern, urban, industrial economies. According to Cell, legal segregation was a political strategy used to rationalize "a particular configuration of caste and class."[10] Residential segregation along with racially stratified access to schools and various kinds of employment and wages, the main tenets of white supremacy, created impoverished conditions for many blacks across North America and in Africa.[11]

The second uprising started in Omaha in August 1966 when groups of young people looted and firebombed buildings on North 24th Street. At the time, black leaders were put on notice that the mayor's office would hold them accountable if the violence did not stop. Sorensen "discounted rumors that there was any relationship between the violence and the shooting death a few days earlier by police of a suspected young black burglar."[12] Embarrassed by the damage to white-owned businesses and his inability to control North Omaha, the angry mayor informed leaders that some whites wanted to help "the Negro achieve first-class citizenship, but this lawlessness stiffens attitudes and makes it difficult to help."[13]

After the disturbances, the Omaha City Council cut the funding for Omaha's Human Relations Department in half. A spokesperson from Sorensen's administration explained, "There seem to be a lot of suggestions that someone stirred up trouble. For some of these men in the council, it is a natural conclusion that any trouble stirred up would be stirred up by those fellows from the Federal government and the Human Relations Board."[14] Chambers lamented the mayor's ignorance—how typical to suggest that local Africans were content with the system of unequal access to schools, jobs, services, and disrespectful treatment in public and that dissatisfaction had to be "stirred up."[15] Like the majority of Omaha whites, the mayor failed to see the deep discontent of African Americans who lived in their midst, nor did they recognize the many forms of resistance that were happening every day.

In an attempt to head off future problems, city administrators opened a North Omaha Community Relations Office, staffed by African American police officers. The officers were to accept citizens' complaints and give recommendations to the Omaha Police Department. However, African American police officers had issued their own complaints against the department, and their recommendations fell upon deaf ears. Marvin McClarty, Sr., who regularly manned the Police Community Relations Office, reported that he had worked for nine months as a detective yet received patrolman's pay because he was black, though "our success record was high."[16] When Bill Bloom, business manager for the city's police union, spoke in the Legislature against open housing, African American officers protested. However, with less than one percent of the police force being African American, the protest of black officers was easily ignored. Seventeen African American officers quit the AFL-CIO afterwards and formed the Brotherhood of the Midwest Guardians, an all-African police union. McClarty, one of the union's founders, spent time with Chambers and Dan Goodwin at the barbershop. McClarty said that he could vouch for the truth of what Chambers told the press. Things did happen in the community at the hands of white police officers.[17]

To distinguish the proverbial "good guys" from the bad, and not knowing what else to do, "Mayor Sorensen personally hired five or six young black 'leaders' to control and report on the Community."[18] Sorensen asked Chambers to keep an eye on trouble spots in North Omaha. Chambers was thoroughly offended at the notion that he would "snitch" on his community.

He flatly refused. That same year, Sorensen told a U.S. Senate subcommittee that urban violence had occurred in his city because "slumlords" had organized to defeat passage of urban renewal ordinances that would have brought in federal dollars. Publicly, the mayor continued to blame outspoken African American activists for inciting the massive destruction of property, but he quietly approved the city's development of two recreation centers for Northside teenagers and gave some support to a job development program for inner-city youth. Chambers considered the mayor's statement about black militants as blaming the messenger. Throughout history they have been dubbed as the cause of problems they point out, and frequently have been persecuted for their vocalness. One example was the infamous retribution by the U.S. government against Du Bois and Robeson whose passports were denied for statements they made abroad about racism in the United States.[19] In Omaha, Sorensen's measures only relieved a tiny part of the economic and recreational shortcomings of neighborhoods where thousands of potential workers remained unemployed. Community members continued to complain of segregated housing, segregated schools, and police harassment. The basic problems in the community still had not been addressed.[20]

In hopes of establishing mutual respect between the "races," several area churches combined resources to open an urban studies center. The center offered sensitivity training for multiple ethnic groups and was run by the Clair Memorial United Methodist Church. None of these overtures, however, would build a bridge between the white majority and blacks. The fault lines between the black and white worlds were systematically reinforced by Euro-American policemen who worked in the African neighborhood and lived out their fantasies and fears unchecked by the city's administrators.

Whether they supported separatist or integrationist strategies for dealing with racial oppression, intellectuals who worked to eradicate the legal and political legitimacy of colonial governments pointed to police as the front line of white supremacy. In June 1964, when Malcolm X (El Hajj Malik El Shabazz) visited his hometown of Omaha, he made it clear that Africans all across the globe were involved in the same struggle and were, in fact, the same people with the same enemy. Malcolm X met with Chambers, Charlie Washington, and other members of the Citizens Coordinating Committee for Civil Liberties (sometimes referred to colloquially as the For Civil Liberties Club or 4CL Organization) privately to discuss the situation in Omaha and the freedom struggle in general. At the Omaha city auditorium, Malcolm explained that his Organization of Afro-American Unity was committed to bringing African peoples' struggle from the level of civil rights to the level of human rights. He said that the United States should cease its support of imperial ventures into Africa.

Malcolm X expressed succinctly what Chambers had been feeling and thinking. Chambers recalled talking with the international leader at his hotel room in Omaha. "He was one of those persons who commands respect just by the way they walk into a room."[21] A year later Chambers would hear news of Malcolm's murder. As wrenching as the loss was, the politically astute on all sides noticed that Malcolm's assassination did not reduce the popularity of his ideas. *The Militant* reported the year after Malcolm's death, that Dr. King's humility was no longer accepted by the young. Chambers was clearly among the young people who rejected the idea of passive resistance. Inevitably, African National Congress President Oliver Tambo would reach the same conclusion: armed self-defense was unavoidable if the liberation struggle in South Africa was to succeed, because of the intensified oppression and brutality of the colonial regime in its efforts to destroy the movement.[22] The idea of retaliation was gaining acceptance among the youth, and it began replacing widespread enthusiasm for nonviolent direct action. In hopes of minimizing the loss of life in Africa, the United Nations organized an economic boycott of the apartheid regime in South Africa on December 10, 1962.[23] Chambers, like other intellectuals of the diaspora, was encouraged by the liberation struggle in Africa; it reaffirmed his view that Africans everywhere were determined to throw off the yoke of colonialism.

From North Omaha, Chambers watched the struggle evolve. The Civil Rights Movement seemed to melt into the black power struggle overnight, following the assassinations of Malcolm X in 1965 and King in 1968. A social critic and reformer at heart, Chambers reached the brink and nearly embraced the idea that liberation would require a revolution inside the United States. Activism spread from Omaha's streets into Technical High School, Chambers's alma mater. The student group Black Association for Nationalism Through Unity (BANTU) formed. BANTU requested the removal of material from the school library that had no relevance for urban youth and demanded that the curricula be updated with classes on Malcolm X, H. Rap Brown, and other nationalist leaders. School officials considered BANTU a secret society and would not allow the group to meet unless the principal was given a roster listing the names of its members. The youth refused to comply because they suspected that administrators would share the information with police—who would then target members with campaigns of harassment. While the extent of Chambers's assistance to BANTU at this stage is not clear, Technical High School students often stopped by the barbershop to discuss issues with Chambers. When the press learned that an invitation had been given to the Black Panther Party to attend a BANTU meeting, the *Omaha World Herald* wrote that "members of a militant student group affiliating with the Black Panther Party [and who] could face expulsion from school."[24] Either the Panthers or BANTU had a member who was leaking information to the press, or the report was concocted to increase public fear of both groups.

At length Chambers agreed to support the youth, and by 1968 was helping to vocalize the grievances of Tech High students in open-air rallies. In May, the students issued a list of twenty-three demands to improve the school for African Americans. Through his speeches Chambers worked to further politicize the students. He argued that African American schools were given the worst teachers, and that drugs were sent into the African community to disrupt and destabilize it. FBI agents noted that Chambers was not a member of the Black Panther Party, "but did associate with [names have been censored in document]" Panther Party members.[25]

Students in Omaha and in other cities were becoming revolutionaries overnight. Human rights violations by police and others in authority, and reactions by African American communities were reported daily in a growing body of alternative newspapers. Soon urban uprisings covered the country in torrents like a chain of electrically charged high-voltage thunderstorms. In August, Chambers wrote an angry letter condemning Governor Norbert Tiemann for sending the Nebraska National Guard into the African community. Tiemann had ordered the troops into North Omaha on July 26, 1967, the anniversary of the death of Eugene Nesbitt. Nesbitt was an African American teenager, who had been shot by officer Floyd Matula, who said that he had suspected that Nesbitt was a burglar. When he heard that Nesbitt had died, Chambers had demanded to know why, if Nesbitt's only verifiable crime was fleeing from police, no warning shots had been fired. The "failure of Safety Director Francis Lynch to conduct any investigation indicates his intent to uphold the first rule of white supremacy: No white man will be punished for an act of violence (even murder) committed against a black man."[26] "We will not docilely and quietly accept the 'legal murder' of our brother by members of the Omaha police division," he said.[27] If it were possible to radicalize Chambers any further in those days, the death of more community children at the hands of the police could accomplish it. Unfortunately, such events were on the horizon.

In March 1968, an African American teen was found hanging from inside a Douglas County jail cell in Omaha the morning after his arrest. Police reported that the youth had committed suicide. Chambers argued that there was nothing in the cell to stand upon and that it would have been impossible for the young man, who was 5'2" tall, to have hung himself. "We are getting tired of having our people killed."[28]

And then there was the killing of Howard Stevenson a few weeks later. A teenager, Stevenson died while standing under the shelter of a North Omaha shop after the right-wing riot that started when George Wallace, candidate for U.S. president, campaigned at the Omaha city auditorium. Wallace was best known for physically blocking a doorway at the University of Alabama to prevent African American students James Hood and Vivian Malone from enrolling there in 1963. Now five years later, protesters holding signs gathered outside the auditorium in Omaha. Minutes before Wallace was to take the stage the activists were allowed into the hall, but they could not find seats. When Wallace began to speak he asked that the aisles—where the demonstrators were standing—be cleared. Upon Wallace's cue the largely white audience metamorphosed into a mob, according to an African American police officer, and helped the police beat the demonstrators. African American youth retaliated that night by looting North Omaha businesses, and Stevenson was shot and killed by police.[29]

Author Frederick C. Luebke observed that the simmering "animosity between many Blacks and the mostly white Omaha police force" was really never far from the surface.[30] Large-scale violence erupted twice in 1966 and once in 1968 in the form of firebombings of Omaha businesses. The last of the 1960s-style revolts, which occurred in North Omaha in 1969, was like no other, primarily because it had the tactical support of the largest cross section of the community. Firebombings and general unrest began after the events that occurred on the evening of June 24. Chambers was probably in the barbershop when a patron reported that a policeman had shot someone in the Logan Fontenelle Homes, a public housing project. When Chambers went to the scene he learned that fourteen-year-old Vivian Strong had been killed by officer James Loder. Loder and his partner were responding to the report of a burglary, but had frightened teens who were playing records in a vacant apartment. The young people ran when they heard police sirens. For some still unknown reason, one officer took aim, hitting Strong in the back of her head. The police had entered the community, and when they left, an African American girl was dead. News of the shooting death of a fourteen-year-old girl flashed throughout the community. Gravity hung on men's faces. Small children were kept out of hushed circles. Women openly grieved the loss of the community's daughter, and then began to organize. Under the name "Fact Finders," Ruth Thomas, Adelaide Turner, and a host of local women allied with the Urban Action Association. They hand-delivered a letter to the Personnel Board of the City of Omaha expressing deep distress over the death of Strong and urging a "complete review of our law enforcement policies and procedures," including the recruiting, testing, and training of police officers. Strong had been shot by police and was dead. Community youth expressed the rage of the entire community when they burned buildings, broke windows, and otherwise destroyed symbols of white power, defiantly protesting the police killing of an unarmed pubescent girl.[31]

Chambers contacted city officials to express his own anger and frustration over the slain child. Here, he communicated, were a people already incensed by abusive police officers in their midst, and by the lack of response from the city to their complaints. These same people would now fear that their unarmed children would be hunted down and killed. Mona Bazaar, a Jewish activist from California, who was in Omaha during the final 1960s' uprising, tried to explain to whites what was happening. Nationwide urban protests, especially the Watts riots in California, signaled a change in black–white relations. Bazaar said, "After 350 years of fearing whites, Negroes have discovered that it is also the other way around. That whites are afraid of Negroes."[32] Bazaar was correct, and a spirit of vengeance momentarily hung over North Omaha. Bazaar would later publish collected speeches and writings that emerged from the community during that era. She printed in its entirety an open letter to the community written by Chambers, entitled "A Message to the Black People of Omaha."[33]

Chambers's letter accused the mayor, county attorney, chief of police, and governor of being accomplices in the young girl's death because of their failure to discipline her killer. Chambers pointed to Police Chief Richard R. Andersen's commendation of white officers' actions as they rode "rough shod" through the community afterward.[34] Chambers reported that officers threatened residents, used profanity and placed loaded guns to the heads of drivers as "they carried out false arrests."[35] Chambers said that it was sickening how cops "felt over the bodies of young Black women" and generally harassed the community while removing their name tags so as not to be identified.[36]

The larger white community did not see any such excesses. In fact, Governor Tiemann praised the police for their work in the community during the riots. The police union even created a fund to supplement Loder's salary while action against him in Vivian Strong's shooting was pending. Bazaar recorded all of these events and published the testimony of the teenagers who were with Strong when she died, who said "we were playing records" when the police arrived and that Vivian had gone to see what was happening.[37] "He shot her right in the head."[38] One witness said, "I saw the policeman and he had a pistol in his hand. The girl was running. I hollered, 'Don't shoot, don't' shoot. But he did." After Strong had fallen face down, eyewitnesses reported that Loder turned her over with his foot and that his African American partner, James Smith, asked, "Why did you shoot her?"[39] Loder didn't reply, Smith said. Smith would eventually testify that before Strong's death, Loder had confided in him that he had to "work himself up" before he could enter the "ghetto."[40] Smith said that he and Loder had argued on several occasions over Loder's racist comments. Strangely, Strong's killing, like other police killings in North Omaha, failed to make the national news. In her notes, Bazaar said that she believed that the media in Omaha suppressed the news of police homicides of blacks.[41]

Within a day of Vivian Strong's death, Chambers led a group of community members to Omaha City Hall to meet with the mayor. He saw the county attorney in the corridor and gave him a list of eyewitnesses that he had gathered at the scene on June 24. When the mayor appeared before the group in the city council chamber, Chambers handed him a list of ten demands, including that Loder be charged with murder and relieved of duty. He also asked that a federal indictment be sought for a probable violation of Strong's civil rights, and that white officers be kept out of the community. Chambers said that the city or state should give Strong's mother $100,000 as compensation for the wrongful death of her child.[42]

At the close of the meeting, Mayor Eugene Leahy promised to address North Omaha residents at Malcolm X Memorial Park the following Monday. At that time the community would hear the city's response to Chambers's demands. The mayor did not keep his promise, and Chambers was outraged at Leahy's cancellation of the meeting. The crowd assembled anyway, and Chambers spoke. He said that the county attorney, whose job it was to file felony charges, had not talked to a single witness from the list of twelve he supplied the mayor. "The only version he had of the killing was that given by the killer."[43] Before the crowd dispersed, Chambers recalled, "the burning started."[44] Fires were set at businesses along North 24th Street. White policemen attempting to enter the community were repelled with bottles and rocks. The uprising and arrests continued for the "six days between Vivian Strong's' killing and her burial," and while Chambers tried to calm the crowds and told the youths to go home, he would not condemn the spirit of resistance.[45]

An animated Chambers told the press that Douglas County Attorney Donald Knowles had "prostituted himself" for political gain when he only filed a charge of manslaughter against Loder, who had long demonstrated that he hated blacks.[46] A complaint filed by Goodwin against Loder prior to the Vivian Strong killing should have been reviewed by the judge, Chambers said. In a previous incident, Goodwin had watched Loder pull his gun on a group of junior high students returning from a skating party. But, when Loder's case went before Municipal Judge Walter Cropper, rather than listen to such facts, Chambers observed, Cropper said that he had much respect for the officer and wanted to release Loder on his signature. To pacify the swarm of citizens who were angry about the girl's death, the judge set a $500 bond. Chambers was livid. The city had orchestrated the investigation so that no one had to pay for the killing of the young unarmed girl. Chambers then tried to express the loss of the girl in a way that anyone could understand:

> To them, we are not human beings. When one of our black children is shot down, it is never murder. . . . As the last four prove. . . . What kind of a charge would have been filed, if Mayor Leahy's daughter were shot in the head. . . . Would Chief Andersen praise the police for killing Mayor Leahy's daughter?[47]

The number of establishments broken into increased nightly. The unrest was not abating. Chambers and Goodwin stood outside of E-Z Drive Thru Liquor Store trying to prevent kids from entering the building when police accosted them. Chambers later recalled that the police officers showed up with shotguns. One "leveled a sub-machine gun at me, and others began forming a circle about me. Dan and another young guy came to my aid."[48]

African American youths targeted white-owned establishments, especially those with a history of disrespecting black customers. The shop where police had killed sixteen-year-old Howard Stevenson the year before was burned to the ground. Some black businesses burned as well, Chambers recalled, but those were connected to white-owned establishments. Firemen claimed that they could not put out those fires due to snipers whom they alleged were shooting from rooftops. For the next several days the community suffered harassment by white police during the day, and smashed symbols of authority by night. Even the religious conservatives could not bring themselves to condemn the youth. Police "shot into the Black Panther Office next door to the barbershop and cut down their flag," Chambers recalled.[49] On Friday, June 27, Chambers phoned the mayor with some suggestions. Chambers asked that the county attorney be charged with negligence since he had failed to file appropriate charges against Loder. Leahy called Chambers back and asked that Chambers keep his concerns confidential for the time being. Chambers replied that he had already been invited to speak about the shooting on KRCB Radio in Council Bluffs, Iowa, and he would keep his engagement set for later that evening.

On June 28 after the radio program on KRCB aired, Chambers and Goodwin went to the barbershop to pick up Chambers's typewriter. They soon noticed that they were being followed by several police cruisers. The officers drove beside them from 30th and Binney Streets heading north.[50]

Chambers remembered the incident in this way:

> That night, Dan drove me across the river. . . . It was near midnight when we returned to Omaha and encountered the police. . . . The [radio] program was picked up in Omaha because the station was so close. I spoke very frankly (as usual) about the killing itself, ongoing police problems, the unwillingness of officials to take corrective action, and criticized the Mayor.
>
> Dan drove to 30th Street. . . . Traveling north . . . we stopped for a traffic light at 30th & Binney. A police car with two officers (at least) pulled alongside and also sat at the light. I was in the back seat behind Dan who was driving . . . We hadn't gone far when the cruiser's flashing, spinning lights came on. Other cruisers materialized.[51]

The squad cars followed Chambers and Goodwin fourteen blocks before pulling them over near North 24th Street. When they stopped, more cars of officers arrived. "Dan and I were ordered from the car with shotguns pointed at us." Chambers heard Officer Philip S. Gibillisco say, "We were told to get the big fish, and we got him."[52] Chambers's gun, which was on the back seat, was taken. The activist yelled to a community member watching the episode to call the mayor. Gibillisco replied, "City Hall ordered the arrest."[53]

Just four days after Vivian Strong's death, Chambers sat in jail on a concealed weapons charge. He plead "not guilty" and was awaiting his hearing when he wrote an essay entitled "Omaha, City of Fascism," which was published a month later in the July 26, 1969, issue of the Black Panther Party newspaper.[54] Chambers described how he had been locked up on a charge that was usually a misdemeanor, but in his case felony charges were filed. Goodwin was also charged with a felony. Both men faced fines of up to $1,000 and two years in state prison. Chambers wrote that if convicted, he would be barred from returning to law school or running for elective office—something he had done unsuccessfully in the past but which he might try again. He said he believed that the mayor and the chief of police had arranged for his arrest because of his refusal to back down from demands that the officer who had killed Strong be fired and charged with murder. Chambers also suspected Nebraska State Senator Terry Carpenter of being part of the group who decided that he was to be picked up because Carpenter's name appeared on a document related to Chambers's arrest that had been given to Chambers's lawyer.[55] The mayor was angry, Chambers wrote, because he had refused to keep quiet about the list of witnesses to the Strong killing. All of this happened because the community protested the killing of one of its children in a city where police killings of black teens "are an ongoing phenomenon," Chambers said.[56] "This is the fifth one in four years. No pig has ever been punished in any of the cases."[57] Chambers's language matched his feelings. Community children were not safe and could be killed at will by police officers, against whom there was no recourse for bereaved parents, and protests brought arrests and the separation of activists from the community. Initially booked on suspicion of possession of a concealed weapon, Chambers noted the "irony" that his bond was set at the same amount as the policeman who killed Strong.

News of Chambers's arrest reached the San Francisco student community by early December, via an advertisement asking for support for the Omaha Frame-Up Defense Committee. The committee pledged support for Chambers who now had to combat a contrived charge of carrying a concealed weapon. "In place of Bobby Seale, read Ernie Chambers. . . . In place of Mayor Daley, read Mayor Leahy, and the cast is complete for yet another sickening chapter of American history. Fascism comes to Omaha, Nebraska."[58] In the end, Chambers proved that the gun had not been concealed at the time of his arrest, the police stop had been illegal, and the charge was ultimately dismissed without a trial. He was released and continued speaking out against police brutality in Omaha and its nexus—colonialism in Africa.

In the meantime, Officer McClarty, who had spent many weekend hours at the barbershop and was there the night Vivian Strong was killed, suffered under the police department's backlash. McClarty recalled the disturbances, which started at Horace Mann School in North Omaha, and that white officers could not get to 24th Street. Several days after the rioting subsided, a police inspector called McClarty to say that a car was waiting outside his home to pick him up—police administrators wanted to talk to him. When McClarty entered the precinct, the room quieted. "They had it from sources that I was in Chambers's barbershop. . . . Passing out rifles."[59] McClarty was relieved of duty while he was the subject of an internal investigation.

A few weeks later, on July 15, 1969, Chambers met with members of the International Association of Chiefs of Police [IACF] to discuss what he felt was corruption and abuse of power that was practiced regularly by the Omaha Police Department in their dealings with North Omaha residents. He later learned that during the meeting, several police officers were sent to investigate a burning car near the community center where his wife, Jackie, volunteered. The officers questioned several children who were playing outside about the fire. One of Chambers's sons was present. The youths later described the incident. The officers, the children said, repeatedly told them that the car fire had been set by Chambers's six-year-old son. The children had replied that they thought another boy had started the fire, and told the officers his name, but the officers repeated their refrain, "No, you mean Ernie Chambers's son."[60] Fortunately, Jackie Chambers discovered that the officers were in the alleyway talking to youths from the center, and went outside to retrieve the youths. She told the policemen that they had no right to "intimidate children" and ushered the children back inside.[61]

In November 1969, the IACF published a report on their investigation of police community relations in Omaha. The IACF found that there was a "disturbing chasm between the police and the minority group persons they serve." On the other hand, the IACF said, the attitude of the police reflected that of the larger community.[62] Across the racial divide, Chambers, and members of Omaha's Black Panther Party (BPP) were busy intensifying their criticism of the local police. Outspoken BPP members included David

Rice, Edward Poindexter, Eddie Bolden, David Poindexter, George Davis, and fifteen or twenty other young men. As tension increased between neighborhood youth and the police, Roger Sayers, Omaha Human Relations director, asked both sides to stay calm and not overreact to the others' comments. Neither the Panthers nor Chambers retreated; they remained in the forefront even as local authorities planned the end of black radical resistance in North Omaha.[63]

The entire situation was such a paradox. What cruel fate that Africans brought to America suffered unimaginable oppression in slavery and its aftermath, and yet, that those who remained in west, central, and southern Africa also faced domination. Chambers recollected back to 1964 when he was with a small group of leaders who accompanied the anti-colonialist Malcolm X to his hotel room after the lecture in Omaha. Chambers listened intently. Malcolm was a student of Africa and had interrogated colonialism, encouraging African nations to rise to independence. America's most vocal and well-known Black Nationalist had long felt the need for an international perspective in dealing with racism in America and in Africa. Malcolm declared that the solution to racism for African Americans was to join the worldwide struggle for human rights. Only by supporting other colonized peoples could African Americans hope for liberation. Solidarity with the international struggle for liberation was the only way to wage the struggle against colonialism within the United States, and not be overcome by a sense of isolation and fatalism. In this context, Malcolm said, black people outnumber whites "eleven-to-one."[64]

By this juncture in his intellectual life, Chambers began preparing to do whatever was necessary to protect the community. He was formally educated, but also studied the history of his people. He was armed and would use his weapon for defense if needed—and the intensification of violence between police and the citizens of North Omaha made it seem that he would. However, a shift in the current of events emerged unexpectedly, starting with news of Senator Edward Danner's sudden death in 1970. Although many young black activists considered Danner too ready to compromise, he was trusted and respected by the older generation on the Near Northside. The need for an effective state legislator to represent North Omaha would significantly alter Chambers's strategy. In 1970, Chambers ran for a seat in the Nebraska state legislature as a representative from the Eleventh Legislative District, which represented the largest number of African Americans among districts in the state. During the campaign, Chambers would not change his basic style; however, his speeches became less rhetorical and were more often substantiated with legal references, as he made the transition from activist to activist-politician. Chambers's core values would continue to anchor his work, and, for the remainder of his life, he would embrace Black Nationalism.

In the weeks before his first election to the Unicameral, Nebraska editors seized on Chambers's rhetorical phrases and advised readers that Chambers's level of acceptance by the Eleventh Legislative District at election time would reveal the mood of the black community and explain the new "expectations for racial relationships" in Nebraska. The press wanted specifically to print Chambers's perspective on the recent murder of a police officer and whether the candidate for the Unicameral felt "remorse" about the policeman's death.[65] The newsmen were referring to officer Larry Minard's death and to the arrests and pending trial of the local Black Panther Party leadership.

Minard died on August 17, 1970, while responding to a call to the Omaha Police Department about a domestic disturbance, or possibly a rape. The caller led officers to an empty house where a wired suitcase exploded and killed Minard. Police launched a massive manhunt looking for anyone involved in the bombing. With the help of the FBI, they soon began focusing their investigation on members of the BPP. On Thursday morning, August 27, Chambers arrived at police headquarters with David Rice, the party's vice chairman and minister of information, Rice's attorney David Herzog, Marvin McClarty, Police Sergeant Pitmon Foxall, and one of the ministers from the neighborhood. They were escorted by two cars in which other Northside community members rode. Chambers acted as Rice's spokesperson, pointing out that the twenty-three-year-old had turned himself in of his own free will after hearing on the radio that a warrant had been issued for his arrest. Since the case involved a policeman's death, Rice feared that other officers would kill him on sight. He went to Foxall and McClarty for help, Chambers said, because they were the only two policemen whom "he had confidence in for his safety."[66] McClarty recalled the day that Mondo we Langa [AKA Rice] turned himself in. A young man in his early twenties, Rice sought out McClarty of the 24th and Erskine Street Police Community Relations Office, who met him and took him into custody. After turning Rice over to the authorities at the police station, McClarty was accused by white officers of hiding him in the community relations office. Joe Friend told McClarty that there was a lot of tension on the force and that he should write a response to the accusations. McClarty said he preferred to be sent home or suspended.

After mass arrests of African American men, Duane Peak, a fifteen-year-old BPP affiliate, was charged as the lone killer, confessing, eventually, to having constructed, set, and detonated the bomb that killed the officer. Despite encouragement by police to implicate higher-ranking BPP members, Peak refused, repeating that he had acted alone. Chambers, who observed the court proceeding was struck by the repetition in Peak's testimony that no one else was involved.

Midway through Peak's preliminary hearing a recess was called. When he returned to the stand, Peak was wearing dark glasses and appeared uneasy. The youth then changed his testimony, claiming that local BPP leaders Rice and Ed Poindexter told him how to design and set the booby-trapped suitcase.[67] Rice's and Poindexter's attorneys believed that Peak was under terrific pressure to implicate the party's leadership. Meanwhile the antagonistic investigation of Minard's death in the segregated community continued and reports of random stops of cars and searches in homes by the police in North Omaha for potential suspects abounded. Under pressure from the police to help identify BPP affiliates as potential suspects in the Minard killing, and given the party's aggressiveness in their relations with white authorities—in spite of the BPP's breakfast, health, and other worthwhile programs—the community was conflicted about how to respond.

Chambers was advised not to defend Rice and Poindexter in public and to stop condemning the police. However, he saw no reason why he or other black men should be associated with the killing of a white officer, which was probably carried out by a lone individual. A student of history and the law, Chambers was aggravated by the presumption of guilt by association for an entire ethnic group. No white officers were checked for possible negative views of blacks after one of their members shot the teenager Vivian Strong. Besides Chambers's irritation at whites labeling all blacks as criminal, he wondered why whites felt that they should be able to count on blacks' alliance in the first place. In September, during his presentation at the University of Nebraska Medical Center, Chambers was again asked about his feelings for the slain policeman, and he gave an answer which would make headlines: "Will I cry for a man who's destroying my people? How many Jews cried when the ashes of Adolph Eichmann were dumped into the Mediterranean Sea, and how many Jews wept when Hitler put a bullet in his head?"[68]

Not only did Chambers fail to show "remorse" over the death of patrolman Larry Minard, but he decided that he would not abandon an individual who had in his own way tried to protect the community. If it were a state of war, and challenging white police control and abusiveness in North Omaha was a war, then the death of a soldier of the opposing army was not murder but a casualty. What did Chambers think about the death of Minard, the policeman who had been killed in his district that August? Although he could empathize with the loss by Minard's children and immediate family, Chambers used the moment to help whites understand the level of ongoing grief suffered by Omaha's African American families.[69]

During his speech at the University of Nebraska–Lincoln before the Afro-American Collegiate Society on September 21, 1970, Chambers said he believed that the slain policeman "was a white cop who volunteered for duty in the black community because he knew he could get away with busting heads."[70] From Chambers's perspective the courts had not listened, and the police department had not listened. The police murders and brutality continued unabated on the Northside and someone had struck back in the only way that would receive attention.[71]

McClarty also tried to put the policeman's death into context. There is "no doubt in my mind, Mondo [AKA Rice] is innocent," McClarty said.[72] Rice testified over and over that he had no role in the killing of Minard, and although the prosecutor could not prove Rice's involvement, the state of Nebraska convicted him by arguing that he conspired with others who did commit the murder. The real problem, McClarty said, was that there was a great deal of fear of the Black Panther Party on the police force. White officers said there were thousands of Panthers out there, "and you could tell them by their afros."[73] McClarty estimated that there were only twenty-five or thirty Black Panther Party members in Omaha, but hundreds of youth were wearing naturals.

> They harassed Mondo and Ed. Just a small group of young men, never threatened anybody. . . . Mondo had never been in a fight. . . . When people say I'm black and proud, white people say we're antiwhite.[74]

When Chambers noted that there had been no outcry of support from the white community for the family of Vivian Strong when the fourteen-year-old girl was killed by a white officer the previous summer, the editors of a Norfolk, Nebraska, newspaper accused Chambers of being blind to the basic difference in the cases, since Strong's death was a mistake in judgment and the Minard slaying was premeditated. Chambers responded that the bombing may have been intended only to be a warning to white officers to stop killing black teenagers.[75]

In 1972, Poindexter and Rice were convicted of murder in the Minard case and were sentenced to life in prison. Many would agree that the wrong men were convicted. Chambers said the collusion of the police and the press in Omaha was part of the problem:

> Let me give you one example of how this works out. An Omaha filling station man was shot. The police department and the press said next day they were looking for Negroes who had done it. The very next day a white father said this son of his had been in a killing and his conscience bothered him. They had arrested a number of Negroes already for it. Suppose the white boy's father had not told that his son had done it? They would still be rounding up Negroes right now in Omaha.... This is the way it always happens.[76]

Chambers believed the combined effects of watching white law violators go free, seeing police abuse the law in the community, and observing the jailing of African Americans on questionable evidence led some people to the cynical view that "there is no such thing as the law."[77] He once said that if a white police officer stopped a black man and the person asked the officer what he wanted, "[H]e can put me in jail for resisting an officer or shoot me.... These are the realities of life for black people. Can you understand that?"[78] When young whites riot like the students did at Fort Lauderdale, Florida, turning over cars and setting fires, no one said they needed more police power. Yet black people who demonstrate for civil rights are jailed, Chambers said.[79] Chambers argued that the entire system was created to favor whites at the expense of everyone else. "You let a white merchant beat some people out of some money ... but if a child in turn throws a brick through that store window," he risks being killed.[80]

The federal government's perspective on urban rebellions and their presumed leaders—who were generally any Black Nationalists in the vicinity—were discussed by President Lyndon Baines Johnson in his "Address to the Nation" on June 27, 1967. In his talk, the president pointed to the causes of urban riots as having roots in poverty, discrimination, and unemployment, and he said that "the only genuine, long-range solution for what has happened lies in an attack ... upon the conditions that breed despair and violence."[81] Publicly, the president expressed his desire for a war on poverty and for a peaceful society. On television, Johnson called for Americans to respond out of conscience, "not because we are frightened." Behind the scenes, however, he supported J. Edgar Hoover's FBI in their clandestine attacks on political groups and the removal of the very men and women who had brought the problem of depravation in their neighborhoods to the attention of the nation.[82]

Chambers's reaction to further interrogation by the media regarding his views on police–community violence was explosive, netting him a fresh wave of condemnations by the Omaha Police Union and the mainstream press. "If justice had been meted out there would have been eight bodies buried," Chambers said, inferring that all eight policemen who responded to the 911 call (in the Minard case) would have died, since that was the number of Black Omahans who had been killed for noncapital offenses on Omaha's city streets by police.[83] The police, Chambers mused, only do what the majority of whites allow.[84]

A few weeks later, the FBI informed Chambers by letter that they had intercepted a death threat against him. A wary Chambers reflected on the possibility that the government itself might have ordered a hit on him. It was quite possible that he was to be next in the wave of political assassinations that had plagued the country. Not sure of where the threat was coming from, discomforted by knowledge that he could be a target, and with zero confidence in the messenger, Chambers gave a Machiavellian response. He had received many threats on his life, he said, but if he were killed or if an attempt was made on his life, a major riot could result in Omaha. The special agent in charge at Omaha relayed Chambers's response back to Hoover.

While the FBI mounted its clandestine attack on Black Panther Party chapters around the country, the U.S. military continued to fight the war in Vietnam, relying on a disproportionate number of urban black youth for infantry. Chambers kept a close eye on news from Vietnam and recounted publicly America's political and military blunders. President Richard Nixon asked for an additional $354 million for the military in mid-1970, all the while vetoing congressional bills for domestic programs. Even Congress was tiring of supporting the president's demands for war funds, and U.S. senators had begun to complain that the president was bypassing Congress in decision-making, such as his issuance of orders for the bombing of Cambodia. Chambers kept up his antiwar rhetoric, arguing that imperialism and racism could not be separated and that all groups of people had the right to self-determination.[85]

Chambers had opinions about virtually everything, and he believed that truly held convictions were demonstrated by action. One of his pledges to himself was to do all that was in his power to keep African American children safe from mental or physical abuse by adults, and to demand adequate schools for community children. To this end, he attended a conference in Atlanta, and worked hard to get petitions signed condemning Georgia governor Lester Maddox for his plea for "massive citizen resistance" to the desegregation of the state's public schools.[86] The editor of *Everybody Magazine* suggested that "if the late Senator Edward Danner could awake for just a few moments, he would probably say a good word for Ernest W. Chambers."[87]

Chambers soon began putting his energies into a different sort of campaign. He had decided to canvass for money for the defense of Angela Y. Davis, the most prominent African woman in the Black Power Movement. A Black Panther Party member and a Communist, Davis was in jail in California, charged with conspiracy to help George Jackson escape prison. Chambers recognized what he considered a frame-up job on Davis as a part of the nationally coordinated FBI–police attack on the Black Panther Party and other activist groups under the code name COINTELPRO, which stood for Counter Intelligence Program. He also noted Davis's sacrifices; she was a woman who stood up in defense of the community and was jailed. His sense of justice and chivalry converged and he worked in her defense. However, Chambers's radicalism was tempered by his knowledge that the misuse of power was occurring at every level of government. During a speech, he told Creighton University students not to "send money to the Angela Davis Defense League" because it was run by the Communist Party and "law enforcement authorities might later use that" information to associate the students with communism.[88] The Communist Party had been designated as an unlawful organization by the U.S. attorney general, and its members were subjected to governmental scrutiny and repression. Chambers said that he would not lead the youth to engage in activities that might sacrifice their futures.

Chambers's occasional statements on the insufficiency of nonviolence to meet the brutal challenge of white supremacists and imperialists kept him high on the FBI's surveillance list. His file, secured after passage of the Freedom of Information Act, notes that the senator's case remained open for years, primarily because Chambers continued to utter what federal agents considered "hate" or inflammatory ideas—as outlined by Hoover under his COINTELPRO agenda. Although COINTELPRO was officially disbanded around 1970, human rights groups would complain that the program's policies continued to be practiced by the bureau for decades. Unfortunately, victims of false evidence manufactured by federal agents would remain in prisons all over the country into the next century. As for Chambers, one federal agent said that he thought "the subject" intended to work politically to make positive changes for his community through the system.[89]

The truth was that Chambers had always been involved in community organizing at multiple levels, and that he himself had not escaped brushes with legal authorities, a hazard of advocacy work that befell nearly all serious activists. In January, the short-lived *Realities* newsmagazine published Chambers's response to being called before a grand jury to disclose his political activities. He, along with David Rice, was one of eight regular contributors to the avant-garde magazine, and it was their writings that authorities wished to investigate. Chambers told the press that the way that grand juries functioned in Omaha was to hold secret meetings and prohibit defendants from confronting their accusers. His summons by the jury indicated that he was under investigation but, Chambers said, instead of being charged with a law violation forthrightly, "the United States District Attorney was hoping that I would say something incriminating. . . . My appearance was pure political harassment."[90] Chambers was correct that the convening of a grand jury was rarely done in Nebraska, and the occasion of his appearance marked only the third conveyance of a grand jury since the 1940s. His guess was that the whole affair resulted from a collaboration between city and federal officials and police administrators to crush African American activism in Nebraska. On the stand, Chambers refused to speak, exercising his Fifth Amendment right:

> Stationed around the courtroom were federal agents in plain clothes. After I invoked my Fifth Amendment right a few times, the judge said something and left the courtroom. The agents began leaving, except for two who remained by the doors. They began to fidget. (I was still sitting in the witness chair.) Finally, the last two agents exited the room, leaving me all alone. When nobody returned, I left also. That was how it went. And that is how it ended.[91]

Chambers later told the press that if he was ordered by the judge to testify he would

> raise questions about the hoax of their investigation of a Black Liberation School while closing their eyes to public schools like Horace Mann and Lothrup where students are abused and cheated

out of their constitutional right to a decent education. . . . And the cold-blooded police murder of Vivian Strong is also worthy of some investigating . . . Or the beating of patrolman Robert Dacus by a white patrolman without any action being taken.[92]

Anyway, Chambers argued, the post of U.S. district attorney had always been a perk and was really only a stepping-stone to political office. He had tried to entrap Chambers because that was the role of the pawn in a much larger game. In the colonial context in which Africans struggled for liberation, whether in Johannesburg, South Africa, or in Omaha, Nebraska, freedom fighters like Chambers would remain the adversaries of the status quo.[93]

3—Grounded Politician

Ernest Chambers's father, Malcolm Chambers, had spent most of his life working as a laborer in the meatpacking industry. The elder Chambers belonged to a generation of men from North Omaha who relied heavily on negotiations with "the better class of whites" for the progress of black people. Improvements in race relations were considered as synonymous with increases in educational and employment opportunities, and progress and regression were calculated by the advancement and notoriety of African Americans in the various fields of endeavor, or, conversely, by a lack of participation of blacks. The *Omaha World Herald* interviewed Chambers's father in the fall of 1969. When asked about Ernest's civil rights work, his father told the press, "I agree with Ernest's goals but I don't always agree with his methods. . . . I probably wouldn't be as outspoken and vociferous as he is," but that they were "still friends."[1]

In 1965, North Omaha voters elected Edward Danner, a member of Chambers's father's generation, to represent them in the Nebraska state legislature. Five years later the community would choose Ernest Chambers, a community activist and Black Nationalist. A veteran union organizer, Chambers's predecessor in the Unicameral was more vocal about social problems than most of his peers. Danner studied his constituency and noted that the African American unemployment rate was ten times that of other ethnic groups. He worked hard, lobbying on and off the floor of the legislature to win passage of the 1969 Nebraska Civil Rights Code, which prohibited employment discrimination. The legislation was also designed to eliminate discrimination in housing, something Danner thought was necessary since ninety percent of Omaha's 30,000 African Americans were segregated on the city's Northside.[2]

Like Chambers, Danner was a community-rights advocate before he ran for political office. In early 1961, after reading Nebraska governor Frank Morrison's plan to root out crime in North Omaha by increasing the police presence there, Danner argued that seventy-five percent of crimes committed on the Near Northside were the result of unemployment. "May I suggest to you while your investigator is looking into the 'Near Northside' situation, that he conduct a survey to determine the non-employment of Negroes, and the industries which do not employ minorities."[3]

Danner continued:

My Dear Governor,
I noted with interest through the public press that you are sending someone to Omaha to investigate reasons for such a high rate of violence and crime in the "Near Northside," Omaha. . . . Being a Negro myself, and handling problems daily which directly affect Negroes, I am well acquainted with the problems Negroes have, especially in obtaining employment in a city and state which just recently boasted that it had no unemployment problems. . . . There are quite a number of industries in the city of Omaha and surrounding areas which do not employee Negroes.[4]

The following year Danner, in his capacity as first vice president of Union Local Number 47, wrote to Omaha Mayor James J. Dworak protesting the fact that the Omaha Urban League had directed their entire staff to work on the nearly all white-District Five election campaign. Danner complained that the league's white leadership could not know the problems North and South Omaha residents faced and that the league's board of directors was controlled by the Omaha Chamber of Commerce, which was on record as opposing passage of a fair employment ordinance. "How does anyone expect us to believe that those who deny Negroes jobs could possibly be interested in our health and welfare? I cannot."[5] Moreover, Danner told the mayor, home improvement loans were not available to blacks and African Americans with enough income to buy housing anywhere in the city were consistently redirected to the ghetto by real-estate companies.[6]

Danner's sponsorship of fair housing and employment legislation was probably his greatest achievement. During his tenure in office, Danner tried to create opportunities for black professionals and academics in governmental posts. For example, the statesman suggested to Mayor A. V. Sorensen that Dr. Claude Organ would be an excellent choice to fill a vacant seat on the city's Personnel Board. Chambers would have taken a different approach to helping African Americans win city and county posts. Instead of seeking patronage, he would prefer legislation to change at-large elections to district-based elections. The switch could make possible, for the first time, winning of those posts by black Nebraskans.[7]

Once in office, a representative for North Omaha would be bombarded with letters from constituents filled with testimonials to the racism that they encountered at work and in seeking services in Omaha and Lincoln. Danner's experiences foreshadowed Chambers's in this regard. A typical case, one that occurred under Danner's watch, was the constituent who had a dental emergency at work and his employer sent him to a local dentist. Upon arriving, the man was refused service and called racial epithets. When he returned to work, he told his boss what had happened and that he was going to report the dentist to city authorities; he was promptly fired. During Danner's five years in the Unicameral, he repeatedly dealt with his constituents' complaints about discriminatory treatment.[8]

Despite all that they had in common, Danner was seen as "reasonable" by Omaha's white leadership in a way that Chambers would never be. An important difference was that Danner kept his confrontations with city officials out of the press. This does not mean, however, that he did not publicize the community's problems. Once Danner organized a tour for thirty-four state legislators to ride through North Omaha to view what he described as the dire need for housing relief programs and antidiscriminatory housing legislation. The tour was scheduled for June 1, 1967—the day before the legislature would begin debating Danner's housing bill. For the most part, however, he did not criticize other officials, or their policies, publicly. In general, Danner was straightforward and relatively predictable, thus, it was not uncommon for Mayor Sorensen to write Danner a confidential letter asking for "guidance." Sorensen wrote Danner on one occasion to inquire about the housing problem in Omaha and how best to approach the U.S. Department of Housing and Urban Development for relief, and Danner sent a private reply.[9] In spite of his acceptability to both Omaha's and Lincoln's elite, Danner was a somewhat controversial figure in Nebraska's outlying white communities. His housing bill polarized the state, and, while activists in Lincoln circulated a petition in support of fair housing legislation, "opposition committees" were organized by segregationists in Hastings and in Kearney.[10]

Although they shared similar convictions, the generation that separated Danner from Chambers affected both the content and style of their activism. Danner ran his reelection campaign on the noncontroversial platform of supporting education for blacks, but once in office used his position as chairman of the Labor Committee to fight for African Americans' employment. Meanwhile, Chambers would fight racism and discrimination in North Omaha, and he kept the public informed of his battles through his manipulation of the press. Determined to win opportunities for African Americans, Danner would likely have approved of the appointments of George Althouse and Woodson Center's renowned director Alyce Wilson to the newly established Equal Opportunity Commission in Lincoln, and would have seen their appointments as a marker of racial progress. Chambers, who came of age during the Civil Rights Movement and grew into full adulthood during the Black Power Movement, considered Althouse's appointment as worthless. Althouse was a conservative who stressed accommodation, rather than confrontation with white power.[11]

Danner and Chambers both received scores of "hate" letters. They each also received information from whites describing racist groups and incidents. An immigrant to Omaha, S. R. Merrer, wrote to Danner of the "hot bed of racial hate at the Eagles Hall at 24th and Dodge.... Once you join they point out to you with pride that no [blacks] are permitted.... Why should a hate organization like the Eagles be tax exempt?"[12] The two also got letters and phone calls describing police assaults on unarmed blacks. In one incident, Danner learned that police officers had followed two African American males around North Omaha after having ticketed them for negligent driving. When the police officers pulled them over for the second time that night, they asked Ennice Lispcomb to get out of his car; they had a warrant for his arrest for petty larceny. Lispcomb later described his beating by the officers. His companion, Gary Kimsey, tried to intervene and was shoved and pushed by the policemen. Lispcomb said that he was beaten again at the jail and was not allowed visitors for a day. Lispcomb was not charged with larceny at all, but with interfering with and assaulting an officer, and his bond was set at $1,000.[13]

In many ways, Danner's career anticipated Chambers's. By networking with the Human Relations Board and African Americans at the Urban League, Danner was able to push his civil rights agenda. The younger man would inherit and broaden this chain of political networks. Chambers was well read in addition to being active in politics. And, although Chambers might not agree, it is possible that Danner's example helped the young aspiring politician shape his own priorities. Danner's career ended abruptly in early 1970 when he suffered a fatal heart attack. Nebraska governor Norbert T. Tiemann appointed an African American Republican, George W. Althouse, to finish out Danner's term.[14]

During the summer of 1970, shortly before Chambers announced his candidacy for the legislature, the Unicameral voted unanimously to pass Resolution Five in support of American prisoners of war and soldiers missing in action. The legislators' position clashed with large numbers of Nebraska youth who protested the American presence in Vietnam. A separate measure would increase penalties for persons who vandalized public buildings and requested the use of the state's emergency fund to help repair damages from riots and to find out who the protesters were. Senator Terry Carpenter backed the resolution, stating, "I don't think it is broad enough. We not only have fire, but we are now having bombs, even to the point of attempting to blow up [in] the city of Omaha, a building which could have had a number of policemen" inside.[15] Carpenter was referring to the firebombings that had occurred in Omaha with some frequency beginning in 1966, and to a suspicious fire that had damaged a structure on the University of Nebraska campus in Lincoln.[16]

The resolution was withdrawn after the state attorney general ruled that the Governor's Emergency Fund was only for actual emergencies and that senators could not appropriate those dollars to pay rewards to persons for information about who started the fire at UNL. Edward Danner had died by the time the foregoing debate took place in June 1970. George W. Althouse, appointed by the governor as the representative of North Omaha, was present—but silent. Already the differences between Danner's leadership and Althouse's approach were in sharp contrast.

Unimpressed with Althouse, Chambers announced his candidacy for the post. The *Omaha World Herald* responded by printing an editorial lauding Althouse's merits: "Sen. George Althouse, the Nebraska Legislature's only Negro member, made a deep impression on his fellow legislators. . . . Althouse let it be known that he was not a meddler but a listener."[17] The newspaper endorsed Althouse's candidacy over Chambers's, arguing that Chambers "has shown no talent or inclination for working with others, a problem solver he decidedly would not be. The quieter Senator Althouse appears to be the kind of man who would get legislative results for his constituents."[18]

Many community members were determined that Althouse not be elected. An article appeared in *Everybody Magazine* questioning "Althouse's Real Age."[19] The caption under Althouse's photo read "Master Liar, Uneducated 'Tom' Quiet as Mickey Mouse."[20] The editorialist revealed the contempt and impatience of young African Americans in Omaha with anyone who tried to appease white racism. During his campaign, Althouse apparently told the reporter that he was sixty-eight years old. A reporter for *Everybody Magazine* did some research to find out that Althouse was born in 1894 and that he was seventy-six years old at the time he was running against the thirty-three-year-old Chambers for a seat in the state legislature.[21] The magazine also charged that Althouse was attempting to gain financially from the community's problems. "Using such institutions as St. John A.M.E. Church, the Y.M.C.A., the Red Cross, the Eppley Boys Club; George has built a vast political machine in Omaha that is solely supported by funds from various white business and political personalities, such as Peter Kiewit, [and] A. V. Sorensen."[22] The paper reported that Althouse had been expelled from the Prince Hall Masons because of charges that he had misappropriated funds.[23]

The same publication included a paid advertisement for Chambers's candidacy and a letter from Nettye Johnson, Chambers's sister. In "Ernie the Man," Johnson gave a rare account of Chambers's private side. Johnson said she "couldn't remember [Ernest Chambers] kissing and hugging—to show affection," but that he showed love and concern in other ways.[24] "He doesn't drink and won't change his course of action because other people don't like it, if it is what he believes."[25] Her brother was "very angry . . . because of racism and 'our silence' in the community."[26] Finally, Johnson said, she was proud of Chambers.

Community activists rallied around Chambers, while the mainstream press kept tabs on the Chambers–Althouse race. After reading the paper's opinion that the contest for the Eleventh Legislative District had besieged the African American community, Chambers complained that the *Omaha World Herald*'s reference to the race as a squabble "was typical of its degrading headings when the subject is connected to Blacks."[27] Ironically, Althouse's sole speech during the Unicameral's special summer session won endorsements for Chambers from the Danner family—and from another opponent in the primary elections, Michael B. Adams. Adams, also a contender for the Eleventh District's legislative seat, had worked in the city's planning department and for Greater Omaha Community Action. His grandfather John Adams, Sr., had served as a Nebraska state senator. A community activist, Michael Adams was outraged at Althouse's behavior in the legislature. Adams recalled that while speaking on the floor of the legislature in June, Althouse had said to his colleagues, "there are two things which can give a man heart trouble—running up hill and meddling in other folk's business.... If it was his [God's] plan that the white man was to be in command, then there's nothing we can do about it."[28] Adams said that North Omaha would not be fairly represented by Althouse and his "plantation antics." Chambers wholeheartedly agreed.[29]

Marian Danner Williams, whose father had died of a heart attack in office, said she was stunned by Althouse's statements. She told the press that, yes, her father had "spent his entire life running up hill in battle and running interference on behalf of all of his people—the poor, the sick... whether white, Indian, Mexican."[30] She said that her dad would "turn over in his grave... if we do not elect Ernest Chambers as our state senator," and if he heard his successor claiming that God chose whites to rule because of the color of their skin.[31] The message from Danner's daughter served as a powerful endorsement for Chambers. It would substitute for being selected as a successor by Danner himself, though Danner had named the young activist among a group of rising North Omaha men whom he felt were particularly promising. The Danner family's support brought the weighty expectations of older community members upon Chambers, those who had witnessed Danner's hard-won battles—lobbying for a fair housing ordinance, equal employment laws, and advocacy for prisoners. Danner's quiet style, however, never caught the attention of the youth, who demanded open confrontation with white power. Chambers himself was mildly critical of Danner as too willing to compromise.[32]

Now Chambers was buoyed with optimism about the upcoming elections, confident that what he brought to any political office would be an improvement over those who preceded him since, in his view, they spent part of their time coddling racist whites. The battle for a seat in the Unicameral had only just begun. Three days after Danner Williams's letter appeared in the press, Althouse made his own statements to the media, ostensibly in hopes of putting out the fire that his comments on the floor had ignited. Althouse said that Chambers would represent only blacks if elected, while Althouse would represent all ethnic groups.[33]

Althouse badly judged the times. Instead of keeping silent on the controversial issue of the American presence in Vietnam, he waved the homeland banner, expressing his support for U.S. policies. In fact, he used loyalty to white America as the subtext for many of his political statements at a moment in history when even many middle-class and conservative whites were resigning segregation to the heap of "noble" lost causes and the conflict in Vietnam as unwinnable. Despite all of the hoopla in the press over the Althouse–Chambers race, Chambers kept sight of the fact that he had two opponents in the 1970 nonpartisan primaries. In addition to the Republican Althouse, there was his friend, Michael Adams. Chambers had known Adams for years and told the press that if he were not running for the same office, he would have voted for Adams. The two activists agreed on many issues, including the need for school board elections by district, the dire necessity for changes within the Omaha Police Department (OPD), and an end to discrimination against African Americans. David Rice, Black Panther Party member and former Greater Omaha Community Action employee, moderated a panel discussion between the two men; Althouse was also invited but did not appear. Although both candidates presented their platforms well, Chambers went further than Adams in condemning the status quo. Chambers argued that labor unions in Nebraska practiced racism. Not only had he learned from his father's experiences as a packinghouse worker, but Chambers had himself encountered prejudice as a U.S. postal worker in Omaha. His platform included a public condemnation of Omaha policemen. They were "the scum of white society.... The police department, from top to bottom, is shot through with corruption and incompetence, and I exclude nobody."[34]

It was his boldness in challenging the establishment and his refusal to bend when the press, city and state government officials, and conservative black leaders came after him that made Chambers unique. Not only could he go toe-to-toe with the powerful, but when the dust cleared, Chambers always seemed to be left standing. He was a heroic type of figure, someone not to be messed with, a freethinker whom nobody could beat. Althouse refused to debate him and failed to attend the candidates' forum at Wesley House. This irritated some community organizers. Rice, an active Democrat, considered the incumbent state senator's failure to show up for the meeting as disrespectful to the community. Rice passed around a petition stating "as far as we're concerned, George Althouse isn't even running."[35]

Althouse had been appointed by Governor Tiemann when Senator Danner died, but when the election results were tallied Althouse's lack of popularity with voters became clear. The incumbent finished behind Chambers in the legislative primaries: 916 to 666 (Adams came in a close third with 543 votes). To be sure, not all whites approved of Althouse, just as not all African Americans agreed with Chambers's style. V. J. Mason wrote to the local paper arguing that it was a sad sight when a legislature of supposedly educated senators applauded Althouse's argument for "a divine master planning for a master white race." Mason was referring to Althouse's statement during legislative debate that God put the white man in charge and there was nothing anyone could do about it.[36] The community's response was embarrassment, and the senator was the subject of some hostility. In mid-June, Althouse told the press that Chambers's supporters had intimidated people who would have voted for him. He complained that during the spring primaries, workers at his headquarters had been threatened by people working for the Adams's and Chambers's campaigns. Chambers did not believe the charges. "The Governor down in Lincoln . . . probably told him to say this, like he has told him to say other things."[37] Chambers said the incumbent knew he was trailing in votes and was "reaching for a straw."[38]

Actually, the police killing of a young teenager over a year before was the catalyst for a marked change in the community. After Vivian Strong's death, young people who grew up in North Omaha could sense deep inward disappointment in the adults. Clearly, changes were in order for the way Omaha police functioned in the African American community. Althouse never expressed the idea that something had to be done about the way that the community was policed. The election of 1970, at some level, involved issues of African survival in the West, and although Chambers had no knowledge of it, Althouse's headquarters probably did receive spontaneous threats. An outspoken African American policeman headed the meager line of courageous community members who volunteered to work on Chambers's campaign. Officer Marvin McClarty was among those who opened a campaign office for Chambers at 24th and Lake Streets, and he was not deterred by the death and bomb threats that were phoned in. The majority of community folk showed their support for Chambers in the privacy of the voting booth.

Across the nation, fear of reprisals for voting against white power was only just beginning to wane. Passage of the Voting Rights Act of 1965 raised black people's confidence in the electoral system and the number of African Americans in state legislatures across the United States surged. The national count of black state lawmakers went from 64 in 1965 to 406 over the next 24 years. In retrospect, Charles Jones and Michael Clemons have argued that black caucuses are the key to leveraging political power within predominately white institutions and the communities they serve. However, in the early years when the number of representatives were few, or where African Americans served alone in their statehouses, the strength of their representation was not necessarily as diluted as one might expect. For example when Leon Jordon, a former policeman, and Bruce Watkins, a mortician, formed Freedom Incorporated in Kansas City, Missouri, in 1962, to create political unity among black voters in order to break the power nexus of white political boss Louis Wagner, they set in motion a series of political events that would result in unprecedented black local representation in the Midwest. Up to then, Wagner had selected candidates for the African American community, namely conservative J. McKinley Neal, the state's only black state senator. Freedom Inc. ran a people's campaign, electing Watkins instead to the city council. Almost immediately, Watkins and Freedom Inc. began lobbying for passage of a referendum banning discrimination in public spaces. In 1964, Jordon and Harold "Doc" Holliday, Sr., were elected to the Missouri state legislature, by the same body, and by 1978, the black political machine had became powerful enough to elect two African American city council members, four state legislators, and a judge, and were behind the appointments of a number of African Americans to local boards. With the exception of one conservative politician who relied on the support of white voters, black elected officials representing twenty-two percent of the city's 500,000 residents were all members of Freedom Inc. The cohesiveness of Kansas City's black political club was unmatched by any other metropolitan area at that time.[39]

In contrast, North Omahans formed only ad hoc grassroots organizations organized around key issues and for the election of specific individuals, but lacked a black political machine that would continuously function over a period of years. A great deal of black politics in Omaha then revolved around problems that ebbed and flowed in form, but that went substantially unchanged for fifty years. The ongoing challenges included the struggle over equality in education, community development through black business opportunities and loans, housing (the problem of discrimination eventually mutated into issues of affordable housing), and the issue of policing. The savvy of the black electorate in determining the community's collective position on proposed laws and on desirable political leadership made widespread personal allegiance to Chambers a cultural and political phenomenon.

Chambers took his popularity in stride, and spoke to his community regularly during the campaign. "I am not a miracle worker and cannot promise the impossible, but following is a list of items to which I'll address my efforts when elected."[40] Himself a parent of young children, Chambers promised to push for district elections for the Omaha School Board and to have some aspects of education mandated by statute. He promised to help provide reliable scrutiny of federal funding for schools to make sure the dollars reached those for whom they were intended. Chambers also promised to urge an investigation of the Nebraska State Penitentiary, and penal reform to rectify segregation and other forms of discriminatory treatment of African American inmates and to ensure educational opportunities for prisoners. He would work for implementation of stiff penalties for child abuse in schools and homes and would press for the punishment of drug pushers. He recommended the establishment of treatment centers for addicts. Chambers also hoped to find an effective method for removing incompetent judges, including those unable to perform their judicial duties due to racism or senility. Additionally, Chambers believed that city government should be liable for abuse and other negative actions by police. Finally, Chambers said that he was basing his candidacy largely on his reputation for honesty and courage.

Although well attended, his constituency's low-income base meant that Chambers's campaign speeches netted just over $1,000 combined. Dan Goodwin collected contributions at the barbershop totaling just under $400. Contributors included relatives of both Chambers and Goodwin; Omaha basketball star Bob Boozer; Carl Peterson; *Omaha Star* writer and editor Charlie Washington; lawyer Bob Broom; and businessman John Standard. Nanette Graf and Elizabeth Koenig were two of several Euro-American women activists who contributed along with more than forty other supporters.[41]

At thirty-three, Chambers was more accomplished than most men in the state. He had earned a degree in history from Creighton University and had completed two years of law school. His advocacy and fearlessness made him, for community members, the candidate of choice. Considered a "militant" by whites, the majority of Northside families who knew Chambers considered him well grounded and trustworthy, although many would hesitate to admit their feelings in the presence of white people. Weeks before the fall election Chambers told reporters, "I don't plan to storm into the legislature and demand things be done. . . . I will identify the areas which have problems and recommend solutions."[42] Chambers said that once elected he would work to get rid of the Omaha Police Court, which "too frequently disregarded rules of evidence and discriminated against the poor in their judgments."[43]

The media continued to pay close attention to the legislative race. In October, *Jet* magazine covered a fund-raising event hosted by the Chambers campaign. As usual, Chambers's sharp words were noted by the press. In a speech given before supporters, Chambers called America "a violent and lawless country" whose president was "conducting the most violent war in the history of this godless, imperialistic nation," while at the same time calling on Africans to be nonviolent.[44] An *Omaha World Herald* reporter wrote that many people wondered whether Chambers could get along with the other forty-eight senators. Chambers wrote a rebuttal that set the tone for what would be a long and often sour relationship with Nebraska's most widely circulated publication. Chambers responded that he could be rational and reasonable when dealing with reasonable people. Piggybacking upon the majority community's expressed fear of Chambers's Black Nationalistic leanings, Althouse called a town hall meeting. Althouse said his purpose was to make it clear that he planned to address all of the constituents in his district and not just the seventy-five percent that were African American.[45]

Occasionally, white activists would contact Chambers and offer support for his campaign and for the black power struggle. Chambers responded to white liberals as Malcolm X (El Hajj Malik El Shabazz) had done, by suggesting that white people go and educate their countrymen. It was, after all, whites who were perpetuating the nation's biggest problems, he said. Naturally, there were a few exceptions. One of these was author Lois Mark Stalvey. Stalvey had been introduced to Ernie Chambers in the late 1960s by Dr. Claude Organ, the African American head of surgery at Creighton University's Medical Center. When Chambers told her that all whites benefited from racism and so were oppressors, Stalvey appreciated his honesty. Several months later, Stalvey told a group of well-educated African Americans in Omaha how important Chambers seemed to the community. To her surprise, many upper-class African Americans inferred that Chambers's outspokenness could be awkward for them. Chambers was clearly loved most by the people who had the least economic and political power. To them, "Ernie" was the archetypal survivor, and the essence of a courageous and just man found in both African American and mainstream American folklore. Stalvey was deeply impacted by her encounter with Chambers. Her first book, *The Education of a WASP*, was published in 1970 and contained many of the lessons that Chambers had taught her. She later wrote to Chambers that "there is no question that my book[s] would not have been written without your influence."[46]

Meanwhile preelection day activities intensified. The *Omaha World Herald* reported in late October that Arthur A. Fletcher, "A high [ranking] official of the U.S. Department of Labor, said in Omaha Tuesday that 'we don't need any more civil rights legislation on the books, for now.'"[47] Fletcher was in town to support fellow Republican George Althouse's bid for election. He was welcomed by a handful of African American Republicans from North Omaha and spoke at St. John's African Methodist Episcopal Church.[48]

On November 4, 1970, when Chambers's victory was formally announced, congratulations streamed in via Western Union from around the state, and supporters cheered at his campaign headquarters. This is a "victory for all our people, even those who do not yet realize it," wrote one Nebraska woman.[49] Other congratulatory telegrams were sent by the Urban League, and from Chambers's mother and family. The Citizens Coordinating Committee for Civil Liberties (4CL), an activist group that Washington belonged to, wrote, "We extend greetings of pride and love to you Ernie on your victory in the election, sincerest congratulations, Senator Chambers."[50] Chambers paused to enjoy the moment with his own family and told his school-age children, Mark, Gayla, and David, they could stay home from school to celebrate along with himself, their mother, Jackie, and young Ernie, Jr. In the following days, Chambers agreed to a number of interviews. He told the press that his electoral success was a result of "Black people who are tired of white people determining who will represent them."[51] Chambers said that his victory

> was a defeat for black preachers, the *World-Herald* and the *Omaha Star,* who endorsed Althouse; Governor Tiemann, who had appointed Althouse to the senate seat . . . and Sam Cornelius, Federal anti-poverty official . . . who brought to Omaha . . . Arthur Fletcher to campaign for Althouse.[52]

Privately, Chambers cast the election results in spiritual terms when he wrote, somewhat sarcastically, that "the forces of evil were defeated."[53] He said that "Althouse was "obviously the white people's candidate," one who had been "bending the knee and prostrating himself before the white people. . . . The only hang up is that he [needed] Black votes to win."[54] Despite the desires of local government and the *Omaha World Herald* who wanted to pick the community's representative, Chambers said, those days were gone. Furthermore, the activist pledged, being in office would not change him. He would continue to wear T-shirts and when it was cold, turtlenecks. He would continue to cut hair at the barbershop on 3122 North 24th

Street. Chambers played a tape-recorded "victory speech" for reporters. The voice recording was of Malcolm X speaking and may have been a recording of the speech that Malcolm gave when he came to Omaha in 1964.[55] Malcolm said that the black community needed leaders with love for their people in their hearts and that "the day is gone when whites can control the Black community or send in other Negroes to do it for them."[56] One reporter noted that among the many political signs on the walls of the barbershop was a poster that read: "If laws strangle and subdue a people, then God damn the laws." Another said: "Feel inferior? Enjoy beating Black people and want the 'thrill' of killing? Join your local police force."[57] To the white community, such statements would appear radical, but to many in Chambers's district, they made perfect sense.

Since Chambers had won fifty-seven percent of the vote, he reasoned that the majority of the community supported him, and at any rate, he expected to serve only one term. Always the pragmatist, Chambers's mind raced forward. His immediate goal was to meet with Public Safety Director Al Pattavina about getting white officers reassigned and "putting black policeman in the Ghetto."[58] Asked if he thought that his views would bring him into clashes with the other senators, Chambers said, "My mind is open toward them as I hope theirs is toward me."[59] However, if getting along meant changing his habit of standing up for what he believed in or stopping his advocacy of African people's political interests, then they would not get along. "The item which was selected by the people of the Eleventh District is the item which will go to the legislature."[60] Chambers could not know that the election of 1970 would set the course for his life.

After the election festivities, Chambers began studying the lawmaking process in preparation for his induction into the legislature in January. He learned that the usual method for drafting a bill was for a senator to take his idea to the bill drafting office whose staff members would then write it up formally. A senator would then file the bill with the Legislative Clerk's Office for introduction during the first ten days of the new legislative session. This would not be overly difficult, and Chambers felt that he was ready for his first day. Senator-elect Chambers spent the months between his November victory and January 1971 researching and speaking publicly. He had two months before the convening of the Unicameral in January and devoted some of his time to contemplating the new stage that the liberation struggle had reached in Omaha and around the world. In a short period of time, one African country after another had declared independence, and black people had dismantled legal segregation via the Civil Rights Movement. Racism was still practiced everywhere but at least it was not upheld by the law. His cautious optimism was interrupted by yet another episode with Omaha policemen. In 2005 Chambers recalled it this way:

> One summer day, in the early evening, I was driving two of my sons to a downtown movie. They were both in the backseat. I had been receiving many threats, but I wasn't going to let that stop me from taking my children on outings. I had the gun on the frontseat. My sister was concerned and said she would let me borrow her pistol whenever I took the children anywhere.[61]

He was pulled over by the police and ticketed. When the press learned that charges were pending against Chambers for possession of a nonregistered gun, the information became a featured news item. Police noted that Chambers had said that the gun was registered, but would not tell the officer who it belonged to. Privately, Chambers made an inquiry with his sister—who had thought that the gun was registered.

The "offense" of carrying a nonregistered gun was misdemeanor according to the Omaha Municipal Ordinances, punishable by up to six months in jail but the usual penalty was a $500 fine. Since it was not a felony, the charge could not have kept Chambers from taking his seat in the legislature. Still, when an article appeared in the news about the incident, Chambers may have had a sense that his life had fallen under even heavier scrutiny since the election. He made a statement, however, dismissing the arrest as typical harassment by police.[62]

The 1971 Unicameral convened on January 10, and seven days later the *Lincoln Journal* reported that sparks between veteran legislator Terry Carpenter and the freshman senator were the "highlight."[63] Both men were extraordinarily witty and were skilled at debate; it made good copy when they locked horns. Chambers would serve during his first term in office with some of Nebraska's most popular Euro-American politicians, including P. J. Morgan, Eugene T. Mahoney, and Jerome Warner. None of these men showed a deep interest in improving the lives of African Americans in the state, but, some would argue, that was not what they were elected to do. They each represented the priorities of their own districts. The reigning theory was that if a politician took care of his or her district, the best interests of the entire state would be served since the interests of the whole would be balanced by the needs of the various citizens. Chambers believed that the process could work if representatives advocated for the majority of their constituents and not only for the wealthy. He would represent everyone, but would place the needs of the poorest people first, and he would strive to make the community in Omaha between Cuming and Pratt Streets to the south and north and from 33rd Street on the west to the Missouri River below 16th Street a safe place to live.[64]

First Days

Chambers wrote a journal entry on his first day in the Nebraska state legislature.

> I arrived at the capitol this morning (10:00 a.m.). Upon entering the building, I was subjected to many stares . . . all new senators were invited to take a seat . . . left of the area where incumbents are seated. . . . Photographers began snapping pictures, and newsmen set up lights for film.[65]

A number of senators approached Chambers with advice:

> Pederson, particularly, came and talked about the great opportunity I have to do something for 'my people' down here, but he warned me 'not to blow it' by being too hasty or too forceful in my presentations.[66]

Chambers told Pederson, "I have an obligation to the people who elected me and I intend to honor it." He reminded the veteran senator of his record of opposition to election of school board members by district.[67] "Rather than all of their being concerned about my conduct," Chambers wrote, "they'd do well to consider that of the other 48 senators."[68] "Even old Batchelder—law-and-order-racist that he is—gave me a firm handshake. . . . Had I been unaware of his past, glaring record of anti-performance, perhaps he could've made me regret that he will not be around for the coming session."[69]

At noon the senators went to the Cornhusker Hotel to meet governor-elect James J. Exon. At Chambers's table, the conversation focused on the conditions of the poorest districts. Chambers recorded his impressions after the new governor rose to speak. "James Exon is a big, rough-hewn man with a friendly ingratiating manner. Time will tell whether it is real or a front."[70] Exon hoped the senators would ignore party differences and work together for the good of the state. Chambers approached Exon afterwards and said there were specific cases that he would like to discuss, and Exon said that he had wanted to meet with Chambers before the legislative session began.[71]

The following afternoon Chambers spent time visiting with a "young white senator" named John DeCamp.[72] DeCamp told Chambers that he had been able to get elected by leading his constituents at Neligh, Nebraska, to think that he was a conservative. DeCamp said that he was considered a crook because of the way he ran his campaign and that he failed to carry his home precinct due to his reputation for "crookedness."[73] Still, Chambers agreed to conduct exchange visits with DeCamp, each touring the other's district. Chambers noted that DeCamp "told a reporter (who published it) that I have the power to start a riot, but have chosen, instead, to utilize 'the system.'"[74] Senator Gene Mahoney introduced himself to the freshman senator. Mahoney told Chambers that he had been stopped by a highway patrolman on the way to Lincoln earlier that day, and that he had been victimized by the state patrol because of his opposition to Governor Tiemann. Mahoney then walked Chambers to the bill drafter's office, and Chambers took the opportunity to bring up his idea of dividing the Omaha School District into several districts in order to arrange for the election of school board members by different sections of the city—an idea whose time had not yet come. Chambers disapproved of his colleague's evasiveness. "Mahoney is tricky, subtle and most slippery. He bears watching," Chambers wrote.[75] "I had a brief chat with Terry Carpenter the first day. . . . He's very different from the way news accounts portray him. He is able to carry on a rational, amiable conversation.[76] Chambers recorded his conversation with Carpenter in his journal:

> Senator, what you do and say outside the legislature is your own concern. We have nothing to do with that. However, if you make a speech on this floor [legislature] which alienates the other senators, you'll hurt your cause and limit your chance of getting anything done here. Senator [Edward] Danner cried and begged his way to more legislation.[77]

Chambers replied:

> Senator Carpenter, I'm not here to do any crying or begging. That's not my style. Nor will I be like Senator [George] Althouse who said,

on this floor, that 'God put the white man in command.' I can't go for any nonsense like that. And even worse than his stupid comment, the other senators applauded him. That tells me a whole lot about what I am dealing with down here.[78]

Chambers knew racism's faces before entering the legislature—overt and subtle, Dr. Jekyll and Mr. Hyde—and that he would serve as the lone African American in a body of whites. "I knew they were products of a white racist culture, and I knew that I'd face the same thing in this legislature that I did everywhere else so I didn't say in my mind 'I'm going to come down here and take time to learn the rules and how they do things.' No. I'm not."[79] Chambers said he would pick up the parliamentary "niceties" with time.

Chambers later reflected upon his initial floor debate:

> First day I was down here I got into a conflict with Terry Carpenter who had everybody shaking and in fear. Nixon was going to come on the campus and that was when they had the anti-war fervor. . . . Terry Carpenter was going to condemn the students because they were going to wear black arm bands and they thought it was disrespectful. . . . [I] talked about academic freedom and freedom of speech. . . . Terry couldn't get the best of me.[80]

Chambers said that before long he and Carpenter were friends, debating over "trivial matters, but on matters of substance it was as if we were joined not just at the hip but from head to toe."[81] Chambers proved the equal of the maverick veteran senator—to the utter amazement of the other solons. But then, Chambers had long before passed the litmus test. He had won his seat in the Nebraska Unicameral in the context of a nationwide trend to use civil rights networks to elect community-chosen "natural" leaders to political offices. The same year that Chambers was elected, three African Americans joined the U.S. House of Representatives for a total of twelve. The state legislatures of Alabama, South Carolina, and California each gained an African American state senator; it was the first time since Reconstruction that African Americans held so many political offices. Most of the successful campaigns were won on the Democratic ticket and yet Chambers would note the disrespect which both the Democratic and Republican Parties treated nonaligned and African American members. Chambers's fate as an Independent was long sealed, however, going back to the 1964 Democratic Party National Convention when the heads of the Democratic Party had refused to seat delegate Fannie Lou Hamer and other members from the Mississippi Freedom Democratic Party. Here represented was perhaps a third of the population of Mississippi, organized on a grassroots basis primarily by women, in order to circumvent the racist machinery of the white-led Mississippi Democratic Party.[82]

In the winter of 1970, Chambers received word that the weapons charge against him had been dismissed. The court decided that the seizure of Chambers's gun had been illegal since no search warrant was presented and officers had no cause to search his vehicle. Although he had been concerned about the pending charge against him, he had refused to alter his political work because of it. Chambers's post-election agenda would be a logical progression of the strident advocacy that he had practiced in the community. However radical his colleagues might consider them, the senator would file his bills with the Legislative Clerk's Office for introduction during the first ten days of the new legislative session.[83]

Chambers's entry into state politics signaled to the community that they had reached a new stage in the struggle. Chambers election was an unquestionable coup by the community and represented what the majority of African Americans wanted all along: a voice in government, a gatekeeper for the community who could help send employment, housing, and other resources in and keep violent repression out. The concept of community did not apply only in a strict geographical sense to people in Chambers's district, but to African Americans wherever they resided. Chambers now represented about one-twelfth of the people in Omaha and roughly two percent of the people across the state. In spite of attempts to keep him from political office through false arrests and by supporting his opposition, local historians Lawrence H. Larsen and Barbara J. Cottrell argue that absorbing a "militant" into government was perceived as less threatening by the Omaha power structure than to continue to exclude blacks from the political process. Federal agents would have their work cut out for them trying to keep up with Chambers after January 1971. Although they knew that he would commute daily between Omaha and his office in the state capitol at Lincoln, they could not know in advance with whom he would meet, either in his office or at the barbershop, or what his speaking itinerary would be.[84] Chambers's election, from the perspective of the status quo, would likely appease and calm the African American constituency. And Chambers's success did give the community hope. However, the establishment underestimated Chambers's prowess as a statesman and his dedication to liberating black and low-income people.

Chambers's first term in office went so well and his skill and aptitude for debate at the legislative level was so high that more than one reporter commented on his shining abilities in comparison to his colleagues. Affirmed in what he felt his talents and abilities were, Chambers tried hard to help those most in need. He was often frustrated during debate by what he perceived as a lack of ethics and a lack of concern for the poor on the part of his colleagues. "I admit that I have always felt a lot of bitterness about the way we have been treated. That bitterness has increased. I can see now that a lot of things which would be beneficial to thousands of people are not being done because of legislative pettiness or indifference."[85] Chambers told the press that his colleagues showed no concern over unemployment, educational quality, poverty, hunger, or racism.

The senator's relationship with the Nebraska press as established that first year would remain intact for the rest of his career. The Lincoln papers, whether the *Journal* or *Star*, frequently noted Chambers's intellect and progressive ideas and used his talks on the floor to help validate some of their own liberal views, such as the notion that government should work to eliminate suffering. The *Omaha World Herald* more often than not criticized Chambers for his "failure to support the police" and for his open critiques of other elected officials. However, the general consensus of North Omaha was that "Ernie has done an outstanding job." An editorial printed in the city's Human Relations Department publication opined at the end of his first legislative session that the Omaha senator had brought thoughtful and carefully researched bills to the floor and worked to represent minority groups as well as low-income whites. By the end of his first year in office, with compliments flowing and with his confidence mounting, Chambers began to consider running for the U.S. Senate.[86]

Adjourned

That summer Chambers was photographed beside his wife Jackie and with his brother Eddie, in front of a crowd of community people gathered at Malcolm X Memorial Park in Omaha. A banner reading "Happy Birthday Senator Chambers" bedecked the platform.[87] That afternoon Chambers had been at the front of a motor parade that spread over eight city blocks—from 21st and Burdette Streets to the outdoor field. At least 500 people (some estimates ran into the thousands) attended the event, and Dr. Earle G. Person, Jr., borrowed words from Ossie Davis's eulogy for Malcolm X, stating "in honoring you [Chambers], we honor the best in ourselves."[88] Harold Adler, a regional officer from the B'nai B'rith Anti-Defamation League, said that Chambers could not be intimidated. Chambers spoke briefly, mentioning the upcoming fight for the job of his brother Eddie Chambers who had been fired by the Omaha School Board. Eddie Chambers had been terminated along with several other African American teachers by Omaha Public Schools (OPS). The school district had hired Chambers the year before to comply with federal directives for integrating their teaching staff. Once they were no longer under the scrutiny of federal authorities, OPS fired the teachers who had been offered positions to satisfy the federal mandate. Even the *Omaha World Herald* condemned the behavior of the Omaha School Board in Eddie Chambers's case.[89] The U.S. Department of Health, Education, and Welfare Civil Rights Office found that Eddie Chambers's application "had been treated discriminatorily," and he had been let go.[90] Senator Chambers quickly filed a complaint on behalf of his brother with the federal Civil Rights Office.

Chambers explained that he was fighting for equal rights on multiple fronts and in several different theaters. Two months into his first term, his own civil rights bill came up for debate. He had sponsored the measure because he did not believe that the city of Omaha would pass a civil rights ordinance with any teeth in it. They had failed to give the power of subpoena to the city's Human Rights Board. He was also continuing to address complaints to city administrators and would deal directly with organizations and individuals who violated the civil rights of his constituency. Before closing out his speech at the park—in an uncommon public display of emotion—the senator thanked his community for placing their trust in him.[91]

Omaha Human Relations Department Director Roger W. Sayers announced that his organization's greatest accomplishment that year was helping to organize "the Community salute to Senator Ernest W. Chambers."[92] Sayers had discovered that a five-minute weekly news slot allowed by KETV to the Human Relations Department enhanced his ability to communicate with the public and improved the organization's standing in the eyes of community members. Using the airtime to ally his organization with Chambers's name had not hurt his popularity either. Sayers vouched that his agency would continue to try to relieve economic conditions in North Omaha by supporting tenants' rights to voice concerns to the Omaha Housing Authority, pressing for improvements in the public schools, and eliminating job discrimination. Looking back, the previous two years had served witness to a number of political changes in the community. The Black Panthers had been attacked and virtually removed from the scene, but on the other hand, the community had achieved a phenomenal stroke in the election of "Ernie."[93]

Mona Bazaar wrote to tell Chambers that news of his election had reached the West Coast. The California activists who had supported the Panthers during their travail with the Oakland and Los Angeles police, and who had attempted to raise funds to defend Chambers when he was jailed the previous year on a weapons charge, now learned of his election to the Unicameral. Bazaar wrote, "How wonderful to see your return address—Senator Ernest Chambers! To think how a short time ago . . . [they] tried to railroad you to jail on a phony gun charge. How galling it must be to them to see you elevated to state senator."[94] Bazaar closed her letter by saying that she loved Chambers. His senior by many years, Bazaar did not necessarily mean that she was interested in romance. It was the simple admission of admiration for Chambers's courage and dedication to the people. It was attractive to her, and she would not be the only woman to feel this way. A busy, but devoted husband, Chambers took the attention in stride. He was too engrossed in planning or countering each new bill to be overly flattered. However, the attention and accolades from women's associations, legal defense funds, activists, and student organizations did not wane.[95]

In May 1971, politically neutral groups like the Urban League of Nebraska quietly acknowledged Chambers's political might and paid political homage to him. If anyone could effectively go to bat for their budgets, he could. Raymond Metoyer, president of the Urban League of Nebraska, wrote to Chambers asking for his stamp of approval on the organization's philosophies and programs: "Your involvement with the board and the community has a definite bearing on whatever effectiveness we hope to make in the . . . change of those that propagate hardships on blacks."[96] Chambers responded positively to the Urban League's overtures. At that time, some of his most trusted associates sat on the board. Marvin McClarty and Charles B. Washington were then two of the league's three vice presidents. Earle Person was also on the board of directors, and so were Rick Davis (owner of Davis Insurance) and Michael Adams (Chambers's opponent in the 1970 legislative primary). Other members of the board included Eugene Skinner, African American educator, Carney Rountree of Upward Bound, and Lawrence R. Myers, who would become the head of the Equal Opportunity Commission. The board was a fair sampling of African American Omaha's educated elite with a smattering of self-educated activists.[97]

Before the end of the year a group of politically minded North Omahans organized a black caucus to help other African Americans win electoral posts and to influence the political process by organizing the community's vote. They had been buoyed by the anticipation of their own rising political power, sparked by Chambers's success. When it was time for the senator to run for reelection, the group readied their endorsement. Many also supported Chambers's friend Dan Goodwin. Goodwin gave his time to a number of community organizations, including the black-run Council for Community Justice, School Community Advisory Board, and Omaha Opportunities Industrialization Center's board of directors. Now he made an unsuccessful bid for a seat on the Omaha School Board. Goodwin ungrudgingly conceded that he did not have the senator's oratorical gifts and thus did not enjoy the wide appeal that "Ernie" could garner. Neither did he have as many enemies.[98]

Chambers received and read hundreds of letters from Nebraskans and from around the country. Hate mail arrived with the rest of the correspondence, and Chambers kept special boxes for it. He collected piles of such letters even before entering office. One letter mailed from New Orleans, Louisiana, in the fall of 1967 was a prototype of dozens that would follow. Bearing both nativist and racist themes, the writer asked Chambers, "if you find living in a white country so disagreeable, why not take a fast plane back to Africa. . . . You are ridiculous to [think] you can change the way of life of a majority of another race."[99] On the other hand, Chambers's constituent correspondence was filled with testimonials to racist treatment that community members encountered while seeking services, working, or shopping in the city and their pleas for justice.[100]

Regardless of his detractors, whom the senator dismissed as unintellectual ideologues, Chambers was determined to fulfill his campaign promises. One of his first steps as a state official was to urge the OPD to move African American policemen into the community. He called for a study of the Nebraska penal system, partially due to his own concerns and also in response to requests from inmates for help. For instance, Chambers arranged for legal assistance for an incarcerated woman at the York prison, as she was unable to fill out papers for herself. "Nothing is academic or theoretical about their need for legal help. Something must be done, and I am prepared to do all I can to shake something loose in their favor."[101]

In a memo to himself, Chambers sketched a record of his first year as a senator. Many of his efforts had been successful. He had taken on a number of issues: condemnation of capital punishment, higher minimum wages, banning corporal punishment in schools, allowing parents to view their children's school records, and school and city council elections by district. Chambers would stay with these issues until he succeeded in getting appropriate legislation passed, or indefinitely. He had spent many hours serving on the Judiciary and Public Works Committees, and had gotten the AFL-CIO's endorsement. Contrary to his initial plan to serve only one term, he was just settling in.

By the fall of 1971, a handful of Chambers's backers were organizing for the 1972 election. His friendship with Goodwin not only survived Chambers's ascent into state politics, but "Dan" was becoming like a brother. Although they spent time together only on weekends and in the summer when Chambers cut hair at the shop, it was Goodwin's name that would appear on flyers urging Chambers's reelection. Goodwin now served as chairman of the Friends of Ernie Chambers Campaign. The two printed answers to criticisms about "Ernie," reemphasizing Chambers's accomplishments, noting that he was a recipient of the Edward Danner Community Service Award, that he he had earned the endorsement of the state's black political caucus, and that had received the Pi Kappa Delta Award from Nebraska Wesleyan University for his outstanding oration.[102]

Despite the predictions of naysayers, the senator had also proven that he could collaborate productively with his colleagues. After all, he had joined the supposedly irascible Terry Carpenter in a campaign to secure funding that would provide educational opportunities for prisoners in trades. The pair had succeeded in getting $200,000 to launch the project. While his election literature listed these strengths and accolades, Chambers ran his second campaign on the platform that his political loyalty belonged *only* to the community. His first session had proven, he argued, that he could not be bought by special interest groups, and that he would not be intimidated simply because he was outnumbered in the Unicameral. Personally, Chambers approached his reelection not only with confidence, but also with the idea that his constituency now knew what they were getting with him as their spokesperson. If they wanted his intense brand of advocacy, they would return him to office. Of greater concern to the senator was whether conditions had improved for the community during his term in office. Chambers noted that at least things had not worsened. Federal works programs that had not operated since the New Deal were being reinvigorated and schools were desegregating their workforces. Conditions for African Americans seemed to be moving in the right direction nationally and also in Omaha.

The few words that Chambers did utter in direct support of his own reelection were, to those accustomed to his usual aggressive banter, surprisingly humble: "I see so much that has to be done, compared to what has been accomplished.... I studied and mastered the techniques of the Unicameral and have used them to help the people of my district and the state."[103]

News of Chambers's reelection was widely circulated. Former Black Panther Robert E. Cecil sent congratulations to Chambers from a prison in Colorado. Cecil said that he was part of a self-improvement group that supported each member in setting goals so that once released they would not return to prison. Their most important task was to eliminate the feeling in themselves and in the other brothers that they were failures, because that feeling led to being locked up again after being paroled. "It is not surprising to find out that most of the inmates here have heard about you," Cecil wrote.[104] Chambers was pleased by the constructive approach Cecil was taking in regard to his imprisonment. "This is a time to think deeply about Malcolm X and the way he transformed prison into an institution of greater learning and understanding for himself."[105] Chambers asked Cecil to describe the federal prison and its programs in case some of them might be helpful for improving the prisons and jails in Nebraska. Chambers confided in Cecil that he might eventually enter national politics. "Someday I may be in a better position to have some impact on the federal system."[106] Chambers earned just $5,000 per year as a state senator at that time, which he supplemented with his earnings from cutting hair. He told Cecil that he was not in a plush job; he still worked at the barbershop in addition to serving as state senator. In fact, Goodwin had purchased a new building three doors down from the old one and they would be moving everything within a month. And, yes, the struggle continued.[107]

For one thing, protesters of the Vietnam War could be found in every city and town, from the shiny waters of the East and West Coasts to the center of the country. Wherever there were young people, there was also opposition. Chambers rejected all justifications for violence, including those for war, other than the degree of force that was absolutely necessary for self-defense. A father of four, he opposed the whipping of children, and fought against corporal punishment in public schools. News that Vietnamese babies had been killed during a U.S. offensive at My Lai back in March 1968 focused Chambers's general antiwar and anti-imperialist sentiments into a shrill condemnation of American presence in Vietnam. Only four months into his career as a state senator, Chambers submitted a biting resolution on the American presence in Vietnam to the Nebraska Legislature.[108]

> Whereas, America declares, in disregard of the Geneva Conventions, that it is not a war crime to inflict a general death penalty on the population at large for the acts of some individuals, and . . . Whereas, a mass murder of unarmed, unresisting men, women and babies occurred at My Lai . . . Whereas Lt. William Calley did not feel that he was killing human beings at My Lai . . . That Lt. William Calley be award[ed], the Congressional Medal of Honor.[109]

If Chambers could not get the Unicameral to condemn the war, he would point out that the senators' silence could be interpreted as approval. If the murder of civilians was wrong, why had they not condemned it? Chambers's highly opinionated statements were perceived by some as self-righteous. Why did Chambers persist in trying to take his colleagues to task for some breach of moral conduct? Who did Chambers think he was, bringing up these things all of the time?

In Chambers's own mind, however, the case was black and white. They could be in league with the murderers of infants or condemn the attack. As with most issues that Chambers took on, his opponents were left with few harbors in which to anchor, other than silence. It was only his opinion, but he possessed a certain moral certitude and used the U.S. Constitution, the Bill of Rights, and the International Conventions on Human Rights to make his case. Chambers had gone beyond Dr. King's pricking of the conscience. Before long the senator's convictions led him into another brief clash with Terry Carpenter. It was over the latter's Legislative Bill 63, which would allow citizen petitioners to protest the public gathering of groups. A reaction to Woodstock and what Carpenter believed was a generation that disregarded social mores, he tried to ensure such expressions of youthful freedom did not take place in Nebraska. Chambers said the bill was draconian, and although the editor did not mention Chambers by name, an *Omaha World Herald* editorial agreed with him that Carpenter's "response to Woodstock" violated the constitutionally guaranteed right to freedom of assembly.[110] Carpenter did not argue with Chambers over the measure's merits. Instead, he condemned piercing speech, which the young lawmaker employed when he wanted to drive home a point. Ironically, long-term Senator Jerome Warner had accused Carpenter of using similar tactics.[111]

A similar episode occurred on April 28, 1971, when Chambers, speaking from his desk on the floor of the chamber, introduced a group of students from Project Excellence. He told the youths that "during the early history of the country, state legislatures like this were considered to have given birth to democracy. Ironically and tragically in 1971, state legislatures such as this one are systematically killing democracy."[112] Carpenter stood and said that he did not approve of Chambers's "persistent condemnation" of his colleagues.[113] He could not see why Chambers insisted on telling his visitors that things were not done properly in the legislature. "I responded that I was elected to this body, just as he was. I have as much right to speak as he does. In the same way that he expresses his ideas freely—no matter how way-out they may seem to be—I intend to do the same."[114] Besides, Chambers said, the legislature should review the record because it would reveal that they had been killing democracy. Senator Richard Proud stood and agreed that some things could be improved upon, but that Chambers should not discourage children about the process. Chambers was readying a reply "when President Frank Marsh arbitrarily" cut off debate.[115] Chambers argued that if he would not be allowed to debate the question, then no one should have. He then went to the balcony and talked to the children. After a few minutes of silence, Senator Elmer Wallwey, a farmer from Emerson, Nebraska, rose to ask the chair to "direct the Sergeant at Arms to escort the gentleman back to his seat."[116] The Chairman and the Speaker of the House whispered over the request. One thing was clear: Chambers was not seeking his colleagues' approval. The senator was a first for many of them. They had never met an African American with Chambers's bearing, skill, confidence, and status. "I stood in the balcony and called down: Mr. President, if you want me to take my seat, why don't you ask me?"[117] Chambers soon returned to his seat, but not without the growing sense among his colleagues of the senator from District Eleven's utter freedom.

By Chambers's second year in office, *Lincoln Star* Reporter Don Walton referred to him as the legislature's "best floor speaker and its quickest mind."[118] His most important success, according to Walton, was his override of the governor's veto of his bill prohibiting the state from prorating welfare payments (giving partial payments in lieu of full checks) to families. Chambers was a cosponsor and introducer of countless bills during the first session, and nineteen bills in 1972. He sponsored legislation to develop a county court system that would replace justice of the peace courts, reform prisons, establish election of Omaha School Board members by district, provide legal counsel to the indigent, require gas and electric companies to send notices before stopping services, and for the social welfare office to give allotments for medical diets to families with sick children.

The senator also demanded respect for himself and for his constituents. "Ernie Chambers is not the first Negro to sit in the Nebraska Legislature.

He's just the first, very probably, in no way ashamed of his blackness," noted a reporter for the *Lincoln Journal*.[119]

> Chambers could very well be the most incurable idealist of the century.... He holds to a textbook notion legislatures should be something like a collection of philosophers, kings, wise and deliberate men, not eating off lobbyists, ever working in the public interest.[120]

Not only was Chambers a topic of discussion in newsrooms and in political circles, his election and legislative maneuvering reverberated through the justice community. The day after Chambers's election to the Nebraska Unicameral, Richard A. Salem, the U.S. Justice Department's Midwest Regional Director for Community Relations, sent a request for an investigation of possible police misconduct in Omaha to Chief William O' Connor, head of the Criminal Section of the Civil Rights Division at the U.S. Department of Justice. Salem wrote, "... our agency had been working [with] city officials and community residents for the past eighteen months in an effort to ease tensions between police and the minority community in Omaha."[121] Complaints against the police were received somewhat regularly at the Midwest Division but two detailed complaints arrived after the bombing death of the Omaha police officer in August of 1970. A Mr. and Mrs. Carl Washington filed a complaint after their home at 31st and Fowler Streets was illegally searched by police on August 25 of that year, and the Washingtons requested a federal investigation of a possible violation of their civil rights. One of Chambers's sister's homes was also searched by police after the bombing, Salem said, and Ernest Chambers had requested a federal investigation.[122]

While power brokers in Nebraska adjusted to having a "militant" in the state legislature, Chambers was also settling into his environment. Before long he felt sufficiently at home in the Unicameral to unveil his expansive humorous and poetic sides. He used his considerable oratory skill to harpoon an opponent with both irony and sarcasm, and sometimes just to lessen the monotony. On such occasions, he poked fun at colleagues and sometimes even at himself. Toward the end of one session, he issued a mock apology for his support of legislation that would have allowed a single instead of a pair of license plates for vehicles, and for which colleagues complained of his naiveté as a senator and stressed the importance of two license plates to police.[123]

Had the wicked bill passed, the sovereign state of Nebraska, doubtless, would have been deluged by crime.... My legislative inexperience and youthful exuberance blinded me to this subtle attack against the moral fiber of society.... Fortunately, some of my older and wiser colleagues rescued the State.... Down with Crime, up with two license plates.... PS Legislative Bill 423 must have originated from the Evil One himself.... Contritely yours, Ernie Chambers.[124]

In spite of his wit, Chambers's recovery after a serious thrashing of his proposal revealed that he was not an especially good loser. Thereafter, he would try to pick battles that interested him enough to continue waging them after a setback.

Chambers's success as a state senator resulted from his keen insight and his unwavering Black Nationalism (manifested by the senator in his pride in black people's intelligence, endurance, humanity toward others, and determination to be free). Questioned by reporters, Omaha city administrators reluctantly agreed that on more than one occasion Chambers had calmed Omaha when rioting seemed imminent. Still, reporters frequently noted the fact that most whites continued to see Chambers as a proponent of "violence and hateful demagoguery."[125] One of the reasons for their perception were the reminders offered by the Omaha Police Union that when a white patrolman was killed in North Omaha, Chambers had said that justice would have been served if all eight of the officers who responded to the call had died. Community activists reiterated again that Chambers's reference was to the number of unarmed Africans killed in Omaha by white police officers and that he had made a numerical comparison. The tension between a semisegregated community and agents of the government sent in to control it emanated from the caste structure that had permeated the United States up to 1970 and which left a subtle but omnipresent racialism in the aftermath of desegregation laws.[126]

Determined to make a difference, Chambers challenged the way things were done in the Nebraska Unicameral, in the public schools, on schools boards, and in city and county government. Responses from Euro-Americans around the Cornhusker State ranged from surprise and respect to rage. Chambers wanted change too fast, they said, and yet as hard as his opponents tried—through hate mail, voting blocs on the floor, bad press, and administrative discourtesy—collectively they could not remove, intimidate, or quiet him. Although Chambers's positions resulted from his own analysis and his personal convictions, as a public official elected primarily by African Americans, Chambers's constituency underwrote his freedom to say and do whatever he pleased. In return for their support at election time, his allegiance belonged wholly to the community. Chambers was obligated to no political party. He was at liberty to do battle with all forces outside of his constituents, and his job could not be threatened by white interests. There was nothing anyone could do. Chambers was functioning effectively and in high gear now in his element. Chambers's political independence did not, however, stop the city and state "fathers" from penalizing other African Americans in highly visible positions. In the summer of 1972, the University of Nebraska Board of Regents canceled Black Studies Director Milton White's contract after White complained of racist treatment by the university's administration. White said that administrators had made repeated attempts to prevent the growth of the Black Studies Department by eliminating key courses. University President Durwood Varner told the press that he had ended White's contract because White was an "open advocate of Black Nationalism."[127]

Depending on one's political persuasion, Black Nationalism was the long-awaited ideological reference point for African liberation or the rejection of white culture and harbinger of the threat of retaliatory violence. African Americans' desire for freedom "crystallized into ideology" not long after their struggle in the Americas began, according to historian Sterling Stuckey. They were encouraged by the American War for Independence, by the Haitian Revolution, and by individuals like Martin R. Delany who began to develop nationalist thought. Stuckey points to nationalist themes in songs sung by Africans on the South Carolina Sea Islands, the lyrics of which called for independence and promoted the guarding of African wives and daughters from oppression and from the sexual aggression of white men: "That no white foe with impious hand. . . . Shall slave your wives and daughters more or rob them of their virtue dear. . . . Pledge your bodies for the prize / pile them even to the skies."[128] Alphonso Pinkney points out that by late 1969, Black Nationalism was the primary "ethos" of the African freedom struggle. California intellectual Maulana Ron Karenga and Imamu Amiri Baraka (aka Leroi Jones) served as the leaders of the North American movement toward African cultural nationalism. For Chambers, as for other Black Nationalists, defining the community in racial and cultural terms and focusing upon group identity was necessary to combat a form of repression that relied upon a racial caste system.[129]

Conservative blacks wanted nothing to do with nationalism, and it so happened that Chambers's enemies soon found a candidate to run against the fiery orator. James Hart, Jr., an African American lawyer, had relocated to Omaha in June 1971, to take a job as Urban Affairs Council manager for the Omaha Chamber of Commerce. Now, less than a year later, Hart agreed to run against Chambers for his seat in the Unicameral. Hart told the news media that Chambers was ineffective. "It does no good to rock the boat of slavery. We've got to update our thinking."[130] Hart's candidacy was challenged by Legal Aid Society lawyer Robert V. Broom, who cited a state residency requirement of a full year before participating as a candidate in a general election. As election day neared, scheduled for November 7, 1971, Hart's efforts were thwarted on a number of fronts. Hart complained to the press that over twenty of Chambers's supporters had "harassed" him at his office, asking him not to run against Chambers and suggesting that he had not been in Omaha long enough to know what problems blacks faced. Questioned by reporters at his office in Lincoln, Chambers said that he did not know Hart and had not asked anyone to visit him. Chambers suspected that racist whites had set up the whole episode to try "to show a split in the black community."[131] Roger Sayers, Omaha Human Relations director, was a member of the group who visited Hart and was acting as an observer. Sayers said that the group had not harassed Hart but merely wanted to know who was backing him and whether he would pay his first loyalty to the community if elected, or to the Omaha Chamber of Commerce. Dan Goodwin had attended the meeting, as had Michael Adams, president at the time of the Nebraska Urban League. Charles Washington, then a consultant for the Urban Housing Foundation, was also present, as was Rodney Wead, executive director of Wesley House; Mel Corbino of the Urban League; and representatives from Mothers for Adequate Welfare. Sayers said that the group had scheduled a meeting with Hart at the Chamber of Commerce headquarters in its First National Bank location, but that Hart may have regretted consenting to the forum because he failed to anticipate the questions that were asked. Hart said that a number of people who liked to think of themselves as "power brokers" told him that if he failed to withdraw from the legislative race, he would be "dealt with."[132] Those present at the meeting conceded that they wanted to know who Chambers's contender was and find out who had put him up to running against "Ernie."

4—The Power of One

When Secretary of State Allen Beermann published the results of the general elections in 1972, Richard Nixon was being returned to office for what turned out to be an abbreviated second term. Former Nebraska state senator Terry Carpenter had been defeated by Carl T. Curtis in his race for a seat in the U.S. Senate, and Charlie Thone was seated in the U.S. House of Representatives from the Omaha District. In the spring of 1972, Rowena Moore, president of the Nebraska Black Political Caucus, had announced the group's unanimous endorsement of Chambers "for his tireless work on behalf of the state of Nebraska."[1] The statement was delivered before a meeting of sixty people at Wesley House and came on the tail of a month-long controversy over the Hart candidacy in the press.

Several months into his new term as a state senator, Chambers saw that his influence had become even greater and that his office had as much power as the individual in it could command. In September, with these musings in mind, Chambers wrote to Omaha Mayor Eugene Leahy and insisted that he be included and informed of any administrative plans that would affect his district. He specifically wanted to know all of the facts related to the Riverfront Development Project, including land use, acquisition, financing, and relocation plans.[2]

> Ordinary and traditional political courtesy (recall your being snubbed recently by a national political visitor to Omaha) would cause an invitation to be extended to me, as the legislative repre-

sentative of the 11th District. . . . A critical state has been reached. No longer can I be excluded.[3]

Chambers was not against progress and the reinvestment of the city into Omaha's downtown, but he would not sit by while his district was broken up by whites who had fled to the suburbs during the late sixties and now wanted to reclaim the land in the "inner city."[4] He would monitor plans for the Riverfront Development Project just as he would continue to monitor police in North Omaha.

He demanded investigations into police killings of citizens, roughly half of whom each decade were African American. Chambers's certainty that some police officers entered the community looking for someone to assault grew out of his own observations, the reports of eyewitnesses and victims, and from tips he received periodically from members of the police department. A handful of policemen admitted privately that they had witnessed racial violence from fellow officers. On one occasion Chambers received an "anonymous" call from an Omaha police official describing a racist beating initiated by high-ranking veteran officers. Chambers took notes during the phone call. "Sgt. Parker was drunk. . . . Parker said 'lets go nigger-hunting.'"[5] An African American officer referred to as Benak and Sergeant Parker were accompanied by Patrolman Shook and Sergeant Tate at a raid on 16th and Wirt Streets. According to Chambers's source, "Parker grabbed Benak's flashlight striking . . . Benak in the face" shortly before the "other cops began hitting blacks."[6] Chambers talked to Omaha Police Chief Andersen about the incident even though Chambers's source told him that "Chief Andersen went down to the station Sunday morning and grabbed reports to conceal them."[7]

Tips like that one would help keep Chambers focused on law enforcement and on ways to improve police accountability. To try and stem the mayhem, Chambers sponsored legislation requiring a grand jury review of all deaths occurring while the victim was in police custody. Deaths involving police actions would go beyond the police department's internal review. Senator Chambers told his colleagues during floor debate that "police watch while drugs are sold" on the Northside.[8] On the defensive, Omaha Mayor Leahy argued that federal agents in the city would have reported any police payoffs for ignoring local drug traffic. Police Chief Richard R. Andersen said that police usually knew who were moving drugs but that it took time to "make a case" before arresting individuals.[9] Al Pattavina, Omaha public safety director, said if he were presented with evidence, he would investigate Chambers's allegations.

In January 1973, during a public hearing on drug enforcement, "Ernest Chambers of Omaha and Terry Carpenter of Scottsbluff" teamed up to attack corruption they believed existed in the Nebraska State Patrol drug enforcement program. Chambers said that it was well known that some members of the vice squad took payoffs. Carpenter asked the press, if ten undercover agents aren't enough, why did the chief of the state patrol fail to request more? "We should get rid of him [state patrol chief Col. J. E. Kruger] and get somebody who wants to do it."[10]

Second Term

Chambers entered his second term in office with questions in mind about state and federal corruption and how far the abuse of powers ran. How would the dust settle after the Watergate crisis had passed? On the day of his second inauguration—January 20, 1973—Nixon was expected to declare a cease-fire to end the fighting in Vietnam. Chambers hoped that the president would follow through. In a memo to himself, Chambers wrote, "Nixon knows what Hoover knew on people," inferring that the FBI's corrupt practices were sanctioned by the White House.[11] He pondered over local issues as well—whether there was corruption involved in the leases of school lands and how long school segregation would remain the de facto situation in Omaha. He planned to write bills on the death penalty and minimum wage, and for the investigation of police-owned bars. He would look into whether Aid to Dependent Children payments were adequate to raise poor families' standards of living and whether workers' compensation laws needed revising. There was a lot to do, but he had boundless energy for this sort of work. He planned to write a number of articles as well, but would not get to most of them.

To deal with his colleagues' nagging over his attire (T-shirts over muscles bulging from his regular weight lifting, and which made him look more like a longshoreman than a state senator), he would present the argument that his casual dress irritated them but that he had to put up with their "foul habit" of smoking on the floor of the legislature. Chambers's effort to ban smoking from the legislative chambers would effectively counter senators who wished to make a rule requiring that their colleague wear a dress shirt and tie. For a while, he brought in a child's folded tie and shirt and set it near his seat on the floor of the legislature alongside a sign that said the senators could talk to the shirt if they wanted or they could talk to the man.[12]

In the election cycle the veteran senator Terry Carpenter had made an unsuccessful bid for the U.S. Senate and while doing so lost his reelection campaign for the Nebraska state legislature. Carpenter had demanded a recount. When the votes from his write-in campaign were tallied once more, Carpenter was declared the winner by just three votes. Now his opponent William Nichol demanded a recount. The tables turned again and Nichol came out ahead, beating Carpenter by only sixty-eight votes. Carpenter argued that many of his votes had been disqualified during the recount because voters misspelled his name. Unfortunately, poll officials had removed the candidates' names from those ballots, making a final check impossible. Chambers, loyal to his friend, said that the legislature should decide the outcome of the election since the voters' intentions were what mattered, not their spelling ability. Chambers was backed by John Cavanaugh and a few others. However, the majority of state senators either took the opportunity to get rid of Carpenter, as the old politician himself suspected, or they believed that Nichol had won fairly. Either way the episode ended Carpenter's career as a state lawmaker. Carpenter left the Nebraska State Capitol sure that the lack of support shown him by his colleagues resulted from the other senators' fear of him.[13]

It was true that some senators felt uncomfortable with the maverick's style. Jerome Warner saw Carpenter as a man who would not back down and who took defeats on bills personally. Biographer Charlyne Berens notes that "Carpenter and Warner did not get along," and yet Warner was chosen by the body to chair the committee considering Carpenter's request for a recount in the election contest against Bill Nichol.[14] Warner disapproved of how Carpenter used his power: "part of his strength was to take on new members early and hard and belittle them. . . . [he] liked to go after a person who was obviously not well-versed on a subject. . . . Or he would manage to pick a fight about the meaning of a word."[15] Warner was referring to devices that Carpenter used to filibuster bills. Carpenter, like Chambers, was often outnumbered but stood fast in support of his own measures and principles; the veteran senator was working the system in a legal, if aggravating, fashion. Chambers would eventually become an expert in the use of all of these tactics as well, since they comprised the few ways in which a person in the minority could outmaneuver the majority.

In 1974, Chambers was easily returned to office, proof that most African Americans in North Omaha appreciated the changes that he was attempting to make in the power structure of the state, and they either approved of his tactics or believed that his ends justified his means. During the next twenty-four months, Chambers would be featured in both the local and national news, appearing in *National Geographic* in the spring 1974. In one photo he was in the barbershop beside Dan Goodwin. Intrigued by Chambers's lack of conventionality—refusing to wear a suit and tie in favor of sweatshirts and blue jeans—and for the changes he was making in the structure of Nebraska's electoral politics, the magazine christened him "spokesman for a troubled minority."[16] Although the attention added to his notoriety, Chambers would privately disagree with such descriptions, since from his perspective it was whites who were troubled. He felt that that African Americans merely found ways of coping with the majority community's lack of ethical and moral health. But, he may have asked himself, why explain such things to those not inclined to listen? Besides, time was speeding up for him. Letters poured in on a daily basis. All sorts of people wanted help and advice. Others wrote to grapple with the senator over his bills, statements, and what they saw as his hatred of white power.

Community Politics

Goodwin's Spencer Street Barbershop served as the senator's storefront in North Omaha, and combined with his office in Lincoln, was the "political headquarters for the city's blacks," especially for independents and Democrats.[17] Community folk sought out Chambers at the shop that Dan Goodwin still ran on North 24th Street. Five years older than Chambers, Goodwin had graduated from Technical High School ahead of his friend and then joined the navy. He later told a reporter that when he met Chambers he liked him right away. "We had automatic rapport. . . . [he] had an uncanny ability to "express the community's needs."[18] Besides, Chambers's presence there, cutting hair on weekends and chatting it up with anyone who stopped by, expanded the shop's reputation as a place to talk politics.

University of Nebraska student Gregory M. Organ wrote a report about Chambers, noting, "A community ombudsman of sorts, he took on the considerable task of monitoring the police, the schools, and city hall to see that the interests of blacks were served."[19] "If someone was having trouble with the city or a landlord, they would go see Ernie," and Chambers did his best to solve each problem presented to him.[20] When not helping constituents or working on legislation, he had several ongoing projects that demanded his attention. For one thing, his lifelong struggle with the racist policies of the

Omaha Public Schools (OPS) was coming to a head. Although he had occasionally wound up as the only African American child in white classrooms, Chambers also had attended semisegregated Lothrup Elementary and Technical High School. He knew how African history was ignored in public school curricula, and that most African American students in segregated schools received inferior educations.[21]

In early 1973, Chambers and other North Omaha parents jointly filed a complaint with the U.S. Department of Justice, arguing that teachers exhibited racism and discriminatory treatment toward black children. In August, Chambers contacted J. Stanley Pottinger, assistant attorney general for the Civil Rights Division of the Justice Department, pointing out how the actions of school officials proved that they had no intention of desegregating Omaha schools in compliance with the Justice Department's order for OPS. Chambers complained that the Justice Department was "double-dealing," claiming to be upholding the rights of all citizens while using an "almost apologetic tone in statements" to white school personnel about the desegregation order.[22] His suspicions grew after the Justice Department failed to consult with the African American parents who had filed the complaint. The representatives from Washington dealt exclusively with the city instead. When Chambers learned that the Justice Department was contemplating the substitution of a consent decree for OPS in lieu of a plan describing in detail what should have been the district's desegregation initiative, Chambers protested. The senator believed that the idea of signing a decree, promising to add teachers and students to schools to affect a racial balance, was the school district's attempt to avoid desegregation. He blasted the plan: "School officials have publicly advocated defiance of the Justice Department and tried to incite public opposition and resistance."[23] After all, he said, the Justice Department's investigation itself found that OPS were intentionally racially segregated, and that this was why it had mandated that a desegregation plan be instituted in the first place.

Eventually, the federal officials came to believe that the only way to integrate the city's all black schools like Conestoga, Franklin, Kellom, Lothrup, and Mann was to bus African American children out and bus white kids into the "inner city" neighborhoods. The Omaha School Board was given two weeks to begin complying with the decision or to appeal it. To their credit, the Justice Department officials cited twelve violations of antidiscrimination laws by the Omaha school system, and it charged that the Omaha School Board was intent on keeping schools segregated in violation of federal law. Specific instances of discrimination were described. One observation of federal officials was that white students in the Technical High School attendance area were given transfers to white schools but African Americans were not allowed to transfer. Special transfers of white students also occurred in Clifton Hill, Franklin, and Saratoga Schools.[24]

It was the persistence of these customs that Chambers addressed. By mid-summer of 1975, opposition by Omaha officials to desegregation peaked. The lawsuit by community members resulted in the Eighth Circuit Court of Appeals ordering the schools to desegregate by the beginning of the fall term of 1976. A decision to fight the integration order of the Eighth Circuit was made by Superintendent Owen Knutzen and Omaha School Board President Paul Kennedy. The school district would not abide by the order of the U.S. Eighth Circuit Court of Appeals and instead appealed the case to the U.S. Supreme Court.[25]

In the meantime, Chambers continued his letter-writing campaign to officials in Washington, including Omaha-born President Gerald Ford. Chambers resented that Ford had publicly sympathized with white Americans who did not want to send their children to integrated schools, and he condemned the president's consideration of using the Justice Department to interfere with court-ordered busing. "Your overtures," wrote Chambers, "degrades the judiciary, it proclaims to the world that constitutional rights of children are based on the flimsiest whim and count for nothing in America."[26] Chambers argued that while busing was used to enforce school segregation, Ford had "uttered not a whisper. Now that it has become a means of vindicating constitutional guarantees to black children, here you come."[27]

Chambers received responses from Ford through the Justice Department and from Bobbie Green Kilberg, associate counsel to the president. Kilberg explained the president's position. Ford had drawn up legislation that he felt would help the nation "deal" with desegregation by declaring court-ordered busing as an "interim and transitional remedy" only.[28] Chambers fumed at Kilberg's explanation. Ford had given the nation a way out—without facing the harm whites had done to African Americans for generations—and so that even the remedy for mending current abuses could be dropped after a year or two. Anger usually came to the senator along with words to express himself. Occasionally, he would allow himself to experience the feeling in silence. When he was completely silent and still, he may have noticed more fully his environs. It came to him, anyhow, that Cynthia Grandberry, his legislative aide, did an excellent job of communicating with callers about problems in the schools. A young mother herself, Grandberry had experienced some of the same hurdles that other parents were facing. Actually, having grown up in North Omaha, Grandberry understood virtually all of the issues that their constituents faced. She was a tremendous help to Chambers and someone to talk over cases with, if he wanted to. Grandberry had, in fact, become an integral part of Chambers's office, and lobbyists, public officials, members of the media, and community people knew her well. Yet the general public would know little about Grandberry, Chambers's legislative assistant for almost the entire duration of his years in office and the senator's "right hand."[29]

Cynthia Baltimore Grandberry was born in Omaha, Nebraska, on July 31, 1951, and grew up in a religious home. By the time she came to work for Chambers in 1972, Grandberry was a military wife, mother of a young son, and a college student with interests in modeling and fashion. She was just over twenty years old. Grandberry would later recall the treatment she received from other Unicameral staff when she first applied to work as a secretary for Senator Chambers:

> At the time I was attending UNL. At a meeting for black students, Lonetta Riley, who was an instructor, spoke of a black senator who was representing North Omaha. She spoke of the need for black students to go to the Capitol and view the legislative process in action, take notes on what this senator was doing, and figure out what we could do to help.
>
> So I went to the Capitol and inquired about working with Senator Chambers. I was sent to Eunice Bradley who headed the Legislature's personnel office. . . . Eunice Bradley told me what I would have to do to be considered for employment with the Legislature. I needed to go through the State Personnel Office and take a typing and shorthand test. If I passed, she would interview me for a position with Senator Chambers.
>
> She asked me if I knew who Senator Chambers was. I told her that I did not. She asked me whether I cared that I would be working for a "Negro." She said that she was glad to have a "Negro" secretary for Senator Chambers and would I be willing to work for Senator Chambers. I told her I would not mind. She then asked that I call Senator Chambers and make sure that he did not object to me working for him as his secretary. . . .
>
> To my surprise, he said no interview was necessary. He said

that if I wanted to work with him that would be okay by him. I was to introduce myself to him on the first Legislative Day. . . .

I had envisioned a man over 6' tall, 200 lbs or more. . . . When I saw him, he was a short, slim, muscular built man in a T-shirt and jeans. No suit, no tie and everyone seeking him out—talking intently to him. Not wanting to interrupt his conversation, I was standing off to the side. He surprised me when he stopped his conversation to introduce himself and ask me what I wanted. I told him my name and that I was to be his secretary. He said, great, and that I should seek him out when the Legislature adjourned.

As the day wore on, Senator Chambers was elected Chairman of the Government Committee. The secretarial position I had was not elevated to "Committee Clerk." All the Committee Clerk positions were pre-assigned by Eunice Bradley. . . . I did not realize that his being a Chairman meant I could not be his secretary, in the opinion of Eunice Bradley and others.

When I returned to Eunice Bradley's office, she informed me that I would not be working as a secretary for Senator Chambers. . . . She said that she could offer me employment as a transcriber until the end of the legislative session. She reminded me that my shorthand skills were poor and that all Committee Clerks were required to use shorthand skills to record the hearings. . . .

Disappointed, I went to the Legislative Chamber and sought out Senator Chambers. I told him what Eunice Bradley had told me. Before I could get it all out, Senator Chambers stopped me and said simply that if I was good enough to be his secretary before he was Chairman, I was good enough to be his secretary now. He told me to come with him so he could let Eunice Bradley know that I would be the Committee Clerk. I told the Senator that I did not have the shorthand skills to record the committee's hearing, but I was an excellent typist. He laughed and explained that hearings were electronically recorded—not taken down in shorthand.

When we arrived at Ms. Bradley's office, Senator Chambers told her I would be the Committee Clerk of the Government Committee. Little did I know that my employment would change how many things that were done—beginning with the process of how senators would hire their staff.[30]

Grandberry earned a degree in business from the University of Nebraska and attempted law school while working for Chambers (with much encouragement from him). She eventually withdrew from the program as she found maintaining her duties at the office and keeping up with her studies, as well as parenting her son, extremely difficult to balance. Chambers had helped as much as he could by answering phones while she was in class, and he hired other part-time workers. Still there was an enormous amount of work to be done. The duty that she never delegated was the keeping of the senator's "black book" in which she entered all of the bills that he would work on for the session.[31]

Grandberry's proximity to the senator gave her an uncommon degree of access and influence with him. Eventually, she would tell Chambers when she was mistreated by visitors and asked Chambers to look more deeply into the motives of his callers. Her faithfulness to his office and her growing demand that reporters, visitors, and constituents respect the senator, the office, and herself reflected Grandberry's commitment to support Chambers in his mission. Her intuitiveness and ability to analyze situations quickly allowed the senator to work undisturbed while she handled walk-ins and dealt masterfully with the press. Grandberry helped to invoke a respectful distance between the senator and those who came to see him.[32]

Over time Grandberry came to know Chambers as well as anyone, and despite Chambers's occasional antireligious statements, she believed that Chambers's work was "motivated by a deep spirituality."[33] He was, after all, raised in a church. His father was a minister and even though Chambers disliked things that he saw "so-called Christians do, he had internalized some basic principles."[34] Grandberry said that although he probably would not admit it, Chambers had learned from the Bible and especially from Jesus's example that the church and "able-bodied human beings ought to stand up for the poor and disenfranchised."[35] She respected Chambers and did what she could to support his efforts. The atmosphere in the office was frequently studious and quiet for part of the day. At other times, constituents or colleagues would stop by and talk. Chambers discussed current issues with guests, and sometimes, to break up the monotony, would tell a joke, do a magic trick, or read a political rhyme. In their world, Chambers was most often at his typewriter, on the phone, or labeling news clippings, and Grandberry was to answer the phone and the door, and refile items when he was finished with them.[36] Chambers was aware of Grandberry's shrewdness and ability to get to the bottom line in scores of phone contacts each day, but the contributions of women to the struggle may have still seemed, at least initially, to fit into a supportive role.

When Chambers felt bombarded with things to do, he would draw or lift weights. For periods of time he stuck to a regime, but even if he worked out for a few minutes it helped him to relax. Generally he would ask Grandberry to hold all of his calls and go into his library and lift weights for an hour. When he finished he almost always felt good. Grandberry would give him a quick summary of his phone calls and her unsolicited (but usually helpful) opinion on which she thought should be given priority, and Chambers came to trust her judgment. Sensitized through conversations with Grandberry, Chambers scanned legislation proposed by his colleagues, looking for sexism.[37]

Chambers focused intently on women and children in the law from the mid 1970s forward. However, when the rights of adoptive children and their mothers were debated throughout the legislative session in 1979, the dispute spilled over into his office. The proposed bill allowed persons adopted as children, upon reaching the age of majority, to see their adoption records and find out the identities of their natural parents. Chambers argued on the floor that "this bill requires a balancing of rights and interests; the adoptive parents, the adoptive person ... The question for me is whether or not those parents can permanently cut off the right of that child to know who his or her natural parents are."[38] Chambers said, "it seems to me that most important person who is the fulcrum has rights which are regarded the least."[39]

The senator was especially concerned that siblings separated by adoption be able to locate one another as adults. Chambers asked one witness why the child's feelings mattered less than the mother's. At the judiciary committee hearing on the bill, Mrs. Jim Helgoth, a witness, argued that a woman could have been unwed at the time that she had given up the child and may have later married and may have a family. "The child would walk in and say, 'Here I am mom.' The bill is created on the aspect that everybody wants to see everybody."[40] Grandberry agreed with Helgoth. She told Chambers, when he returned from the floor, that a woman who has given up her child does so because of horrible circumstances. If she is able to move on with her life, she has already suffered overwhelming grief from losing her child, and she should not have to see that child unless she wants to. Chambers demanded to know, Grandberry later recalled, "What about the child?"[41] The argument went on for as long as the discussion was on the floor, and was accompanied by uncharacteristic door slamming by Grandberry. Chambers maintained his position, however, in floor debate. "As far as I know, I haven't been adopted, but I can tell you this. As a race, we don't know who we are or where we came from and it does mean something. . . . It may not matter to some people, but others do want to know how [sic] they are and where they came from because there is a totality of existence which isn't explained in terms of your being here right now."[42]

But Chambers and Grandberry saw eye to eye on the issue of a woman's right to control her own body. No subject polarized Nebraska more than abortion, and Chambers championed the rights of women in this regard. In 1979, during what Chambers's considered a herculean effort to make each fetus community property, Senators John DeCamp, Don Dworak, and Bernice Labedz rallied behind Legislative Bill 316, which would limit the circumstances under which a physician could lawfully perform an abortion. The bill included a forty-eight-hour waiting period before a woman requesting an abortion could undergo the procedure. Chambers debated an amendment to the bill that focused on the definition of the "viability" of the fetus, arguing that the U.S. Supreme Court had just, in the *Colautti* case, redefined the term. In *Roe v. Wade*, the court defined "viability" as the stage when a fetus could survive outside of the mother's womb with or without life supports.[43] Chambers's language mirrored the Supreme Court's.

> Then states began to enact legislation attempting to push backward toward the point of conception the point of viability or reducing the period of time during which a woman and her physician have sole say as to whether an abortion would be performed. . . . The Supreme Court expanded the whole issue of viability in such fashion, that the matter is to be determined by the attending physician.[44]

The attending physician must have "a right unfettered by the state, to make a medical judgment" in determining when a fetus could survive on its own.[45] Chambers told his colleagues that the legislature must enact a bill in agreement with the standards set by the U.S. Supreme Court or they would create an unconstitutional law that would eventually be stricken.[46]

Women's rights activists applauded Chambers's efforts, and women's rights advocates began conferring with the senator frequently. The following year Chambers argued for women's right to insurance coverage of medical treatment, regardless of what outsiders felt about specific procedures like abortion.

> Mr. Chairman . . . I think this amendment even as amended is very arrogant. . . . There is nothing that a male could get that would not be covered. So I think what we ought to do is put "No male who gets

V.D. or any other ailments connected with the sexual organs should be covered by this type of insurance program. . . .[47]

Chambers recognized that according to some religions a human being was created at the moment of conception, and he was well acquainted with Catholic doctrines because of having studied at Creighton University. However, he knew that even in the Catholic Church the issue was controversial. "By reading Thomas Aquinas [and] St. Augustine, that is how I learned that the church fathers even disagreed on the issue of abortion."[48] The rights of the fetus are weighed against the rights of the mother, Chambers argued, and "the court has said if a balance has to be struck, it has to fall in favor of the mother."[49]

Grandberry supported Chambers's stand on the abortion issue. She fielded hostile calls from anti-abortion groups and filed scores of hate-mail letters from conservative Christians. Like Chambers, she believed that until a fetus could survive outside of the womb, it was not fully a human being. Grandberry appreciated the senator's position on the right of women to control their own bodies as well as his willingness to confront agencies and individuals who practiced racism. As an African American woman, she had experienced sexual discrimination, but, because she grew up both black and female, she understood how racism and sexism converged. Moreover, as the front line, so to speak, in Chambers office, Grandberry would note the irony that in an age of "progress" in race relations, she heard complaints about racist incidents from constituents every week.

Despite improvements, like an increase in the number of African Americans hired by the Omaha Police Department, white police violence would rear its head again, eroding the optimistic view that things had gotten better. Bad times would, in turn, call for a reexamination of African America's relationship to the majority population in Nebraska. Years earlier Chambers had explained his thoughts on state violence. In his speech entitled, "The Way It Is Today," Chambers said policemen were "the symbol of white supremacy in the black ghetto."[50] It is the police who are assigned and carry out the "dirty work" for the rest of the racist society.[51] That dirty work is the regeneration of racist ideology, which, the senator believed, infected Euro-Americans from "the White House down to the little white man pushing a broom."[52]

Police officers, back in the day, were hired without college degrees, and Chambers felt that they suffered from insecurity as a result. Chambers argued, "So you might ask him, 'What are you stopping me for? Which you have a right to know. . . . But he takes it as a challenge and pulls out a pistol, if you are black, and then he [blows] you away."[53] If citizens complain about police murder, "a clamor erupts" from politicians and others who say you should be supporting the police.[54]

As farfetched as Chambers's interpretation could sound to people who had never seen the police in anything but a protective role, a number of incidents supported his claims. The summer before Chambers first won his seat in the Unicameral, Arvid Sherdell Lewis's name began to appear from time to time in the local newspaper. Twenty-one-year-old Lewis owned a gas station on 27th and R Streets in Lincoln. As the proprietor of one of the few African American businesses in the city, Lewis's station and his conduct drew the attention of local police. He was charged in 1970 with purchasing stolen goods, mainly guns, after the police searched the gas station and then Lewis's home. Lewis plea-bargained, admitting to having "concealed knowledge of a felony."[55] He was acquitted of the gun charges. Lewis continued to run his business and became a Youth Counselor for Lincoln Action Program. Within three years, his arrest record would multiply, and he would be the subject of a sting operation for drugs by the State Patrol and Lancaster County law officers.

Less than a month after his first acquittal, Lewis was again in the press. He joined Lewis Cooper and Cleveland Randolph as the spokespersons for a group of African Americans who met with Lincoln Mayor Sam Schwartzkopf to demand the suspension of three Lincoln policemen who had beaten eighteen-year-old Randolph. Randolph said that on October 14, 1970, three Lincoln police officers had stopped him on suspicions of "bicycle violations," and then beaten him. Lewis, Randolph, and Cooper told the mayor the problem would "stop here or on the streets," and newsman Dick Haws wrote that Lewis's comment sounded like a threat "that bloodshed and deaths could result if some action was not taken by the mayor."[56] The mayor refused to suspend the officers involved.

A short time later, Lewis was driving by a fraternity house known in the black community of Lincoln for its segregationist policies. He turned onto R Street and was pelted with water balloons from the frat's open window as he drove past. Lewis stopped his car and went into the fraternity house. He used a stick to hit two white men who were nearest the window. The UNL students were checked over at the University of Nebraska Health Center and released, and Lewis was arrested and charged with two counts of "assault with a weapon."[57] He was found guilty and fined $200.

Three months later, twelve officers met outside of Lewis's house with the intent to search the premises. Five Lincoln police, four state patrolmen, and three members of the Lancaster County Sheriff's Office went to the home intent on delivering a warrant. Lewis, a former high school football star and coach for a Lincoln Police Department midget league football team, was shot to death in the doorway of the 23rd and Potter Street home that he shared with his Euro-American girlfriend. Lewis was killed by plainclothes deputy sheriff Rodney Loos at 10 p.m. on September 24, 1975. Afterward, over forty community members demanded that County Attorney Ronald Lahners tell them what the search warrant of Lewis's home was for. Some members of the group yelled, "cold blooded murder."[58]

In February of the same year another African American man, Elijah Childers, Jr., had been shot to death in his home by Police Officers Don Buckner and Mike Williams. The officers had gone to the Childers's home to investigate a disturbance that had occurred at a bar earlier that day. After killing Childers, the Lincoln police declared Buckner and Williams innocent of any wrongdoing. Childers's death was on the minds of community members when they met at Anna Hopkins's home at 1550 North 23rd Street, a block from Lewis's place—on the night following his death. Some of the neighbors referred to Lewis's slaying as a "gangland killing" and said that the "police are the gangsters."[59] A white neighbor said his son saw police rushing Lewis's house in the dark with sawed-off shotguns. The same neighbor, Jacob Schiermann, said that Lewis had approached him earlier in the week asking if he had any "problems with peeping Toms." He suggested that the police may have done a practice run on the Lewis place the night before and that Lewis had spotted them.[60]

The official version of the incident was released a day after the shooting, and said that Lewis was fired upon when he went to answer his door with a weapon in his hand. City Councilman John Robinson remarked, "Obviously, things have grown out of control. . . . We have a gut issue of whether or not our law enforcement agencies have gone completely mad."[61] Some community members indicated that they believed police officers feared African men who refused to act docile. Marvel Nevels, a young African American friend of Lewis, asked, "How is the police department going to replace Barbara Kelley's son?"[62] Over thirty people visited Governor J. James Exon's office to complain. It was announced shortly thereafter that the FBI had been asked to look into the shooting.[63]

The day after Lewis died, Chambers said that he would investigate the death himself. He did not know whether the investigation initiated by U.S. District Attorney Daniel Wherry of Omaha would take part in any cover–up.

Chambers said it was appropriate that Lincoln Mayor Helen Boosalis and County Attorney Ron Lahners had called in outside agencies, but that they also seemed to be stating that the police actions were legitimate. Later, when the city announced that a grand jury would not be called, and the U.S. Department of Justice said that Lewis's rights had not been violated, Chambers and Barbara Kelley, Lewis's mother, led a group of demonstrators down the streets of Lincoln to protest the findings in the case. The press noted that eyewitness accounts differed from those of police. Carol "Dolly" Spitznogle, Lewis's girlfriend, said that Lewis did pick up a rifle when they heard a noise outside, but they did not hear a police identification or warning. They thought that their house was being broken into.[64]

On October 6, 1975, Chambers published information on the Lewis killing that he read in police reports but that were not made public. Chambers argued that based on the police reports, "Sherdell was the victim of a criminal homicide committed by Deputy Rod Loos."[65] What Chambers found out was that several Lincoln Police Department officers had asked an informant to try to buy cocaine from Lewis. At 5 p.m. on the day of Lewis's death (September 24), the informant was given three twenty-dollar bills with recorded serial numbers and was dropped off at 2284 Potter Street where Lewis lived. When the informant left the Lewis home, he said that he had purchased twenty-three dollars in cocaine from Lewis and that there was more cocaine in the Lewis house. A warrant was prepared, and fourteen law enforcement officers arrived at Lewis's home that night. Chambers noted that none of the marked twenty-dollar bills was ever found on Lewis or in his residence, nor was there any cocaine found in Lewis's home.[66]

There were also conflicting accounts from police officers. Sergeant Al Curtis, a uniformed patrolman, and Officer S. A. Miller of the Lincoln Police Department both said that Lewis had set his gun down and did not have a gun in his hand when he was shot by Loos.[67] Officer Miller reported:

> I then observed a black hand [sic] and half of a forearm I believed to belong to Sherdell Lewis, I observed the rifle and the hand was holding onto the barrel of the rifle, placing it against the wall at the west side or to the west of the door. As the gun was being brought down placed against the wall, I then heard the shotgun held by Rob Loos go off. I then heard the sound of a body hitting the floor, Sherdell Lewis was moaning.[68]

Chambers concluded that the story of the unnamed "informant," like the elusive search for cocaine in connection with Lewis, "was a mere smoke screen to justify exactly what happened: the calculated gunning down of Sherdell Lewis."[69]

According to reporter Nancy Hicks, Lewis lived with a young white woman, drove expensive cars, and was self-employed. He had confronted the previous mayor of Lincoln, saying that if city officials would not control the police and stop their abusive behaviors in the African American community that African people would fight back. Lewis was seen by the police administration as a troublemaker in a city in which the most outspoken human rights activists, other than Chambers, had been women. A group of citizens, including Jessie Payne, director of Lincoln Action Program, community activist Donna Polk, and Lincoln Equal Opportunity officer Gerald Henderson, arranged for a meeting with Mayor Boosalis because some members of the community "perceive the shooting of Lewis and Childers as [similar to] nationwide examples of white police killing Blacks."[70] In the end, Lewis's death was found to have been justifiable or, at worst, accidental. The small African American community of Lincoln did not accept the decision as valid, but, aside from Lewis's family, who would forever feel the sting of his death, in time they turned their attention to other issues. Chambers added Lewis's death to the train of abuses by the status quo—justifying all-out resistance.

Chambers's early career established him as a definite force in the Nebraska legislature. As a politician, the senator's persuasiveness with the other solons was established very early. It was not a matter of popularity, but rather of follow through that earned him respect. To be an effective legislator, one must master the art of knowing which bill is important to each senator. The giving or withholding of support at crucial junctions was one of the first major lessons that Chambers gleaned from the Unicameral and its mastery his primary political accomplishment. At the start of Chambers's career in the Unicameral, he had sponsored a measure for district elections to school boards. The bill required that school boards be elected "on the basis of geographical districts."[71] In the mid-1970s Chambers reminded his colleagues that they had passed such a measure previously, but that the governor had vetoed the bill after the legislature adjourned. That OPS faced a lawsuit by the U.S. Justice Department because of its practice of "drawing district boundaries to maintain segregation" made the debate over the measure more timely.[72]

Thus, when Senator George Syas moved to indefinitely postpone Chambers's bill for district elections, Chambers responded that Senator Syas "often obtains a ride down here and back home with Bernie Geiger who is a lobbyist for the Omaha School District. He can deny that that has anything to do with the way he votes or the issues that he decides to expound, but we all know."[73] The Speaker interrupted Senator Chambers because he said he felt that the remark was personal. "All right, strike that from the records, but it is true never-the-less," Chambers said.[74] Senator David Stahmer rose:

> Mr. President, members of the body . . . I think that if we were to characterize this debate, we could characterize it as . . . disingenuous . . . because we are talking about in essence of putting a band-aid on a problem that needs major surgery. . . . The leadership of the city of Omaha does not have the moral fiber to stand up and do what is right for children. Basically they are selfish they are interested in serving their own interests and they could care what the hell happens to the kids in the ghetto schools. If I am wrong, let the Omaha School District publish the report of the test scores in the ghetto schools and you will find out who is right and who is wrong. . . . I suspect that no harm could come from adopting Senator Chambers's bill, possibly hopefully some good could come from it.[75]

As the collective opinion of the body moved toward favoring Chambers's measure, Senator Gene Mahoney quipped, "I ride with Bernie but I'm going to vote with Ernie."[76]

Chambers's success in Lincoln enhanced his popularity in North Omaha even more. His groundedness and his resolve to stand up to any force that functioned to oppress his people's aspirations resulted in deep respect for him by his constituency. While he fought day-to-day battles on behalf of the poor, Chambers also established his importance in the history of resistance by African American intellectual leadership. Bertha Calloway, curator of thousands of African American artifacts and a founder of the Negro Historical Society of Nebraska, as well as an employee at the African American–owned *Omaha Star*, once said that Chambers stood apart because after graduating from Creighton University Law School in 1974, he used his education for the benefit of the community. Chambers, Calloway argued, fought for African cultural survival. He dedicated his life to ending police misconduct, and demanded equal treatment for black children in public schools and in the university system. The restoration of the community's political and physical health were notions that lodged themselves in Chambers's heart, charting the course of his life.[77]

Chambers's activities outside of the legislature spoke as loudly as his arguments during a scorching debate. He had attended the National Black Political Convention back in 1972 along with more than 2,500 other delegates, including a large number of intellectuals who identified themselves as part of the Black Nationalist Movement. One of those leaders, Amiri Baraka (formerly Leroi Jones) helped to organize the Congress of African Peoples in Atlanta, Georgia, in the fall of 1970, as well as the National Black Political Convention. However, as the Black Nationalist agenda became divided, with the larger segment increasingly committed to focusing on electoral politics, Chambers abandoned the organizing arm of the movement and gave his allegiance—once more—to the black working class, the poor, and the youth. For a new generation of radical activists had begun to emerge in the late 1970s and their gaze was trained upon ending the most unapologetic racial regime on earth. They spent their time and youthful energy on college campuses and in their communities protesting U.S. support of apartheid in South Africa. The grassroots and student-led Anti-Apartheid Movement focused on U.S. collusion with the racist regime. When the United States abstained from voting in a condemnation of South Africa's segregationist laws in the United Nations Security Council, many of the activists who had been content with conducting educational seminars about South Africa's racism now turned to direct action tactics, targeting corporations inside the United States with ties to the apartheid state. University of Nebraska–Omaha's student group Black Liberators for Action on Campus (BLAC) and the African People's Union (APU) at the University of Nebraska–Lincoln, for a time, made anti-apartheid their major political organizing focus. Both organizations held teach-ins where audiences were educated about the poverty and injustices that South Africans endured. On the University of Nebraska–Lincoln campus, students Elizabeth Burden, Doreen Charles, Shomari Ashberi (Mark Jones), Lateefah (Sherry Hale Coleman), Hadari Sababu (Kenneth Jackson), Jaha (Deresa Oliver), and others clad themselves in black armbands and held posters describing the injustices of apartheid. They passed out TransAfrica publications that provided the latest available statistics on the region and news from the African National Congress (ANC).[78] The reigning party of South African whites, who dubbed themselves Afrikaners, the students said, held all of the soil-producing lands, forcing the majority black population to live on reservations where the earth was too rocky and poor to feed the people. Husbands were forced to live in barracks in urban centers close to the mines, so that their bosses could maximize the number of hours that they could get from the labor force. Prostitution and vice were high in urban areas where men were separated from their wives and families for most of the year. Health care was almost completely lacking. Married women, those who could find work, nursed white babies in town while their own small children took care of infant siblings on the Bantustans (tribal reserves).[79]

The senator intensified his research on Africa and made comparisons between black South Africans and African Americans in the United States. He reviewed rates of mortality, malnutrition, and access to basic health care by black people in South Africa and in the United States and found that racism had a profoundly negative effect on African people's health. The situation was despicable in South Africa, where a law required that only black doctors and nurses treat African patients. During this period there was one nurse for about every 128 whites and one nurse for every 756 black South Africans. As a result, many African people suffered from preventable illnesses. One year a count was taken of persons with tuberculosis, and 759 whites had the illness while 47,692 blacks suffered with the disease. Children fared the worst, and deaths from preventable childhood diseases were frequent occurrences. The infant mortality rate for white children, Chambers noted, was 18.6 per 1,000, while for African children it was 112.2 per 1,000, or one in ten.[80]

Senator Chambers spoke about South Africa on several occasions at the invitation of university students. The senator believed that freedom fighters in the United States, who were struggling to end police repression in their communities, and South African revolutionaries confronted the same enemy. Although colonialism and segregation were constructed somewhat differently in the United States and South Africa, the problems that African people faced in both places were also similar, and resistance took whatever form was most likely to succeed. The South African government responded to the black South African–led international resistance movement by increasing their repressive measures. They had already instituted the Terrorism Acts under which suspects could be kept in detention without formal charges being filed for up to 180 days. But then, government repression in South Africa had a long history. The South African police had arrested 8,000 black persons in 1952 in order to squelch the ANC's Defiance Campaign, in which protesters practiced civil disobedience in segregated facilities. One outcome was the Treason Trials of 1958, held in Pretoria, the nation's capital. When the prosecution finished presenting its case, the government declared a state of emergency, presumably to keep foreign reporters from gaining firsthand information on legal aspects of the trials and to inhibit investigations of police killings that had occurred during demonstrations organized by the Pan African Congress (PAC) and ANC.[81]

By the late 1970s Chambers kept up regularly with the South African freedom struggle. He would have noted the occasion when Randall Robinson published ANC President Oliver Tambo's call to the international community to step up their organizing efforts if they wished to help the nation, already in "civil war," to keep the bloody phase of the revolution brief. Building on years of Pan-African and anticolonial theorizing through the writings of intellectuals like Delany, Douglass, Fanon, Cesaire, Guevara, Nkrumah, Shabazz, and others who condemned racism and colonial repression in Africa and in the United States, Chambers heeded the call. Chambers's ingenuity lent itself to the practicality of how to wage a freedom struggle from inside "the belly-of-the-beast" (a popular way of describing resistance to apartheid inside of prosegregationist societies). Chambers kept abreast of African freedom struggles throughout the diaspora as a senator in the Nebraska Unicameral, denouncing the oppression of African people in Africa and in America on the floor of the statehouse. He rejected propaganda that described ANC freedom fighters as terrorists, and condemned as evil the refusal of the United States to support the United Nation's anti-apartheid initiatives, including a voluntary arms embargo of South Africa. The urgency of the movement and the notion that Afro-Americans were similarly situated were clear to him. For Chambers, police shootings and killings of hundreds of black children in Soweto, a township outside of Johannesburg, as they marched from Naledi High School in defiance of repressive measures (including being forced to speak the Dutch-inspired Afrikaans in school) was not unlike the killings of young people in North Omaha.[82]

By the late 1970s, Chambers could be heard conveying the idea to diverse Midwestern audiences that the quickest way to end the suffering in South Africa would be for the twenty-four million blacks there to kill the five million whites who were determined to hang on to their racial privileges and their apartheid state. However, he unfailingly added the postscript—sanctions were the least violent way of furthering the goals of revolution. One only had to read from Stephen Biko to learn that the best way to support the South African revolutionaries was to cease supplying financial and military support to the Afrikaner government. At great personal risk, South African black consciousness leader Biko corresponded with U.S. Senator Dick

Clark, chairman of the Senate Subcommittee on Africa, to communicate his message to the world: "At this stage of the liberation process we have become very sensitive to the role played by the world's big powers.... In a sense, America—your country—has played a shameful role in her relations with our country."[83] For Biko, the United States could choose to continue its support of the existing white minority in power or offer real help toward the formation of South Africa as a nonracial democratic society. Although it was a crime punishable by death for South Africans to call for divestment, Biko did so. The activist acknowledged that blacks would suffer materially under sanctions, but that the level of suffering was already intolerable, and sanctions would support the greater good by helping the revolution succeed more quickly.[84]

The idea of divestment of U.S. corporations from South Africa had been heralded by activists and students for some time. Countermovement forces voiced their opposition through a handful of conservative African Americans and hundreds of corporate leaders with ties to South Africa. New rumors were started and old accusations were recirculating, namely that the ANC was Soviet-controlled, and that TransAfrica—Robinson's direct aid and lobbyist organization—was sympathetic to Marxists. Chambers, however, considered reports that he received by way of Robinson's organization as reliable, primarily because TransAfrica maintained communication with the ANC. The murder of Biko in detention in 1977 enraged anti-apartheid activists around the world. It appeared that the young intellectual was murdered in retaliation for his outspoken resistance to the oppression of his people. The news of Biko's death impacted activists in Nebraska. Chambers was incensed at the murder of the black freedom worker, and condemned the brutality of the South African police.

Chambers's perpetual anger over racism was suspended momentarily in the spring of 1978, and he was moved by compassion and sorrow over the death of a friend. Chambers served as a pallbearer at the funeral of Terry Carpenter, who had been a white man and a brother in the struggle against the powerful. Carpenter had represented his constituency in Nebraska's panhandle passionately. He had fought the senators from the urban centers of Omaha and Lincoln who sometimes seemed to forget the western end of the state. Much of what Carpenter said about power dynamics in Nebraska was true. Omaha and Lincoln each had multiple state legislative districts within their metropolitan areas (17 and 4, respectively). Collectively the cities were home to twenty-one of the Unicameral's forty-nine state senators. Lincoln, as host to both the flagship campus of the University of Nebraska and the seat of government—as the capital city—commands much of state budget allocations as well as federal funds for higher education. Nearby Omaha, with a population nearly double that of Lincoln followed as the second-greatest recipient of state revenues and federal funds allocated to Nebraska. Considered by some a luxury and by others as fundamental to the functioning of a democracy, an Office of Public Counsel or Ombudsman's Office was enacted through legislation in 1971 to help mitigate some of the differentials in power between rural and urban, wealthy and poor, and to generally provide more equitable government across Nebraska and between people of upper and lower economic classes. Ombudsman Marshall Lux and members of his staff became known for insisting that public agencies follow written procedures when dealing with clientele and for investigating complaints by the people of the state against public agencies. With Senator Chambers's full support, and sometimes insistence, the ombudsman had been known to intervene with other public agencies in response to citizens' complaints about excessive red tape or lack of services. As such, the Ombudsman's Office had investigated disputes over farmland taken by the Nebraska Department of Roads, and investigated the service delivery of other state agencies. However, the largest portion of the Ombudsman's caseload related to the state penitentiary and county jail system and came from prisoners who complained that their rights were violated by prison personnel, or that their medical needs had been neglected. Whatever the subject or category, roughly one-quarter of the complaints considered by the Ombudsman's Office in a given year were found justified. The Nebraska Equal Opportunity Commission (NEOC) also concerned itself with the rights of citizens but focused its investigations on violations of federal and state civil rights mandates. These cases fell under laws protecting citizens' rights in the areas of public accommodations, equal pay, housing discrimination, and especially fair employment practices (in compliance with the Fair Employment Practice Act). The NEOC maintained intake offices in Omaha, Lincoln, and Scottsbluff (Carpenter's home) and regularly received the greatest number of complaints in the realm of employment discrimination, accounting for over seventy percent of the commission's caseload. The cases included issues of excessive discipline or termination based on race, failure to promote or denial of training, and failure to hire. Thousands of dollars in awards to complainants over time were assigned for violations determined valid by the NEOC. In spite of claims by Chambers's enemies that ongoing racism and oppression of the poor were figments of the senator's overactive imagination, data from the NEOC seemed conclusive. Since its inception, the NEOC received complaints against offices within government as well as from privately owned establishments. Those accused of some form of discrimination during a two-year period alone included the city of Omaha's Fire Department, Vickers Incorporated, University of Nebraska Medical Center, Farmland Corporation, Western Sugar, Cracker Barrel, Mutual of Omaha, and American Tool Company, among others. While not all of these cases resulted in an award for the complainant, all were considered plausible enough for the commission to schedule a public hearing. Carpenter used unequal power relations among rural and urban whites to develop a generalized understanding of how the abuse of power by any majority works, and he came to understand that the same abuse of power that his constituents faced impacted African Americans without any social sanctions to rein them in. For Chambers, Carpenter's growth at understanding racialized politics and the nexus of power and domination reaffirmed that the world was not just divided by color, but by the greedy against the poor. Back when Carpenter was diagnosed with cancer, Chambers recalled that Carpenter had told him that he knew he was going to die. The forewarning did not help, and when he received news of his friend's passing, the senator felt the loss severely. Carpenter's respect for Chambers had never stopped growing. Commenting on "Ernie's" ability to debate an issue, Senator Carpenter once said that he "watched [Chambers] plant land mines, and then had seen them go off one after another."[85] The most fitting salute to Carpenter, it seemed, would be for Chambers to fight on.

In April 1979, Chambers cosponsored a resolution in the Nebraska state legislature to remove the state's financial investments from corporations doing business in South Africa. He argued that Nebraska should reaffirm its stated concern for human rights by withdrawing its support from a system in which the ruling class of four million white people controlled the political and economic life of nineteen million black people. Chambers told his colleagues that apartheid meant that in their own country blacks were restricted to certain areas, were not allowed to vote, own land, hold public office, join white unions, or go into urban areas unless they were working for a white person. He said that investment in the apartheid regime was utterly immoral and destined blacks to a life of servitude, poverty, and neglect. Moreover, the South African government had broken several international conventions because it "denies basic human rights."[86]

Resolution 43

That spring Chambers and his cosponsor Senator Steve Fowler introduced a resolution calling for the divestment of state funds from South Africa. The measure recommended that the state of Nebraska's Investment Council remove funds from "any bank or corporation which has investments in the Republic of South Africa."[87] On March 31, 1980, the Nebraska legislature voted twenty-eight to zero to adopt the measure. At the time that they offered their divestment resolution, Fowler noted that Nebraska had twenty-five million dollars invested in South Africa through twenty-six different American corporations. Chambers argued that investment in South African companies equated to support for the apartheid system so that "Black people in a mineral-rich country live in dire poverty."[88] The success of the resolution caused elation among anti-apartheid activists, and North Omaha residents exuded a certain pride that their senator had accomplished such a feat. In the backlash that followed, members of the business community tried to demonstrate that the presence of their companies actually helped South Africa make progress in human rights. Other warned that the economic outcome would be disastrous for the state. Meanwhile members of BLAC and the APU and the politically conscious reveled in victory.

Chambers knew that Resolution 43 frustrated bankers, investors, and other power brokers across the state. He was, however, accustomed to swimming against the tide. His growing power in the legislature proved that with determination and skill, the tide could be harnessed. The senator's South African resolution was the first divestment measure to be passed by any state legislature in the country, and thus led the way to dismantling U.S. support for the racist South African regime.[89]

Knowledge of Chambers's stand against apartheid spread outside of the Midwest, and anti-apartheid activists began intensifying their protests. Churches hosted teach-ins around the world, with participants at single events numbering into the hundreds and thousands. Activism expanded the movement even further, and people increasingly rejected the federal government's policy of cooperation and "Constructive Engagement" (President Ronald Reagan's term) with the apartheid regime. Disenchanted, freedom fighters in the states scaled up their efforts, targeting universities, banks, and labor unions as well as major U.S. companies in South Africa, including Shell, Mobil, Ford, General Motors, IBM, and U.S. Steel, as locations for nonviolent but direct action demonstrations. Not since the Civil Rights Movement had so many Americans rallied to confront a social evil.[90]

On May 6, 1980, Franklin A. Thomas, chair of the Study Commission on United States Policy Toward Southern Africa (funded by the Rockefeller Foundation), invited the senator to submit a statement describing his resolution. Board members of the commission had just returned from a fact-finding trip to South Africa and hoped to incorporate Chambers's perspective in their report. Chambers used the opportunity to call for sanctions at the national level. Released in the spring of 1981, the study recommended broadening the arms embargo, endorsing the Sullivan Principles (prohibiting discrimination against Africans in American firms located in South Africa), but stopped short of calling for divestment or direct action campaigns.[91]

Disappointed though he was, the senator noted that his resolution had garnered the attention of the South African press. A popular African newspaper, *Sechaba*, reported that the "American imperialists" were encouraging the Botha regime to attack the ANC and other anti-apartheid revolutionaries taking refuge in the front-line states. Fortunately, the editorialist wrote, "Reagan is aware that the black Americans are very sensitive—and justifiably so—about U.S. policy towards Africa. The Afro-Americans who understandably identify with the struggles of the African people, regard an attack on the African continent as an attack on them."[92] The white South African press had also, by this time, learned of the passage of Nebraska's divestment resolution and the *Rand Daily Mail* reported that it was "ominous." It was horrific news for the Botha regime, partly because Nebraska had over twenty-four million dollars invested in businesses with interests in South Africa and because "it is the first time an individual American state has taken such an action.... Its vote could well set a bandwagon rolling."[93] History proved the Rand editorialist correct. By 1982 the U.S. divestment campaign was snowballing. That year the mayors of thirty-three U.S. cities joined an international group demanding the "immediate and unconditional release" of Nelson Mandela, the ANC president who had been imprisoned since 1962.[94] A few months later, Chambers named as his priority bill an additional divestment measure, one meant to "provide teeth" to the divestment resolution. The bill would prohibit the investment of state monies in South Africa by providing guidelines for the phasing out of pension funds, and prohibiting the investment of stocks in any company with South African investments. Chambers told his colleagues that "Nebraska should not be underwriting the most racist, repressive regime on the face of the earth."[95]

In the spring of 1981, Chambers had been one of eighteen state legislators from across the country who were invited to address the United Nations' Committee on Apartheid. Chambers told the UN Conference on Public Investment and South Africa that "South African racism and apartheid exist for the same reason as did slavery in America.... Racism is profitable."[96] Paraphrasing Malcolm X (El Hajj Malik El Shabazz), Chambers said his main purpose in fighting for divestment had been to "give encouragement to those oppressed people . . . who are willing to use any means necessary to speed their freedom."

When Chambers took the fight against apartheid into the Unicameral he was at the crest of a formidable movement. University students around the country considered apartheid to be one of the great moral injustices of their day. Between 1977 and 1982 twenty-three states tried to initiate some form of divestment measure, with Michigan (December 1980) and Connecticut (1981) passing the first divestment laws.[97] However, Nebraska was the first state to successfully pass *any* South African divestment mandate. Chambers's Divestment Resolution 43 was approved by the solons in Nebraska in March 1980. The senator wrote the following journal entry that spring:

> The real momentum for my legislative action came from the dispute over the 1300 krugerrands donated to the University Foundation for the benefit of the University of Nebraska Engineering school.... I pressed the point that the university was to benefit from the krugerrands which were minted on the backs of Black South Africans. The Senators expressed the usual disgust with apartheid but didn't wish to 'punish' the university. Because of their expressed opposition to apartheid, I was able to parlay that into an agreement to pass my resolution banning the state of Nebraska from investing funds in companies doing business in South Africa. Thus, Nebraska became the first state to act.[98]

For the remainder of the decade Chambers was involved in activities supportive of freedom fighters in South Africa. In a last-minute effort, in June 1983, coordinated in part by Nebraskans for Peace, Chambers sent a telegram to U.S. secretary of state George Schultz asking for help in preventing the "execution of three ANC members by South Africa tomorrow."[99] The three had been accused of high treason for their alleged attacks on police stations, but the international community believed that their confessions were "extracted by torture."[100] The U.S. State Department replied that they could not stop the executions, and Marcus Motaung, Jerry Mosoli, and Simon Mogocrane were put to death by the South African government.

A few days before the senator's forty-sixth birthday, Chambers received two unusual calls and he noted them. First, a constituent called and "cussed me out; hung up"; and secondly, Senator Don Wesley called to ask what to look for if he participated in the all-expense-paid South African trip that some of the senators were going to take.[101] Chambers had heard of plans for the "junket," which he opposed since the senators would not be allowed to take pictures, move about among the people, and interview the indigenous South Africans with whom they wished to speak. A handful of senators went anyway, but Senator Chambers tried hard to sabotage any public relations value that the trip might have. During their absence, the senator shared with the media and with the legislature a postcard that he had seen on top of a pile of mail in the Associated Press mailbox. The postcard, signed by Senator Rex Haberman, pictured a young, bare-breasted South African woman. Haberman wrote what he would later pass off as a joke. He wondered if the reporter would like her as a gift.[102] She would, he thought, make a good housekeeper. The note was obviously sexist and derogatory—an allusion to domestic work as black women's natural occupation—and because Haberman had chosen a card with frontal nudity, he seemed to suggest that the woman could be sexually exploited. Chambers contacted the press about the impropriety of Haberman's actions, and he said that the episode proved that those who were supposed to be on a trip to determine whether South Africa was moving toward treating indigenous African people with human dignity were in no position to know.

The senator had done all he could to help the freedom fighters win the struggle for the liberation of South Africa. He provided facts and information for his colleagues, worked with the student-led African Peoples Union of the University of Nebraska campus at Lincoln and BLAC at UNO, joined forces with the Coalition Against Apartheid (a North Omaha political action group lead by Paul Penny), spoke at the De Porres Center in Omaha, and worked to educate the public on the anti-apartheid effort along with other community folk. The indigenous freedom struggle in South Africa was growing in strength and with foreign investment to the country vanishing the people could not lose.[103]

In June 1981, at the invitation of the American Committee on Africa, Chambers spoke at a Conference on Public Investment and South Africa. He joined Nigerian ambassador B. Akporode Clark, chairman of the UN Special Committee Against Apartheid, in giving a press conference on sanctions in New York City. In 1983, his ideas were again solicited by the UN Special Committee Against Apartheid. Chambers told the international body, "I am from the State of Nebraska which is Midwestern, predominately white, agricultural, very conservative and in some ways manifests a racism similar to that found in the Republic of South Africa."[104]

Chambers's name became familiar to at least some visitors to the United States from Africa. On August 24, 1983, Chambers had an unexpected surprise when representative J. L. T. Mothibamele from Gaborone, Botswana, stopped by his office to discuss African affairs. Some other senators failed to meet with the African delegation and one of their members suggested that they try and speak with Senator Chambers. Chambers and Mothibamele discussed the Anti-Apartheid Movement, current affairs in Botswana, and issues affecting central and southern African nations and Africans in the heartland of North America.[105]

5—Statecraft

Chambers's evolution as a lawmaker was nothing less than magnificent. He and Senator Steve Fowler's divestment resolution literally started a domino effect, as one state after another followed Nebraska's lead in ending economic support for apartheid. The Anti-Apartheid Movement swept though the nation and the world, drawing its strength from regular community folk, and enjoying widespread participation in North Omaha. It would leave behind changes in the political consciousness of North Omahans. One group of activists succeeded in simultaneously purchasing Malcolm X's (El Hajj Malik El Shabazz) birthplace and the old telephone building on the Northside. The latter would become the venue for Bertha Calloway's Great Plains Black History Museum. The senator wrote letters of support to assist in the building black institutions.[1]

Odyssey West Magazine ran a special on Chambers in the spring of 1985, querying how "an ultra-conservative predominately white state" where African Americans make up at best three percent of the state's population, was the third state in the United States to enact a divestment law—and the first to successfully pass any anti-apartheid divestment measure. Chambers's reply explained his motivation, but not his power to impact the law:

> To be Black and conscious is to be in a perpetual rage. The only way you can walk through this life as a Black person and be docile is either to be drugged and have narcotics in your system or be asleep mentally; asleep intentionally because you can't face what is being done to us and you feel helpless to do anything about it.[2]

A more feasible explanation was that Chambers's prowess as a legislator and as an intellectual were constantly evolving. Back in January 1979, J. James Exon had given his farewell speech, and Charles Thone was sworn in as the new governor of Nebraska. Chambers continued his service on the Unicameral Government, Military, and Veterans Affairs and Judiciary Committees. That year, he supported Senator Dave Newell's bill to eliminate tax on food sold in grocery stores, and he submitted his own measure to eliminate all tax on food. Chambers said he opposed taxing food because "it is immoral to tax a necessity of life."[3] Later that year, Chambers would vote to upgrade the pay structure for inmates at the state penitentiary who worked jobs, and as always he sponsored a bill to repeal the capital punishment statutes. This time Chambers won first-round approval of a thirty-year mandatory prison sentence in lieu of the death penalty.[4]

The process of getting a bill passed into law in Nebraska is as arduous as introducing them is easy. Any number of bills can be sponsored, and likewise all of them can be killed at any of several intersections along the process. A bill is introduced by a senator during the first ten days of the session; a clerk assigns a number to the bill, which is then referred to committee. The committee kills the bill or has a public hearing on it. This system of a Unicameral was instigated by the U.S. senator from Nebraska, George Norris, who did not want bills to have to go through a conference committee in which senators met in secret. Norris believed the very concept of a conference committee was undemocratic. At any rate, after the initial phase, successful bills go to General File and in turn the full legislature can debate and vote on the bill. It takes twenty-five senators to move the bill (or amendment) to the next level. Bills that survive this far go forward to Enrollment and Review where they are checked for grammar, and any successful amendments to a bill are added before the bill goes to Select File for a final round of debate. If it is not killed, the bill moves on to the governor's desk for a signature or veto. In spite of this apparently rigorous procedure, Nebraska's one-house system simplifies the process compared to that of the other forty-nine states. Still, the Unicameral's unique structure allowed a single forum over which Chambers developed considerable influence. More than one observer has said that Chambers could never have exercised as much power as he eventually wielded if Nebraska's state legislature had a two-chamber house.[5]

The development of black electoral power in Virginia bears some similarities to Nebraska. William Ferguson Reid was elected to the Virginia House of Delegates in 1968 and was followed into office by William Robinson, Sr., the same year, and by L. Douglas Wilder who was elected to the State Senate in 1969. Wilder would serve as the lone African American in the Virginia Statehouse until 1980, and he would continue to serve as a state senator until 1985. Unlike Chambers, however, Wilder's platforms generally included his pledge to be tough on criminals, and he supported the death penalty as an appropriate punishment for heinous crimes. In 1990, Wilder became the first African American governor of a state in the Union. During the decade that he served as Virginia's only black senator Wilder's influence grew largely out of his adeptness at understanding the law and his willingness to be criticized for being overly adamant about his positions. The will to use the power of his position to halt legislative business became Chambers's hallmark, but was a practice that was applied by other black elected officials around the nation. However, the art of melding street-level activism with the political process among African Americans was trail-blazed by Adam Clayton Powell, Jr. As a civil and labor rights activist in Harlem, New York, Clayton Powell organized rent strikes and led demonstrations demanding fair hiring practices in civil service jobs for blacks. His legacy was in part the establishment of a tradition of black political maneuvering between the seat of government and the neighborhood, a facet of his style that remained in force for most of his tenure as a member of the U.S. House of Representatives from 1945 to 1971. In 1977, during the Ohio General Assembly's debate at the statehouse in Columbus, Senator C. J. McLin Jr., and his African American colleagues utilized some of the tactics that Chambers employed in the Nebraska legislature. In one instance, the black members abstained from voting in a close contest, preventing passage of a bill on the state's budget. With so few African Americans in state legislatures before 1980, relying on the filibuster and refusing to cast a vote were some of the few tools that African Americans in majority white-governing bodies had at their disposal to shift the course of events during the legislative proceedings toward the interests of their constituencies. Yet, no state senators had the powers that urban mayors exercised: they could not appoint cabinet members or make personnel decisions for top political posts. However, because Chambers was the elected leader of the Eleventh Legislative District in Omaha, he was at once the spokesperson for the section of the state with the largest number of African Americans and for the greatest concentration of black people in an urban setting in the state. As a result Chambers functioned, practically speaking, as state senator and as the unofficial mayor of North Omaha. Four years prior to Chambers's initial election to the Unicameral, there were no African Americans serving as the mayors of metropolitan cities anywhere in the United States. That changed in 1967, when both Carl Stokes (Cleveland, Ohio) and Richard Hatcher (Gary, Indiana) became the first urban black mayors in the nation's history, starting a new trend in electoral politics. At a time when white flight was rapidly contributing to increases in the black population of cities, black political machines grew in strength. By the close of 1989, African Americans were mayors of over 300 North American cities. Black mayors used their power as city administrators to appoint African American police officials, but frequently engaged in power struggles with the local political machine. For example, Stokes (mayor of Cleveland from 1968 to 1971 and representative in the Ohio House from 1967 to 1968) boycotted the city council meetings because the members regularly tried to circumvent him.[6]

While the legislature was in session from January until early summer, Chambers regarded his many projects as somewhat peripheral to the task at hand, as he thoroughly prepared for debate on the bills under discussion each day. Political astuteness on the floor demanded that he read each senator's bills in advance, study existing Nebraska law, and occasionally check with with the Legislative Research Office to find cases from other states with which to buttress his arguments, and then, of course, there was the preparation of his own bills. What would help his community most? The answers came readily. Chambers had lived in the community all of his life, and the obvious problems were still the police department's racism and brutality, the lack of jobs due to poor quality education and discrimination, and racist judges. The latter was harder to deal with, but not impossible. Chambers would commit himself during those years to waging the major battles on issues in floor debate, battles he had fought all of his adult life. Irrespective of temporary defeats and the lack of tangible forms of support by his constituents—like showing up regularly to observe the legislative process—he became increasingly influential in the Unicameral. Chambers's level of preparedness involved knowing which bills were most important to each senator, and he tried to impress upon his colleagues that they would need his support, sooner or later, in a close vote. If he did not get some of what he wanted, then he would filibuster when one of their bills was on the table.[7]

By now Senator Chambers was an influential member of the Government, Military and Veterans Affairs Committee and he utilized his power to help his constituency. He was pleased when, after a good deal of educating and persuasion, several senators supported his measure for city council elections by district. "We have 38,000 people who spend fifty-six million dollars in Omaha annually. Yet we have not been able to make a major decision as to where or how our tax money is being spent," Chambers said.[8] He also sponsored a legislative bill that would require governmental agencies to hold open meetings when making policy changes. Chambers wrote the bill when the Omaha Housing Authority raised rents after going into closed session for discussion. Another measure (Legislative Bill 112) would enable the Nebraska Equal Opportunities Commission to enforce laws against companies practicing discrimination in public facilities. Opponents said if the bill became law the new rule would allow individuals to "harass businessmen over maybe nothing."[9] Chambers countered, ". . . we're talking about giving an agency the power to do something it has already been given responsibility for."[10]

Throughout the late 1970s and early 1980s, in addition to preparing for debate and working the floor of the statehouse, Chambers kept up his scrutiny of law enforcement practices. One policing issue that caught the senator's attention in the late 1970s was the loss of "evidence" in an "under-monitored" special fund set up by the Nebraska State Patrol for drug sting operations.[11] With the "no fault" ruling in the slaying of Sherdell Lewis still smoldering inside of him, Chambers looked on while Lincoln defense attorneys Kirk Naylor, Jr., and Dennis Keefe issued a report arguing that two undercover agents had used what were supposed to be police drug dollars to store up drugs for themselves. Chambers had long suspected corruption in the use of informants. He wanted a thorough review of every police and sheriff's department in the state and had proposed such a study back in 1974. Ironically, when the Judiciary Committee agreed to conduct the investigation, they refused to appoint Chambers as chair of the subcommittee for the study that he had proposed. Chambers sent a memo to the entire body. "Dear colleague[s], an ugly event occurred at the May 6th meeting of the Judiciary Committee."[12] Fear of the Nebraska State Bar Association (NBA) had persuaded his colleagues to keep him from a leadership position on the committee to investigate law enforcement practices in Nebraska, Chambers said.[13]

When Legislative Resolution 132 first "authorized the study" of Nebraska's legal system,[14] Chambers was back in law school. He contacted Creighton University's law dean to say that he would be unable to attend summer sessions because of his role in the study. His supposition that the NBA did not want the investigation to go forward was proven correct when the association expressed displeasure with the Judiciary Committee for agreeing to it. The response of the association lent credence to the impression of some community members that the police, courts, and judges were part of a protected union and not only did the NBA fail to monitor these agents of the law, but it actually shielded those entities from public scrutiny. That the NBA was opposed to the study had been made clear enough to Chambers on March 3, 1974, when Governor Exon decided to "publicly denounce" Chambers "and the study at the Lincoln Law Day Conference."[15] Chambers said he knew that other members of the Judiciary Committee were contacted and told to oppose Chambers's chairmanship of the subcommittee, and he believed that Senator Richard Fellman was one of the first to "cave in" to the NBA's demands. "As a result of this concerted effort by the Nebraska Bar Association, I was denied Chairmanship of a subcommittee authorized by my own resolution."[16] Chambers told the press that he wondered what NBA feared people would learn. "The primary question is whether adequate legal services are being delivered to the public."[17] In contrast, the relatively progressive Nebraska Association of Trial Attorneys wanted the investigation.[18]

Ultimately, the Judiciary Committee backtracked on its decision to support the study. Chambers had a pretty good idea about what had transpired— "pressure was applied on the Reference Committee to kill it."[19] "For some reason, the Judiciary Committee is very beholden to the NBA."[20] Chambers guessed that committee members seeking reelection feared that NBA lobbyists' funds would dry up, or that some of their law practices could be "audited" by the powerful agency. At any rate, the senator's faith in the legislature, which had grown during his first years in office, was permanently damaged. "After this wrenching, tearing episode involving betrayal of trust and violation of promises, the Judiciary Committee can never be the same. Its former effectiveness has been successfully destroyed."[21]

If denial of Chambers's leadership of his own subcommittee were not enough, months earlier Chambers was denied the chairmanship of the Government, Veterans, and Military Affairs Committee, a post which he had previously held. One citizen wrote his opinion of what had happened.[22]

> It would take a pretty naive individual not to believe that Senator [Dennis] Rasmussen used racial sensitivity as a tool to garner votes to outbid Senator Chambers for the Chairmanship of the Government Committee. . . . At any rate, Nebraska is the real loser. Sena-

tor Chambers knows what checks and balances mean in our democratic system and has continued to go about his job under some fairly trying conditions. There is no way one can clip the wings of an individual with his energy, intellect and dedication.[23]

Chambers's popularity among working-class whites across the state grew in measure with his willingness to expose and fight policies that favored only the wealthy and the politically well positioned. The *Lincoln Star*'s Unicameral reporter, Don Walton, recognized Chambers's legal and intellectual skills. As a result, Walton had a different take on Chambers's loss of the Government, Military and Veterans Affairs Committee chairmanship. Walton argued that the conservative older senators tended to win the chairmanship seats over the younger, more aggressive senators. Rasmussen, a fifty-five-year-old farmer, had defeated Chambers, the barber and law student. Walton pointed out that John Cavanaugh, III, had also failed to win against the reigning chair of the Public Health and Welfare Committee over Tom Kennedy. Both of the younger men were highly opinionated on the floor, and both had supported Terry Carpenter's right to challenge the election results in the Forty-Eighth Legislative District. Still, Chambers was the only incumbent committee chair removed by in-house elections. The episode set the stage for the circumscription that Nebraska's Euro-American representatives would attempt to put on Chambers's political career by never again allowing him to win a leadership seat within the Unicameral. An unintended result of what would become one of the legislative body's institutionalized practices also revealed the limits of their power to control Chambers.[24]

In many ways, the loss of the committee chairmanship was for Chambers like the proverbial line drawn in the sand. The secret ballot voting process meant that no one had to confront the senator directly and risk political retaliation for excluding him, and yet the bottom line was that despite his abilities he would never again rise to a position of official leadership within the legislature. Chambers experienced for the first time the absolute political nature of the legislature. If one played the game and catered to business and other powerful lobbyists, one advanced; and if one hammered at the body to be a protector of all of the state's citizens, including the weak and unorganized, then that person would be cut out of the political pie. It was at this juncture that Chambers consciously reconfirmed for himself the values and goals that he had long held. He had come into office as a man of the people. His return to law school and the lessons of the legislature as to how the game of politics was played in Nebraska made him even more determined not to acquiesce to what he saw as others' corrupt, self-seeking style of representation. Chambers would change his vocation in the legislative roster of solons. He had been listed as a "Barber," now he called himself "Defender of the Downtrodden."[25]

Veteran Senator

Foretelling Chambers's future legislative prowess was passage of his bill for district rather than at-large elections back in 1975. The new law ultimately changed the structure of the Omaha City Council and Omaha School Board. Chambers had succeeded at persuading the conservative legislators of the state to force open Omaha's all-white power structure and allow the representation of nonmajority peoples. It was a major breakthrough for African American politics in Omaha.[26] To the city of Omaha, however, Chambers was scarcely less a thorn-in-the- side as a state senator than he had been as a community activist. Years into his service in the Unicameral, Chambers's views about American society remained intact. In general, Chambers's "radical ideology" matched that of other African American nationalists. Paradoxically, however, Chambers would condemn capitalism and yet did not adopt Marxism or socialism. Instead he pointed to racism as the underlying cause of inequalities in America.[27]

> [T]he political and economic systems of a country reflect the ethos, ethics, or philosophy of a people who make up that country. . . . In fact, there is no salvation for a people in any system. The goodness or badness of a people who happened to be in control at a given time determine what is.[28]

Chambers said neither socialism nor communism would end racism and discrimination if the new system remained in the hands of Euro-Americans whose cultural outlook went unchanged. A nationalist philosophically but also a pragmatist, Chambers ultimately decided that although reform efforts would probably fail, they had to at least be tried. Chambers said that his life would "prove that when a man does all that he can and achieves against overwhelming odds," people will eventually see that nothing really changed and that "other perhaps more drastic measures have to be resorted to."[29]

Despite all of his talk of failure, Chambers knew that he had succeeded.

> There is no Senator in this legislature who is as productive as I am . . . as a man having to struggle for everything, abilities and insights are developed which white people don't develop when they are always in the majority, when they always have someone to prepare the way for them . . . always have a scapegoat to blame . . . they become soft.[30]

Chambers argued that whites have a sense that blacks are superior because they accomplish more with fewer resources and networks.[31]

It was true that Chambers's victories resulted from his high level of preparation, which he achieved through an intense work regime. Early on in his career he memorized the legislative procedures, and then he used them to derail pieces of legislation. On these occasions, Chambers's remark was, "I stand up and remind them that when I first came to the Legislature, I was the one who was considered destructive of the system. . . . Rather than master those rules, they would move to suspend them."[32]

By the early 1980s, national interest in guaranteeing equal opportunities for African Americans in order to reverse the residual effects of slavery and segregation had collapsed. Descriptions of Chambers appeared in the Midwestern press that suggested the senator frequently beat a proverbial "dead horse" by complaining of racial discrimination, which some people claimed no longer existed. Experts on racialized societies like George M. Frederickson would argue that racist social practices typically continue even after a dominant group has "intellectually condemned" racism—but most Nebraskans would not lean toward such an understanding.[33] The increasingly conservative take on affirmative action by Euro-Americans paralleled the rise of the women's rights movement. Conservative males charged that feminism, like affirmative action, had gone too far, disrupting the home and the economy. While Nebraska joined the rest of the country in moving back to the right during this era, Chambers watched the reaction of the national black leadership. He sent out letters criticizing Coretta Scott King and other black people who endorsed the white candidate, Walter Mondale, in the 1984 presidential primaries, over the African American Reverend Jesse Jackson. His sense was that many middle-class African Americans had moved on with no regard for the poor and working class. He would never have to endure criticism for abandoning his roots. As the 1980s opened, Chambers kept up his protests of police slayings of unarmed citizens and other forms of discrimination.[34]

By this juncture, above all of the other characteristics that Senator

Chambers exhibited, his political staying power was undeniable. Not only would he remain in the legislature, but he would continue to wage battles over many of the same issues because they were vitally important to his constituents. In the 1980s and 1990s, Chambers would fight against the death penalty and for the rights of student athletes, children, prisoners, farmers, and anyone else in need of protection. Chambers would keep up with his itinerary of speaking engagements and, as far as possible, with his family. Meanwhile, the nationwide economic recession of the 1980s had given rise to two related crises in the state: the failure of the family farm and excesses in the banking industry.

At the time, Chambers served on two legislative committees (Government, Military and Veterans Affairs Committee and Judiciary Committee) and on the Executive Board. The senator was serving as vice chairman of the Judiciary Committee under his colleague William Nichol. The Judiciary Committee opened its first session of the decade by holding a two-day conference to review changes in the Nebraska Department of Corrections, partly as a result of Chambers's lobbying. The committee directed the Department of Corrections to ensure that the state penitentiary in Lincoln, the women's' prison in York, and other correctional facilities were following the department's guidelines with respect to the treatment of prisoners. Chambers dislike how society seemed to write off prisoners. He had file drawers full of inmates' letters and had responded to most of them; however, keeping up was time consuming. By the 1980s, the State Ombudsman's Office was working cooperatively with the senator in trying to resolve prisoners' complaints. Chambers began gradually to refer more and more of his prisoner cases to that office. His strong opinions about prisoners' rights only added to his renown, and Chambers was constantly in the public eye. At this stage in his career Chambers's self-confidence could hardly have been higher. He was excellent at debate, and knew that his ability to sway others to his side of an argument was unusual. But there was something happening to him internally that was difficult to pinpoint.[35]

Somewhere between his first and second decades in office, Chambers lost the optimism that he had had as a freshman senator. He would not be able to change the nature of the Nebraska Unicameral into the empathic servant of the people that it should be. He had seen the political games that were played by committees and had noted the partisan nature of most political dealings. All that he could do to bend the process toward justice was to hold his colleagues' "feet to the fire" during his watch. In the end, what would he have accomplished?[36]

When he arrived in his office in January 1981, Chambers was welcomed into the new year by a pile of hate mail. Most of the letters were from professed Christians who were furious about the suit he had filed in U.S. District Court to stop the Unicameral from hiring a chaplain to pray each day before the opening of legislative debate. Chambers told the press that "paying for prayers [was like] paying for sex."[37] The comment did not win him many new friends, and Chambers received more hateful letters than usual, including threats and racial epithets. "Stay out of prayers so some one don't shoot you," one read.[38] Another suggested Chambers emigrate to another country. "You don't pray in the Jungle, why don't you go back."[39] Chambers shared the notes with the local press, but said it was not the first time that he had received angry letters or threats on his life.

When U.S. District Court Judge Warren K. Urbom ruled that the legislature could no longer pay for prayer services but that they could accept prayers from volunteering ministers, Chambers emerged victorious. After he won in court, a Lincoln paper published an editorial praising Chambers for bringing a lawsuit that resulted in wider denominational participation and multiple-faith representation in the Unicameral (since volunteer preachers emerged from various religions and denominations). However, the victory was only a partial one. His suit against the state of Nebraska in federal court was successful, but the U.S. Supreme Court reversed the lower court's decision in 1983. Despite the reversal, Chambers continued to believe that the presence of a paid chaplain in the legislature violated the principle of separation of church and state, and he made it a point not to enter the legislative chambers until the daily prayer had been said.[40]

When Chambers first joined the legislature, he would point out the foolishness or the lack of constitutionality of proposed bills—only if they could have a negative effect on his immediate constituency. As the years went by, however, he increasingly saw it as his responsibility—as a state representative and for the credibility of the Unicameral—to prevent passage of all bad legislation. It took a considerable amount of time to become knowledgeable of each of the bills that the other senators proposed. Chambers began driving to his office in Lincoln on Saturdays, and sometimes on Sundays, in order to stay abreast. To make up for the loss of valuable time that he spent preparing to combat bad bills, Chambers took pains to ensure his accessibility to his community. Any citizen in need of help could contact him (and call collect) at his Lincoln office and he would personally return their call. Constituents could also stop by at the barbershop, like they had done for years. Chambers could still be found cutting hair on weekends and during the summer. It was there in the community that Chambers was rejuvenated. The barbershop was one of the places where men and women came just to talk, or to update him and Dan Goodwin about what had transpired during the week. The senator was sometimes congratulated for his handling of issues with the city administration or on the passage of legislation, or just for "winning" a particular debate on the floor of the legislature. Things were going well, but Chambers was restless. He continued to watch less talented men rise politically by making decisions that served only the elite.[41]

In 1982, the senator made a bid for career advancement, challenging Paul Douglas for his seat as attorney general. He made his decision to run after the primaries were over, and so his name had to be added to the general election ballot by petition. Douglas argued that since Chambers had not taken the state bar exam and was not a licensed attorney, he therefore was not qualified to serve as attorney general. Chambers countered that he was more informed about legal issues than most practicing lawyers and challenged Douglas to a series of debates—an offer Douglas quickly declined. Now, as ever, Chambers's style made excellent headlines. For a decade, the Lincoln press covered Chambers's activities in the legislature, editorializing on the many constitutional and political issues he raised. Now, as he sparred with Douglas for the incumbent's seat, the *Lincoln Journal* published a cautious statement in support of Chambers. They argued that the U.S. Supreme Court did not require its justices to be attorneys and neither did the Nebraska State Constitution require that of its attorney general.[42]

The senator claimed that the attorney general's refusal to debate him was an attempt to lock the independent out of the political process by taking the posture that Chambers was not a serious candidate. Chambers would use Douglas's refusal as a part of his campaign rhetoric. He wrote an opinion piece on Douglas, and the *Lincoln Star* published the article. "The true motivation behind his refusal to debate me is fear—cold, hair-raising, sweat-producing, unmitigated fear. And who can blame him?"[43] In retort to an editorial sympathetic in tone to the incumbent attorney general, Chambers wrote that it was unfortunate that the *Lincoln Star* had failed to defend the "public's right to know" the candidates and instead "has encouraged Mr. Douglas to flee."[44] Chambers said the public ought to be suspicious about a man who, after serving as attorney general for eight years, was afraid to debate a contender whom he deemed unqualified. The senator would use the episode to help spread news of his candidacy throughout Omaha. One of Chambers's campaign flyers read: "Wanted: Attorney General Paul Louis Douglas, Republican, for fear of debating Ernie Chambers, candidate for Attorney General."[45]

Politically active members of the African American community of Nebraska galvanized their resources in support of Chambers in his stab at a new political office. Leola Bullock, perhaps the leading civil rights activist in Lincoln since the 1960s, supported Chambers's candidacy. She used her base as an organizer for NAACP and her membership in the progressive, multiracial Newman United Methodist Church to recruit workers for Chambers's campaign. Bullock and her friend Lela Knox Shanks, another well-known civil rights advocate and outspoken Lincolnite, put their networking skills into play, organizing voters for the Chambers for Attorney General Campaign. As a result, an interracial committee formed in Lincoln. Its active members were almost all women and included Alice Roach, Patricia Sims, and Jan Wahl. In addition to helping collect signatures, the group, eventually known as the Lincoln Committee to Elect Ernie Chambers for State Attorney General, held campaign fundraisers. In October, they hosted a chili feed at Newman Church, promising the public that Chambers would be available to answer questions—which he was—and the turnout was good. The group sent all proceeds to the care of Goodwin who served as the official treasurer of Chambers's campaign.[46]

Chambers reminded voters of his accomplishments during his first twelve years in the legislature: extensive service on the Judiciary Committee, upgraded training for county sheriffs and the University of Nebraska–Lincoln Police Department, co-sponsorship of a self-defense bill.[47] Voters were also asked to recollect Chambers's fight against the building of the North Freeway. The senator had written to Mayor Mike Boyle, challenging Boyle's statement that laying the freeway through North Omaha would not harm the African American business community, "only a very dumb man would say that the North Freeway will not separate the community."[48] Chambers and Grandberry worked in tandem organizing opposition to the North Freeway, which city officials planned to build through the middle of his district. This would be the "only place in Nebraska where a freeway goes through a residential area."[49] The road would not allow access between the district's busiest thoroughfares at Lake Street and Ames Avenue, and businesses would be bypassed. Chambers argued that the community in between the two access points would die, and that the city's claim that there was no protest against the project was a lie. "I have over 3,000 signatures against it," Chambers said.[50] He added that the road was primarily a way for whites to get to the airport without having to go into the African American neighborhood. Unfortunately his efforts to stop the North Freeway from dismantling North Omaha neighborhoods were not successful. In the final phases of his hard-fought battle, Chambers resigned himself to helping one family at a time fight the city's claim of eminent domain or, at least, to demand a fair price for their property and hardship. By May, Chambers was visiting with Gene Crump and other local officials about the assurance that minority contractors' bids would be fairly considered as builders of the new road.[51]

The senator informed voters that the Federal Highway Administration had agreed with him that the lucrative utility companies forced to relocate power lines by the building of the North Freeway had to pay their own relocation costs, whereas Attorney General Douglas argued for the use of public tax revenues to bail them out.[52]

At length, the *Omaha Star* printed a full endorsement of Senator Chambers for attorney general.

> Thanks to the efforts of Ernie Chambers in the Unicameral people in Omaha can, through district elections, put our own candidates into city council and school board seats . . . Senator Chambers has announced his intention to run for the Office of Attorney General.[53]

The editorialist argued that since African Americans made up only five or six percent of the population, every eligible voter-of-color had to go to the polls. Chambers was running as an independent and would not benefit from financing through the Democratic or Republican Parties: his campaign would therefore need donations. Chambers's strongest assets, the editorial said, were that he was "probably the most astute and intelligent member of the legislature and the most honest and courageous person currently holding any political office in Nebraska."[54]

Although engulfed in Chambers's campaign, politically active North Omahans also kept their eyes on the national political scene. Representative Shirley Chisholm would be in town in November, and Washington D.C. mayor Marion Barry was running for a second term. It seemed that the Congressional Black Caucus chair, Reverend Walter E. Fauntroy, would also retain his seat. In an effort to grasp some of the burgeoning black vote, the Republican National Committee gave $30,000 toward a black Republican Party dinner at which President Ronald Reagan was the keynote speaker.

Over 1,000 upper-income African Americans would attend that event. However, the majority of African Americans in Nebraska felt that their earnings suffered under the "trickle-down" economics of the Reagan years, in which job programs and other monies that had been funneled into urban centers as a result of the 1960s' uprisings were cut back or eliminated.[55]

In the spring and summer of 1982, Chambers gave speeches across the state. In preparation for the fall elections, he addressed varied audiences sharing his vision for an improved Nebraska. A successful campaign would require an effort by the entire community, and activists in North Omaha utilized all of their affiliations to try to garner votes for Chambers. Erven McSwain, Jr., deputy public safety director, and a community member, asked the pastors in his denomination to "encourage every eligible member in your congregation to register and then vote on November 2, 1982. . . . Take an offering on Ernie's behalf for expenses in this campaign."[56] McSwain would later make the rounds to pick up checks from each church and to deposit them with Goodwin. For the second time since Chambers's initial campaign for the legislature, a substantial segment of the community was working cooperatively and optimistically in the electoral process.[57]

Despite the best wishes of Chambers's North Omaha constituency and other supporters, Douglas prevailed in the November election. Summing up segments of his own history, Chambers would assess his bid for attorney general in this way: "Though virtually penniless and without the support of either political party," in 1982, Chambers ran as an independent candidate for attorney general, winning over 85,000 votes. A substantial segment came from his power base in Omaha.[58] Certainly a large section of Nebraska's African American population voted for Chambers. Community member and activist Vickey Parks said that people saw Chambers in the same way that he saw himself—as one who "dresses and carries himself as a man of the people."[59]

Chambers was not surprised at losing in an at-large bipartisan election, but would eventually introduce legislation to elect the attorney general on nonpartisan basis. At home in North Omaha, momentum from the campaign kept activists focused on increasing the community's political power, in spite of the lost election. Although Chambers was not victorious in statewide polls, he won in North Omaha and community members looked for a way to maintain the communications networks they had established during the preelection season.[60]

Parks was instrumental in rechanneling residual momentum into a related project. The Parks (Vickey and her husband Charles), along with photojournalist Ben Gray and others, would open the Ernie Chambers Information Center in North Omaha. The group's mission was for local people to have greater access to the senator. Headquartered at the historic Jewel Building on North 24th Street, by mid-1986 the center's thirty-four volunteers helped clients write up their complaints against the Omaha Housing Authority, the police department, and other agencies and then forward the write–ups to Chambers's office in Lincoln. Chambers would review the memos and address those that he felt that he could help with. In this way, the senator gained firsthand knowledge of what was transpiring across the community. The information center made Chambers more accessible than ever. He was quite busy and the demands on both his and Cindy Grandberry's time stretched even further than usual. In a way, the call center was an attempt at spreading Chambers's influence among less famous community organizers, all of whom were willing to work under him. For a brief while, the system worked well. However, the economic downturn plaguing the country deepened, and community members had an increasingly difficult time fulfilling their pledges that were to cover expenses for the office. Chambers did not want "us begging for money in his name," Parks said, "but the phone was constantly ringing with people needing help."[61] The office lasted six months before Chambers demanded that it be closed or disassociated from his name. What Chambers gleaned from the experiment was that the community wanted more direct contact with him. This was an issue that he would later resolve by participating in televised talk shows and "open mike" public access television.[62]

In the summer of 1983, a producer from CBS's *Nightwatch*, a syndicated television news program, called to ask Chambers for an interview. Of interest was the senator's bill to pay University of Nebraska football players. Chambers agreed to appear on the show, as he would to a request for a *60 Minutes* television interview, and to an appearance on the *Phil Donahue Show*.[63] On national television Chambers explained that African American athletes who arrive in Nebraska on scholarship were not given stipends by the university and that the National College Athletic Association had rules prohibiting them from working and from receiving gifts. At the University of Nebraska–Lincoln (UNL) that meant that athletes could not purchase a soft drink, buy clothes, pay their own way into a movie, or pay for a meal if they had a date. To live, student-athletes had to sneak around the rules, lie, and, in the worst cases, enter a relationship with someone who was willing to share resources. Chambers felt that the policies created an unhealthy dependence by the athletes on the football scholarship, and on other entities, and that many athletes suffered academically while trying to find ways to reduce their financial straits. Alarmed by the stories he heard from football players, who described being abandoned after exhausting their athletic eligibility or suffering an injury, Chambers requested data on their matriculation rates. Not surprisingly, African American football recruits, if injured, typically did not graduate. Chambers compared the university's football program to slavery, and the football field to a plantation. In the frenzy of the moment, with all of the national publicity surrounding the issue, Tom Osborne, UNL head football coach, announced support for paying the players, but he would later change his mind.[64]

In addition to attempting to help athletes, Chambers could often be found responding to inmates concerns, especially when their complaints involved racism or the arbitrary use of power by guards or administrators. The inmates drew a picture of a racist institution in which unprofessional guards bullied incarcerated men behind the stone prison walls and kept drivers along the heavily traveled 14th Street from a full view of the prison yard. Often the mistreatment was psychological, or it could result from a simple lack of concern. In June 1983, Chambers wrote a letter to U.S. District Judge Warren Urbom, detailing inmates' complaints regarding the failure of the magistrate to file their cases. That same month he called the director of prisons to gain permission for an inmate to attend his mother's funeral. In late July, Chambers made an unannounced visit to the state penitentiary in Lincoln. While there, he talked to the warden and to prisoners. The media quickly learned about his visit and requested interviews. Chambers said that he had received a number of letters and had decided to visit to see their living conditions for himself. Perhaps the long-term result of Chambers's visit was a deepening respect for him by the prison administration. In the future, Chambers would be able to command the attention of the director of corrections who frequently thereafter had the warden intervene in specific prisoners' situations without Chambers having first gone to the media or to the legislative body.[65]

Chambers's activities were rapidly becoming a favorite fare of broadcasters. In January 1983, Chambers was back in the news, this time for criticizing Governor Robert Kerrey, a Democrat, for failing to hire African Americans in key positions of his administration. A young politician and

Vietnam veteran, Kerrey's thinking was representative of the post–affirmative action era. When his appointments were challenged by Chambers, the governor claimed that few qualified blacks had applied. In Omaha, on the other hand, seven new police officers joined the force, and Tariq Al Amin (aka Terry Thompson) was one of those recruits. Al Amin respected men, like Marvin McClarty, James Patterson, and Senator Chambers, who stood up against repression by the majority population. He and the senator would communicate regularly, and they worked on joint projects from time to time.[66]

Black Political Agendas

For the moment, anyway, Chambers was not alone. His small circle of friends seemed to be expanding. His work galvanized and emboldened the black clergy who formed a citizens' organization to combat police brutality. The pastors wrote a letter to President Jimmy Carter demanding that the proposed freeway not be lain through the African community of North Omaha. A new generation of leaders arose in North Omaha, organizing around these issues and cutting their teeth working in the Jesse Jackson for President Campaign. Most of these politically minded young adults had more education and were more upwardly mobile than the "race men" of the past, and their political alliances were more varied. During the late 1980s, Rodney Wead served as the director of the United Methodist Church Community Center's Wesley House. Eddie Staton founded Omaha's Mad Dads, an antidrug and antigang coalition sponsored by local police precincts. Fred Conley, as Omaha's first African American city councilman (and a political moderate), was recognized by the community and by the city administration as a liaison between blacks and whites. The community knew that Conley had won his seat as a result of Senator Chambers's handiwork, through passage of district elections for the city council. Ironically, Conley's moderate political outlook made him more welcome than Chambers among Omaha's power elite, and as a result Conley was more often celebrated. George Dillard, another figure in the community, served as executive director of the Urban League of Nebraska in the mid-1980s. Chambers added these leaders to his network of associations with African Americans in key posts. With the support of some of these community spokespersons, the city of Omaha sponsored the renovation of a few of the businesses on the east side of 24th and Lake Streets. The Blue Lion Center was opened in 1985. It would house a job location program, shops, and other businesses. Chambers wanted improvements in other North Omaha facilities, but also he cautioned the new politicians to be careful not to lose control of what had been key properties for North Omaha businesses for decades.[67]

It was common knowledge among community members that one could tell when an individual had taken a stand in defense of North Omaha. If they were successful, their efforts would bring them into conflict with city administrators who were accustomed to overlooking the African American neighborhoods when it came to making expenditures for new schools, street and sidewalk repairs, decent lighting, and other amenities, and they would be "catching hell." Although Chambers never worked within groups himself, he was pleased when he saw other men and women looking out for the community in their voluntary associations. The vocalness of Chambers's associates made it difficult for the press to label the senator's complaints those of an attention-seeking politician, at least for a while. The presidency of Buddy Hogan over the local NAACP was an encouraging and progressive move for North Omaha. Chambers read Hogan's weekly "Buddy's Byline" in the *Omaha Star* and noted with interest a forthright article describing an audit of Omaha realtor firms, which revealed that several Omaha companies were "contributing to segregated housing patterns" by steering African American clients into predominantly black neighborhoods. Realtors quoted different mortgage rates to blacks than they did to whites and some used racial references to steer Euro-American buyers toward white-only areas. Hogan wrote that all such activities by brokers, especially references "to school busing must cease immediately."[68]

Even as Chambers mastered the workings of the Nebraska political machine and interjected his thoughts into national and international debates, the political environment outside of Nebraska shifted, and class divisions sharpened within the African American community. Manning Marable, renowned scholar of African American life and culture, argues that propagandists in the United States usurped the phrase "Black Power" and restructured its meaning by associating it with "black capitalism."[69] When the dust settled, it was obvious that there had been a pendulum swing and African American elected officials realigned themselves so as not to appear left of center, paralleling the movement to the right by mainstream America. In fact, Marble argues, most black officials elected after 1972 owed their posts to their local Democratic Party and not to Black Nationalist organizations. Their voting reflected that they feared the "disapproval of the apparatus."[70] The result was that even though the number of black political officeholders had doubled in some areas (especially mayors), the autonomy of black elected leadership had declined. Throughout much of the country an "elite" enjoyed the fruits of the protest movement and were in place to direct federal relief dollars, but those funds frequently failed to reach the low-income people for whom they were intended.[71]

Many black officeholders seemed convinced that African Americans as a group had made substantial progress and that the crisis of oppression was over. In fact, however, nearly all of the Black Nationalist revolutionaries who had dramatized the problems facing their communities had been systematically disconnected from the people in a secret attack by the FBI.[72] They were dead, in prison, or had been offered deals and were co-opted. The exceptions like Angela Davis (although crucified by the press who made her appear as dangerous and anti-American even to much of the rank and file of the black community) were able to find refuge in positions in which they demanded and won the freedom to continue their pre-1970 work of organizing, educating, and generally looking out for the community. The absence of revolutionary thinkers drained the movement of its vitality, and the majority of African Americans fell back upon the "old guard" of conservative religious leadership instead of supporting the remaining nationalists.[73]

Chambers was on his own. He had to chart his political course independently, and under the circumstances it made sense for him to refrain from joining community groups or any political party. He would make his own decisions, fight his own battles, and deal with the consequences, good or bad. The truth was that even as a child Chambers had been a freethinker. He did not change this habit when he entered the legislature in 1970. Nor, looking back, was he silent in August 1979, when, along with Senator Orval Keyes, he accepted an invitation to join 140 other politicians from across the nation at a White House briefing by President Carter on the Strategic Arms Limitation Treaty (SALT) II. Chambers did not know why he'd been invited, but he hoped to use the opportunity to talk about affirmative action and other issues that he considered important. He arrived in Washington in mid-August and entered the White House with the other invited guests. When President Carter came out, Chambers listened to his promotion of the SALT II treaty. However, during the question-and-answer session afterward, Chambers asked the president whether the recent purge of upper-level personnel had created a climate where military men were afraid to speak out against SALT II, and he asked Carter why he had called for Ambassador Andrew Young's resignation after Young met with Palestine Liberation Organization leaders.[74] The national press had reported that Young was let go because he was out of line with the president's policy that did not recognize the Palestinian leadership as legitimate and in keeping with the country's friendly relations with Israel. President Carter responded angrily that Young had resigned voluntarily, and "if you doubt that, why don't you ask him."[75] Chambers expressed his feelings about the pervasiveness of American racism, and Carter sought and won a show of support from the white majority in the room when he said, "I don't believe ours is a racist nation. I'm proud of this country."[76] One Nebraska business representative in attendance told Chambers that he was "a disgrace."[77] Chambers disagreed. He took the time to pen a letter to Ambassador Young, arguing that it would have been better if he had forced President Carter to fire him, "Then the political scenario would have been cleanly completed."[78]

When he returned to Nebraska, Chambers learned that his exchange with Carter had resulted in a torrent of editorials and public opinion articles at home. A general sentiment was that "Ernie was wrong; wrong in his contention America is a racist nation."[79] Scores of other angry Nebraskans claimed that Chambers had shamed the state by talking disrespectfully to the president. In the midst of the uproar, while speaking before the Falls City Rotary Club, Chambers told his audience that the same Nebraskans who claimed to be embarrassed by his dialogue with the president "will go back to their tractors and . . . complain about Carter." He said, essentially, that they were being dishonest.[80]

Chambers had taken the best hits that Nebraska press outlets could muster, along with their publication of piles of letters to editors condemning him. He withstood negative editorials, hate mail, threatening and derogatory phone calls, and he did not flinch; he never apologized, either. Many in the community saw Chambers's firmness as a cause célèbre. Ben Gray, local photo journalist for KETV Channel Seven in Omaha, had just started broadcasting a weekly television show called *Kaleidoscope*, which aired issues of interest to Omaha's African American population. Gray invited Chambers on his show to discuss his comments to President Carter.[81]

It was during the show in September 1979 that Chambers had expressed his view, once and for all, that Carter had let Young go to appease Jewish American supporters of Israel. American Jewish leaders were incensed that Young had met with Palestinian Liberation Organization representatives, thereby formally recognizing the leaders of Palestine and "legitimizing" their struggle. Chambers argued that (white) ambassadors had met with the PLO in the past but that "Young was a fall guy" whose removal would calm angry and influential American Jews.[82] Gray would eventually offer Chambers time on the show whenever Chambers was involved in an issue that he felt the community needed to be informed about. Soon it mattered little what the mainstream press printed about Chambers's clashes with other politicians because the community could detect where their interests lay in any new controversy by listening to Gray discuss issues from the perspective of an African American community member.[83]

Now in his mid-forties, Chambers was certain that the racism embedded in majority-group Nebraskan culture would prevent his ever being elected to a higher political office. He had decided to try to influence national politics in another way—by working on the political campaigns of African Americans who might be able to be elected and whose hearts were in the right place. Over the winter, Ajamal Byndon, Buddy Hogan, and others hosted a chili feed where citizens could learn how to get involved with the Jesse Jackson for President Campaign. On such occasions, Chambers condemned the argument that Jackson could not win because of African Americans' numerical disadvantage in electoral politics. Jackson's "Rainbow Coalition" platform spoke to the interests of all working-class folk. If Chambers believed that regular people of various ethnic backgrounds had enough in common to support a solid African American presidential candidate, then maybe it was true. Chambers's involvement stimulated interest in the campaign throughout the community.[84]

The senator remained optimistic about the outcome of the 1984 presidential election until he learned that Jackson had come under attack. Reporters overheard Jackson utter the words "hymie town" in reference to the Jewish population of New York City.[85] The Jewish Coalition pressured Jackson to quit the presidential race and they demanded that the Democratic Party distance itself from the African American candidate. After Jackson's comment made headline news, threats were issued against his life. Minister Louis Farrakhan, imam and national leader of the Nation of Islam, quickly stepped forward to offer Jackson protection through NOI security. The Jewish community and mainstream America pressured Jackson to reject Farrakhan's offer. Chambers's response was that Frank Sinatra was guarded by the Mafia, and President Richard Nixon, "a gangster," by the Secret Service, "but when a black man who is risking his life against overwhelming odds, against a racist system, speaks out in our behalf, and another black man" comes to his aid, the original black man is told to reject the help.[86] "The Jews [are] no different to me than any other group. If he treats me decently, he has decent treatment coming."[87]

Chambers published an open letter to Farrakhan in the Nebraska press applauding the NOI for offering to provide Jackson with bodyguards. The senator had raised the ire of the national Anti-Defamation League (ADL) a few years earlier by supporting Young in his attempts to discuss the Palestinian–Israeli conflict, openly condemning the Israeli occupation of Palestine, and pointing to Israeli racism—since Israel and the United States were among the few members of the United Nations who refused to condemn apartheid in South Africa. Now, the ADL issued a report on Chambers declaring the senator "Anti-Semitic."[88]

In Omaha, a meeting was called between the African and Jewish communities to discuss the ADL's report on the senator. At the Omaha Club in mid-winter, leaders of the Jewish community said that they regretted that the report had been released before Senator Chambers could comment on it, but that Chambers was a right-winger "who acted like Adolph Hitler."[89] Northside community leaders in attendance had mistakenly thought that an apology or in-depth explanation and compromise were the goals of the meeting. They soon learned that they were being called on to discredit and condemn Senator Chambers. Chambers addressed his constituency through Gray's *Kaleidoscope* television show. He explained that the attack on him was actually tied to his activism in the Jackson presidential campaign. "Jackson is interested in bringing about equality," and some groups in America still feel threatened by the possibility that someone could bring that about, he said.[90] In the end, prominent North Omaha figures Hogan, Dillard, and Wead apologized to Chambers for having attended the meeting where the statement was made comparing Chambers to Hitler, which the senator saw as worse than the original report. "They were too hard on themselves; they went in good faith," Chambers said, "the worst thing that can happen is to let the Anti-Defamation League divide the [African] community."[91]

Loss of the Chairmanship, 1985

Privately, Chambers believed the purpose of the ADL report was fulfilled. It was meant to keep him from getting the chairmanship of the Judiciary Committee, and it was timed perfectly. "There was no other reason for its release."[92] Although the damage had been done, Chambers took the opportunity to clear up some of the falsifications that had been printed about him. First, he was not racist and did not believe in discrimination against anyone, including Jews. Further, he had written bills and resolutions to aid Jews. Chambers said that the ADL had grown into a Zionist organization, and they did not like the public position that Chambers took regarding the state of Israel. He argued that the ADL's strategy was to brand anyone who condemned "Israel's connection to white-racist South Africa, 'anti-Semitic.' . . . I'm not one who's going to cut and run. They picked the wrong man this time."[93]

The political power of the ADL could hardly be overstated. On the other hand, elections to leadership posts in the legislature were often accompanied by "charges of betrayal and double dealing." But, as a *Journal Star* reporter noted, the "realignment" in January 1985 was worse than usual.[94] Chambers was angry because he was again refused a chairmanship position despite the extra hours that he spent researching for the benefit of the entire committee. In a speech on the floor, Chambers charged that racism and his "refusal to 'lick anybody's spit'" kept him from the chairmanship of the Judiciary Committee for the fourth time, even though he had served on the committee for fourteen years.[95] This time, Chambers lost to Peter Hoagland, a six-year veteran of the legislature and an Omaha attorney. "If ability and dedication counted for anything, I would have obtained that chairmanship a long time ago. . . . Down here, I'm like Rodney Dangerfield. Among the Senators, I get no respect."[96] The *Omaha World Herald* inferred that Chambers's lack of membership in the NBA and his being a political independent hurt his chances. It was true that Chambers's refusal to join either of the two major political parties limited his access to posts that required political patronage and that the arms of both parties had ways of reaching into the Unicameral and influencing his colleagues. In everyday terms, this meant that the price of Chambers's independence, his rejection of invitations to social events where political aspirants rubbed shoulders with political and economic power brokers, meant that they also rejected him. Furthermore, his reputation as a freethinker, one who would not hold to a party line but would speak his own mind, made him of little use to the special interest groups that heavily influenced the state's political culture. Moreover, the press frequently reminded readers that Chambers was the "Legislature's only black," as if people did not know who Chambers was.[97] Chambers continued to serve on the Judiciary Committee as a member with Senators Chris Beutler, Peter Hoagland, and five others, even after his 1985 defeat. He also became a new member of the legislature's policy-making Executive Board that year.[98]

Chambers knew that his independence caused some people, including many of his colleagues, to fear him. His unharnessed assertiveness also served as a source of embarrassment to a small but growing segment of Omaha's black middle class. But Chambers would not hide his aggravation over the lack of fairness in the system. Chambers wrote a one-page journal entry in January 1985 after he lost the chairmanship position for the fourth time. In it, he noted his personal qualities and legislative victories. He was strong, on the cutting edge of social issues; he had a conscience and was tenacious. His list of legislative successes was by now lengthy: because of him, third-party victims of high-speed police chases would be compensated; additional training would be required of law enforcement personnel; and "bounties" on Native American prisoners in county jails would be eliminated. The list went on: passage of the Nebraska Civil Rights Act, district elections, no pension discrimination against women by the state, no death penalty for juveniles, and abolition of the death penalty—vetoed by Governor Thone. Chambers also wrote down the things that he had done which he considered lasting contributions to Nebraska. The list included getting travel and food expenses paid for legislators who received neither benefits nor a pension, and who were paid only a $12,000 annual salary. Perhaps his greatest accomplishment had been his international victory in helping to unravel the apartheid regime in South Africa by sponsoring successful landmark divestment legislation. It was an impressive record for fifteen years of service and probably more than most other politicians would do in a lifetime. Chambers wrote that, with all of these things in mind, he was still not surprised at being kept out of a leadership post in the Unicameral, only "bitter."[99] He lived in a world, he said, where ability and expertise have "no significance."[100]

By 1985, Chambers abandoned any form of nationalism that would include racial separation. He was completely invested in his battle to reform Nebraska's state government into an apparatus that helped, rather than hindered, the life chances of all citizens, and he simultaneously limited his sphere of activity according to his interpretation of the U.S. Constitution. He was so engulfed in the state political process that his rejection for a leadership position in the Unicameral made him feel as if he had been "cut off at the kneez [sic]."[101] On the other hand, Chambers did little lobbying to court the vote of his colleagues. Incumbent Judiciary Committee Chair Chris Beutler had sent a letter to the other senators in November 1984, announcing his intention to run again for the chairmanship of the committee. To Chambers, he added a personal note: "Ernie, your committee needs you more than ever. I hope you will be there this time around to keep us on an even keel."[102] Beutler's gesture was not unusual. Privately, the senators acknowledged that they respected Chambers's understanding of the law and insight into political and social issues, but his formal leadership as a committee chair was not desired.[103]

One reason that he could not rise to the top of the body was his constant criticisms of white power for both overt and systemic racism. A case in point was Chambers's battle against special police tactics, which he said were reserved for black citizenry. Instead of making peace with the Omaha police administration, his criticisms intensified throughout the 1980s and were a source of annoyance to the status quo. Besides, there was substantial evidence that police killings in Nebraska had their counterparts in police behavior in other states and that certain trends in police interactions in "minority" neighborhoods were a national phenomenon. *Police Practices and the Preservation of Civil Rights*, a pamphlet produced by the U.S. Civil Rights Commission (1980), confirmed Chambers's suspicion that police across the country continued to violate the civil rights of African Americans citizens.[104] A disproportionate number of the victims of police brutality were members of minority groups, the report said. Police also provided slower service to minority communities; officers who were the subject of repeated complaints typically went undisciplined; and efforts to promote officers of color were lacking. Chambers had been saying these things for years.[105]

Outside of politics, ordinary people continued to struggle to make ends meet as the economic recession of the 1980s wore on. Farmers were particularly bad off as grain exports to overseas markets sharply declined, and transport and shipping costs were up. In the fall of 1984, news of the fatal police shooting of a Nebraska farmer over a bank foreclosure made the front pages of town presses. Arthur L. Kirk was killed by a special forces unit of the Nebraska State Patrol on October 23, hours after Hall County sheriff's deputies attempted to serve papers on his farm. At the request of a Grand Island bank, lawmen served Kirk papers demanding he pay over $300,000 in loans or vacate his property. Kirk had drawn a gun on the deputies and asked them to leave his premises. They did but called in the Nebraska State Patrol's Special Weapons Team.[106]

Chambers heard about the killing, which the police ruled as a legitimate use of force, through the local media, and was outraged. He told the press, "that man . . . went back to work and they called in the state patrol . . . and they blew him away."[107] Drawn into the incident because it involved an impoverished family versus big money interests, Chambers circulated a memo calling for a complete investigation. He argued that there was a land grab going on across the country, and that small farmers were being pushed off of their land, and as a result many of them were under enormous psychological strain. "The state patrol must be instructed that it works for the people, not bankers."[108] Chambers promised to do all that he could to make sure that what happened at Cairo, Nebraska, did not happen to anyone else. A bank loan, Chambers argued, is not worth a person's life. Chambers urged the legislature's Judiciary Committee to demand an investigation into Kirk's killing.[109]

Two months later special investigator Samuel Van Pelt revealed inconsistencies in the reports of the officers involved in the shooting, including Kirk's location when he allegedly fired at lawmen. Chambers argued that their inconsistencies raised the question of whether Kirk had fired at all. Addressing his report to Governor Robert Kerrey and the Judiciary Committee, Van Pelt said "this case is one of perspective," with the farm economy being "the stage" and part of the cause of Kirk's death.[110] Chambers insisted that the forty-nine-year-old farmer had done nothing that justified his being killed on "his own home soil."[111] Many of the senators received calls from farming communities where people were angry and frightened. One woman asked her local sheriff's office why they killed the poor farmer and what they were going to do to her for having inquired. In fact, the Kirk shooting was not an isolated incident. A SWAT team had also been called out on October 17, 1984, to help the Thurston County sheriff remove Ruben Leimer from his farm after a court ordered him to vacate. Leimer was thought to be a member of the Posse Comitatus, a right-wing organization. Leimer did not resist when the SWAT team arrived and so escaped with his life. Ironically, the concept of SWAT teams had originated in response to protest movements of the 1960s, for the purpose of increasing law enforcement officers' personal security in urban conflicts, specifically with black protesters and antiwar youth.[112] Chambers requested reports from the State Patrol and the governor in order to answer the question of why the officers and troopers had failed to wait the "distressed farmer out rather than rushing in."[113] He received no satisfactory answers.[114]

Meanwhile the country's economic crisis was wreaking havoc with Nebraska's financial institutions. By the early 1980s, the senator knew that the Commonwealth Savings and Loan in Lincoln was struggling and had entered bankruptcy. The company was not federally insured, and hundreds of the state's citizens lost their life's savings at the very time that they might have needed them. By mid-November Commonwealth depositors were frantic. Chambers and his colleagues received hundreds of calls from citizens praying that the state would make good on the financial institution's failure. The senator argued that depositors should also question Attorney

General Douglas and Governor Kerrey, who had connections to the institution, as well as contacting Nebraska state banking director Paul Amen. As soon as Chambers announced his support for the depositors' claims, he began receiving confidential information about management problems within the Commonwealth. He was told that Sumner Edward Copple, a bank administrator, had signed off on loans for friends in exchange for taking half of the amounts for himself. Later Chambers was told that Copple would write the loan off as "uncollectable." [115] Worse, a citizen named Charles Gove told Chambers that Douglas was receiving "kick-backs" off sales of state property.[116]

Chambers suspected that unethical, even criminal, activity had weakened the Commonwealth. He wrote the state banking director to say that the attorney general probably had violated the law in his dealings with the failed financial company. With mounting incidents of impropriety surfacing, Chambers began looking into the formalities required to impeach the state's attorney general. In late November, he mailed copies of his "Impeachment Memo" to colleagues and to Commonwealth depositors.[117] The legislature adopted Chambers's Resolution of Impeachment, and Douglas was put on trial before the Nebraska Supreme Court. During the proceedings, Douglas said that he had made some poor choices, but he did not think that they should result in the loss of his post. The seven-member court split four to three over whether or not to remove Douglas, but, Chambers lamented, the "Constitution requires a 'supermajority' of five affirmative votes. Hence Douglas was acquitted."[118] When the ruling in Douglas's case came down, Chambers noted in his journal: "impeachment decision came today and allowed the Attorney General off the hook."[119] Chambers then wrote a letter demanding Douglas's resignation in order, he said, "to get some things into the record."[120] Although he would not face prison time or be forced out of office, the impeachment effectively ended Douglas's political career in Nebraska. How ironic, it seemed to Chambers, that he would have to "rescue" depositors from the man whom voters had preferred over himself.[121]

Funeral of Vivian Strong at the Greater Bethlehem Temple in Omaha (July 1, 1969). Reprinted with permission from the *Omaha World-Herald*.

An aerial view of North 24th Street in Omaha during the uprising that followed Strong's death (June 30, 1969). Reprinted with permission from the *Omaha World-Herald*.

(above) Chambers arrested by Omaha police (c. 1960s). Photo courtesy of the *Lincoln Journal Star*. (below) Chambers (left) cuts hair in Dan Goodwin's Spencer Street Barbershop with Bill Armstrong and Goodwin (far right) (February 1968). Photo courtesy of the *Lincoln Journal Star*.

Chambers's victory celebration after he was elected to the Nebraska State Legislature (November 5, 1970). Photo courtesy of the *Omaha Star*.

(above) "Happy Birthday Senator Chambers." North Omaha salutes Chambers after his first session in the Unicameral. Chambers and Mrs. Jacklyn Chambers (both seated) with brother Eddie Chambers standing at the microphone (July 1, 1971). Reprinted with permission from the *Omaha World-Herald*. (below) Chambers and Senator Terry Carpenter (1974). Photo courtesy of the *Lincoln Journal Star*.

(above) Chambers, Senator John DeCamp (left), and farmer Virgil Taylor (center) survey a Nebraska farm. Photo courtesy of the *Lincoln Journal Star*. (below) Chambers and son David in the Nebraska Statehouse (January 22, 1979). Photo courtesy of the *Lincoln Journal Star*.

Barbara Kelley and Chambers lead a protest after the fatal police shooting of Sherdell Lewis, Kelley's son (1975). Photo courtesy of the *Lincoln Journal Star*.

(above) Lincolnites register to vote in order to be eligible to sign a petition for an investigation of Lewis's death (1975). Photo courtesy of the *Lincoln Journal Star*. (below) Chambers takes the oath of office again (January 1985). Photo courtesy of the *Lincoln Journal Star*.

(above) Chambers makes an anti-apartheid speech behind the student union at the University of Nebraska (October 12, 1985). Photo courtesy of the *Lincoln Journal Star*. (below) Chambers and Mel Beckman look at a replica of the electric chair used at the Nebraska State Penitentiary (February 5, 1976). The chair was given to Chambers by anti–death-penalty activists, and remained a conversation piece in Chambers's office in Lincoln for decades. Photo courtesy of the *Lincoln Journal Star*.

Chambers's T-shirt, bearing the caption "Reagan Hood: from the needy to the greedy," was designed in response to President Ronald Reagan's welfare reforms that cut benefits to low-income households (May 29, 1987). Photo courtesy of the *Lincoln Journal Star*.

North Omahans organize a demonstration on the steps of the Douglas County Courthouse in response to the initial "not-guilty" verdict in the Rodney King police assault case in Los Angeles, California. Chambers held a placard that read "Injustice and Racism Reign in the U.S." (May 1, 1992). Reprinted with permission from the *Omaha World-Herald*.

(above) This cartoon by *Lincoln Journal Star* artist Paul Fell is one of scores of caricatures of a legislature beaten by Chambers's legendary prowess at statecraft. Courtesy of the *Lincoln Journal Star*. (below) Chambers and two new friends (left to right) Rodney Jones and Matt Cannon at the Million Man March in Washington, D.C. (October 16, 1995). Photo courtesy of the Chambers Collection.

(top) North Omaha residents stage a mock funeral as part of a campaign to stop police killings of unarmed citizens. Photo courtesy of the Chambers Collection. (middle) Cynthia Grandberry and Nicole at the author's house in Lincoln, Nebraska, May 6, 2003. Author's photo. (bottom) Chambers speaking at the United Nations Conference on Public Investment and South Africa. (left to right): George M. House, American Committee on Africa; Senator Chambers; Ambassador B. Akporode Clark, Nigeria, Chairman, United Nations Special Committee Against Apartheid; Senator Jack Backman, Massachusetts (others unidentified) (June 12–13, 1981). Photo courtesy of the Chambers Collection.

6—"Defender of the Downtrodden"

Turbulent economic times in the 1980s and early 1990s were accompanied by a lessening of public trust in high-level officials. The Nebraska state legislature would accumulate its share of the fallout, and Chambers, along with his fellow senators, would stumble through the debris. The Commonwealth Savings and Loan of Lincoln had collapsed early in the decade, and Chambers fought to make the state cover depositors' losses. When the Franklin Credit Union, located in the heart of Chambers's district, also failed, a special committee was created (in 1988 and again in 1989) by the Nebraska state legislature to investigate. The special committee, also known as the Franklin Committee, was made up of Senators Loran Schmit (chair), Bernice Labedz, Dan Lynch, Dennis Baack, James McFarland, Jerome Warner, and Ernie Chambers (vice chair). The committee was charged with investigating the circumstances behind the failure of the Franklin Credit Union in North Omaha and other related unsavory allegations.[1]

What Chambers knew about Franklin at the outset was that the institution's African American president, Lawrence E. King, Jr., was an influential and well-connected member of the Republican Party. During the course of the investigation, photos of King with U.S. presidents and other prominent national politicians surfaced. King was so well regarded, it seemed to the special committee, that his institution, which was supposed to be regulated, went largely without oversight. The Franklin Committee noted that they were, in effect, being asked to figure out why the institution had existed without being monitored. To help the committee uncover the facts in the case, Senator Schmit retained the services of Kirk Naylor as counsel, and Jerry Lowe of the Lincoln Police Department as their primary investigator. The case became more serious as the investigation moved forward. In addition to the losses of depositors' money through alleged embezzlement, high-level banking officials and community members were accused of sexual misconduct with teenagers at parties hosted by King. Some witnesses testified that funds from the bank were used to host elaborate parties for wealthy men. Lowe acted swiftly, conducting ninety-six interviews before he announced his view that the key issues in the case—the misuse of depositor's funds and a child sexual abuse ring and related drug abuse scandal—were intimately connected. The committee was especially concerned about reports of "abuse of authority by law enforcement and other regulators that reached high into government and touched persons of prominence and wealth."[2]

By the summer of 1989, the depths of the scandal seemed unfathomable. A *Washington* [D.C.] *Times* headline read "Homosexual Prostitution Inquiry Ensnares VIPs with Reagan, Bush."[3] The paper reported that King may have transported youth who lived in foster care or other out-of-home institutions to provide sexual services for well-to-do politicians both in Omaha and in other cities. After a preliminary review of the facts, the special committee reported that its members had been surprised to learn that the Nebraska Attorney General's Office had known about the allegations of child sexual abuse in connection to the credit union for over a year, but did not follow up with any sort of investigation.[4]

The committee requested that the Attorney General's Office turn over the reports written at the time the allegations were made. Two assistant attorneys general were subpoenaed by the committee and were instructed to produce law enforcement reports, including any investigations of King. The Attorney General's Office refused to allow the reports to be turned over to the committee, basing the objection on "separation of powers" and Nebraska state law, which said the reports of the attorney general were privileged. Shortly thereafter, the committee made public the results of their preliminary investigation. In an addendum to the interim report, Chairman Schmit said that the committee did not have any prosecutorial powers and that the most the committee could do would be to suggest laws to "prevent something like this from occurring again."[5] In frustration over the chairman having effectively limited the powers of the special committee, Senator Chambers and Naylor, who had already encouraged several young people to come forward and tell their stories of abuse by persons in connection to Franklin, resigned from the committee. News of the resignations contributed to an even greater level of public distrust of government officials in Nebraska. Was the committee itself a part of a cover-up? To improve their image and to get a better handle on the Franklin case, the remaining committee members decided to hire a private investigator who would take a fresh look at the ordeal. Schmit selected Gary Caradori, a member of the Nebraska State Patrol who had a reputation for thinking independently. Caradori's professionalism and the quality of his work were challenged, however, as soon as he produced videotaped statements by victims of sexual abuse. One young woman, Alisha Owen, described ritual and satanic sexual abuse of "street kids" by King and the male guests of his elaborate parties.[6] Other victim-witnesses, including Troy Boner, Danny King, and Paul Bonacci also gave video statements. The young people corroborated each other's stories and described the sexual and social activities that they had engaged in with wealthy and prominent men, including Peter Citron and Alan Baer. The youth also described the availability of drugs, which guests could access at the events. Caradori told the Franklin Committee that he believed the youths' allegations were true and feared the pressure that would be brought to bear on the witnesses to recant their stories.[7]

Upon the advice of the U.S. Attorney General's Office, the Franklin Committee shared tapes of the victim witnesses telling their stories of abuse with members of the Nebraska State Patrol and the Nebraska Attorney General's Office. Within days, leaked copies of the videotapes were made available to the press. Owen, who was in jail, said that she was contacted by the Nebraska State Patrol and told to be careful of whose names she gave to the committee. She felt that she had been threatened, she said. Caradori's fears about the repercussions of the investigation were seemingly accurate. Chairman Schmit said that both the U.S. attorney general and the state attorney general promised to investigate the matter. The Franklin Committee reported that they "lost direct contact with the law enforcement investigation" after the Attorney General's Office stepped in. A grand jury investigation was called, but instead of producing more witnesses, the grand jury accused Caradori of coaching the teenage victim-witnesses. On June 12, 1990, Caradori contacted Schmit to say that an *Omaha World-Herald* reporter had called to say that he would be indicted by the grand jury who would hear the Franklin case. He asked Schmit to tell the committee not to "abandon" the youths.[8] A month later, Caradori died in his private plane, which Schmit told the committee had mysteriously dissembled in the air. Schmit inferred that Caradori might have been murdered.

After Caradori's death, Chambers's withdrawal from the Franklin Committee was criticized in hushed corners as having been motivated by fear. Some people speculated that the senator had initially not anticipated the level of corruption and was backing out. In general, however, Chambers's constituents repeated the explanation that Chambers had refused to go along with the pretense that an in-depth investigation was underway. The case continued to reek of a cover–up, especially after Owen was indicted for perjury for accusations that she made against Omaha Police Chief Robert Wadman. Owen said that she had had sex with Wadman when she was a teenager and that Wadman was the father of her child. Bonacci, Danny King, and Boner corroborated Owen's testimony about Wadman. Later, however, the three recanted, in exchange for immunity, presumably for drug and prostitution charges. Boner came to Schmit's office in the capitol building in Lincoln to say that he had told the truth about Wadman, but that the FBI had said they would charge him with perjury. To those who assumed that Chambers had resigned from the investigation as a form of self-preservation, Chambers could answer that the special committee had proven, beyond a doubt, that it would not get to the root of the problem. Schmit and the remaining Franklin Committee members considered Owen's statements about Wadman as "most controversial" and wondered why the chief refused take a paternity test so that the allegations could be put to rest. In the end, it was Owen who was discredited in the eyes of the grand jury—since she no longer had corroborating witnesses—ultimately she was convicted of perjury. Larry King was eventually convicted of banking violations in federal court and was sent to prison for misappropriating Franklin Credit Union funds. The grand jury said they had evidence that Larry King may have solicited teenage boys for homosexual acts of prostitution, but failed to indict King, or any of the other men named by the victim-witnesses, for sex offenses. When the Franklin Committee asked why, Schmit was told that King would spend enough time in prison for his financial crimes. In the committee's final report, Schmit wrote that the sexual "allegations remain unresolved."[9]

Both Baer and Citron, whom the victim-witnesses named as being at King's parties, were indicted in separate cases, Baer for pandering, and Citron for child molestation. The thirty to forty million dollars that was missing from the credit union in the heart of North Omaha was never recovered. Wadman went on the offensive, filing suit against the Franklin Committee, which he claimed had destroyed his credibility. Chambers was in the news again in regard to the case in February 1990. Special prosecutor Van Pelt made an appeal to the senator for help identifying additional witnesses for questioning by the grand jury. Chambers flatly refused to help. The senator said he had already encouraged young people to come forward and that they had become targets. "I had told them [the young people] any leads would be pursued and there would be no repercussions.... I cannot assure the young people they will not be subjected to the same type of disparagement."[10] The senator ultimately persuaded the Nebraska Supreme Court to have the grand jury report expunged from court records.

On several occasions animated newspaper editorials appeared featuring discussions of what legislative beat reporters considered Senator Chambers's political naiveté. With respect to the Franklin ring and the legislature's will to root out high-level corruption, perhaps it was true. They described Chambers's concept of the legislature, as a neutral institution that could be made to serve the people without bending to the will of powerful interests groups, as philosophically attractive but highly unrealistic. The media pointed to the senator's refusal to be entertained by lobbyists as his unwillingness to recognize a fundamental if unsavory aspect of the process. Chambers's response was that he was merely unstained by a generalized corruption and that service to the people was an intrinsic part of the purpose of government. As if to underscore his position, during his second decade in office, Chambers identification of his vocation as the "Defender of the Downtrodden" was no longer expressed tongue-in-cheek.[11] The title came from the notion that the people most in need of help deserved focused assistance and the swiftest relief.[12]

In 1989, Chambers waged a battle in defense of Native American rights. Chambers's proposed adoption of an Unmarked Human Burial Sites and Skeletal Remains Protection Act by the legislature was to give force-of-law to the demands by Native American tribes that the bones of their ancestors, which were then on display and in boxes at the Nebraska State Historical Society, be returned to their people. Proponents of the bill included the Pawnee and the Winnebago Tribes, who sent Native American author Walter Echo Hawk to represent them, along with a representative from the Indian Commission. Nebraska Attorney General Robert M. Squire also spoke in support of the measure. Opposing passage of the act were the National Park Service and Rob Bozell of the Nebraska State Historical Society.[13]

In his opening statement, Chambers explained that "the Pawnee Indian Tribe ... feel their ancestors cannot rest until they have been given proper burial, including proper internment of remains and burial goods."[14] Chambers said that he had recently read an article about how the remains of 100

Jews killed during World War II had been reburied and funeralized. From the Vietnam War more than "172 sets of remains" were repatriated to the United States. Chambers argued that those who said "these bones of the Native Americans ought to be left in glass cases" were racist.[15] "I understand what it means to be treated like an object, to have those things that are most dear to you trampled upon."[16] Chambers's labors paid off, and the human remains that had been housed at the Nebraska State Historical Society were returned to the tribes.

Police Violence

Double standards seemed to abound in the West where persons of color were concerned. The nature of police work, the senator noted, created opportunities for self-sacrifice and leadership as well as for the abuse of authority. Chambers was not surprised by the difficulty that many white people had in believing that police abuse their power. He knew that, for the most part, officers of the law act professionally in white communities. Even rookies perform appropriately, he once said, when they are among people whose experiences with officers matters to central command. Each incident that occurred between the community and the police added to Chambers's conviction that the police themselves were in need of monitoring. Chambers had been arguing for legislative review of police procedures since he had arrived at the Unicameral. Back then, he had fought passage of a section of the Criminal Code of Nebraska, dealing with disorderly conduct, after one of his colleagues had suggested that throwing snowballs should fall under the disorderly conduct statute. Chambers lost his patience with the debate: "There is tremendous ignorance in force on the floor of this Legislature. . . . In order to prevent the abuse of certain rights that are intrinsic to a democratic system of government, certain provisions were put into the Constitution."[17] Chambers said the addition of the "snowball" rule would be detrimental to his community since any police procedure left vague seemed to invite misinterpretation and abuse. Besides, the senator said that one section of the code was aimed at allowing officers to break up the free assembly of people.

> I call these the black-community-amendments. . . . In the community that I live in, they come in people's houses without warrants. They beat people without warrants and I have two cases like that brought to me over the weekend. . . . So although you don't face the menace, there are people who do.[18]

Over the course of his career, Chambers remained engulfed in battles to get police "killers" of citizens prosecuted, while representatives from the Omaha Police Union responded by venting their wrath at Chambers in their publication, *The Shield*.[19] Chambers recalled how in the fall of 1980, James Powell of North 33rd Street in Omaha had been shot and killed by Nebraska State Patrol officer Jimmy Wayne Burns. The police report on the incident said that Burns had been helping a stalled motorist when Powell sped by on the interstate. Burns had pursued Powell at high speeds and said that because the "dome light" was on in the vehicle that he could see "a Negro male and a female passenger" were present.[20] When sirens did not induce Powell to stop, Burns forced the car onto the shoulder of the road. The trooper said that he told the driver to get out and was opening the car door when the car lurched forward, causing Burns to fall on his pulled revolver, which emptied itself into the head of the unarmed man. The Douglas County coroner reported that nineteen-year-old Powell died of a "gunshot wound" to the head.[21] To the police, it was an accidental homicide. To members of the community, it was another police murder. Why did accidents on the part of the police always seem to result in the death of another black person?

Increasingly, conservative African Americans joined Chambers in vocally condemning the police for their aggressive behaviors in the neighborhood. Two months before Powell's death, the heads of the Interdenominational Ministerial Alliance, Luke Nichols, a personal friend of Chambers, and Reverend Wilkerson Harper, had written a joint letter protesting police abuse of African American citizens and had delivered it to Mayor Al Veys and City Council President Steve Rosenblatt. Nichols and Harper said that they realized that most officers were trying their best but that the persistent "brutality and abuse, physical, verbal and psychological, that is visited upon black citizens by a *few* members of the Omaha Police Department (OPD) with immunity from administrative or legal consequences" had to stop.[22] Moreover, the ministers called for an increase in the hiring of black officers to a level reflective of the proportion of African Americans in the city. They also wanted a police community relations office reestablished in North Omaha, and for the mayor and city council to make a public statement "that you will not tolerate and will deal severely with those who mistreat black citizens in Omaha."[23] The men copied the letter to the Douglas County District Court and requested the conveyance of a grand jury to investigate charges of police abuse of African American citizens.[24]

Demands for equitable treatment with respect to law enforcement activities by the conservative religious sector of the African American community surprised the city administration. Confronted with the specter of possible court proceedings and negative press, Mayor Veys took a middle-of-the-road approach by publishing an open letter to the police and to members of the Ministerial Alliance. Veys pledged to support lawful police activities, but said that he did "not condone misuse of police powers. . . . I urge and demand that police officers become familiar with the neighborhoods that they serve. Officers should, in addition to carrying out their professional duties, realize that they are public servants."[25] The mayor said that he was caught in the middle "between the black community leaders and the police division."[26]

Veys was not the first mayor of Omaha to find himself in such a predicament. In fact, the fight that the current mayor had stumbled into was the same struggle that Chambers had had with Mayor A. V. Sorensen years before. Veys suggested that in return for his condemnation of the abuse of police powers, African American leaders should help police to locate and arrest "criminals" in the black community. Officers would feel supported by a "show of cooperation" such as that.[27] Veys also promised to institute a community relations office to be housed on North 24th Street and directed the public safety director to explain appeal procedures to the public so that they could take their grievances to the next level if not satisfied by the findings of internal police investigations.[28]

In a separate news release, the ministers described the nature of the abuses.

> We are receiving many reports reflecting the number of men and women, some women pregnant, young men and women, even children being unfairly treated, called names not fit for any human being, denied human rights, kicked, forced to disrobe, black women approached by white officers for sexual favors, flagrant disregards for the dignity of black people.[29]

On the crest of rising vocalized support from his community, Chambers placed his signature at the top of a list of African American community members (including George Garnett, James Hart, Luke Nichols, and Talmadge Owens), who sent a formal request for an investigation into the shooting death of Powell to the U.S. attorney for the District of Nebraska. The U.S. District Attorney's Office sent a speedy reply. An FBI investigation into the shooting would be initiated, and their findings would be passed on to the Civil Rights Division of the Department of Justice. Before he received a response, however, Chambers had to file yet another complaint about police brutality. This time his letter accompanied a petition signed by fifty-eight residents of the Hilltop Homes Housing Project and nearby neighbors. All signers condemned what had amounted to a generalized police assault on the projects on the night of September 28. That evening neighborhood folks were attending a Bible study at 2414 North 33rd Street when a neighbor lady ran into the apartment with two small children to find shelter from gunfire. A moment later, shots could be heard outside of the apartment.[30] One resident recalled, "Police were steadily shooting out windows, cussing at us . . . made us lie down on the ground and kneed us in our backs."[31]

Chambers said that, despite an apology to the occupants of the unit and the explanation that police had been told that a burglary was taking place but had entered the wrong apartment, people were enraged. Most felt that such an episode would have never happened in a white community. Chambers filed another complaint with the U.S. Justice Department and with the newest mayor of Omaha, Mike Boyle. When the Omaha police administrators refused to discipline officers for their "outrageous behavior," Chambers condemned the whole department, including the lousy job the city did training the policemen who went into the apartment where the Bible study was being held—on their own—without getting the approval of supervisors. In the confusion, Chambers reminded the mayor, officer Paul Briese shot officer Alan Abbott all because of the "disregard of the chain of command."[32]

Worse than the assault itself was the aftermath in which police officials worked with the mayor and the press to "whitewash" the episode. Chambers argued that the *Omaha World Herald* had turned the story onto its head by casting it as case in which the community failed to support the police. The leading local paper reported that "several hundred people gathered after the shooting, shouting racial slurs and foul comments at police," effectively twisting the nature of the incident from one of police misconduct, poor judgment, and disorganization into African Americans' failure to support the law.[33] Diligently, Chambers copied his complaint to forty-five media personnel, police officers, community members, and city officials, including Ben Gray (of KETV), Charles Washington, Fred Conley, John Evans (FBI), Joe Friend, Marvin McClarty, Matthew Stelly, Tal Owens, Al Goodwin, Buddy Hogan, Deputy Public Safety Director Erven McSwain, Stella Standifer, Harold Andersen, and Larry King of the *Omaha World Herald*.[34] In the end, one police officer came forward, admitting to Chambers that he had witnessed the pogrom and that police reports of the events were not true.[35]

The hostility between the police and the African American community spilled over into the corporate world.[36] One winter morning, Chambers called Omaha Police Chief Wadman to complain that off-duty police were distributing a "cotton patch flyer" that pictured a brown "cotton patch doll" and racist commentary.[37] Chambers had learned about the flyer from constituents at the Omaha Metropolitan Utilities District who said the same item was being circulated at work, apparently as some sort of "joke."[38] Public Safety Director Al Pattavina met with Chambers at the barbershop to discuss the incident. Chambers reiterated to Pattavina and to Chief Wadman that North Omaha needed to be patrolled by officers who were from the community.[39] The benefits of having black officers assigned to a largely African American precinct were demonstrated by policemen like Marvin McClarty, Sr., who lived and worked in North Omaha.[40] McClarty was especially trusted by the community because he refused to cover up the bad conduct of fellow officers and because he worked to get the police department to make reforms. What North Omaha needed was not more powers for police, but more police who knew the people that they were supposed to be protecting.[41]

McClarty was one of a handful of African American policemen who made it clear that their primary allegiance was to the community that they served.[42] By the mid-1980s, McClarty was running an anti-gang unit in North Omaha, trying to stop drugs from entering the city at the source. He believed that large quantities of narcotics were being brought into Nebraska from high-level dealers in Colorado.[43] However, the OPD, McClarty quipped, "wanted to take pictures of [random] kids."[44] The veteran felt that he was getting less than full cooperation from headquarters. "I asked for ten black officers but they put white boys in instead.[45] Then, rather than take directions from McClarty, "the white boys stopped and harassed the youth. . . . Their job was to report back to [Chief] Wadman what I did."[46] McClarty felt the whole project was a sham, and that the real goal of the department was to ensure that Nebraska received federal drug enforcement dollars, which required that a certain number of "gang members" be identified. McClarty believed that since only a small number of Northside youths belonged to gangs at that time, the OPD photographed "inner city youth" indiscriminately, telling parents that the photos would be useful in case their children were ever on a missing persons list.[47] In fact, McClarty said, the department placed those photographs in "federal reports of gang members. . . . Police Chief Wadman is crooked."[48]

One bright spot in all of the chaos was when Terry Thompson—who later changed his name to Tariq Al Amin—joined the Omaha police force. A young man fresh out of the marines, Al Amin became a confidante of both McClarty and Senator Chambers, and he would became an outspoken member of the African American police union, the Brotherhood of the Midwest Guardians. It was members of the Midwest Guardians who had some years earlier sued the city for discriminatory hiring and promotional practices on the police force. The lawsuit revealed that in the decade between 1970 and 1980 not a single African American was hired by the OPD. In the end, the department settled out of court and agreed to a "consent decree," which would require that a certain number of officers be hired or promoted in order to integrate the OPD.[49]

Unfortunately, problems between police officers and African Americans in Nebraska did not wane. One particularly notorious policeman named Dan Clark was known as "Red," dubbed so for his red hair and alternatively as "Dirty Red" for his tendency to use intimidation and violence out of an apparent pleasure in bullying people. Chambers often expressed his view that cops like Clark, who was assigned at that time to North Omaha on the Weed and Seed Drug and Gang Unit, were rather slow-witted. He agreed with the contention by some scholars that white people with the least education were most susceptible to racial bigotry, because they "saw themselves in competition with striving blacks."[50] Historian William Loren Katz provides some support for this position when he notes that a spike in attraction to racist organizations during the 1980s and early 1990s reflected high inflation in combination with high unemployment. Like their predecessors who organized after the American Civil War, Klansmen and Klanswomen in the late twentieth century often professed Christianity and patriotism. They could be identified in the 1980s, according to scholars of the Klan, by their uses of slogans such as "reverse discrimination."[51] Katz writes that despite its lack of intellectual appeal, the "strength and impact of the secret order in this century stems from its ability to strike a resonate white chord . . . it has hit upon a simple truth. . . . White people do not want to surrender their privileges."[52]

Chambers was well aware of the increase in the visibility of the Klan. At several hearings of the Judiciary Committee, he listened to the Anti-Defamation League discuss the rising membership of hate groups and heard testimony that eleven other states had adopted antiparamilitary training bills. However, Chambers refused to lend his support to a similar measure. Of more pressing concern to him than militarized fringe groups were the local police who abused unarmed African Americans people, and the OPD and city administration, which continued to provide no meaningful response. Over the next two years, Chambers would receive news of police assaults and harassment by officers nearly every week. Complaints against another officer, named Charles Matson, who was identifiable by his large stature and known as "Big Head," ranged from frightening children to physical assault. Matson's worst actions would catapult him onto the political battlefield between the OPD and North Omaha residents.[53]

In *Black Bourgeoisie*, E. Franklin Frazier provides the classic description of the African American middle class. He depicts a group that has lost both their cultural grounding and their sense of purpose, and he argues that the black bourgeoisie of the diaspora are indistinguishable from any other middle class in the world. One could pick them out if you listened to them talk, Frazier believed, as they place property rights above all else and are able to disregard the suffering of the working class and unemployed. Class differences sharpened among African Americans in Omaha in the late twentieth century, their edges brocaded by hard ideological perspectives. In the new century, middle-income African Americans began adopting mainstream contentions over the notion of lawlessness. The prevailing argument was that high incarceration rates of inner-city youth resulted from personal choices. Moreover, the failure of the public schools to educate African American children (indicated by too many low test scores) was not systemic, but was the result of a child's home life. To address what church-going centrists had long considered deficiencies in the homes of lower-income, unchurched blacks, a series of programs sprung up around the city and would continue apace into the new century. Churches held temperance rallies to discourage youth from using alcohol or drugs and to obtain from sex. For their part, the Urban League of Omaha hosted parent forums and workshops meant to strengthen the structure of the home and give parents tips on preparing children to learn at schools. But Chambers and a handful of others would continue to address the systematic economic and educational disparities affecting the youth. Though members of Omaha's African American community held sharply differing opinions on the causes of the community's growing impoverishment, the education gap between black and white youth, and street gangs, they closed ranks behind Chambers when it came to the question of police violence. In 1986, when Richard L. Kellin died of injuries sustained in a police interrogation room and the Douglas County Grand Jury returned the verdict that no state or municipal laws had been broken, the black community's class divisions melted into a pervasive anger. Omaha

City Council Member (for District Twenty-One) Fred Conley, a political moderate, introduced a resolution regarding Kellin's death. Conley asked the council to declare that the police officers implicated in the killing had acted outside of the policies of the city of Omaha. Conley also requested a legal opinion on whether the municipality could avoid liability in the Kellin case by showing that the officers were not acting within the scope of their official duties. Conley hoped that the city would not have to provide legal defenses for abusive police officers. He argued that all police personnel who were part of the Kellin interrogation should be fired and prosecuted—a popular sentiment in North Omaha—and proposed that the city council support a petition drive (the petition itself was drafted by Chambers) demanding that a grand jury convene and investigate the case. However, Thomas O. Mumgaard of the city of Omaha's Legal Department discouraged the council members from passing Conley's resolution, expressing his view that it was unconstitutional for the body to champion a cause. There was sufficient public outcry to demand a grand jury investigation without the Conley resolution, and a grand jury did convene to hear the complaint. However, to the disappointment of many in North Omaha, the grand jury determined that the actions of the officers had not been illegal. Meanwhile Chambers's office phone rang continuously about the behaviors of white officers. Tom Reilly, Omaha Public Defender, called Chambers and asked to be put in touch with African American police officer Terry Thompson (Tariq Al Amin). Reilly wanted information on a patrolman by the name of Kyle who the public defender said had a reputation for being racist and mistreating citizens. The problem, Reilly told Chambers, was that the judges believe police officers whether they lie or not. So it was in the spring of 1986, sixteen years after Chambers was first elected to the Unicameral, that he was waist deep in yet another investigation of a Nebraskan who had died at the hands of police. The reality that the killings had gone unabated created an unwelcome sense of déjà vu. After looking into the circumstances leading to the death of Kellin, Chambers wrote to Omaha Mayor Mike Boyle outlining the events leading up to the man's death. To prepare the report, Chambers reviewed twenty-eight different police records, each explaining how Kellin died in police custody. He also interviewed Kellin's pastor, the Reverend Elijah Hill, who was with Kellin at the time of his arrest. Hill reported having seen a male officer manhandle Kellin.[54]

Chief Robert Wadman had refused to give Chambers copies of the police reports on the Kellin arrest. So Chambers went another route and got copies from Douglas County Coroner James Keenan and from County Attorney Donald Knowles. Chambers told Keenan that he needed to check the reports again, because it was not clear why the County Attorney's Office had publicly announced the opinion that the police had done nothing wrong. When Chambers phoned Boyle, the mayor said that the city had nothing to hide. To Chambers's surprise, the mayor asked him to "obtain a list of the witnesses at the scene of the arrest because the police had failed to do so."[55] Cynthia Grandberry accompanied Chambers as he went to get information and a list of witnesses. The senator became furious when he learned that neither the chief of police nor the county attorney had read all of the police reports of Kellin's death, and yet both of them had expressed their official opinion that the city had no liability. An *Omaha World Herald* editorial condemned anyone who criticized the police. "Society would be better off if . . . it is assumed that the person who engages in a fight with an officer is in the wrong."[56]

Members of the African American community disagreed. Aside from a congenital problem with his spine, Kellin was in good health when Officer Charles Matson and a female officer arrived at his residence to settle a domestic dispute. He seemed in good health when he got into the back of a squad car and rode toward the police station, but hours later he was dead. The community insisted on meeting with Chief Wadman to find out why. Chambers pointed out that Kellin weighed less than 120 pounds and that he had been questioned by four police officers in an interrogation room. Chambers suspected that Kellin had been "manhandled by three officers, one of whom (Matson) is a competitive weightlifting bodybuilder."[57] Chambers said the police had no real reason for arresting Kellin who had been arguing with a teenage niece about butting into a conversation that he was having with his mother. The order of events are somewhat sketchy, but by most accounts Kellin was taken into an interrogation room when he arrived at the police station. The officers said that Kellin was intoxicated and that he was knocked down after resisting an officer who had hold of him. At some point in the interrogation, the officers said, Kellin pushed against a table and hit his head on it, all in an effort to resist the officers who were restraining him.[58] In his private investigation of what happened that night, Chambers learned that when Kellin was finally turned over to the booking officer, she refused to accept him into custody until he received medical care for his closed left eye and the blood coming from his nose and mouth. Kellin was subsequently treated at the hospital for cuts and returned to the jail, where he was discovered dead early the next morning.[59]

On May 15, 1986, community members met with Chief Wadman at the

United Methodist Community Center's Wesley House at 34th and Parker Streets. Rodney Wead, the center's director, was present, as was Buddy Hogan, NAACP president, and Mike Jones, KETV reporter and community member. The following weekend Ben Gray replayed Jones's interview with the police chief on his weekly television show *Kaleidoscope*.[60] The chief of police repeated that the officers involved in Kellin's death had done nothing wrong. Hogan asked Wadman whether the police officers would be asked to sit for lie detector tests since a polygraph test had been used previously on an African American officer when a white prostitute said that the policeman had sex with her in his squad car. The chief replied that the cases were different because the one with the prostitute involved "a member of the public accusing an officer of impropriety."[61] Wadman's comments evoked a smoldering silence from his African American audience.

During his research, Chambers talked to witnesses who said that Kellin was drunk and was inadvertently spitting saliva, and that some of the saliva got on Officer Matson. He learned too that Kellin actually weighed only 105 pounds and that he had scoliosis of the spine. At least one witness said they saw Matson slam Kellin's head into the back of a police car. Kellin's wife arrived and asked Matson why her husband was being treated so roughly. Matson told her to get back or they would arrest her, too.[62]

Chambers argued that the officers should have given Kellin a citation and should not have arrested him at all. The normal course of action for domestic disturbances was to defuse them and not to escalate the situation into one where someone could be hurt. After the arrest, Kellin was not charged with a crime beyond disturbing the peace. Police procedure required the officers to book him immediately, but they did not. After he had sustained injuries in the interrogation room, Kellin was made to walk to a squad car rather than be taken to the hospital on a stretcher. All of those "mistakes" contributed to Kellin's death, Chambers argued, and they constituted a denial of "due care."[63] The senator said that he believed in such cases "liability attaches" to the city.[64] Chambers also suspected that the officers committed criminal acts by assaulting Kellin. An autopsy revealed that Kellin's skull had been fractured and that his brain had hemorrhaged. In spite of the story about Kellin bumping his own head against the table, it seemed quite possible that Matson had beaten Kellin to death.[65]

Since neither the OPD's Internal Affairs Division nor the County Attorney's Office seemed likely to investigate what had happened to Kellin, Chambers filed a request for an investigation into Kellin's death with the Federal Bureau of Investigation office in Omaha. He alleged that one or more police officers had used excessive force against Kellin, thereby violating his civil rights. "Mr. Kellin died while in police custody as a result of injuries inflicted. . . . In a country ruled by laws rather than men," Chambers wrote, "even the police function must be subject to the constraints imposed by the Constitution."[66] The truth was that Chambers knew that the FBI was only slightly more likely to find evidence that a law officer had violated a citizen's rights than was the local police department. He continued sending complaints anyway for, if nothing else, it would establish a federal record of police misconduct in Omaha.[67] Practically no one from the Northside believed that an unarmed white man could have been killed in police custody without the officers involved being found guilty of at least negligence. Vickey Parks, Tariq Al Amin, and many others joined Chambers in calling for the convening of a grand jury in the Kellin case.[68] Their efforts paid off in early 1987, when a petition drive succeeded in forcing the convening of the fourth grand jury in Nebraska since 1941. The grand jury's instructions were to indict the police officers involved in Kellin's death only if probable cause existed that criminal wrongdoing had occurred. The grand jury returned their verdict quickly, finding "no wrongdoing" by the officers.[69] They did, however, recommended changes in the handling of prisoners at the city jail. The jury's ruling left Chambers bitter. The courts at every level were unwilling to convict Euro-American policemen for their brutality against his people.[70]

An interesting phenomenon occurring within the ranks of police officers at the time was described by McClarty. He said that whenever a community member died at the hands of a policeman, African American officers felt pressured by white officers to "choose sides."[71] McClarty had worked under a number of police chiefs, and he had experienced pressure to defend police actions under each of them.[72] An insider in the Police Department, McClarty admitted that the automatic defense of a police officer after killing an unarmed citizen was to say that the victim attacked them or that police thought that he or she had a gun. McClarty was sure that the story police told about Kellin falling and hitting his head was to cover up the truth that they "beat Richard Kellin" for no reason.[73]

There was one outcome of the tragedy that made it seem that Kellin had not died in vain. Namely, that it changed the young police officer, Tariq Al Amin, who now vocalized his observation that there was pervasive racism at all levels in the OPD. Before he became a vocal community advocate, Al Amin had been awarded commendations for his police work. After he openly criticized the department, he was accused of various infractions, including allegedly sleeping on a stakeout, for which Al Amin was suspended for several days. Al Amin said that police supervisors came up with the idea of writing negative evaluations of his work in order to silence him, as well as by various other punitive means. In defense of their colleague, the African American police union, the Brotherhood of Midwest Guardians, held a press conference divulging their experiences with racism on the force and with cover–ups of police misconduct.[74]

The horrific circumstances of Kellin's death also inspired Hogan, head of the local chapter of the NAACP, and George Garrison, chair of the University of Omaha's Black Studies Department, to set up a course in diversity training for police. Although some officers may have benefited from the course, others walked out midway through the training program because they disapproved of what was being said. McClarty noted that the OPD had ordered the officers to attend the class, but when they left partway through, the administration did not reprimand them in any way. McClarty said, "Garrison, myself, and [Officer] Patterson" argued with the police administration about the officers' utter disrespect and determination to maintain their racist views.[75]

Chambers tried to think of new ways to help his community. However, in his forties now, and having recently gone through a divorce, he was uncharacteristically unsure. He had been a faithful but very busy husband, and it seemed that his wife felt that he had abandoned her for his career. Compounding the loss in his personal life, he had also reached the proverbial fork in the road. At midlife, he had already served in the legislature longer than he had ever expected. And he had no reason to believe that voters would cease returning him to the post, nor did he see anyone more qualified or more given to service than himself. In an interview that revealed his ambivalence about his future plans, the law school graduate (he had returned to law school in the mid-1970s and earned his J.D. even while serving in the Unicameral) doubted whether he would ever take the bar exam and enter the domain of his frequent adversary, the Nebraska State Bar Association. As far as serving in the Unicameral, Chambers told a reporter that "the next term could be [his] last."[76]

In spite of everything, he had seen major successes during his tenure, beginning with district elections for the Omaha City Council, which he had secured during his first years in office. At the time, the issue of district elections was on the agenda of African American politicians across the country and the Seventh Circuit Court of Appeals ruled (1975) that for cities with a history of racial discrimination, at-large elections represented continuing discriminatory behavior. At-large elections were not in themselves unconstitutional, but they could be when they "operate to dilute, minimize, or cancel out a minority group's voting strength," the court said.[77] Chambers was well aware of the historical and political significance of his successful bill to eliminate citywide elections for the previously white-only seats on the Omaha City Council. An article about his feat was the focus of an editorial in the *Lincoln Journal*. "He has changed the governmental structure and power relationships in the state's most populous city, county, and school district by obtaining passage of legislation to require election by district."[78] The results had surfaced long ago, starting with the election of an African American to the city council for the first time.

In December 1984, Chambers found himself contemplating a run for mayor. He reasoned that his best chance of winning an electoral race in an at-large election was to Omaha's mayoral post since his constituency base was there and because the mayor was elected on an "officially non-partisan basis."[79] He weighed his chances of success. The incumbent mayor, Mike Boyle, though he had a number of critics, was popular with white power brokers in the city. Another drawback to running was that community member Fred Conley, who was then serving his second term in the Omaha City Council, had all but announced his candidacy. After careful thought, Chambers again decided not to run.[80]

A Partner and a Friend

Part of the reason for Chambers's success on the district elections bill was that community members turned out in support. Wayne Lowden of North Omaha testified that he had "no representation whatsoever on the present city council."[81] The Omaha Association of Social Workers also publicly supported Chambers's bill. Yet it was Cynthia Grandberry, his legislative aide, who had been the first to sign a petition in support of the bill. She supported almost all of his projects and had inspired a few. He had known for some time that "Cindy" was his best friend.[82]

By 1987, Chambers had seen the state go through several years of bad economic times, and the failure of the Commonwealth Savings and Loan had only made morale worse. The senators voted to adopt a resolution that would reimburse depositors of the insolvent Commonwealth Savings and Loan Company for over twenty million dollars, partially due to Chambers's effective lobbying. This did not eliminate the suffering of the poorest Nebraskans, who typically had no savings at all. Chronic unemployment was straining many Americans, and most African American families in Nebraska struggled to make ends meet. With no relief from the recession in sight, Chambers told his colleagues that Nebraska's poorest citizens were in dire straits. They could not provide their families with basic necessities due to high inflation. The senator expressed his view that the legislature was ignoring the problem. He soon joined a small cadre of senators in trying to raise the Aid to Dependent Children monthly stipend from $280 per month to $400. A committee amendment supported the idea that a change in the monthly subsidy was needed, but only recommended a twenty dollar per month increase.[83]

The reluctance of the legislators to help Nebraskans in need was repugnant. It stood to reason that bad economic times would hurt the financially vulnerable the most. Chambers told his colleagues, "There are occasions that arise where my emotions are affected more than at other times, and this is one of those occasions . . . even if we make the modest increase to $325 it is not adequate to meet the needs that we say we're trying to meet."[84] Chambers suggested that his colleagues think about how difficult it would be for them to survive on so little: "I'm keenly aware of the problems that people are having, not just in the cities, but on the farms too."[85] Chambers said that he received calls from all sorts of Nebraskans in need of help to pay their utility bills and to feed their families.[86] In the end, the senator decided that something was better than nothing and supported the meager increase.[87]

Chambers sponsored numerous bills to alleviate the financial shortfall for low-income Nebraskans, such as setting maximum fees that attorneys could charge clients. Although generally opposed to gambling, when debate over a Nebraska lottery was underway, Chambers offered a sports wagering bill to legalize bookmaking (a form of gambling popular in North Omaha). Chambers also spent a great deal of time countering special interest group legislation that was of no benefit to ordinary families. When Senator Loran Schmit sponsored a bill that allowed city and county governments to establish ethanol facilities, Chambers said the bill benefited only the rich because of its provisions allowing property tax exemptions to companies that own aircraft and computers. Legislative Bill 775 was being backed by lobbyists from the wholesale producer ConAgra.[88] Chambers said it was "the first—and biggest—corporate-welfare bill," ever debated by the Unicameral; the senator offered more than thirty amendments to the bill, which he used to filibuster the measure.[89]

Surely the economy would have been better for working-class people if Jesse Jackson had become president. Although not surprised, Chambers remained disappointed that the Jackson had not won the Democratic nomination in 1984, and especially at how Jackson had backed out of the presidential campaign—folding under pressure from whites to "get out" of the presidential race because some Jewish Americans considered him anti-Semitic.[90] How ironic and what masterful and twisted reasoning it was that succeeded in getting the African American candidate to exclude himself from the competition by calling him a racist. The political system perpetuated racism with which Jackson had contended all of his life. It had been hard for Chambers to watch a proud black man, who actually had a vision for the country, throw his support behind Democratic nominee Walter Mondale.[91]

Chambers still respected Jackson, however, and spoke with the civil rights leader when he made an appearance before the Nebraska legislature in February 1987. During his visit, Jackson expressed concern about industrial workers and farmers: "Ours is not a struggle of black versus white. . . . It's the merger maniacs versus the locked out."[92] Jackson's populist message sat well with Chambers, whose major criticism of Jackson was his "unwavering loyalty" to the Democratic Party, which accepted black votes but neglected black interests.[93] Chambers's Black Nationalist perspective, with its emphasis on black-controlled institutions, was the guiding principle behind his preference for voting as an independent. A third-party alternative was not unheard of in the Midwest where the remnants of a populist tradition could still be found in state lore pointing pridefully to William Jennings Bryan, who (around the turn of the century) supported an agenda heralding the interests of the common man.[94] Bryan's perspective symbolized white Nebraskans' attitudes on race relations. They denounced obvious racial violence, *if* it could be proven to exist, but insisted that "complainers" get to the hard work of pulling themselves up by their bootstraps. Chambers, along with fellow Black Nationalists and critical race theorists, would argue that this point of view is based on unconscious denial of the inherent harm in a cultural outlook that disparages anyone not of European origins, and of the privileges that are reserved only for whites.[95]

For years Chambers had explained these concepts to his audiences; Chambers's speaking itinerary during the last years of the 1980s was extensive. He appeared at four or five events each month in 1988. These included lectures at a host of educational settings, including Boys Town, the Nebraska School for the Deaf, Young Democrats, and the University of Nebraska at Omaha. He also gave scores of interviews, both in person and over the telephone, sometimes speaking to as many as five or six reporters in a week. A great deal of Chambers's energy was spent rallying his community to vote. For the second time, Chambers was active in a presidential campaign. Now he channeled his support toward the independent candidate of the national New Alliance Party, Dr. Lenora Fulani, a psychologist from New York. Fulani represented many of the people who had worked hard on the Jesse Jackson campaign four years earlier and who had lost hope that the Democratic Party would ever represent the interests of African Americans, Latinos, working people, women, or gay and transgendered populations. An articulate African American woman, Fulani was a people's candidate and Chambers felt that she would provide the moral leadership which the country needed.[96]

Fulani's supporters noted that Democratic presidential hopeful Michael Dukakis agreed with precious few of the themes from Jesse Jackson's campaign platform, most of which Fulani adopted. Among Fulani's campaign messages was the notion that African American voters would no longer give their votes to a Democratic Party that took them for granted. Her New Alliance Party beat out Ron Paul and the Libertarian Party, and was the only independent party to appear on ballots in each of the fifty states. She did not expect to win, she said, rather hers was a "crusade for fair elections."[97] Critics of the New Alliance Party, though, saw the organization as "avenging the [Democratic] Party leadership's treatment of Jesse Jackson."[98] Although very popular with activists, many African Americans were hesitant to support a campaign with the kind of socialist rhetoric that was a part of Fulani's platform. Alvin Thornton, Howard University professor, said that Fulani's campaign was not necessarily in line with African Americans' best interests.[99]

Chambers, who had supported Jackson by functioning as a lead local organizer in 1984, now gravitated toward Fulani and quickly became the Nebraska head of the Fulani campaign. Simultaneously, Chambers removed his name as a contender for his own seat in the Nebraska Unicameral, running a write-in campaign instead for his legislative post, and at the same time announcing a full-fledged campaign for the U.S. Senate as a candidate from the New Alliance Party.[100]

As soon as his candidacy for the congressional seat was official, Chambers demanded an invitation to participate in scheduled debates with major party candidates, former Nebraska Governor Bob Kerrey, and State Senator David Karnes. But Kerrey told the press that he would not attend the debates if Chambers were permitted to participate. The former governor saw the New Alliance Party as extremist and said that Chambers was an opportunist who was going along with the party's platform for the purpose of seeking attention. The New Alliance Party's calls for an end to poverty, affordable housing, an end to U.S. imperial ventures overseas, Native American land rights, reinstitution of trade unions, and increased taxes on the wealthy, among other imperatives, were in Kerrey's view, contrary to the tenets of capitalism. Kerrey also felt that Chambers was unwittingly being used by the New Alliance Party, which, he said, sought legitimacy by attaching its name to a local state senator.[101]

In full support of Fulani's bid for the presidency, Chambers made appearances throughout the summer, frequently speaking at the De Porres Center, on Al Jamal Byndon's Cox Cable television program, and in other community forums. In May, a crowd turned out for a rally at Omaha Central Park Mall where Chambers gave the keynote speech, "The State of North Omaha."[102] Chambers advised his fellow community members to remain vigilant in demanding solutions to old problems but he also talked about hope. He believed that with good voter turn-out and solidarity among working and low-income people, a candidate with moral fortitude could be elected president.

In spite of everything, it seemed that Chambers maintained something akin to faith. Though he still believed that strict adherence to religious rituals actually separated humans from each other, he would not discount the possibility that a greater power might exist. Chambers expressed these thoughts in regard to his old friend and former colleague Terry Carpenter:

> Do you remember his pallbearers? There was Irish Catholic Gene Mahoney, Jewish Dick Fellman, what I suppose was a Protestant in Chuck Davey, and there was me, this man supposedly totally irreligious. There was a real message in that and most people didn't catch on.[103]

The excitement and momentum in North Omaha stemming from the buzz of organizing for the upcoming election was pierced by bad news and attended by refreshed anger and despair. On a quiet April night in 1987, Kevin Watson was driving his motorcycle in the neighborhood and, according to a police report, ran several stop signs. Officers Kris Jacobson and Gary Schnebel chased twenty-five-year-old Watson down North 24th Street at high speeds. When Watson stopped, they said, a struggle occurred, ending in the wounding of the two officers, who were hit in their bullet-proof vests, and in Watson's death.[104]

Senator Chambers believed a different account of what happened. On April 20, he wrote, a twenty-five-year-old unarmed man was out riding his motorcycle for pleasure. Police decided to interact with him and ended up killing him. For Chambers's community the loss of another unarmed young man produced nightmarish recollections and rage. In their defense the officers argued that Watson had committed a felony assault upon one of them. Chambers's view was shared by most Northside residents, who had seen far too many cases like Watson's. On May 6, Erven McSwain, Jr., of the Human Relations Office and a friend of the senator, attended a session of the Black Forum, a series of community meetings held at Wesley House. After the meeting, McSwain wrote to Chambers, telling him that he had raised the issue of whether police needed sobriety tests after these killings of unarmed citizens: "With the kinds of complaints the Human Relations Department are getting against police, it's reasonable to conclude that other Kevin Watsons will meet their death, due to the unnecessary force used by police."[105] Things had never been good between the community and the police, and economic crisis seemed to bring out the worst. Police killings on Omaha's Northside polarized the state along racial lines. Most white people continued to count on the police to "control" the African American community. Perry W. Hadden wrote to Omaha Mayor Bernie Simon, arguing that whites were afraid to go into North Omaha because of the area's reputation for excessive crime.[106]

> In my opinion, Ernie Chambers should promote, not condemn, the actions of the police. He should promote law obedience to all citizens, to include the black community.... Why was the man being chased?... Maybe Ernie Chambers's objections in the past to his several traffic and/or speeding tickets caused this young man to think that he too, was not subject to police department enforcement of laws.[107]

Omaha Police Officer John P. Newell wrote a letter to the *Omaha World Herald* calling Chambers's theories fanciful. "To suggest that the officers shot each other [in bullet-proof vests] is repugnant.... Who shall spare us from this impetuous, presumptuous pseudo-guardian of the people."[108] Newell's letter could be interpreted as subtly suggesting that Chambers be silenced. Written by an Omaha police officer and published by the state's leading newspaper, the publication of Newell's comments did not help to convince the community that the city cared about dealing with African Americans justly. Newell said that Chambers's ranting broke up the serenity of the city.[109]

Chambers responded with his own letter to the press. There were conflicting accounts by the officers of what happened that night, he argued. Both officers agreed that they were planning to arrest Watson for a traffic violation. However, one policeman said that Watson turned to fight them simultaneously, while the other officer said that his partner was fighting Watson when he emerged from the car. A witness saw both officers grab Watson, force him to lie on the sidewalk face down, and drag him. Another community member heard the sound of someone being hit. One bystander reported that the police officers were on top of Watson hitting him. There were other disparities in the officers' stories. While both claimed that Watson had grabbed a gun out of officer Schnebel's holster, "each officer claimed that the other was shot first."[110] It is difficult to envision a 160-pound man tackling two, two-hundred pound police officers while they were "each lying across his upper body. . . . [Chief] Wadman refused to order residue tests on the hands of Schnebel."[111] The senator interviewed Watson's family, and they and his employers said that Watson was an extremely quiet and nonaggressive person. Chambers believed that Watson had set his motorcycle on its kickstand and was not fleeing, but waiting for the officers.[112]

In the end, the city refused to prosecute Kris Jacobson, who shot and killed Watson, and in October of that year, the Omaha Police Department gave Jacobson the Medal of Valor, their highest award, for his actions in the Watson case. Gary Schnebel, Jacobson's partner, received the Survivor's Club Award for the shot that he took in a bullet-proof vest. LaDonna Watson, Watson's widow, told the press that the city of Omaha not only allowed police brutality in the black community but rewarded it. President of the Omaha NAACP Buddy Hogan argued that the Omaha Police Union gave the award to give "comfort to those officers on the force who feel it's necessary to exert their macho image in the black community."[113] Hogan said that the union had pressured the police administration to give the award. George Dillard, executive director of the Urban League of Nebraska, said one of the officers involved in the Watson killing had long enjoyed a reputation for corruption. Dillard said that it was odd for such a person to be rewarded for contributing to the death of a citizen. Al Amin, who was now president of the Midwest Guardians, met with Chief Wadman to express his group's opposition to the presentation of awards to officers Jacobson and Schnebel.[114] The following day when an award ceremony was held for the police officers who shot Watson, an *Omaha World Herald* headline read "Chambers Blasted Wadman For Approving Police Award."[115] Chambers told the press that Police Chief Wadman "is rewarding two cops for killing a black man.... You don't give people rewards for tragedies."[116]

For the first time in over a decade, and in utter frustration with a state whose laws he had tried to reshape for the protection of all citizens, Chambers publicly suggested that his constituents might have to take up arms to defend themselves. I am not encouraging violence, the senator said, but "I won't try to stop it any more. There are different ways of dealing with problems, and my way has failed."[117] On the day of the award presentation, Chambers stood outside of the Omaha police headquarters, utterly alone. He wore a large sign that read "Killing Is Not Valorous—To Reward It Is Immoral."[118]

A short time later, Al Amin, Brenda Council, an attorney with Union Pacific Railroad, Mike Jones, KETV reporter, and Buddy Hogan, NAACP president, all appeared with Chambers on Ben Gray's *Kaleidoscope* program to discuss the severity of the problems between police and the community. Chambers said that there had been a number of recent complaints about police stops of elderly women near Bakers' Supermarket on Ames Avenue, and Hogan said that Watson could have been any one of their sons.[119]

Nationally, the end of the twentieth century witnessed a resurgence of public concern over racial strife—exemplified by a rise in incidences of police conflicts with minority citizens. In May 1992, the burning and looting of businesses in California received nationwide attention. The uprising was a spontaneous protest against the verdict in state court in the case of the Los Angeles police officers who were caught on videotape beating Rodney King. Activists in Omaha held demonstrations when the verdict of not guilty was announced. Chambers, a featured speaker, addressed a crowed outside of the Douglas County Courthouse. The senator carried a sign to the open-air demonstration that read "Injustice and Racism Reign in the U.S."[120] The local press noted that many Omahans, fearing that riots would break out in the city, had kept their children home from school. Protests continued around the country until a federal indictment led to the officers' convictions.

The community remained roused and damnation of abusive police officers could be heard at barber and beauty shops and at the local grocery stores across North Omaha. A strange and surreal message cut through the clamor when Chambers received news that his long time friend Charlie Washington had died. "Charlie" had been a "race man," a human rights activist, a writer, an editor, a good person, and one of the few people whom Chambers had been able to look up to.

Washington was born in 1923, and went to work for the *Omaha Star* in 1938. In the early years he served as a reporter and sold advertisements. Later he led desegregation efforts in Omaha, working to integrate Peony Park swimming pool in 1955; in 1963 Washington joined with Kelsey Jones and Rudolph McNair, holding sit-ins at the Woolworth's store in downtown Omaha. Washington's funeral marked the passing of a giant from the civil rights era. Community, city, and state dignitaries took part in a formal send-off. Senator Chambers was accompanied by Governor Kerrey, Mayor Boyle, and Fred Conley as the official dignitaries. Also on the program were Brenda (Warren) Council of the Omaha School Board, Attorney General Bob Spire, George Dillard, Heisman Trophy winner Johnny Rodgers, Buddy Hogan, Roger Sayers, Larry Myers, Bob Boozer, Dorothy Eure, Sonny Foster, Linda Newby, and Al Goodwin. The senator mourned Washington's death in private, as well as joining North Omaha in making formal tribute. Chambers had publicly expressed skepticism about religion, and he was considered by many to be an agnostic, but it was difficult to know what his views of the afterlife really were. He did claim, with confidence, that living right would satisfy any requirements for existence after death. He would share little else about his own spirituality. University of Nebraska–Lincoln students analyzed Chambers's theology in their publication, *The Daily Nebraskan*, and found that the senator did appear to try and help anyone in need, but whether he did this out of a sense of spiritual duty to other humans was not known.[121]

The sheer number of human rights bills that Chambers had sponsored was daunting. One controversial measure that the senator sponsored was a bill prohibiting discrimination against persons with HIV/AIDS. The bill covered all aspects of life—schools, housing, public accommodations, and employment. The bill went before the Judiciary Committee in 1990, and Chambers argued during the bill's hearing that persecution of homosexuals was immoral. His sensitivity to the idea that people had a right to their sexual orientation may have been kindled by one of Chambers's favorite authors. The Irish writer, Oscar Wilde, author of *The Importance of Being Ernest* and *The Picture of Dorian Gray*, was imprisoned in 1895 for practicing a homosexual lifestyle. Wilde was released from prison twenty-four months later, but died in 1900 from illnesses that he had developed during his incarceration. The world had robbed itself of Wilde's talent as a result of parochial thinking and prejudice. But most people would have no concept of the harm that they did. Chambers blamed the fact that people often accepted what they were taught without thinking.[122]

Some things in life truly were black or white. For instance, if Chambers supported your cause, you could not ask for a greater ally. On the other hand, if you became a foe, Chambers could be merciless. In 1991, Chambers helped to thwart the career of a young politician. The recipient of Chambers's offensive was Paul Bryant, candidate for the Omaha City Council who was running against the incumbent Fred Conley. Although an African American, Bryant's support base was not North Omaha, but seemed to come from some of the businesspeople downtown. Bryant sought out Chambers before he announced his candidacy and the senator did not oppose the idea. However, the younger man did not tell the senator about having sold drugs in the past. When Chambers found out, he felt that he had been misled. He met with Bryant and threatened to publicize the young man's past involvement with drugs if "Paul" did not withdraw from the contest against Conley. Despondently, Bryant's campaign manager told the press that he had not planned to discuss Bryant's drug "use" as a college student, until Chambers brought the issue up. "To say a drug dealer should represent us is the crowning insult to our community," Chambers said.[123] In the end, Bryant withdrew from the race and Conley retained his seat.

To Chambers, the ends had justified his means. The community had been protected from one who was seeking political opportunities and not, in the senator's opinion, looking to serve. In a very different case, Chambers would challenge an entire town in an effort to protect the rights of a handful of individuals. Chambers defended an interracial couple in York, a town fifty miles west of Lincoln, after a Confederate-flag-bearing crowd of men descended upon the home of Les Blyden and Jennifer Manire. York police, who were informed of the assemblage of a mob early on, failed to intervene until after the men had reached the couple's home. Shortly thereafter, Chambers addressed an audience of over 300 hundred persons in York's city auditorium. Denying that racism is a problem, he said, "only makes it worse."[124] The senator promised to hold the York Police Department and Charles Campbell, York County attorney, accountable for the lack of an appropriate response to the family's plea for help. Albert Maxey, an African American police officer from Lincoln, attended Chambers's talk, and shared Chambers's concern with how York officials were handling the incident.[125]

As the economic downturn continued, vigilantism and extremism became increasingly attractive to some. James F. Ahearn, Omaha Division special agent in charge of the FBI, wrote a letter testifying that groups were organizing in Nebraska whose mission was the "overthrow of the lawful government by means of force and violence."[126] G. L. Kuchel, professor at the University of Nebraska–Lincoln, agreed that low-income whites were organizing for what they saw as inevitable communist invasions and race war. Groups like the Klan, Posse Comitatus, the Christian Patriots, Neo-Nazis, and others had "gained tremendous momentum in the past five years."[127] These militants considered their enemies to be Jews, bankers, lawyers, African Americans, and government agents. The problem, which had started small, grew over several years. The Judiciary Committee had tried to cope with the growing crisis back in January 1986, when they held hearings on a bill to criminalize training procedures by paramilitary groups.

The senator had said repeatedly that the popularity of the Neo-Nazis and other groups resulted from the problem of "economic insecurity," and that the citizenry's financial straits needed to be addressed, not its symptoms. When Kuchel said that the bill would protect the state's citizens, Chambers countered, "But [are not] the citizens . . . the ones who would be in these groups?"[128] Chambers's reasoning could only be perceived by those who understood his feelings about the Second Amendment. He told his colleagues again that the tendency of police to ignore citizens' constitutional rights was a far greater hazard to the public than any paramilitary groups.[129]

In January 1990, Chambers had served in the Unicameral for twenty years. He wondered privately whether that was long enough. He sponsored a legislative resolution that year to authorize a person to practice law in Nebraska so long as they had graduated from an accredited Nebraska law school. Chambers sought a way for a person to gain accreditation as an attorney without taking the bar exam from the highly politicized Nebraska State Bar Association. At midlife, Chambers may have been trying to expand his options. His popularity among North Omahans remained high, as was indicated by their perpetual selection of him at the polls. His battle to save the homes of elders from demolition during the city's eminent domain claims for the North Freeway project, though unsuccessful, endeared the senator even to many politically conservative community members. Chambers seemed an example of the best that their community had produced, someone who could be trusted and who would stand his ground against the powerful.

As Chambers looked back over his era in the Nebraska state legislature, it was hard to deny that present conditions marked the worsening of times for African Americans in his state and in the country. The Ku Klux Klan was on the rise—segmented but updated and growing in membership. The economy was bad, and Africans in America were among the hardest hit. Meanwhile, a number of police officers continued to exploit their power in the African community. On the other hand, Chambers had changed the way many Euro-Americans went about interacting with African people, as if the respect that those in authority felt for Chambers in some small way covered the lives of regular people who suffered the inconvenience of being without wealth or political clout. More tangible were his winning of district elections for the Omaha School Board, Douglas County Commissioners, and the Omaha City Council—giving African Americans their first real opportunities to win seats on Omaha's governing bodies since Nebraska achieved statehood.

Jim Raglin, Nebraska Press Association writer, mailed a draft of an article about Chambers to the lawmaker. Chambers had shared with Raglin that he was shy and quiet as a child. "I had trouble in [grade] school with letters. A lady, white teacher—all my teachers were white—stayed over noon hour to help me. . . . Then and now, my mind was like iron—hard to scratch, but once scratched it stays there."[130] The result was the development of a powerhouse of intellect and energy. Raglin said that after two decades in the Unicameral, Ernie Chambers remained what he was all along, "an army looking for a war."[131] Raglin had captured the essence of the senator's personality. Chambers would have fought injustice in any context into which he was born. However, this truth does not lessen the severity of the battles that the descendants of Africans faced in Middle America and across the postcolonial world in the final decade of the twentieth century.

7—"Dean"

Considered a pariah by many Nebraskans, Chambers's importance in select international circles held little sway in his home state. It was undeniable, though, that his contributions to the Black Power and Anti-Apartheid Movements had created a place for him in history. Fittingly, Chambers's name would appear with those of Julian Bond, Benjamin Chavis, Jr., David Dinkins, Carol Mosely Braun, Randall Robinson, and thirty-nine others in a "Statement on the Announcement of Elections and the Call for End of Sanctions" in September 1993. The South Africans had liberated themselves of the apartheid regime—with limited bloodshed due to the enactment of international sanctions. Now political prisoner and African National Congress (ANC) leader Nelson Mandela was released from prison, and democratic elections with universal suffrage were scheduled for the following year.

Chambers had played a role in the South African freedom struggle. It would be difficult to argue that the senator was less than brilliant. But in spite of his extraordinariness the *Lincoln Star* reported in January 1991 that Chambers was not likely to be elected as chair of any legislative committee. Although he was the third-longest-serving member still in office in the Unicameral, a local newspaper editorial opined that racism and distrust of the audacious senator from North Omaha made his formal leadership of a committee unattainable. Chambers had chaired the Government, Military, and Veterans Affairs Committee back in the early 1970s, but the development of his style as an "institutional obstructionist" now obstructed him. But then a cursory look around the nation at black elected officials revealed that those who used the power of their positions to improve the lot of "the People" sometimes had to endure retaliatory measures. In spite of this reality, a few of Chambers's peers in other states fought for economic and political relief for their constituents. Richard Hatcher in Gary, Indiana, appointed African Americans to a number of posts within his administration and Coleman Young in Detroit, Michigan, hired African American civil servants from other states, refusing to accept the excuse that there were not enough qualified black applicants. An undaunted Marion Barry, mayor of Washington D.C. (1979–1991), who was arrested on drug charges and served a six-month prison term but was reelected (1995–1999), worked to create jobs for the low-income unemployed in both terms in office. Northern elected officials like David Dinkins, mayor of New York City (1990–1993), also won hard-fought gains for blacks. He instituted hiring programs for low-income people even while contending with the Crown Heights riot of 1991. The first African American mayor of Chicago, Harold Washington (1983–1987), had first served in the Illinois House of Representatives (1965–1976) and Illinois Senate (1977–1980), but was too independent for then Mayor Richard J. Daley and the Daley Machine. Washington lost the support of political backers when he sponsored legislation suggested to him by Police Officer Renault Robinson, who had formed an African American Patrolman's League to fight racism within the Chicago Police Department. While Robinson was suffering reprisals in the form of write-ups and a suspension, similar to what Tariq Al Amin suffered in Omaha, Washington proposed legislation for a Civilian Review Board to hear charges of police brutality and racism. According to political pundits, Washington survived the loss of support by Daley largely because, years earlier, he had helped to found the Chicago League of Negro Voters, which proved essential in electing Washington to the U.S. House of Representatives in 1980, and as mayor of Chicago in 1983. In the latter post, Washington battled with Chicago's City Council in order to win economic concessions for low-income workers in a fashion not unlike Chambers who fought political wars on the floor of the Nebraska Statehouse, elevating the issue of economic distress of the poor and in support of initiatives to help his constituency combat racism and other working-class peoples improve their lives and life chances.[1]

Since Chambers did not have the power as a state legislator to appoint other African Americans to political posts, he worked doggedly to change existing laws so that district-based elections could replace at-large elections. His success in this realm meant that neighborhoods could elect persons to represent them on the city council, county board, and school district. Chambers's strategic approach fit the pattern of other African American elected officials nationwide. Scholar Charles E. Jones notes that in many cases African American state senators were able to obtain additional positions of power, but had more difficulty in passing legislation favorable to their constituencies. The social composition of American cities was in flux during this period, and white flight meant decreasing tax bases for urban centers at the same time that the cost of services were on the rise. The result was an increased dependency by cities like Omaha on federal expenditures—a fact that put African American politicians in a precarious situation during sequential Republican administrations, especially after funds in support of social programs were cut back. Even then, not all black elected officials who were Chambers's contemporaries insisted on immediate measures to relieve the financial distress of African American urban communities. Atlanta's mayor, Andrew Young (1982–1990), adopted the rhetoric of "trickle down" economics from the Reagan administration and supported the interests of business in the hope that new jobs would result for his constituency. Philadelphia's Wilson Goode (1984–1992) plowed new ground for conservatives in 1985 when he refused to take steps to slow the increasing impoverishment of his city's North Side residents. Goode also distinguished himself by ordering police to drop a bomb on the home of members of John Africa's MOVE organization. MOVE members had barricaded themselves indoors and were resisting the city's initiatives to enforce sanitation and other codes on their back-to-Africa environmentalist organization whose members were attempting to practice a rural lifestyle in the city where they lived as an extended family. As a result of the bombing, fires raged within a square city block and eleven people died during the police assault. That African American Philadelphians reelected Goode in 1987, symbolized a growing class divide among urban black people. By this juncture, Chambers clearly no longer fit the prototype of the black state representative, most of whom tended to be from elite social and economic backgrounds and were Christian, male, and middle-aged or young. There remained thirty-three old guard senators in the early 1990s, including Arthur Eve, a New York assemblyman (elected first in 1967); Robert G. Clark, senator from Mississippi (elected first in 1969); Maryland Senator Clarence W. Blount (elected in 1971); and Senator Chambers, who began serving the same year. Though most similar in his political persuasion and politics to the old guard, Chambers was also different from the other "warhorse legislators" as a result of his relative isolation in the Midwest. Getting results for his constituents required that he sometimes make use of the filibuster in the extreme. Despite his sense of isolation, Chambers did take steps to stay abreast of news from the National Black Caucus of State Legislators; however, as an independent, agnostic, mature man from a working-class family, he had even less in common with the new class of state-level politicians after 1990. The one exception to this rule was that in spite of their affluent origins, the newest African American state legislators also served as the representatives of low-income urbanites, who put a great deal of their trust into their elected leaders. The largest number of African America legislators in the United States during the first decade of the new millennium served in southern states, with forty-seven in Georgia and forty-five in Mississippi, respectively. Black representation in the statehouses of the middle west remained sparse, with no more than five serving at any one time in Oklahoma, three in Colorado, two in Minnesota, and one—or at best two—in Nebraska. A full seventy percent of these new black legislators had been elected after 1993, the majority of them Democrats. Many of the younger legislators owed their seats, in part, to the support of the local arm of the Democratic Party and were under pressure to deracialize their agendas in order to be seen as responsive to their wider constituencies. Meanwhile black communities demanded that their elected officials serve as representatives of the race. The new black legislators sometimes had to choose between acceptability—the reward for supporting the status quo—and becoming a maverick.[2]

Chambers made his choice before he ever entered the Unicameral, and he would ultimately expand his political quest for justice for African Americans to an attack on all systemic corruption. More than mere determination to keep his campaign promises, and to maintain his convictions, Chambers was also responding to the growing impoverishment of working-class folk in North Omaha—a macrocosm of the effects of postindustrial market forces—which was wreaking havoc in his hometown and especially among his constituency. As Chambers neared retirement age, he could have counted an ever-increasing number of black candidates with conservative agendas running with the support of conservative political action committees and the Republican Party. In a state like Nebraska where the community traditionally had the power only to elect one state senator from Omaha, the importance of the legislature as a space where the economic and political rights of African Americans are defended by a lone senator—his or her abilities and political persuasion remained critical to the interests of the community. As such, Chambers made it his policy to disregard what his colleagues might think of him and to focus instead on vocalizing the concerns and issues faced by his constituency to the best of his ability. Although respected by his colleagues, Chambers could name few true friends among fellow legislators.

One editor correctly judged the mood of the solons, especially Chambers's colleagues' frustration with the senator's monopolization of debate. Chambers had filibustered for hours on end during a recent session to prohibit passage of an anti-abortion measure. Their failure to contain Chambers had been difficult for the other legislators to explain to their constituents, and at length the senators overwhelmingly voted for a new rule allowing the body to invoke cloture—to cease debate after eight hours of debate on a bill at each stage of consideration. Chambers response came quickly. "It's obvious the legislature can't stomach full and unfettered debate on serious issues." Whether the new rule would stymie Chambers, who was "known for his ability to play the legislative rules like a piano," was another question.[3]

From the senator's perspective, any rule that the legislature adopted could also be used to hem in opponents. Undaunted, he conducted his research and filed his bills in preparation for what would be one of the battles of his lifetime—the fight to rid Nebraska of that antiquated and barbaric phenomenon of state execution. For Chambers, the 1991 session began with his offering of a bill that would replace the death penalty with life imprisonment without parole. In spite of the coup against him by the other senators, a week into the new session Chambers had secured the twenty-four co-signers that he needed to get the anti-death-penalty bill passed. A confident Chambers relished the fact that adding the thirty-year minimum in actual prison time before the possibility of parole had convinced his colleagues that public safety and justice could be simultaneously served by the new measure. The only wild card would be Governor Ben Nelson. Nelson had told Chambers that he would keep an open mind, but Chambers recalled that Nelson had said that he supported capital punishment during his campaign for governor. Though Nebraska had had its present death penalty law since 1973, no one had been executed by the state since the mass murderer Charlie Starkweather met his fate in 1959. The fight took on more immediacy now because a number of men on death row were approaching their execution dates.[4]

Although they had committed crimes, Chambers believed that the humanity of death row inmates should not be forgotten. He interacted with death row inmates on a personal level, making it difficult for anyone to discuss the prisoners as though they were less than human beings, at least in Chambers's presence. After a trip to the state penitentiary that Chambers made to show concern over reports that prison guards exhibited abusive behavior, Chambers received a letter from Harold Lamont Otey. Otey said that Chambers's visit had angered prison administrators who had thundered, after Chambers left, that no one from the outside would manipulate what went on inside of the prison. Otey also complained about members of the State Ombudsman's Office—who were charged with overseeing the welfare of prisoners. "Hassan Muhammad acts as if he is [in] Harold Clarke's [the African American director of corrections] hip pocket."[5] Muhammad's investigations of inmate's complaints seemed to Otey to be half-hearted. Worse, Muhammad had not confronted the prison's director about a "miniature electric chair, complete with light bulb where the man's head is" on the desk in his office.[6] Otey said that Clarke's message was clear.

One of nine death row inmates, Otey was sentenced to die for the 1977 rape and murder of Jane McManus. Otey's execution was scheduled for July 1991, and emotions ran high throughout the spring and summer among anti–death-penalty activists. When Assistant Attorney General Sharon Lindgren voiced her opinion on television that Otey should be executed, Chambers retorted that Lindgren was "seeking sexual gratification" in Otey's pending death.[7] Chambers told the press, "She will have to achieve that elsewhere. Maybe with a vibrator. I doubt she can get a man."[8] The senator's comments caused a shrill uproar that was exacerbated by the media. Lieutenant Governor Maxine Moul asked Chambers to apologize for his comment, which she said was sexist. Chambers had no intention of taking back his words. "My comments were addressed to one person who happened to be a woman. . . . because of what she is doing, not because of what she is."[9] Chambers had meant to be harsh and insulting; he would not tolerate Lindgren's smirking before the cameras, he said, as if killing a citizen of the state were a joke. Otey barely escaped execution in July, coming within six hours of his scheduled death. At the last minute, a Lancaster County judge issued a delay.[10]

By mid-1994 Otey was again running out of time. His lawyers filed a civil rights suit in U.S. District Court claiming that Otey's right to due process might have been violated because Attorney General Don Stenberg was Nebraska's chief prosecutor, and because he also was one of three people who sat on the pardons board and had heard and rejected Otey's request for clemency. But Assistant Attorney General J. Kirk Brown said that the public would lose respect for the criminal justice system if Otey's execution were delayed any longer. When a memo surfaced featuring Brown's joke that a television show on Otey's life would air opposite the attorney general's holiday party, Chambers filed a complaint against Brown with the Nebraska Bar Association. Brown was unprofessional and should be reprimanded.[11]

On August 21st through the 22nd, one week before Otey was scheduled to die, 200 death penalty proponents and opponents faced off outside the Nebraska State Capitol. The banners, slogans, emotional speeches on both sides, and bickering between camps drew the press, and the demonstration was a featured news item. U.S. District Judge Warren K. Urbom ultimately denied Otey's request to halt the execution, and Otey was executed. Chambers responded to Otey's death with lethargy. He told the press that he considered his inability to preserve Otey's life a "deep personal failing."[12] Omaha resident Michael Welborn wrote the Public Pulse section of the *Omaha World Herald*, agreeing that Chambers had failed Otey, but not because he had not fought hard to prevent Otey's execution. "Chambers failed to learn the lessons of compromise ... preferring to browbeat lawmakers. ... He has failed to place the welfare of his constituents above his personal agenda, preferring to make himself a martyr while others suffer for the sake of his pride."[13] Chambers would be accused by more than one person of being egotistical. The lawmaker's retort was that he would love to have ten people with his stamina, who would not cut and run when trouble came. Imagine, he said, how much work could get done. Besides, the majority of Chambers's constituents were pleased with him. If not, would they have continued to send the senator back to Lincoln to represent them? Whatever eccentricities Chambers had were a part of the package.

Three more execution dates were approaching and the struggle against them would keep the political scene tumultuous. Chambers worked every angle that he knew to enact legislation to end state killings. He sponsored yet another bill to eliminate the death penalty and to provide a sentence of life without parole in 1997, but did not prevail. The following year during a special session of the Nebraska legislature, Chambers again lobbied for passage of a bill to prevent persons with disabilities from being subject to the death penalty. In 1999, he would sponsor Legislative Bill (LB) 76, calling for a moratorium on the death penalty while a study on the equity of the sentencing of death by state judges, by race and class, could be undertaken.[14]

In spite of Chambers's hard work, two more men would be executed in Nebraska before the end of the decade. Robert E. Williams was convicted of the rapes and murders of three women in the 1970s, Catherine Brooks, Patricia McGarry, and Virginia Rowe. Williams asked the senator to be present when his death sentence was carried out. Williams was executed in December 1997, and although Chambers did not witness the moment of death, he stayed with Williams until the executioners were ready, and remained at the prison until the convicted man's ordeal was over.[15] Otey and Williams were both African American and their victims white; however, the execution of John J. Joubert, a white man, was carried out in July 1996 with less hoopla. A child molester and murderer, Joubert had killed three boys, one in Maine (Richard Stetson) and two in Nebraska (Danny J. Eberle and Christopher Walden). Joubert's death discouraged public support for use of the electric chair, because during the electrocution Joubert's head blistered. Anti–death-penalty activists raised the question of whether Nebraska's electric chair constituted cruel and unusual punishment. Chambers remained hopeful that the impending execution of Native American inmate Randolph Reeves could be prevented. The senator again introduced a bill to abolish the death penalty in January 1999, one week before Reeves was scheduled to die. If Reeves were killed, it would be the state's fourth execution in just five years. Senator Kermit Brashear would eventually introduce LB 52, proposing that lethal injection replace the electric chair in Nebraska.[16]

Briefly, Chambers tasted victory when a moratorium replacing the death penalty with a life prison term (LB 76) was adopted by the legislature. However, before the end of the term, Governor Mike Johanns vetoed the measure. The stroke of a pen erased what had taken years to construct. For the senator the turn of events was like a bad dream. The one remaining positive aspect was the senator's sponsorship of a mandated study on the fairness of application of the death penalty (LB 76 A), passed into law when the solons overrode the governor's veto.

Chambers's commitment to end the death penalty had been recognized in November 1995 when the National Coalition to Abolish the Death Penalty presented Chambers with an award for his efforts. Now, in recognition of Chambers's valiant fight against state executions, the National Association of Criminal Defense Lawyers honored him with their Champion of Justice Award. The attorneys saluted Chambers for his introduction of anti–death-penalty legislation "every session of his thirty-two year career as a state senator."[17]

The death penalty battles had been fierce. Mid-decade, Chambers took time for some other political activities. Partially resulting from his disappointment with the slate of candidates running in the 1994 gubernatorial race, Chambers launched a "write-in" campaign for the governorship. In so doing, he skirmished with Allen Beermann, secretary of state, over what Beermann said was a requirement that a write-in candidate have a running mate. "I probably have better name recognition than anybody (else) in this state," Chambers quipped.[18] In the end, though, he chose Hispanic activist Jose Soto as his lieutenant governor hopeful. His campaign ultimately failed, however, in the at-large election against Ben Nelson.[19]

In October 1995, Chambers would set his sights elsewhere. He set his work aside momentarily to travel with other African American men to Washington D.C. to take part in the Million Man March. Chambers joined at least 400,000 brothers on the National Mall where the throng listened to Nation of Islam Minister Louis Farrakhan challenge black men to support each other's businesses and to take care of the black family. In contrast to then-retired General Colin Powell, who found the decision about whether to attend the march a "tricky issue," Chambers embraced it.[20] Nearly half a million men attended the event, with a significant contingent from North Omaha.

The march was an invigorating break from the regular day-to-day struggles of the community and the "hypocrisy" of the legislature. The latter had come to the fore for Chambers that spring when publicity over the publications of Neo-Nazi Gary "Gerhard" Lauck stirred the state legislature to consider a resolution condemning the racist literature that Lauck authored. German Consul General Gabriele von Malsen-Tilborch from Chicago told the press that Lauck's anti-Semitic materials had "flooded Germany," and made it appear that Lincoln, Nebraska, (where Lauck mailed his materials) was the headquarters of the U.S. Neo-Nazi Movement.[21] In spite of a resolution signed by many supporters, including the NAACP, the Lincoln Interfaith Council, and the Jewish Federation of Lincoln, among others, Chambers promised to oppose any resolution banning Nazi publications. Chambers said the measure was inappropriate as it would not have the force of law and would only add to the Nazi's stature. Anyway, Chambers said, the senators were being hypocritical: "The legislature did nothing" to stop "harassment by police" or to investigate "housing discrimination suits filed by blacks and a cross-burning at Southeast Community College in [nearby] Beatrice."[22] Moreover, the senator supposed that many "Nebraskans believe in the hate-filled doctrines that Lauck preaches."[23] The real reason for Chambers's lack of support for the measure was obvious only to those closest to him. The senator would never support a resolution limiting freedom of speech.

A report entitled the *Disproportionate Confinement of Minority Youth in Nebraska* supplied data to back up Chambers's complaints about inequalities in policing and in the criminal justice system. The study, published in 1993 by the University of Nebraska in cooperation with the Nebraska Commission on Law Enforcement, found that in 1991 twice as many minority youth were arrested as white youth, and that once inside of the criminal justice system, their rates of confinement—compared to white youths who committed the same offenses—were staggering. African American youth in the state were five times as likely to go to secure detention as their white peers who were arrested on similar charges and three times as likely to be sent to secure correction. Four times as many went to adult jails and five times as many African youth compared to white youth went to adult lock-up facilities. The report noted that in Douglas and Lancaster Counties, "minority youth were arrested at roughly two to three times their representation in the population.[24] Chambers was given a copy of the report and soon afterward took issue with Senator Jim Cudaback who offered an amendment to Crime Bill LB 371 calling for mandatory minimum sentences and the construction of a juvenile facility. Cudaback said that the juvenile facility could be built anywhere in the state. Chambers retorted that the "juvenile facility should be located near the area where most of the youths, who will be sent to the facility are from. These juveniles need to be near their families so they have some sort of support system," Chambers said.[25] "It is repugnant to view the juvenile facility as potential economic development for a rural area of the state."[26]

Chambers's criticisms of his colleagues could be unrelenting. In 1996, in an effort to silence the lawmaker at least some of the time, his fellow senators proposed a rule that would empower the speaker of the legislature to change the order in which amendments were debated. The problem confronting the solons was that they found themselves spending "all of their time debating minor amendments or amendments intended to delay action, a technique Chambers often use[s] to get other changes that he wants, before voting to shut off debate," wrote one newspaper reporter.[27] Senator David Landis said that the purpose of the new rules was "to cut into Ernie talking all the time . . . [but that] they do not work."[28]

Chambers's enemies sometimes commented on the senator's unusual confidence; supporters and foes alike would, with increasing frequency over the years, refer to the lawmakers' egotism. One reporter noted that Chambers claimed to transform "the Nebraska Legislature just by entering the Chamber."[29] All things considered, Chambers could not have been surprised when he lost another "bid" for the chairmanship of the Judiciary Committee. As usual, he would continue to serve on the committee anyway, this time noting, "I wouldn't miss it for the world."[30]

During standoffs like these Chambers found pleasure in writing poetry or in art, and the senator participated in a display of his artwork at the Black Rainbow Art Gallery in Omaha in February 1996. Gallery owner Oral Belgrave had opened the site at 1240 South 13th Street, to show and sell art by local artists. Chambers's sketchings of Malcolm X (El Hajj Malik El Shabazz) and Jacqueline Kennedy Onassis—depicted with fangs—were much discussed pieces at the exhibit. Chambers also lent his support to cultural activities such as the Malcolm X Memorial Foundation, which sponsors annual tributes at Malcolm's family's former home at 3448 Pinkney Street in Omaha. The celebrations are held each year on May 19, Malcolm's birthday, and not infrequently, Chambers was the featured speaker. Eventually, National Public Radio (NPR) would recognize the impact of Malcolm on the city of his birth with a Story Corps Project. NPR reporters interviewed North Omahans about Malcolm's impact on their lives. Chambers's old friend Charlie B. Washington would also be recognized, posthumously, when a branch of the Omaha Public Library was named after the North Omaha activist.[31]

As the twentieth century came to a close, marking Chambers's thirtieth year as an elected official, the senator's methods and his struggle were vindicated in unexpected places. In 1998, Dennis Smith, president of the University of Nebraska, wrote Chambers of his five-year plan to increase faculty diversity. Chambers had condemned the university for its failure to hire and retain a diverse body of professors. Smith wrote that "the benchmark calls for a minimum net gain of 12 minority faculty members per year for five years."[32] Another piece of vindication came in the form of an Omaha Conditions Survey compiled from data by the U.S. Bureau of the Census. The report revealed that unemployment rates for African American men exceeded those of all other groups combined. In the state's largest city, African American men were two to three times more likely to be unemployed at any age than any other member of the population, with the exception that African American males from twenty to twenty-one years of age were four and one-half more likely to be unemployed.[33]

The data suggested that problems Chambers had for so long described as confronting members of his community were not conjured up out of ego as some of his critics had suggested. In 1998, the Omaha Human Relations Board issued a report on police community relations. The board initiated their study after Marvin Ammons, an African American veteran of the Persian Gulf War, died in police custody of a gunshot wound, and in consideration of the subsequent indictment of Police Officer Todd Sears. The board responded to complaints that "some city residents were being unequally treated by some Omaha Police Officers."[34] Citizens complained about racist, unprofessional, and rude conduct by police. The board acknowledged that there was "little trust between law enforcement officers and minority citizens."[35] Board members offered recommendations to relieve problems, some of which Chambers had made as many as thirty years before. One suggestion was for the chief of police to devise a communications policy with "special emphasis on minority affairs."[36] The Omaha Police Department (OPD) needed to recruit more women officers and persons of color. Additional training and the formation of a complaint process that would be responsive to citizens was also needed, they said. Chambers was years ahead of his time, and there was something satisfying about having some of his message understood.

Although only a few Nebraskans probably read the essay in the *Washington Post*, the paper had published a one-page article on Chambers that attempted to explain the "method to the madness" in the senator's work.[37]

> Representing some 32, 000 citizens of Omaha in Nebraska's Eleventh Legislature District. . . . It is an impoverished constituency, with a high concentration of blacks and the twin scars of unemployment and blocked opportunity. . . . In the conservative state politics of Nebraska, the best he has been able to do on some bills is merely to ease the assaults on poor people instead of eliminating them. . . . In 1992, Chambers filibustered for eight hours against an amendment to cut welfare payments to pregnant mothers, seen by the by the majority as an enlightened way to save money.
>
> . . . Among his constituents, Chambers's caring about quality schools, job training and helping families secure medical and legal care is not seen as the work of a radical but of an honest, aggressive politician. It is only elsewhere that that is dismissed as effrontery.[38]

The new millennium opened with Chambers working long hours at his office in Lincoln. The more his colleagues tried to stifle his voice the more determined he became to work their rules to his favor. After a decade that had opened and closed with the other legislators united against Chambers and his filibusters, the senator seemed to relish taunting them. "I own this legislature, you all are my white folks. If a law must be passed, I will allow you to pass it. If I want to bring the legislature to a halt, I will do it."[39]

It was difficult after the turn of the century to deny that Chambers had enormous power. Some of the senators made him a plaque bearing the title "Dean" of the Legislature, and Chambers placed it on the wall in his office. By the year 2000, Chambers had served the legislature longer than any other senator still living. He was the Unicameral's most senior member and "master" of legislative rules. "Maybe I am like Houdini," Chambers once said, "you can put me in a box and in chains and when you open the box I'm gone."[40] For an article about his length of service, Chambers named some of his most important accomplishments: winning district elections for Omaha's City Council, Douglas County Board, and Omaha Public School District; the resolution to impeach Attorney General Paul Douglas; a statute to divest funds from apartheid South Africa; legislation opposing the death penalty; sponsorship of a bill allowing gay marriage; and his fight against a bill denying women the legal right to have an abortion.[41]

Back in 1997, Chambers had been the lone member of the Unicameral to oppose Nebraska's ban of partial birth abortions. During debate over the measure Chambers argued that the bill was not in line with U.S. Constitution or the U.S. Supreme Court's interpretation of the law. To the senator's delight, three years later, in 2000, the U.S. Supreme Court found the Nebraska law unconstitutional. Justice Sandra Day O'Connor had cast the deciding 5 to 4 vote. The high court ruled that "the Nebraska law included an exception only to preserve the woman's life."[42] O'Connor said that she would have been more likely to view the bill as allowable under the Constitution if it had included as an exception "to preserve the woman's health" and not just her life.[43] The state law was also too broad and too vague, according to the justices.

For his efforts on behalf of women, the Lincoln chapter of the National Organization of Woman (NOW) organized an "Ernie Chambers Appreciation Day."[44] On an afternoon in June, women from across the city gathered to recognize Chambers in the Park Middle School auditorium. The women's group had initially sought and received the governor's pledge to sign a proclamation from the state honoring Chambers for his years of service as a lawmaker. However, the venom that surfaced between Chambers and the governor had not dissipated with the end of the session. Chambers refused to participate if Governor Johanns attended. Chambers's habit of locking horns with Nebraska's governors had not diminished with his youth. In 2001, a *Lincoln Journal Star* reporter noted that Chambers and Johanns had dominated the legislative session all year. All eyes were on the "tenacious governor . . . and the clever senior senator, a master of the rules."[45] It was

Chambers's colleagues who approved the majority of the governor's proposals and who mustered the strength to override only two of Johanns's vetoes. In fact, one reporter wrote, most "senators spent the session seeing how close they could come to the Johanns plan. Meanwhile, the voice of Senator Ernie Chambers of Omaha filled the legislative chamber, slowing debate for days, forcing some senators to change or abandon their bills, and in the end assuring there would be no time for the controversial fetal homicide bill, which would make it a crime to kill an unborn child."[46]

NOW rearranged the program and had the proclamation come from their organization rather than from the state. The affair, without the governor and the pomp and circumstance that he would bring, still turned out well. A long-time member of the NAACP, Lincoln's Leola Bullock presented Chambers with some memorabilia that she had collected over the years. The items included a Chambers write-in for governor T-shirt and Chambers for attorney general buttons. Bullock's good friend, Lela Knox Shanks, read poetry. Some of the poems were written by Mondo we langa, the former member of the Black Panther Party, still in prison in Nebraska, and Willie Otey, who had been executed by the state. Shanks said to Chambers, "you lead us all kicking and screaming into the twenty-first century for human rights."[47]

Just weeks before the ceremony, Johanns had vetoed proposed legislation by Chambers intended to protect gay people's rights, and Chambers would probably never forgive the governor's vetoing of the death penalty moratorium for which the senator had labored long and hard, finally winning the approval of his colleagues. He's made "a mockery of everything I've done," Chambers said.[48] At sixty-three, Chambers did not feel that he had to go along for the sake of ceremony. NOW uninvited the governor so that Chambers would show up. The tribute was intimate, and Chambers made a rare public announcement in appreciation of Cynthia Grandberry, his legislative aide: "Anyone who could spend 29 years in my presence is entitled to this gathering far more than I."[49] After the formal ceremony, individuals approached Chambers to express their personal appreciation for the senator's diligence.

Chambers received many other commendations and compliments during his final two terms in office. Usually the recognition was sincerely meant, but on other occasions accolades were tongue-in-cheek. An example of the latter was a *Lincoln Journal Star* Opinion Page cartoon featuring caricatures of two of Chambers's colleagues. One of the solons held a book of legislative procedures and was practicing hitting his colleague over the head with it. The caption read, "opponents of veteran senator Ernie Chambers begin annual preparations to curtail his legislative maneuvering."[50] The inference was that the other senators' efforts to control Chambers using the legislative rule book were valiant, though futile.

Before the end of his career, Chambers would sponsor upwards of 500 bills, offer over 350 amendments and more than a dozen constitutional amendments, and would stop many pieces of what he felt was bad legislation from becoming law. His successful legislation included banning the death penalty for persons under eighteen years, "opening Omaha School Board meetings to the public . . . district elections . . . increasing training for sheriffs . . . providing medical services to low-income women with high-risk pregnancies . . . ending sex discrimination in state, county and city retirement programs," banning the rescinding of an athlete's scholarship because of injury, and requiring grand juries to convene in cases of the death of any person while being apprehended by police or in police custody.[51]

Noting his successes, Chambers sometimes emphasized that he had done much of the work while being criticized and standing alone. It would have been easy for anyone in his position to imagine—at times—that they had been abandoned even by the community that they served. Aside from a long-standing clique of socialites made up of teachers, doctors, and ministers and their wives (the airs of the latter were mitigated by church responsibilities), there was really only one class of African Americans in North Omaha when it came to political representation prior to 1980. However, class differences sharpened as the region became poorer as a result of the failure of family farms and of the packinghouses, and as opportunities for educated blacks simultaneously opened up. Omaha lost over 10,000 jobs as a result of the closure of the meatpacking plants and the end of employment for blacks who worked on the railroads was almost immediate. The number of unemployed African Americans began to rise sharply at the same time that job requirements began demanding training in computer technology. With inadequate preparation by many public schools, a number of urban youths became engaged in the dual "underground" economy. The scholar Clarence Munford argues that Rust Bowl deindustrialization impacted the Midwest severely during the 1980s, turning it into the region with the most extreme and widespread black poverty, surpassing even conditions in the American South. The region had the lowest black income in the nation, and no greater disparities between white and black incomes could be found. Though most of the old problems remained, by the turn of the twenty-first century many of the movers and shakers from the 1970s and 1980s were aging or moving on to other interests or locales. Rodney Wead, executive director of Wesley House, and Buddy Hogan, former head of the Omaha NAACP, were gone from Omaha but not forgotten. Bernice Stephens Dodd, who directed the Omaha chapter of the Opportunities and Industrial Center passed away on October 17, 2006, and Mildred Brown, publisher of the *Omaha Star,* died on November 1, 1989. Marshall Taylor, a member of the mature set, founded the Aframerican bookstore in the mid-1990s. During this time a new generation of leaders came to the fore in North Omaha. The younger set of educated African American elites in North Omaha were more inclined to speak out when they disagreed with Chambers than their parents generation had been. This trend created a tension between the old guard who stood behind Chambers because of the senator's practice of identifying with all community members—including those with very low income—and the new guard whose tendency was to believe that African Americans who remained impoverished did so, at least partially, out of a lack of initiative. This difference in perspective created some aggravation between the younger crowd of up-and- coming North Omahans and Chambers. Chambers took the opportunity to chide middle-class black men and lay bare the difference between them and the older, more inclusive tradition of leadership. When John Enslin of *Rocky Mountain News* in Denver called Chambers for a story he was writing on Mad Dads since a Denver coalition that was thinking about founding a chapter of the Omaha-based organization to combat their own problems with gang activity, Chambers's reply was tongue-in-cheek. He advised the reporter to tell the group to define their role in advance. Would they be an actual arm of the police department or would they simply be informants? At all costs the Denver group should avoid the gimmicks of the North Omaha Mad Dads (primarily ministers and other middle-class black men), who had used a helicopter to follow African American youths suspected of gang activities. Chambers's critique suggested that Eddie Staton and other members of a new class of African American leadership wished to avoid identification with African American urban youth, and were using their organization to demonstrate for the white power structure the separation between adult black men and the largely unemployed undereducated teenagers. Rather than make the effort a community initiative, which Chambers would likely have supported, the Mad Dads reported to the police. Those who care, Chambers said, should seek out the underlying problems that give rise to the undesirable behaviors.

Middle-class African Americans who held contracts from OPS were sometimes caught between the OPS district and the predominately African American community's interests. The senator tended to aggravate these delicately balanced relations by intermittently demanding an end to racist practices by OPS personnel. The alleged injustices included preferential placement of the city's best teachers outside of his district, lagging improvements in construction and technology, low expectations of students, and the occasional physical assault on an African American student by OPS personnel. Chambers noted that there were similarities between arbitrary violent beatings of African Americans under slavery and brutality on blacks in his district by persons in authority. In his *Omaha Star* article "The Fourth of July Barbecue, Bugs and Bondage," Chambers wrote that violence was meant to keep black people in their place. That police brutality was especially reserved for black citizens was acknowledged in the Kerner Commission Report of 1968, but Chambers charged that it remained a problem in Omaha into the twenty-first century. Police beatings or killings of unarmed black people also continued to occur nationwide. In 1992 alone, police assaults on unarmed citizens were reported in Teaneck, New Jersey; St. Paul, Minnesota; Indianapolis, Indiana; Los Angeles, California; and in other major cities. In one case, an African American police officer was killed by fellow policemen who claimed the shooting of their colleague was a case of mistaken identity. Mistrust between white and African American officers prompted the formation of the Guardians, a national black fraternal police association. Chambers supported the local black police fraternity, working closely with Marvin McClarty, Sr., and Tariq Al Amin, who were part of the leadership of the Brotherhood of the Midwest Guardians Association in Omaha.

In spite of North Omaha's expanding leadership base, most of the small but growing black middle class in Omaha would continue to show deference to Senator Chambers. They were apt, however, to exert their independence, collaborating at times among themselves without consulting the statesman, and working to build constituency bases both within and outside of the African American community. New politicians included Frank Brown, a former news reporter who had attended St. Benedict Church as a child, and who was elected serve on the Omaha City Council in 1997. Brown earned Chambers's endorsement for reelection as District Two Councilmember over Ben Gray in 2009, but Gray won out. Preston Love, Jr. (son of the renowned musician Preston Love, Sr.) was active in the state's Democratic Party. Joseph P. "Sonny" Foster served as an aide to a number of white mayors of Omaha, and Tommie Wilson took over the reins of the NAACP's Omaha branch following Reverend Everett Reynolds's tenure. Reynolds held the post for years after it was vacated by Buddy Hogan. Another well-known member of the black elite was Dick Davis. The Davis family opened Davis Insurance in 1971, and watched the agency grow into a multistate brokerage. Dick Davis now served as the chief executive officer for Davis Companies. As a way of giving back, Davis initiated a minority student scholarship for African Americans attending the Nebraska university system. On the other hand, his service on predominately white foundations as well as community development boards meant that he could act as gatekeeper to funds earmarked for African American community development. Tim Clark, the only African American on the Board of the Omaha Community Foundation, became well known for the Blues and Jazz Fest, which he organized annually beginning in the early twenty-first century at the Lewis and Clark Landing on the Missouri River. Of the newer public figures Chambers remarked, "all of the others . . . were tied into organizations and could expect support. . . . I'm not like those others. I've never been able to get support. I was alone out there. I was on my own."[52] Chambers said that he had only his conscience to lead him and that his reward was the reassurance that what he did was right. "I am what you might call a free radical."[53]

Last Stands

The senator's final years in office were bittersweet. Chambers reached the pinnacle of success as a lawmaker and politician through his unparalleled power in the Nebraska Statehouse, although he was resented in corresponding proportion by many people in the state. He also suffered personal losses through the deaths of a few very close friends, betrayal by members of his constituency, and the ultimate loss when he was forced from office by the passage of a constitutional amendment limiting each legislator's period to two consecutive terms. The accolades were numerous and the victories satisfying, but when set beside the repetitions of old injuries directed at Chambers personally or at his constituents, there was a marked muffling or at least abbreviation of the moments of celebration.

In February 2001, Chambers moved to amend a bill by striking its enacting clause. Chambers's amendment would in effect, make the bill null and void. The senator unraveled the riddle for his colleagues when he spoke on the measure. "When somebody who means something to me is publically embarrassed and humiliated, then I'm going to deal with the ones who did it in public."[54] Chambers introduced his comments with a parable.

If we have a situation where two people are involved, one white and one black, and let's say that there has been an advertisement in the paper that an apartment is for rent and people have made complaints that there's discrimination of a racial nature here because whenever a black person comes he or she is turned away, and that happens so regularly, white people would go into denial as some people around here are in denial and say, well, I don't believe there's anything racial.[55]

Chambers went on to describe an incident that had occurred that week in the State Capitol Building. A white woman was in front of Grandberry in line at a staffer's desk in the rotunda outside of the legislative chamber. The white women, another senator's legislative aide, was served politely. However, when Grandberry made the same routine request from the assistant sergeant-at-arms, she was ignored. During his inquiry about the failed interaction, Chambers was told that the worker in question could not hear Grandberry. "Well, he couldn't understand Cindy. That's the worst racist stereotype you can give when you say white people cannot understand a black person who is speaking English, and this is the first time I've ever heard anybody around here say they could not understand Cindy when she spoke."[56] The senator was livid; and given Grandberry's three decades as his legislative aide, he did not buy the argument that the staffer did not know Grandberry, either.

So that tells me if a Black person comes up and he doesn't know the Black person, the Black person can't get the service, but any White person can who is not known. . . . When I was critical of the Governor for not appointing women, nobody came and said, Ernie, you shouldn't say that . . . When I go after these judges who have sexually assaulted, literally, white women . . . I intervened . . . And now it comes to somebody who means something to me and I'm supposed to sit and be quiet after I've done all these things for white people?

I've got a kill motion on my bills, and if you want to really go through it and kill mine I don't care. . . . Nothing else matters. The sun that gives light and life has been eclipsed and I wish this had been a situation where I was in a restaurant or any place and a white man insulted this black women. . . . I'm not going to inflict physical violence on anybody, at least that's not my intention, so some people better stay away from me. . . . Now, we can decide how much that man [Hungate] means to this body and how much racism the Legislature is going to tolerate and put up with. It's going to be a long, long session.[57]

When Chambers finished speaking, Senator Landis rose to offer an apology to Grandberry on behalf of the Unicameral for the insensitivity that the legislative staffer and his supervisor had displayed.

Chambers continued:

We haven't dealt with teacher salaries or school aid. . . . There's a budget to be built. . . . And it may be necessary for the Exec Board to take over the hiring of some of these people so that the Clerk is not a buffer.

Can you try to conjure up a notion of what that may make you feel like. . . . You have two lines of people. They form a corridor and you put a camel between those lines and a basket on his back, and each person in that line, and by the way, the line stretches from here to California, each person takes a little pebble and throws it in a basket. In the same way that the ocean consists of a large number of droplets of water. . . . At some point an amount is going to be on that camel's back which the camel no longer has the strength to support, and when that final pebble is thrown in, that point of no longer being able to endure is reached. The camel collapses and the basket of pebbles crushes the camel . . . And nobody is responsible, but the camel lies there crushed as a result of the collective actions of like-minded people engaging in the same kind of conduct.[58]

Chambers said that the incident was not the first time that Grandberry had had problems with employees under the jurisdiction of the clerk of the legislature. Nor would it be the last time that Chambers defended a woman's right to be treated with respect in public spaces.[59]

A year and a half after the incident with Grandberry, Chambers publicized the verbal abuse of a woman, allegedly by Assistant Omaha City Prosecutor Michael A. Goldberg, using the case as an example of abuse of authority. The woman parked in Goldberg's parking stall. Goldberg used his vehicle to block her in. When the woman returned to her car, Goldberg allegedly held a can of mace close to her and demanded that she pay fifty dollars or all of the money that she had. Goldberg took eighteen dollars as payment for her having parked in his parking spot. Chambers felt that Goldberg had abused his authority, and recommended that he be charged with robbery. The senator filed a grievance against Goldberg and notified the state attorney general and the members of the legislature. The case against Goldberg was not pursued by the state.[60]

Born into a segregated world where racial thinking permeated much of American life, Chambers would fight even subtleties that begrudged African Americans equal treatment as citizens, and that submerged public acknowledgment of their accomplishments in any field of endeavor. For example, when sportswriters announced that Hank Aaron's record for home runs in baseball had been surpassed by Barry Bonds, Chambers felt that racism affected the tenor of the announcement. He sent a scathing letter to the Public Pulse section of the local paper, which the editor published.

> All of this hypocritical bleating and yakety-yakking by white sports commentators about an asterisk accompanying Barry Bonds' breaking of Hank Aaron's home-run record is cloying in the extreme. . . . If asterisks are to become the order of the day in the realm of sports records, one should accompany every so-called record established by any white athlete in any sport while black athletes were locked out of competition due to their race.[61]

The 2002 legislative session opened with Chambers's colleagues initiating another bill designed to make it easier to invoke cloture. Patrick O' Donnell, clerk of the Nebraska legislature visited Chambers's office that morning, while the senator and Grandberry were still having their coffee. O'Donnell wanted to discuss possible changes in the rules that would result from the bill. After the clerk left, Chambers said, "I'm like Muhammad Ali"; Ali always tried to beat his opponents psychologically before getting into the ring.[62] That year and the next would be especially poignant for Chambers and would call for some of the statesman's most effective leadership skills. Chambers would also see the cessation of political wars in some of the theaters to which he was accustomed.

By the turn of the twenty-first century a new generation of activists formed businesses, nonprofit corporations, and political alliances in North Omaha. Since most of the new cadre had grown up together, they easily combined in networks of interests groups. The turn of the millennium witnessed the growth of an Economic Empowerment Committee, which worked at organizing black-owned businesses, and which was headed by a popular married couple, Paul and Quinzola Penny. Ajamal Byndon and Lerlean Johnson were involved in a school desegregation suit against OPS; Reverend Everett Reynolds and the NAACP would continue to investigate complaints made against Douglas County Corrections. Barron X and Minister Bruce Muhammad organized the Omaha contingent of the Million Family March; Councilman Frank Brown continued the decades-long effort to create a Civilian Review Board to hear complaints against police officers. Brown's work met with some success when the city council created the Office of Independent Auditor. An old group of activists reformulated themselves under the name of Nebraskans for Justice, and sponsored a lecture by Angela Davis who was asked to speak on behalf of Mondo we langa (formerly David Rice) and Edward Poindexter, the local Black Panther Party leaders who had been incarcerated since 1970. Chambers, himself, would speak on an August afternoon in 2000 at the Douglas County Courthouse in support of "Mondo and Ed."[63]

Problems with police in North Omaha had not improved significantly over two or three decades, but they were no longer refutable. The OPD's *Annual Report for 2001* provided arrest data demonstrating that its officers arrested African American teenagers at rates entirely disproportionate to their numbers in the city's population. In terms of the numbers of arrests made, more African American teens were arrested for robbery, felony assault, burglary, motor vehicle theft, misdemeanor assault, fraud, buying stolen property, and sex offenses than whites or any other group. More African American adults were arrested for murder, robbery, felony assault, and drug violations than whites. These figures seemed more alarming considering that African Americans made up only about thirteen percent of the population of the city of Omaha. Most community members believed that the higher rates of crime reflected more intense scrutiny of black people by police and those stereotypes increased the likelihood that those arrested would be entangled in the criminal justice system.[64]

In July 2002, Chambers phoned Nebraska Director of Corrections Harold Clarke about the well-being of prisoners. Clarke said that he would abide by Chambers's request to stop relying on electronic drug detection to determine who could visit inmates. A number of women had complained to Chambers that the drug machine at the prison could be set off by household products, even hair coloring. The victory was a large one in the lives of families trying to visit their incarcerated relatives. The previous year, Chambers had sponsored legislation requiring the Department of Corrections to hire a medical director due to the excessive number of complaints from inmates about inadequate health care.[65]

Chambers's political power was undeniable, and a number of his fellow solons would, along with lobbyists, approach him requesting the personal favor that he let their bills survive. The senator was busy preparing for debate one April morning, when a lobbyist named Jim Cavanaugh stopped by. To Cavanaugh's salutation, Chambers answered, "I'm fighting it."[66] Cavanaugh said, "I have two bills up this morning."[67] "Well what's your other one, because I'm fighting the first one," Chambers said.[68]

In the middle of a whirlwind of work, constituents, and the always present media requesting interviews—Mollie Rae died. Chambers grieved openly the loss of the miniature poodle that had been his and Grandberry's pet for more than twelve years. On his public access television program on Channel 22, in his *Omaha Star* column, and on the floor of the legislature, Chambers memorialized Mollie Rae as his "best and truest friend."[69] After what was thought to be a routine surgery to remove a lump from the dog's side, Chambers found her at home lying near his bathtub. Chambers told the world, "I am being eaten alive daily. Sleep is broken; my appetite has fled." Chambers said he had been "rescued from being consumed by bitterness" by the pure spirit of Mollie Rae.[70]

Chambers's public expressions of deep grief over a dog raised a few eyebrows among non-pet owners. Some wondered aloud in the *Omaha Star* whether age had finally crept up on the senator. On the other hand, accolades over Chambers's beautiful eulogy of his pet flowed in from animal lovers across the Middle West and beyond. In spite of his depression, Chambers would press on that fall, preparing for a third special session of the 97th Legislature. It seemed that 2002 marked the entry of the other forty-nine states into step with international opinion that electrocution as a means of carrying out the death penalty was cruel and unusual punishment. All of the other states with death penalty laws still on their books had dropped electrocution as the means of carrying out capital punishment sentences. At the request of the governor and on the advice of some observers who felt that the U.S. Supreme Court might see Nebraska's mode of electrocution as in violation of constitutional provisions, the legislature considered changing the method of execution from electrocution to lethal injection.

During special sessions of the Unicameral, the solons debated LB 2, To Change the Method of Execution to Lethal Injection, and LB 1, which proponents argued added another layer of protection for Nebraskans against unfair application of the death penalty to the older provisions that the death penalty could not be imposed upon anyone under eighteen at the time of their crime (1982) and that the death penalty would not be imposed upon "any person with mental retardation" (1998).[71] The law would now require that a three-judge panel (voting unanimously) must decide if aggravating circumstance warranted use of the death penalty.

Chambers fought LB 1 and leveled heavy opposition against the switch to lethal injection, because the measures might have the undesirable effect of making execution *appear* more just or more humane. After a private meeting between Chambers and his colleague Kermit Brashear, "Brashear pushed to have the bill killed that would have changed Nebraska's method of execution to lethal injection." Reporters speculated that Chambers and Brashear had made a deal and that Chambers was "betting that because Nebraska [was] the only state with the electric chair as its sole means of execution, a court will deem it cruel and unusual punishment—leaving Nebraska without a means of executing people."[72] A buoyant Chambers told the press, "I doubt seriously that anybody will be executed in Nebraska again."[73] The proposal for LB 2, intended by the governor to strengthen the death penalty law, may have actually weakened it. A local newspaper reported that while Chambers appeared to have gone down in defeat, in fact, "the session bolstered his decades long quest to abolish the death penalty."[74]

Chambers's efforts were applauded by human rights activists in Nebraska. University of Nebraska Foundation Professor Paul Olson presented Chambers with a 2002 Peacemaker of the Year Award. Olson issued a statement in honor of the senator's lifetime of work.

> Nebraskans for Peace's Motto is "there is no peace without justice." Senator Chambers has lived that motto.... Justice for Senator Chambers has meant accepting no lunches from lobbyists and refusing no request from the downtrodden. It has meant stopping at least two bad pieces of legislation per session. It has meant enduring spoken racism and insult year after year and perennially living with a more insidious silent hatred. It has meant growing grey in the fight for peace and justice without growing stale in it. We shall not look upon his like again in Nebraska.[75]

Leola Bullock, long-time member of the Lincoln NAACP, agreed that Chambers deserved accolades. He could have been a wealthy man, she said, had he not chosen to dedicate his talents to public service. Other commendations would come, some of them in private by people who had quietly observed the senator over the years. Lela Knox Shanks, civil rights activist and former member of the Congress of Racial Equality, who made her home with her family in Lincoln after the 1960s, said that Chambers "used language in the public forum to achieve his ends."[76] He had his own style. She conjectured that Chambers's three-plus decades in the Nebraska legislature had probably cost Chambers close relationships and a feeling of safety. He became, she said, "a voice for the voiceless."[77] Others would describe Chambers's legacy in terms of his impact on the wider populace. State Ombudsman Marshall Lux once wrote that "no one has had more influence over Nebraska government in the last twenty years than Senator Chambers. When, one hundred years from now, historians write about Nebraska government, names like [Governors] Kerrey, Nelson, and Johanns will be footnotes."[78]

For many, Chambers's motives were less obvious, shrouded, as it were, by his rhetoric. Still others have found clues to the senator's thinking in his metaphors or in his references to verses in the Bible. In spite of his commentary over the years emphasizing human beings' lack of concrete knowledge about the existence of God, some of Chambers's remarks paralleled the deism that was popular among the nation's founders. A sect of Christianity, Deists believed that God set the world in motion and then left humans to work out their own affairs. "We don't need supernatural intervention to do the kind of things that have to be addressed." Chambers once explained his life's work in terms that could be construed as admitting the possibility of a final judgment. There might be another realm of existence, he said, and "it is an obligation . . . I've got a destiny to meet."[79] If good works were sufficient, then Chambers would certainly have paved his way to heaven.

On Monday July 21, 2002, Omaha City Council member Frank Brown and County Commissioner Carole Woods Harris joined Chambers in delivering a letter to the Douglas county attorney asking that charges be filed against the police officer who on July 19, 2000, had killed a man from Chambers's district. Chambers had been told that he would be accompanied to the Attorney General's Office by a throng of African American preachers, but only two or three ministers showed up. Brown, who had sent 100 letters to community members, appeared disappointed at the showing. The senator was not surprised. Most people were willing to talk, but few were willing to act.[80]

Chambers would use his use both his call-in show on public access television and his regular column in the *Omaha Star* to outline the George Bibins case. Quoting from his letter to County Attorney Jim Jansen, Chambers posited his appeal to Jansen to ask that he reconsider his "decision not to re-file charges against officer Jerad Kruse in the shooting death of George

Bibins."[81] Chambers noted that even Police Chief Don Carey could offer the public no justification for Officer Kruse's shooting of Bibins. Chambers described the scene. Bibins, an African American man, was in the jeep, and "Officer John Gruidel was standing on the driver's side of the jeep right by George Bibins and did not feel menaced or threatened. He did not do the killing. Kruse did as soon as he reached the vehicle."[82] When the grand jury declined to indict Kruse, Chambers informed Jansen that he would request an investigation by the U.S. Justice Department since "the shooting death of an unarmed citizen is of extreme concern to society."[83]

Police Officer Tariq Al Amin also condemned the killing of Bibins. Al Amin discussed the killing and a subsequent event on his television call-in show "Protecting the Village," and afterward endured threats from fellow police officers. More controversy arose when, in the wake of the Bibins's shooting, a local African American bishop named William Barlow gave $100 to the children of officer Jason Pratt, a policeman, who had been killed earlier that year. Instead of giving the memorial in his own name, Barlow made the donation in the name of the children of Albert Rucker, Pratt's killer, and an African American. Pratt and Rucker had each shot the other on September 11, 2003, while Pratt was attempting to arrest Rucker. Rucker died immediately, and Pratt passed away just a week later.[84] On his television talk show, Al Amin argued that Barlow's gesture was out of place. Barlow had not given money to any of the black families whose members were slain by white officers, including the still grieving Bibins household. On television, Al Amin held up a straight razor and said that "this" would be his gift to the children of Rucker so that they could "cut Barlow's throat." Acting Chief of Police Al Pepin interpreted Al Amin's commentary to be damaging to the image of the OPD and recommended that the veteran police officer be fired. In October 2003, Chambers dedicated much of his time to defending Al Amin. Chambers noted that Al Amin's comments were obviously rhetorical and that his intended viewing audience, the African American community, recognized them as such. After a formal hearing and an outpouring of community support, Al Amin's attorney successfully argued that Al Amin's comments were protected by his First Amendment right to free speech, and he was reinstated by the OPD. Shortly thereafter, Thomas Warren, the brother of Brenda Council, was sworn in as Omaha's first African American chief of police. Although he had not supported Al Amin in the Barlow controversy, Warren took steps to try and improve the policing of North Omaha. He challenged the tradition of allowing veteran officers to bid first for their "beats," assigning inexperienced officers across the city before the bidding process took place. Warren did not want to continue the long-standing practice of sending rookies into neighborhoods disdained by those with seniority. His plan to "ensure that rookie police officers didn't dominate one crew, one shift or one precinct" was interpreted succinctly by one commentator: "What it boils down to is that they just don't want all the rooks in North O." The police union filed suit against Warren, and Douglas County District Judge Joseph Troia ruled against Warren's plan and in favor of the police union. It seemed that one of Chambers's longstanding foes retained its power, despite years of battle.[85]

Signs portending a sad end to a long and in many ways magnificent career appeared in 2004. That the year would go badly was foreshadowed by the death of another close friend. Word had come that renowned jazz musician Preston Love was near death. Love, in his day, had played with the likes of Ray Charles, Aretha Franklin, Count Basie, Smokey Robinson, and Billie Holiday. He worked at Motown during the 1960s and had been Omaha's leading jazz artist after returning home. Chambers noted in his news column the week of Love's death that he had gone to the hospital to say goodbye. The senator no longer attended funerals, but he had to acknowledge Preston's transition from what had been an artistic and rich life. It was Love who had convinced Chambers to write a column for the *Omaha Star*, and Love was one of the people who read Chambers's essays and provided the senator with culturally based intellectual feedback. Out of respect, Chambers gave $1,000, or a month's wages, to the Preston Love Music Scholarship at Creighton University. "Au Revoir, Maestro," Chambers wrote in the *Omaha Star*, meaning literally "until we meet again."[86]

The other piece of bad news for Chambers was that his court battle against term limits for state legislators was failing. Four years earlier, residents of the state had voted in the affirmative for a constitutional amendment limiting members of the Nebraska Unicameral to two consecutive terms. The idea of term limits was fundamentally in opposition to the idea behind district elections, and, in Chambers's view, any attempt by the majority to control the choice of his constituency was nothing less than tyrannical.[87] Chambers told the press that the law's purpose was to circumvent the will of the people and remove him from office. Now it appeared that the majority would succeed in overwhelming him, and that the end was drawing near.

In the meantime, Nebraska would continue to be Nebraska and Chambers would be himself. A hate rally was held by members of the Neo-Nazi Party in conjunction with the Ku Klux Klan on the steps of the State Capitol building. Forty or so Nazis and Klansmen exchanged epithets with more than 100 protesters outside of the statehouse in mid-July. Nearby, a thousand of the state's citizens attended a diversity and peace rally in Pioneers Park, Lincoln's largest and most beautiful green space. Citizens had been invited for a day of fun and frolic to offset the negative press and ill will that the Nazi rally would generate. Chambers, who had other fish to fry, attended neither event. He felt compelled to condemn the American war in Iraq in writing, which he said was immoral and which could not be won. A few individuals argued that Chambers should support the troops regardless of why they were in Iraq and contested the senator's position on Chambers's open-mike cable television program. Chambers, however, thrived on debate and argued his own position using history and, occasionally, the Constitution as his primary sources of authority.[88]

Another horrible thing happened that year. Chambers was furious when he learned that Omaha police officers had obtained DNA samples from "dozens of black men who roughly fit the description of a serial rapist."[89] Many of those tested were professional men, who were contacted by police at their places of employment. The men who were tested ranged in height from about 5'8" to 6' tall, and many did not fit the description of the attacker at all. The senator soon learned that the episode had another purpose—that of acquiring names in order to fill the requirements for a federal grant. When none of the men's DNA matched the sample taken by police, Chambers argued for oversight in police use of DNA testing in criminal investigations. In the wake of the police sweep of black men, the lawmaker expressed his bitterness to a *Mother Jones* reporter. Nebraska is "a terrible place to be. It is an ultraconservative, ultraracist state. I would not advise anybody black to come here."[90] Back in the Unicameral, the senator sponsored a bill to address the use of DNA in police work. Chambers's bill would require probable cause of a suspect's involvement in a crime before DNA could be sampled. The measure passed unanimously.[91]

Awards were presented to the senator with increasing frequency during Chambers's final term in the Unicameral, and 2005 was especially punctuated with accolades. That year Chambers joined a host of other famous midwesterners in an Omaha-Lincoln Hall of Fame special report edition of the *Lincoln Journal Star*. The cast of greats included William Jennings Bryan, Johnny Carson, Malcolm X, Bob Gibson, Hilary Swank, as well as convicted mass murder Charles Starkweather, and other luminous as well as unsavory but still famous figures. Since the requirement for inclusion was only that one be well known, the value of having been included in the Hall of Fame was somewhat dubious. An honor bestowed upon Chambers in Omaha was more clear. Chambers's name was set in stone when the Omaha Housing Authority partnered with the city of Omaha and the Department of Housing and Urban Development to open an affordable housing complex, which they christened "Ernie Chambers Court."[92] Chambers's acceptance of the honor was signaled by his attendance at the groundbreaking ceremony on site near 17th and Grace Streets.

In January, Chambers and Dr. Marguertia Washington both received the state's Dr. King Humanitarian Award for "Living the Dream" in recognition of themes from the life and work of Dr. Martin Luther King, Jr., in their careers. Washington, the niece of the *Omaha Star*'s founder Mildred Brown, served as editor of the state's only surviving African American weekly, and Chambers was the lone African American legislator in the state.[93] Chambers would also receive a "Hero of the First Amendment" award that year. He traveled to Orlando, Florida, to accept the commendation during the Twenty-eighth Annual Convention of the Freedom from Religion Foundation. The senator gave an address to mark the occasion titled "First Amendment: Last Bastion."[94]

Aware that his days in office were numbered, Chambers guarded, as carefully as anyone could, his own legacy. He disdained any gesture that pointed to him as second best. Once, he mistakenly thought that he had been selected as the recipient of the Humanist of the Year Award, only to find out that the nominating committee had recommended him for their distinguished service commendation and not for the Humanist Award itself. The latter went to Pete Stark, the U.S. Representative from California who made a public announcement of his atheism—a first for a member of Congress. Chambers refused to accept the lesser award.[95]

Another year that had begun on an extraordinarily high note turned shrill with condemnation—this time from home. In 2005–2006, the senator ran into an unprecedented and emotionally embittering mutiny, spearheaded by members of his community. The ordeal began in the statehouse, when Chambers's colleague Senator Ron Raikes introduced Legislative Bill 1046 to reorganize the OPS district into a "learning community" that would focus on improving the education offered to area students. Omahans had long complained that OPS was too large. Senator Chambers added an amendment to LB 1046 providing for the division of OPS into three separate school districts. Ben Gray, host of the *Kaleidoscope* television program, on which Chambers had appeared with some regularity for years, publically criticized Chambers's amendment. Attorney Brenda Council—whose seat on the Omaha City Council was owed to a similar measure (one which allowed for district-level control of the elections of city council members)—also criticized Chambers's amendment. Gray and Council were joined by Charles Parks. All three reacted to what they felt was a measure that would resegregate OPS.[96] Although they had each held the senator in high regard over the years, some of Chambers's commentary of late, including his public doting over his pets (Chambers and Grandberry acquired a second poodle after the death of Molly Rae), raised questions for some people. On the other hand, a thorough reading of Chambers's amendment made it clear that any claim that Chambers was attempting to resegregate the public schools in Omaha was a gross misinterpretation of Chambers's intentions. The amendment made no recommendations relative to the race of the future student population that would make up the student bodies of each district. Rather the amendment referenced only current student populations. The district proposed for Omaha's Northside would fall between fifty-one and fifty-five percent African American. Chambers's amendment did not address students at all, but instead offered a plan for the existence of three separate smaller school districts. One consequence of the change would be to enhance local control of public schools, including those schools in the proposed district where most of Chambers's constituency resided.[97]

Attorney Council opposed Chambers's amendment to LB 1046 for the formation of three separate school districts. Council had remained in good standing with the Democratic Party over the years and Chambers's plan was highly unpopular in political circles. Council said that she feared the change would "only institutionalize racial isolation."[98] Gray, in addition to being a journalist, was co-chair of the OPS African American Achievement Council. Gray said that passage of the school reorganization bill and Chambers's amendment in particular was "a disaster."[99] Chambers responded to Omaha's black elite who criticized his strategy by pointing out that the plan included a requirement for shared financial resources with the other districts. "I have a plan that will work . . . and that's what has got the 'important' white men and these Negro stooges squealing. When have you ever seen rich and powerful white men worried or concerned about anything Mr. Parks said or anything that poor Ben Gray, my friend, has said?"[100] "My intent," Chambers said, "is not to have an exclusionary system, but we, meaning Black people, whose children make up the vast majority of the student population, would control."[101]

Having had his idea disparaged by some of the leading figures in the community—people who had previously admired him—was greatly unpleasant and left Chambers feeling betrayed. The only upside was that regular working folks did not seem to fall in line behind the upper- and middle-class blacks who opposed him. As usual, Chambers stood his ground, pointing out the dismal test scores—on average—of North Omaha pupils at their current schools compared to the average scores of youth attending West Omaha schools. Urged on by the members of Omaha's black middle class and OPS district personnel, the national office of the NAACP filed a lawsuit against Chambers whom they said was trying to resegregate OPS.

To its credit, the *Omaha Star* continued to run Chambers's column (in good times and in bad), showing support for the politician in spite of the complaints of some readers about the adversarial tone of Chambers's essays. The *Star*'s editorials, some of which focused pointedly on subjects that the senator had indicated were of importance to him, also expressed the newspaper staff's political leanings. For instance, the *Star* was in support of the family of a missing child. For months the paper ran a front-page advertisement asking for any information about a missing twelve-year-old girl named Amber Marie Harris. There was considerable frustration in the community over why police seemed to have no leads with respect to the case. Omaha's African American Police Chief Thomas Warren said that when the girl did not go home on November 29, 2005, after exiting her school bus about four blocks from her house near Pinkney Street and Florence Boulevard, the police did an initial search and then listed Amber as a runaway. The police changed Amber's status to that of an endangered child four months later when they received an anonymous tip on where to find Amber's backpack. In the meanwhile Amber's parents, Michael and Melissa Harris, were asked by police to take lie detector tests, as they waited in vain for news that their child had been found and was safe. Finally in May 2006, Amber's body was found in Hummel Park in a shallow grave. Roy Ellis, a convicted child molester, was charged with her death. From the time Amber was reported missing until the day her body was found, the *Omaha Star* ran the front-page advertisement asking anyone who had seen the child to come forward, ensuring that no one forgot the girl in spite of what some charged was the OPD's lack of effort in the case because the missing child was black.

Other activists followed Chambers's example and began taking up the mantle of police criticism in hopes of holding the OPD administration accountable. Paralleling Chambers's stance, Matthew C. Stelly, who ran an unsuccessful campaign for a seat on the Nebraska state legislature from District Eight in 2006, condemned a rash of invasions by police into people's lives and homes. He described one case in which a fourteen-year-old African

American boy was interrogated at police headquarters for two hours without his parents or an attorney present. Stelly reported that the officers involved in the ordeal told the boy's mother that her child had better "tell on someone by Wednesday" or that they would kick the door in and get him. In another scenario, a ten-year-old boy was home alone when officers searched the house then shot the boy's dog before ransacking the parents' bedroom. The family's "crime was that their grown daughter who lived across town had a boyfriend who police thought may have robbed a bank. Chambers was so frequently disgusted with the abuse of authority by officers of the law, that even kindly gestures by law officers did not set well with him. When a member of the Nebraska State Troopers Office called to ask Chambers's birth date in order to send a card, Chambers asked Grandberry to send the reply that they could keep the card and just stop harassing him on the interstate. Misunderstood and increasingly alone, a disgruntled Chambers would remark to those who could hear him that whenever trouble came, most people "cut and run."[102]

Underlying the social problems in Omaha of expanding black and white working-class poverty and eroding hopes for improved race relations was the failure of the Omaha city fathers to replace Omaha's industrial core after the demise of the meatpacking plants and railroads with anything beyond telemarketing (which offered few benefits, lower wages, and were nonunion). The absence of living-wage labor jobs took an enormous toll on North Omaha. Organized street gangs began to surface in the city, and rank-and-file members worked efficiently, cordoning off territory for their trade networks. By the early twenty-first century, the shootings of and by gang members resulted in black-on-black killings that rivaled the number of police shooting of African Americans in Omaha over a period of years. Another result of the economic downturn was increased pressure on the poorest sector of Omaha's population to find ways to survive. As a result, the number of arrests and incarcerations for African Americans, which had always been disproportionally high, spiraled upward. At the same time, rural whites were under similar economic straits and also sought relief. However, whites' survival strategies converged with blacks in ways that were still more harmful to the life chances of African Americans in North Omaha. An ongoing discrepancy in the U.S. justice system since the heyday of sharecropping has been that the percentage of African Americans (and more recently Latinos and other Spanish-speaking persons) fill prisons out of proportion to their percentages in the population. The ratio of African American prisoners at the Nebraska State Penitentiary for decades held at slightly over forty percent, despite that the population of African Americans in the state was at best three percent. Some scholars have drawn comparisons between prisons—reconstructed in the 1990s to yield profits—and the plantation system of the American South. Thus, in spite of what more than a few local commentators described as Chambers's rants about institutional racism, the senator prepared one well-documented argument after another damming racial and economic injustice. His weekly column in the *Omaha Star* condemned Nebraskans for considering the construction of for-profit prisons. "I have always taken deep offense at white communities seeking prisons in order to boost their local economies while being adamantly opposed to nonwhite people moving into their communities as residents." Chambers and his colleague DiAnna Schimek fought against the entry of for-profit prisons into the state of Nebraska. Chambers's rationale was that once constructed the private prisons would need to be filled and that those without adequate legal representation, those already stereotyped, would become fodder for the prison mills. Some community members hoped that the African American community's struggles in Omaha could be alleviated by electing or appointing even greater numbers of folk to serve on the local governing boards. Thus, some individuals worked to get blacks selected to serve on the Metropolitan Entertainment and Convention Authority (MECA) of Omaha. At that juncture, MECA had an all-white board due to its failure to reappoint Michael Green, the lone African American incumbent, and overlooking the nomination of Phyllis Hicks, marketing director from the *Omaha Star*. When Hicks was rejected, the *Star*'s publisher and editor Marguerite Washington was livid. Washington, niece of the late Mildred Brown, wrote a front-page condemnation of MECA, warning African Americans in Omaha that they had better wake up and run for seats on some of the boards in the city in order to "make your discontent and voices heard. There are enough of us talented and articulate people to make a difference. This will force them to deal with us. Aren't you tired of always being controlled and led by others?" Searching for a way to explain his middle-class constituency, Chambers would spend some time philosophizing. People are like "children playing in a sandbox. They need to be cared for and sometimes even need to be talked to bluntly."[103] Anyone who knew Chambers could see that betrayal by community members, especially those who had looked to him for guidance and strength over the years, was unforgiveable. On the other hand, if their refusal to condemn the senator was any indication, Omaha's African American working class, Chambers's real constituency, for the most part assumed that Chambers was catching grief (as always) because he was representing their best interests. Most working-class African Americans in North Omaha would have agreed with *Washington Post* reporter Colman McCarthy, who a decade earlier had described Chambers's methods and the subsequent reaction of the status quo with the adage, "in a world of stagnant air, a strong breeze is called a hurricane."[104]

With time winding down Chambers went on the offensive, attempting to convince the Nebraska Supreme Court to suspend state executions until the court could be assured that the death penalty was handled in a way that was permissible under both federal and state constitutions.[105] He had repeatedly argued that a disproportionate number of men-of-color wound up on death row and that whites who committed similar crimes were given life prison sentences instead. In a letter to the court at the impending electrocution of Carey Dean Moore, Chambers wrote, "I approach this court in my capacities of lawmaker, citizen, human being."[106] Chambers asked that the dignity of condemned persons not be disregarded in the haste of the system to inflict punishment. Moore's death order was subsequently stayed by the court, which a short time later declared that electrocution was cruel and unusual punishment. It would be difficult for anyone disagree with a *Mother Jones* article that reported that local people thought Chambers fit into the tradition of populist leaders in the state. "Ernie comes out of the 1960s, but if you take a step back you can see that it's another aspect in the same vein.... Instead of oppressed farmers it's oppressed minorities."[107]

The senator's colleagues were queried by reporters during his last term in the Unicameral. What would the legislature be like without "King Cobra" (one of the many nicknames Chambers had given himself)? Most said that they did not know. They could tell the press, they said, about Chambers's quests for vengeance on the statehouse floor. When upset, the senator's wrath became infamous in its own right. The media had long ago caught on that the metaphor "King Cobra" referred to Chambers's "venom."[108] Though he had lived seven decades, Chambers would still take on the entire body of the Unicameral in battle. "Freshmen lawmakers responded with a mixture of admiration and trepidation," primarily because of Chambers's habit of cross-examining his colleagues on the details of their bills.[109]

Chambers would leave office in January 2009 along with fourteen other solons whose terms of service had expired. Near the end, Chambers's colleagues surprised him by voting to have the Judiciary Committee Hearing Room in the state capitol building named after him. The reasons that they gave were that Chambers was the Nebraska state senator with the greatest seniority and a long-time member of the Judiciary Committee. But there were those who would say that Chambers's uniqueness as an intellectual and dominance as a political figure were so great that even his enemies had to pay him homage. The members of the Unicameral knew better than anyone that he had never deviated from his impassioned commitment to protect regular folks from the interests of the powerful and wealthy.

From the leading Black Nationalist in Middle America to one of the region's most influential statesmen, Chambers's political journey was truly unparalleled. He spent his first decade as a senator fighting institutional racism, which had a direct daily impact on his constituency and consolidating his power. His Black Nationalist sentiment and legislative skill converged in 1979–1983 with his South African divestment measures. Conscious of his unusual ability to debate the law, Chambers ran for leadership positions within the Unicameral, for state attorney general, for a seat in the U.S. Senate, and for governor. His lack of allegiance to the Democratic Party and his failure to participate in the patronage of the two-party system would prohibit his rise to the top leadership positions in Nebraska, thereby denying him entry into national politics. Chambers adjusted his strategy, and from 1985 forward the senator used his prowess as a statesman—having long become master of the legislative rules—and his political aptitude (making it his business to know which bills were most important to each of his peers) to dominate the legislative process. He threatened and delivered filibusters to coerce his colleagues into cooperating with him in hundreds of instances. Having risen as far as he could without leaving his community behind or softening his demands for social justice, the senator would spend another twenty years fighting oppression from within the body politic. Lela Knox Shanks was invited to speak during a formal dedication ceremony of the Judiciary Committee Hearing Room in Chambers's name, even as the senator was being forced from office. The community activist noted that it was poignantly appropriate to dedicate a chamber where justice issues are debated to the indomitable Senator Chambers.[110]

After thirty-eight years of public service, Chambers hurriedly packed in order to move out of his office in the state capitol building by opening day of the 2009 legislative session.

On the drive home, it would have been difficult not to assess his career. He had won a good share of his battles, yet he had the feeling that fate had played a trick on him: what started out as a mere temporary expedient in the overall struggle had appropriated much of his life. Along the highway, remnants of corn and soybeans lay motionless on the dark Nebraska soil. The same grey sky that had accompanied him on many winter days on his way into work was overhead. Beside him, his companion of so many years sat reading. Nothing seemed to have changed during the decades that he had held office. As for himself, he was still both hated and loved by the state's population, and the forces against him—by some cruel fate—had been granted this final victory. After much musing, the former senator no doubt found solace in the fact that he had given his all.

In interviews during the early days of his retirement, Chambers told reporters that he did not like the way that his career ended, saying, "I got kicked out."[111] But it was impossible to miss the pride that he exuded for having served his constituency and the state with such single-minded purpose and for so long. Floor debate without him, he surmised, would probably be dull. "You'll have to listen intently to hear a heartbeat now," Chambers said. "That's not a boast . . . it's just the way that it was."[112]

Afterword

His career in the Unicameral behind him, the former state senator would now turn his attention to the Douglas/Sarpy County learning community. The body, to which Chambers was duly elected, formed after passage of the controversial School District Reform Bill (LB 1046). Chambers was sworn in on January 9, 2009, and at seventy-one years of age, set his hands to improving Omaha's public schools for all children.[1] A day earlier, on January 8, the first day of the 2009 legislative session, senators brought members of their families to observe the swearing-in ceremony and festivities. Brenda Council, North Omaha resident and attorney, had won the legislative seat vacated by Chambers. As Council took the oath of office, the former senator looked on from the rear of the legislative chambers. "It was essential . . . for the constituents in the district I once represented to see [I support] her and the changing of the guard."[2] The most significant news of the day, however, appeared to escape the press. Cynthia Grandberry, Chambers's legislative aide of thirty-six years, appeared with Council and would work for the new senator in her usual capacity for at least one session. Chambers would continue to influence the legislature, for now, and Council would benefit from Grandberry's expertise in both the mundane matters of legislative protocol and in weighty deliberations in the interests of the community. Although he had not directly groomed a successor, in the end, Chambers made sure that the power and prestige that belonged to the representative of the Eleventh Legislative District did not perish.

Acknowledgments

The following individuals and agencies deserve recognition for their helpfulness in making this research possible. Thanks to the staff at the Charles B. Washington Branch Library in Omaha, Nebraska, for making sure that I had access to all of the available historical documents on North Omaha. Karen F. Koka, former curator of manuscripts, Library/Archives Division of the Nebraska State Historical Society, trained me in the processing of manuscript collections. Diana Bridges, legislative records historian, Brad Boesen, and the staff in the Clerk's Office at the Nebraska state capitol building gave helpful hints as I went through microfilmed copies of floor debate and legislative hearings. Casey Coleman, librarian at the *Lincoln Journal Star*, searched for articles that I could not find anywhere else. Phyllis Hicks and Dr. Marguerita Washington allowed me to peruse photos at the *Omaha Star*. Michelle Gullet of the *Omaha World Herald*, Matthew Lutts of the *Associate Press*, and Tami Pederman of the *Lincoln Journal-Star* all helped me to find needed photographs. Miranda Rivers scanned photographs with care as did my dear friend Neville Murray, who later served as executive director of the Love's Jazz Arts Center in Omaha. Wyatt Houston Day, a nonresident fellow at Harvard University's Afro-American Studies Department, and a manuscript appraiser, looked over the Chambers Collection, read the prospectus for the research that has grown into this book, and gave useful feedback. Chambers's lifelong friend, Dan Goodwin, supported Chambers in most all of his endeavors, and so an outline of Goodwin's own much needed biography may be hinted at in the present work. Journalist Ben Gray willingly shared his extensive cache of videotaped interviews of Senator Chambers. I am appreciative of my dissertation committee, who laid the foundation for the present work: Drs. Jeannette Jones, Kwakiutl Dreher, Learthen Dorsey, and especially Venetria K. Patton, director of African American Studies and Research Center at Purdue University, who has become a friend as well as a mentor. I am also especially pleased to thank my primary advisor from graduate school and through my first posts as an assistant professor, Dr. John R. Wunder. His belief that there are multiple reference points from which to approach the past and his love of historical inquiry allowed me to survive graduate school. He has also, I am happy to say, become a friend. Dr. Brian Johnson, former chief of staff at Johnson C. Smith University, supported my application for the sabbatical that allowed me to complete this manuscript.

A generous grant from the UNCF Mellon Foundation provided financial support for my research and was made possible through the wise collaborations of Dr. Cynthia Neal Spence, director of Mellon Programs for UNCF, and the late Dr. Rudolph Byrd, director of the James Weldon Johnson Institute For Interdisciplinary Studies (JWJI) at Emory University. I also benefited from being in the presence of (at nearly every JWJI event) Beverly Guy-Sheftall, Anna Julia Cooper Professor of Women's Studies and English at Spelman College. The welcome that I received from my colleagues at the JWJI and the intellectual environment that they shared with me has been the richest experience of my academic life thus far. I am (again) most appreciative of JWJI Director Dr. Rudolph Byrd for his vision and execution of plans to create a space for research for scholar-activists; Dr. Calinda Lee, assistant director of the JWJI; Dorcas Ford Jones, administrative assistant; and visiting scholars Drs. Robbie Lieberman, Trimiko Melancon, and Joshua Price, for their determination to forge a nexus between the pursuits of excellence and justice. The JWJI has modeled this path.

This book would not have been published without both the guidance and the patience of Judith Keeling and everyone at Texas Tech University Press. My children, Akhenaten, Eliga, and Daleelah, while busy with their own creations (as it should be), communicated perfect confidence in me—feeding my spirit like nothing else can. Matt J. Johnson, my husband of many years and a lifelong friend, helped me with the technical aspects of this book. Julie Ann Brown, Lateefah Coleman, and Deresa Hall offered encouragement and recollections from their lived experiences in Nebraska. My play nephews Mark Johnson and Amirre Micah (Prince) William Brown provided heartfelt and soul-refreshing smiles. My mother, Anna Ruth (Mead) Hopkins, read a near-final draft and gave excellent suggestions on style as well as on content. Finally, thank you to Senator Ernest Chambers and Legislative Assistant Cynthia Grandberry for embracing the project in its earliest stage and for allowing me access to their rich historical documents.

Notes

Introduction

1. Jeanne Theoharis and Komozi Woodard, *Ground Work: Local Black Freedom Movements in America* (New York: New York University Press, 2005), 4.
2. Ibid., 11–12.
3. Ibid., ix, 7, 12; John Dittmer, *Local People: The Struggle for Civil Rights in Mississippi* (Chicago: University of Illinois Press, 1994).
4. Robbie Lieberman, scholar of American Studies, and others have noted that building a movement and building an organization are not synonymous. See *Building Movement Inspiring Activism in the Nonprofit Community* (New York: Building Movement Project) available at: www.buildingmovement.org, retrieved July 2009. Chambers's brand of Black Nationalism with its insistence on self-defense and the expectation of self-reliance, which it inherently implied, has a parallel of sorts in the independent zeal of activists from other largely agricultural states where movements took shape in the "outback" or in places where the ideal of nonviolence in a physical wilderness had little appeal. See Theoharis and Woodard, *Ground Work*, for a more detailed explanation. See also Charles Payne, *I've Got the Light of Freedom: The Organizing Tradition and the Mississippi Freedom Struggle* (Berkeley: University of California Press, 1995), 204–5.

Chapter One

1. Chambers, letter to A. V. Sorensen, Omaha, 28 March 1967; "Police Reinforcements Go on Duty in Omaha," *Lincoln Star*, 6 March 1968, 3; Frederick C. Luebke, *Nebraska: An Illustrated History* (Lincoln: University of Nebraska Press,

1995), 336; "Funeral Program of Malcolm D. Chambers," 6 November 1995, 2. Ernest Chambers obtained his Federal Bureau of Investigation file by filing a request with the federal agency as allowed under the Freedom of Information Act (1977), see "Ernest William Chambers Omaha, Nebraska 1961–1976," Black Nationalists and Hate Groups Files (Washington DC: Federal Bureau of Investigation, 1977) [hereafter cited as "Ernest William Chambers," F.O.I. File, *page number*)], 9. "Chambers's Father Is Dead at Age 88," *Associated Press*, November 5, 1988; Lowen V. Kruse, *Omaha the Prairie Blossoms: Accounts of Religious Initiative in Relation to Social Change* (Omaha, NE: Paradise Publishing, 2001), 226–35. Slavery was made illegal in Nebraska in 1861. Bertha W. Calloway and Alonzo N. Smith, *Visions of Freedom on the Great Plains: An Illustrated History* (Virginia Beach: Donning Co., 1998), 11, 61, 67–69, 80. The September 29, 1919, lynching of Will Brown occurred after weeks of local newspapers warning citizens about attempted rapes of Caucasian females by black men. Douglas and Emma Williams Chambers, migrated from West Point, Mississippi, about 1917. Cynthia Monroe, a lay genealogist, has traced Chambers's family history back to the plantation in Mississippi where they were held as slaves. For more information, see the Chambers Family Papers in the Chambers Collection. Robert McMorris, "Sun-Up Interview: Malcolm Chambers," *Omaha World Herald*, 23 August 1969, 14. "Funeral Program of Malcolm D. Chambers," 1–3.

2. See also Robert D. Miewald, *Nebraska Government and Politics* (Lincoln: University of Nebraska Press, 1984), 123–24, 152.

3. Calloway and Smith, *Visions of Freedom on the Great Plains*, 11, 61, 67–69, 80. Kruse, *Omaha the Prairie Blossoms*, 232, 234–35. Scholar Trimiko Melancon and the author discussed a mutual observation that African American communities experience the greatest degree of racial group identification in inverse proportion to their percentage of the population.

4. Calloway and Smith, *Visions of Freedom on the Great Plains*, 66; Kruse, *Omaha the Prairie Blossoms*, 226–34; Harry B. Otis and Donald H. Erickson, *E Pluribus Omaha: Immigrants All* (Omaha: Lamplighter Press, 2000), 124–27. See "Social Settlement (Omaha, Nebraska)" Archives Collection Record, Lincoln, Nebraska: Nebraska State Historical Society, (March 2002).

5. Otis and Erickson, *E Pluribus Omaha*, 226–34.

6. Calloway and Smith, *Visions of Freedom on the Great Plains*, 64–65. For a description of kingship and royal leadership among the Palmares of Brazil, Stuart B. Schwartz, *Slaves, Peasants, and Rebels: Reconsidering Brazilian Slavery* (Chicago: University of Illinois Press, 1996), 122–23; Chambers, "The Voice of Thy Brother's Blood Crieth from the Ground," in Mona Bazaar's *Black Fury II* (Los Angeles, CA: Open City L.A., 1970), 11; William Loren Katz, *The Black West* (Garden City, NY: Doubleday, 1971), 167. In 1914, H. J. Pinkett helped to start an Omaha Branch of the NAACP, see H. J. Pinkett. *An Historical Sketch of the*

Omaha Negro (Self-published, 1937), 7–8, 31–35.
7. Pinkett, *An Historical Sketch of the Omaha Negro*, 34.
8. Ibid., 35.
9. Ibid. Information on the geographical dimensions of North Omaha was provided by Nancy Cyr, director of research for the Nebraska state legislature, July 7, 2011. In 2011, District Eleven—which roughly equates to North Omaha, the area represented by Chambers—measured at 8.84 square miles.
10. Ibid.
11. Chambers, interview by author, 9 April 2002.
12. Ibid.
13. Chambers, interview by author, 23 July 2002.
14. Pinkett, *An Historical Sketch of the Omaha Negro*, 36.
15. Ibid.
16. Ibid., 36–40.
17. Ibid., 40–45.
18. Ibid., 41, 52; Chambers, interview by author, 27 May 2003. For an explanation of African secret societies, see Margaret Washington Creel, *A Peculiar People: Slave Religion and Community Culture Among the Gullah* (New York: New York University Press, 1989).
19. Pinkett, *An Historical Sketch of the Omaha Negro*, 40–45, 53–55.
20. Lawrence H. Larsen and Barbara J. Cottrell, *The Gate City: A History of Omaha*, (Lincoln, NE: University of Nebraska Press, 1997), 156.
21. Ibid., 163.
22. Ibid., 163–65.
23. Ibid., 165–66, 168, 171. The higher-ups that Pinkett referred to included Jack Broomfield, who was a leading politician in Omaha after 1900. James Dahlman was the mayor of Omaha from 1906–1930.
24. Larsen and Cottrell, *The Gate City*, 169, 171. An estimated 5,000 people witnessed the lynching outside of the courthouse.
25. "Fifty-percent of Negro Homes," *Lincoln Star*, 1 March 1950, 12; Calloway and Smith, *Visions of Freedom on the Great Plains*, 86–87, 91.
26. "Dreams Realized by SBA Loan," *Omaha World Herald*, 20 July 1969, 8; Kruse, *Omaha the Prairie Blossoms*, 239–40.
27. "Church Segregation Attacked at Forum," *Lincoln Star*, 7 February 1958, 2; Rayford W. Logan, *The Negro in the United States: A Brief History* (Princeton, NJ: D. Van Nostrand Co., 1957), 96–97; Chambers, interview by author, 26 February 2002.
28. Chambers, interview by author, 26 February 2002.
29. Calloway and Smith, *Visions of Freedom on the Great Plains*, 105, 111, 116. Young spoke in Omaha to the local Urban League on April 27, 1966. "Eloquent Testimony of a Nebraska Barber at Riot Probe," *Ebony* (April 1968), 29–38; Chambers, interview by author, 23 July and 25 September 2002.

30. Calloway and Smith, *Visions of Freedom on the Great Plains*, 153; Otis and Erickson, *E Pluribus Omaha*, 132–33. In 1964, Bob Myers became the first African American to serve on the Omaha Board of Education.
31. Otis and Erickson, *E Pluribus Omaha*, 33, 133.
32. Chambers, "Public Pulse," *Omaha World Herald*, 11 October 1958.
33. "Ernest William Chambers," F.O.I. File, 14. See Richard M. Rogers, Deputy Chief Freedom of Information Under Privacy Act, Washington, DC, letter to Chambers, Omaha, 8 July 1976.
34. W. M. McVoy, memo to Officers and Membership, NAACP-Omaha [c. 1963], Great Plains Black History Museum Collection of Omaha, Nebraska; Calloway and Smith, *Visions of Freedom on the Great Plains*, 98, 134, 136; Chambers, note to author, 25 March 2005; "Ernest William Chambers," F.O.I. File, 14.
35. "Ernest William Chambers," F.O.I. File, 7–8, 14–15, 61; Kruse, *Omaha the Prairie Blossoms*, 238.
36. "Ernest William Chambers," F.O.I. File, 9, 16.
37. Kruse, *Omaha the Prairie Blossoms*, 237–238.
38. "What Progress in Rights Fight," *Dundee and West Omaha Sun*, 18 June 1964, 12.
39. Ibid.
40. Ibid.
41. Ibid.; "The Omaha Star Makes Its Debut," *Omaha Star*, July 27, 2006; Regional Director Frank Cronin, letter to Executive Board Member of CIO Local Union in Omaha. St. Martin De Porres Club minutes, 11 June 1953. (Note: Oren Belgrave would open the short-lived Americana Black Museum in 1991.) Lodge Records, Great Plains Black Museum, 5 December 1955; Pinkett, *An Historical Sketch of the Omaha Negro*.
42. "What Progress in Rights Fight," *Dundee and West Omaha Sun*, 18 June 1964, 12.
43. Drew Pearson and Jack Anderson, "Negro Firebrand Tells Hill Why," *Washington Post*, 24 October 1967.
44. Ibid.
45. Chambers, remarks to the National Commission of Civil Disorders, Washington, DC, 23 September 1967, 1.
46. Ibid., 2–3.
47. Ibid.
48. "The Black Revolution," *Ebony Special Issue* (Chicago: Johnson Publishers, 1970), 20; *Report of the National Advisory Commission on Civil Disorders* (Washington, DC: Government Printing Office, 1968), 3–4, 19–21, 64.
49. "The Black Revolution," 157.
50. Ibid., 160–63.
51. Chambers, remarks to the National Commission of Civil Disorders, 5. See also John Hope Franklin and Alfred A. Moss, Jr., *From Slavery to Freedom: A History of Negro Americans*, Sixth Edition (New York: McGraw-Hill, 1988), 440–44.

52. State of Nebraska v. Ernest William Chambers, Transcript, Douglas County Municipal Court Number 92010, 6 May 1965, 1; Edward Danner, letter to Thomas Carey and Wilbur L. Phillips, 5 March 1965.
53. State of Nebraska v. Ernest William Chambers, 6 May 1965, 1, 3.
54. Ibid., 3–4.
55. Ibid., 3, 10.
56. Ibid., 1.
57. Ibid., 4, 10–16; Cindy Lange-Kubick, "Civil Rights Marchers Took to Streets Here As Elsewhere," *Lincoln Journal Star*, 20 January 2002.
58. "Editorial," *Everybody Magazine*, 1–5; "Ernest William Chambers," F.O.I. File, 52, 54–55.
59. José M. Ferrer III, "A Real-Life Glow for a Familiar Theme," *Life Magazine*, 62: 10 February 1967, 12.
60. Ibid.
61. "Eloquent Testimony of a Nebraska Barber," 36.
62. Ibid., 37.
63. Ibid.
64. Chambers, "The Way It Is Today" (speech, Ghetto Crisis Forum, 4 May 1967), 157. See also "Ghetto Crisis Theme of Forum," City Commission on Human Rights Reporter (New York), August 1967, 1–2.
65. Chambers, "The Way It Is Today" (speech, Ghetto Crisis Forum, 4 May 1967), 157, 160–63. See also James Baldwin, Martin Luther King, Malcolm X, "The Negro and the American Promise," interviews by Kenneth Clark, 1, 15 (transcript).
66. John T. McCartney, *Black Power Ideologies: An Essay in African-American Political Thought* (Philadelphia: Temple University Press, 1992), 93, 96. See also Peter J. Paris, *Black Leaders in Conflict: Joseph H. Jackson, Martin Luther King, Jr., Malcolm X, Adam Clayton Powell, Jr.* (New York: Pilgrim Press, 1978), 96, 105–8, 140–41, 159.
67. Paris, *Black Leaders in Conflict*, 95.
68. Ibid.; Chambers, "The Way It Is Today," 164.
69. Chambers, "The Way It Is Today," 165–70.
70. Ibid., 171–72.
71. "Ernie Chambers," *Black and White: Six Stories from a Troubled Time* (Newton: MA: Education Development Center, Inc., 1968), 23. Chambers's experiences were included in a handbook for use by public schools throughout America to help students understand the Civil Rights and Black Power Movements.
72. Larsen and Cottrell, *The Gate City*, 272.
73. Ibid.
74. Ibid.
75. "Ernest William Chambers," F.O.I. File, 7, 8–14.
76. Ibid., 7, 9–13.

77. Ibid.
78. Ibid., 11.
79. Ibid., 12.
80. Ibid., 13; Chambers, Creighton University Law School Fall Semester Class Schedule, 1961–1962, Chambers Collection; Chambers, "Omaha's Segregated Schools," unpublished essay, 1962.
81. Chambers, interview by C. Joseph Coleman, ed., *Creighton University School of Law Docket*, Omaha (Fall 1970), 1–3.
82. Ibid.
83. "Ernest William Chambers," F.O.I. File, 10, 19.
84. J. Edgar Hoover, letter to Director Bureau of Personnel Investigations, Washington, DC, October 8, 1961. Hoover, letter to Assistant Attorney General Internal Security Division, 18 October 1961, in "Ernest William Chambers," *Report*, 21.
85. "Ernest William Chambers," F.O.I. File, 10, 21.
86. Ibid., 15.
87. "Ernie Chambers," *Black and White: Six Stories from a Troubled Time*, 23, Chambers Collection.
88. Calloway and Smith, *Visions of Freedom on the Great Plains*, 136; "Eloquent Testimony of a Nebraska Barber," 38; Cynthia Grandberry, interview by author 18 June 2002, notes the Chambers children are: Mark, Gayla, Ernie Jr., and David.
89. Lange-Kubick, "Civil Rights Marchers Took to Streets Here," 1; "Ernest William Chambers," F.O.I. File, 26.
90. "Ernest William Chambers," F.O.I. File, 26–27.
91. Ibid., 27. Chambers's Omaha Police Department number was 65212. Chambers, letter to U.S. Attorney Theodore Richling, Omaha, 10 May 1965, in "Ernest William Chambers," F.O.I. File, 108.
92. Chambers, letter to U.S. Attorney Theodore Richling, Omaha, 10 May 1965, in "Ernest William Chambers," F.O.I. File, 108.
93. "Ernest William Chambers," F.O.I. File, 106.
94. J. Edgar Hoover, letter to Special Agent in Charge, Omaha, 15 June 65, in "Ernest William Chambers," F.O.I. File.
95. Special Agent in Charge, Omaha, letter to J. Edgar Hoover, Washington, DC, 14 May 1965, in "Ernest William Chambers," F.O.I. File, 108. In 2005, Chambers said that he was aware that he was under surveillance but did not know the extent to which he was being monitored.
96. Chambers, letter to U.S. Attorney Theodore Richling, Omaha, 3 and 10 May 1965, in "Ernest William Chambers," F.O.I. File, 110.
97. Larsen and Cottrell, *The Gate City*, 276; "Police Reinforcements Go on Duty in Omaha," 3.
98. Larsen and Cottrell, *The Gate City*, 276.

99. Ibid.
100. "Police Reinforcements Go on Duty in Omaha," 3.
101. "Mayor Deplores Chambers's Violence Only Way Speech," *Omaha World Herald*, 2 October 1967.
102. Ibid.
103. Ibid.
104. Ibid.
105. Pearson and Anderson, "Negro Firebrand Tells Hill Why."
106. Ibid.
107. Ibid.
108. Ibid., 31; "Ernest William Chambers," F.O.I. File, 33; Chambers, note to author, 25 March 2005.
109. "Ernest William Chambers," F.O.I. File, 32; Pearson and Anderson, "Negro Firebrand Tells Hill Why."
110. Chambers did not profess Christianity. Douglass Hall, "We Demand Rights Now," *Dundee Sun* (6 March 1966); "Ernest William Chambers," F.O.I. File.
111. See Chambers, letter to Paul A. Miller, Omaha, 12 April 1966; Chambers, letter to Charles Krumme, Omaha, 16 February 1967; Chambers, letter to Owen Knutzen, Omaha, 24 January 1968; "Open," *Letter,* from Chambers, Omaha, 25 January 1968; Chambers, letter to Owen Knutzen, Omaha, 24 January 1969 (all letters housed in Chambers Archival Collection in Omaha, Nebraska); Larsen and Cottrell, *The Gate City*, 275; "Ernest William Chambers," F.O.I. File, 33; Kruse, *Omaha the Prairie Blossoms*, 249–50; Luebke, *Nebraska: An Illustrated History*, 334.
112. Chambers, letter to Owen Knutzen, Omaha, 24 January 1968.
113. Chambers, letter to Charles Krumme, Omaha, 16 February 1967.
114. Ibid.
115. Chambers, letter to Owen Knutzen, Omaha, 24 January 1969.
116. Ibid. Long concerned about the OPS, Chambers eventually helped to initiate a school community advisory board and "almost single-handedly brought national attention to the administering of Ritalin and amphetamines to children in public schools." See Geoff Cowan, "The Chambers Affair: The State Senator as Black Militant," *Village Voice*, 14 October 1971.
117. See Chambers, letter to Paul A. Miller, Omaha, 12 April 1966; Chambers, letter to Charles Krumme, Omaha, 16 February 1967; Chambers, letter to Owen Knutzen, Omaha, 24 January 1968. "Open," *Letter,* from Chambers, Omaha, 25 January 1968; Chambers, letter to Owen Knutzen, 24 January 1968; Chambers, letter to Owen Knutzen, Omaha, 24 January 1969. Letters are housed in Chambers Archival Collection in Omaha. Larsen and Cottrell, *The Gate City*, 275. "Ernest William Chambers," F.O.I. File, 33. Kruse, *Omaha the Prairie Blossoms*, 249–50. Luebke, *Nebraska: An Illustrated History*, 334.
118. "Open," *Letter,* from Chambers, Omaha, 25 January 1968.

119. Ibid.; Chambers, letter to A. V. Sorensen, 18 October 1965. See "Ernest William Chambers," F.O.I. File, 35, 37.
120. Hall, "We Demand Rights Now," in "Ernest William Chambers," F.O.I. File, 37.
121. Ibid., 38–39.
122. Ibid.
123. Ibid. 40.
124. "Chambers Wants Drive to Aid Angela Davis," *Omaha World Herald*, 6 December 1970, in "Ernest William Chambers," F.O.I. File, see 90. On 19 January, 1968. Chambers spoke at Northwestern University in Evanston, Illinois. See "Ernest William Chambers," *Report*, 46; Chambers, letter to Mayor Sorensen, no date; "Ernest William Chambers," *Report*, 112; Special Agent in Charge, Omaha, memo to J. Edgar Hoover, 10 March 1968, in "Ernest William Chambers," *Report*, 113–14.
125. Wilson Jeremiah Moses, *The Golden Age of Black Nationalism* (Oxford: Oxford University Press, 1988); Chambers, speech delivered at Midwestern College, Denison, Iowa, 9 December 1969, in "Ernest William Chambers," F.O.I. File, 78.
126. Chambers, speech delivered at Midwestern College, Denison, Iowa, 9 December 1969, in "Ernest William Chambers," F.O.I. File, 78–79. Chambers was referring to the police killings of Black Panther Party members Fred Hampton and Mark Clark.
127. "Ernest William Chambers," F.O.I. File, 48–49, 56. Chambers, speech at a rally held in commemoration of Malcolm X's birthday at Malcolm X Park (Omaha), 18 May 1969. See "Ernest William Chambers," F.O.I. File, 57.
128. Velton Randall, "Is Anyone in White Society Listening," *Lincoln Evening Journal*, 24 April 1968.
129. "'Militant Negro' to Blame for Part of Racial Tensions," *Lincoln Star*, 12 June 1968, 3.
130. "Ernest William Chambers," F.O.I. File, 103. Gloria Bartek was for years the editor of the *Buffalo Chip Newsletter*.
131. "Ernest William Chambers," F.O.I. File.
132. Ibid., 104–5; "Peace & Freedom Party Will Not Have a Candidate on the Nebraska Ballot in November," *Omaha World Herald*, 25 August 1968. It would have taken 750 qualified voters to put a party on the ballot.
133. Otis and Erickson, *E Pluribus Omaha*, 164.

Chapter Two

1. Hall, "We Demand Rights Now," in "Ernest William Chambers," *Report*, 40; "Ernest William Chambers," F.O.I. File, 33; John Dugard, *Human Rights and the South African Legal Order* (Princeton, New Jersey: Princeton University Press, 1978), 133–35.

2. Janice Love, *The U.S. Anti-Apartheid Movement: Local Activism in Global Politics*, (New York: Praeger Publications, 1985), 14.
3. Paul Robeson, *Here I Stand* (Boston: Beacon Press, 1958), xx, 72; "Ernest William Chambers," F.O.I. File, 33. Du Bois had joined Robeson's organization in 1949, acting as vice chair of the African Aid Committee, and in that role he was instrumental in sending aid to the families of men killed in indigenous African coal mine strikes in Nigeria.
4. Larsen and Cottrell, *The Gate City*, 273, 334.
5. Ibid.
6. Ibid., 273.
7. Ibid.
8. Ibid.
9. Ibid., 274.
10. John W. Cell, *The Highest Stage of White Supremacy: The Origins of Segregation in Southern Africa and the American South* (Cambridge, MA: Cambridge University Press, 1982), ix.
11. Cell, *The Highest Stage*, ix; Love, *U.S. Anti-Apartheid Movement*, 1, 14.
12. Kruse, *Omaha the Prarie Blossoms*, 241-50.
13. Ibid.
14. Ibid., 240, 274.
15. Ibid.; see also Tera Hunter's *To Joy My Freedom* (Boston: Harvard University Press, 1997).
16. Marvin McClarty, Sr., interview by author, 21 May 2003.
17. Ibid.
18. Kruse, *Omaha the Prairie Blossoms*, 241.
19. Ibid., 249–50; Robeson, *Here I Stand*, xx, 63, 72, 117–19.
20. Kruse, *Omaha the Prairie Blossoms*, 241–2; Larsen and Cottrell, *The Gate* City, 274–75.
21. "U.N. Is Goal of Malcolm X: Omaha Native Seeks 'Human Rights'" *Omaha World Herald* (30 June 1964); "Malcolm X: Anything Whites Do, Blacks Can Do Better," *Omaha World Herald* (1 July 1964), 4; Chambers, interview by author, 25 July, 2002.
22. "Reports and Reviews," *The Militant* (26 September 1966), 1; "Spear of the Nation," San Francisco: CA Newsreel, 1989, videocassette.
23. Love, *U.S. Anti-Apartheid Movement*, 3, 35. Civil rights leader Dr. Martin Luther King, Jr., and Chief Albert J. Lutuli of the African National Congress jointly issued a call for sanctions against South Africa.
24. Vickey Parks, interview by author, 19 May 2003; "School Laws May Exclude Bantu Unit," *Omaha World Herald*, 8 April 1969, 4; Richard M. Rogers, Deputy Chief Freedom of Information Office, Washington, DC, letter to Chambers regarding "Ernest William Chambers," F.O.I. File.
25. "Ernest William Chambers," F.O.I. File, 49.

26. Chambers, letter to Governor Norbert Tiemann, Lincoln, 11 August 1967. "Ernest William Chambers," F.O.I. File, 17, 41, 112.
27. "Ernest William Chambers," F.O.I. File, 17, 41, 112; "Eloquent Testimony of a Nebraska Barber, 37.
28. Ernest William Chambers," F.O.I. File, 17, 41, 112.
29. Marvin McClarty, Sr., interview by author, Omaha, 21 May 2003.
30. Luebke, *Nebraska: An Illustrated History*, 334.
31. Ibid., 334–35. In 1969, the Nebraska Unicameral passed the Civil Rights Act. Chambers, "The Voice of Thy Brother's Blood Crieth from the Ground," 1; Urban Action Association, 3701 N. 24th Street, letter to Personnel Board City of Omaha, 25 November 1969, available in the Great Plains Black History Museum Collection of Omaha.
32. "Ernest William Chambers," F.O.I. File, 58.
33. Chambers, "The Voice of Thy Brother's Blood Crieth from the Ground," 9, 38, 47.
34. Ibid., 9.
35. Ibid., 6.
36. Ibid.
37. Ibid.
38. Ibid.
39. Ibid., 6, 11.
40. Ibid., 11.
41. Ibid.
42. Ibid.; Chambers, "Loder Preliminary Hearing," *Journal*, 11 September 1969; Chambers Collection.
43. Chambers, "The Voice of Thy Brother's Blood Crieth from the Ground," 1, 11.
44. Ibid., 13
45. Ibid., 8, 18.
46. Ibid., 18, 20.
47. Ibid., 1.
48. Ibid.
49. Ibid., 7.
50. Ibid., 7–8, 12, 20.
51. Chambers, note to author, 25 March, 2005; "Is Omaha Burning Over Black Frame," *Berkeley Tribe*, 27 November and 5 December 1969, 5; Dotti Hrabik, "Peace and Freedom Convention," *Asterisk*, 1, 3 (September 1968): 5; Luebke, *Nebraska: An Illustrated History*, 334; Chambers, "The Voice of Thy Brother's Blood Crieth from the Ground," 13, 15.
52. Chambers, note to author, 25 March, 2005. Chambers, "The Voice of Thy Brother's Blood Crieth from the Ground," 20, 21.
53. Chambers, "The Voice of Thy Brother's Blood Crieth from the Ground," 22, 32.

54. Ibid., 23; Chambers, note to author, 25 March 2005.
55. Chambers, "The Voice of Thy Brother's Blood Crieth from the Ground," 23–24.
56. Ibid., 24–25.
57. "Omaha, City of Fascism," *Black Panther Party Paper*, 26 July 1969. A copy of this article can be found in "Ernest William Chambers," F.O.I. File, 56. The weapon in question was a .38 caliber revolver.
58. "Ernest William Chambers," F.O.I. File, 59.
59. Ibid., 60.
60. Ibid., 61.
61. Chambers, "The Voice of Thy Brothers Blood Crieth from the Ground," 24; "Is Omaha Burning Over Black Frame"; Hrabik, "Peace and Freedom Convention."
62. McClarty, interview by author, Omaha, 21 May 2003.
63. Ibid.
64. Chambers, "The Voice of Thy Brothers Blood Crieth from the Ground," 24, 27; "Malcolm X Declares: Negro Must Prepare to Defend Himself or Continue at the Mercy of Racist Mob," *Omaha Star*, 3 July 1964; Chambers, interview by author, 26 June 2002.
65. "Vote in Chambers Race Will Tell Much," *Norfolk Daily News*, 20 October 1970; "Chambers Raps NU Med. School," *Lincoln Evening Journal and Nebraska State Journal*, 23 September 1970, 1. For a discussion of Black Nationalism historically as well as in Omaha, see Leon Trotsky, *Leon Trotsky on Black Nationalism and Self-determination*, edited by George Breitman (New York: Pathfinder Press, 1978), 1; Tony Martin, *Race First: The Ideological and Organizational Struggles of Marcus Garvey and the Universal Negro Improvement Association* (Westport, CT: Greenwood Press, 1976), 5–6, 33; Sterling Stuckey, *The Ideological Origins of Black Nationalism* (Boston: Beacon Press, 1972), 2–5; Kruse, *Omaha the Prairie Blossoms*, 255–56; Calloway and Smith, *Visions of Freedom on the Great Plains*, 135.
66. "Vote in Chambers Race Will Tell Much," *Norfolk Daily News*, 20 October 1970; "David Rice Surrenders in Minard Bomb Case," *Omaha World Herald*, 17 August 1970, 2; Kruse, *Omaha the Prairie Blossoms*, 254.
67. Kruse, *Omaha the Prairie Blossoms*, 254.
68. "Chambers Raps NU Med. School," 1;"Rice and Poindexter," London: British Broadcasting Corporation, 1994, video recording; Marj Marlette, "New Habeas Corpus Action to Be Filed in Court," 16 April 1978; J. Edgar Hoover, memo to Washington, DC, from Special Agent in Charge, Omaha, 13 October 1970.
69. "Chambers Raps NU Med. School," 1.
70. Ibid.; Chambers, speech at the University of Nebraska–Lincoln, Afro-American Collegiate Society, 21 September 1970. See "Ernest William Chambers," *Report*, 86.
71. Chambers, speech at the University of Nebraska–Lincoln, Afro-American Col-

legiate Society, 21 September 1970.
72. McClarty, interview by author, Omaha, Nebraska, 21 May 2003.
73. Ibid.
74. Ibid.
75. "Rice: Had No Role in Death of Minard," *Omaha World Herald*, 13 April 1971; McClarty, Interview by author, Omaha, Nebraska, 21 May 2003.
76. Chambers, "The Voice of Thy Brother's Blood Crieth from the Ground," 20.
77. Ibid.
78. Dave Hassenstab, "Police Image Isn't Same from Both Sides of Fence," *Lincoln Star*, 15 January 1971, 17; Chambers, "The Way It Is Today," 173.
79. Chambers, "The Way It Is Today," 175–176.
80. Ibid., 177–80.
81. *Report of the National Advisory Commission on Civil Disorders* (U.S. Government Printing Office, 1 March 1968), 1.
82. Ibid.
83. "Chambers, Black Choice for 11th District," *Omaha Star*, 5 November 1970, 1; Dave Hassenstab, "Police Image Isn't Same from Both Sides of Fence," 17; *Unicameral Update* 9: 1, 10 January 1986, 9. Nebraska has 49 legislative districts.
84. Dave Hassenstab, "Police Image Isn't Same from Both Sides of Fence".
85. Special Agent in Charge, Omaha, letter to J. Edgar Hoover, April 1970; Barbara Connell, "A Time for Burning," Augustana Lutheran Church, 1967.
86. Chambers, letter to *Atlanta Journal Constitution*, 28 January 1970; "Ernest William Chambers," F.O.I. File, 85; "Chambers Said He Won't Alter Talks Just to Get Elected," *Omaha World Herald*, 14 October 1970.
87. "Chambers Index," *Everybody Magazine* (March 1970), 9, Chambers Collection.
88. "Chambers Wants Drive to Aid Angela Davis." See also "Ernest William Chambers," F.O.I. File, 86.
89. "Ernest William Chambers," F.O.I. File, 86; "Scholarly Omaha Barber Is Candidate for State House," *Jet*, 15 October 1971; "Chambers Wants Drive to Aid Angela Davis." See also "Ernest William Chambers," *Report*, 82, 89–90. Chambers was elected November 3, 1970, from Nebraska's Eleventh Legislative District.
90. "Grand Jury Equals Grand Injustice," *Black Realities* 1, 3 (January 1970): 2, 11.
91. Ibid., 12; Chambers, note to author, 25 March, 2005.
92. Ibid.
93. Ibid., 1–16; "Chambers, Black Choice for 11th District"; "Police Forerunners Crucified Jesus," *Lincoln Journal*, 16 January 1971, 14.

Chapter Three

1. McMorris, "Sun-Up Interview: Malcolm Chambers."
2. Luebke, *Nebraska: An Illustrated History*, 334–35.
3. Edward R. Danner, Omaha, letter to Governor Frank B. Morrison, Lincoln, 13 March 1961, Danner Collection.
4. Ibid.
5. Edward R. Danner, Omaha, letter to Mayor James J. Dworak, Omaha, 13 April 1962, 1–2.
6. Ibid., 2.
7. Helen M. Stowell, Omaha, letter to Edward Danner, Omaha, 8 June 1966.
8. Robert J. Jones, Omaha, letter to Edward Danner, Lincoln, April, 2, 1967, Danner Collection.
9. A. V. Sorensen, Omaha, letter to Edward Danner, Lincoln, 5, February 1968.
10. Ibid.; "Danner Confident on Housing Bill" (editorial), *Omaha World Herald*, 25 May 1967. The article referred to LB 358. Fred Harrington, Nebraska Real Estate Association Legislation & Taxation Committee, flyer, 25 May 1967, Danner Collection.
11. Edward Danner, memo, 25, October 1968, Danner Collection; Equal Opportunity Field Representative Lawrence W. M. McVoy, Lincoln, letter to Danner, Lincoln, 19 March 1968.
12. S. R. Merrer, Omaha, letter to Danner, Lincoln, 18 April 1967.
13. Gary Kimsey, "Statement to police," Omaha, 4 March 1969, 2–3, Danner Collection.
14. Danner, Omaha, letter to Dworak; Danner, Lincoln, letter to Thomas D. Carey and Wilbur L. Phillips, Omaha, 5 March, 1965, Danner Collection; Danner, Lincoln, letter to Harvey I. Anderson, Omaha, 7 April 1965. The Human Relations Board was created on November 6, 1956, by the city of Omaha electors. Also see "The Home Rule Charter of the City of Omaha" 6 November 1956, Danner Collection. The Nebraska Civil Rights Act (NCRA) of 1969 was originally a bill introduced by Danner, Don Elrod, and seven other senators. The NCRA prohibited housing and employment discrimination and established an Equal Opportunity Commission to oversee compliance with the law.
15. "Resolution 8," Floor Debate, Nebraska State Unicameral, 15 June 1970, 43–44.
16. Ibid.
17. Ibid., 45; "Senator Althouse: 'We're on Way to Better Things'" (editorial), *Omaha World-Herald*, 19 June 1970.
18. "Senator Althouse: 'We're on Way to Better Things'" (editorial), *Omaha World-Herald*, 19 June 1970.
19. "Editorial," (Omaha) *Everybody Magazine* (July–August 1970): 6.
20. Ibid., 6–8. Chambers, note to author, 25 March 2005.
21. Ibid., 7.
22. Ibid., 8.
23. Ibid.

24. Nettye Chambers Johnson, "Ernie the Man," (Omaha) *Everybody Magazine* (July–August 1970): 53.
25. Ibid.
26. Ibid.
27. David Tishendorf, "Squabble Over 11th District Seat Continues," *Omaha World Herald*, 22 June 1970, 4.
28. Ibid.
29. Ibid.; "Editorial," (Omaha) *Everybody Magazine*, (July-August) 1970: 6.
30. Tishendorf, "Squabble Over 11th District Seat Continues."
31. Ibid.
32. "Chambers Index." Danner had also pointed out Kenneth Shearer, Gayle Sayers, and Bob Gibson as especially talented young men. Chambers, note to author, 25 March 2005.
33. Warren T. Francke, "Commentary: Speech Twangs Cy's Heartstrings," *Omaha Sun*, 25 June 1970, 4; Dick Mezzy, "Chambers and Althouse Campaign in Controversial Legislative Race," *Lincoln Journal*, 22 October 1970.
34. Don Pieper, "Legislators Applaud Althouse Speech," *Omaha World Herald*, 17 June 1970. The special legislative session held in the summer of 1970 was Senator Althouse's debut on the Unicameral floor; "Chambers, Adams Agree on Issues," *Omaha World Herald*, 30 March 1970.
35. "Chambers, Adams Agree on Issues," *Omaha World Herald*, 30 March 1970.
36. Pieper, "Legislators Applaud Althouse Speech"; V. J. Mason, "Master Race Rejected," *Omaha World Herald*, 22 June 1970.
37. "No Charges by Althouse," *Omaha World Herald*, 16 June 1970.
38. Ibid.
39. Ibid.; Vickey Parks, interview by author, Omaha, 19 May 2003; Kerry Lee Haynie, *African American Legislators in the American States* (New York: Columbia University Press, 2001); "Kansas City Missouri," *Black Enterprise* (March 1978); Michael Clemons and Charles E. Jones, "African American Legislative Politics in Virginia," *Journal of Black Studies* 30 (2000): 744, retrieved 16 August 2010 at http://jbs.sagepub.com. See also Charles E. Jones, "Black Lawmakers in the Quaker State: An Overview of the Pennsylvania Legislative Caucus, 1970–2002," *Journal of Race and Policy* 4, 2 (2008): 1.
40. "Chambers Index."
41. Ibid.; "The Chambers Candidacy," campaign flyer, 1970, Chambers Collection; "Contributor list," campaign material, 1970, 2, Chambers Collection.
42. Mezzy, "Chambers and Althouse Campaign."
43. Ibid.
44. "Scholarly Omaha Barber Is Candidate for State House."
45. Mezzy, "Chambers and Althouse Campaign"; "Chambers Says He Can Cooperate," *Omaha World Herald*, 23 June 1970.

46. Lawrence W. Levine, *Black Culture and Black Consciousness: Afro-American Folk Thought From Slavery to Freedom,* (New York: Oxford University Press, 1977), 397; Lois Stalvey, Sedona, Arizona, letter to Chambers, Omaha, 24 February 1984, Chambers Papers. See Lois Mark Stalvey, *The Education of a W.A.S.P.* (William Morrow & Co., 1970). Fourteen years later, Stalvey wrote to Chambers and told him that if she had not met Chambers, WASP would never have been written.
47. "Rights Laws Need Enforcement," *Omaha World Herald,* 28 October 1970.
48. Ibid.
49. Dorothy Holly Price, message, Western Union Telegram, 4 November 1970.
50. Citizens Coordinating Committee, memo, Western Union Telegram, 4 November 1970.
51. Fred Thomas, "Ernest Chambers Won't Change as Senator," *Omaha World Herald,* 5 November 1970, 3; "Chambers, Black Choice for Eleventh District."
52. "Five, Maybe Six, New Faces Join County Senator's Ranks," *Omaha World Herald,* 4, November 1970.
53. "Note," election material, 1970, Chambers Collection.
54. "Chambers Says He Can Cooperate."
55. "Chambers, Black Choice for Eleventh District"; Thomas, "Ernest Chambers Won't Change as Senator."
56. Thomas, "Ernest Chambers Won't Change as Senator."
57. Ibid.
58. "Chambers, Black Choice for Eleventh District."
59. Ibid.; Thomas, "Ernest Chambers Won't Change as Senator."
60. Thomas, "Ernest Chambers Won't Change as Senator."
61. Chambers, "Other Gun Incident," essay, 10 April 2005; "Unicameral Kids: A Student Guide to the Nebraska Legislature" (Lincoln, NE: Unicameral Information Office, 2001), 4; "Transforming Ideas into Laws," *Unicameral Update* 18, 1 (6 January 1995): 30–31; State of Nebraska Legislative Records Historian Diana Bridges, interview by author, 11 February 2004.
The legislature was on a two-year cycle at the time Chambers was elected in 1970, and Chambers was inducted into office in January 1971. After 1970 the Unicameral began holding sessions every year. A special session of the Unicameral was held June 9–16, 1970.
62. "Ernest Chambers Charged with Gun Possession," *Lincoln Star,* 28 November 1970; "No Determination Made Yet in Chambers Case," *Lincoln Journal,* 30 November 1970, 20.
63. "Legislative Life," *Lincoln Journal,* 17 January 1971.
64. "Who Is Your Senator," *Omaha World Herald,* 3 March 1971, 51.
65. Chambers, "First Day," journal entry, 5 January 1970, 1.
66. Ibid.
67. Ibid.

68. Ibid.
69. Ibid.
70. Ibid., 2.
71. Ibid.
72. Ibid, 2–3.
73. Ibid.
74. Ibid., 2.
75. Ibid," 2–3.
76. Ibid., 3.
77. Ibid, 4.
78. Ibid.; Chambers, interview with author, 25 July 2003.
79. Ibid.
80. Ibid.
81. Ibid.
82. "The Real Black Power" (editorial), *Lincoln Evening Journal and Nebraska State Journal*, 6 November 1970, 4; Thomas, "Ernest Chambers Won't Change as Senator"; Kenneth Nunn and Gregory M. Organ, "Ernie Chambers: In the System But Not of the System Black Politics and Social Movements of the 60's and 70's," unpublished paper, 17, Chambers Collection.
83. "Ernest William Chambers," F.O.I. File, 83; *Report of the National Advisory Commission on Civil Disorders*; "Unicameral Kids"; "Transforming Ideas into Laws"; Bridges, interview by author, 11 February 2004.
84. "Ernest William Chambers," F.O.I. File, 83. In the Nebraska general election of 1970, the contestants for governor were Norbert T. Tiemann (Republican incumbent) v. James. J. Exon, among others. In the Eleventh District it was incumbent George W. Althouse, Omaha, v. Michael B. Adams, Omaha, and Chambers, Omaha. See "Nebraska Primary," *Omaha World Herald*, 14 March 1970. In the Fortieth District incumbent seat was William M. Wylie, of Elgin, v. John DeCamp, of Neligh. Larsen and Cottrell, *The Gate City*, 277; Chambers, interview with author, 25 September 2002.
85. "William O. Dobler, 'Events in Perspective," *Lincoln Star*, 29 May 1971, 4.
86. Ibid.
87. Randy Ownes, "Speakers Laud Senator Chambers," *Omaha World Herald*, 12 July 1971.
88. Ibid.
89. Cowan, "The Chambers Affair."
90. Dobler, "Events in Perspective"; Ownes, "Speakers Laud Senator Chambers"; Cowan, "The Chambers Affair"; "Ghetto Crisis Theme of Forum," 1–2; Nunn and Organ, "Ernie Chambers: In the System But Not of the System."
91. Ownes, "Speakers Laud Senator Chambers".
92. Roger W. Sayers, *Annual Report, Omaha Human Relations Department*, December 1971, 1–7; Nunn and Organ, "Ernie Chambers: In the System But Not of

the System," 1–5.
93. Nunn and Organ, "Ernie Chambers: In the System But Not of the System," 1–5.
94. Ibid.; Mona Bazaar, Los Angeles, California, letter to Chambers, Lincoln, 12 June 1971, 1–3.
95. Omaha Housing Authority, letter to Chambers, Omaha, 17 May 1971; Bazaar letter, June 1971; League of Women Voters of Nebraska President, Mrs. Fred L. Wupper, Lincoln, letter to Chambers, Lincoln, 22 March 1971.
96. Wupper, letter to Chambers, 22 March 1971.
97. Ibid.
98. "Black Caucus Endorses Three," flyer, campaign material, 1971, 1, Chambers Collection.
99. Anonymous, New Orleans, letter to Chambers, Omaha, 25 October 1967; Danner, letter to Dworak, 13 April 1962; Robert J. Jones, Omaha, letter to Danner, Omaha, 2 April, 1967, Danner Collection.
100. Jones letter, 2 April, 1967.
101. Chambers, Lincoln, letter to Burton Berger, executive director Nebraska State Bar Association, Lincoln, 17 July, 1972; Chambers, memo to self, 1971, Chambers Collection.
102. Friends of Ernie Chambers Committee, "You've Heard a Lot About Ernie Chambers: Now Read the Facts," campaign material, fall 1971, 1, Chambers Collection.
103. Ibid.
104. Robert E. Cecil, Englewood, Colorado, letter to Chambers, Lincoln, 29 August 1972.
105. Chambers, Lincoln, letter to Robert Cecil, Englewood, Colorado, 5 September 1972.
106. Ibid.
107. Ibid.
108. Chambers, Legislative Resolution 43, "Vietnam," Nebraska Legislative Journal 1st Session, 13 April 1971, 1245.
109. Ibid., 1–2.
110. Ibid.; "Full of Mischief," *Omaha World Herald*, 5 February 1971; "Chambers on Right Track," *Omaha World Herald*, 3 February 1971.
111. Charlyne Berens, *Leaving Your Mark: The Political Career of Nebraska State Senator Jerome Warner* (Seward, NE: *Nebraska Times*, 1997), 45–46.
112. Chambers, "Democracy Is Being Killed," journal entry, 28 April 1971, 1–2, Chambers Collection.
113. Ibid.
114. Ibid.
115. Ibid.
116. Ibid.
117. Ibid.

118. "Chambers Termed Senate's Quickest Mind," campaign material, 1972, 1–2, Chambers Collection.
119. Dick Herman, "Statehouse Letter," *Lincoln Evening Journal and Nebraska State Paper*, 13 May 1971, 4.
120. Ibid.
121. Midwest Regional Director U.S. Department of Justice Community Relations Service Richard A. Salem, Des Moines, Iowa, letter to William O'Connor, Chief, Criminal Section Civil Rights Division U. S. Department of Justice, Washington, DC, 4 November 1970, 1–2, Chambers Collection.
122. Ibid.
123. "Chambers Delivers Mock Apology," *Lincoln Star,* 13 May 1971.
124. Ibid.
125. Cowan, "The Chambers Affair."
126. "Racism Charge 'Unsubstantiated,'" *UNO Gateway* 71, 61 (23 June 1972).
127. Ibid.; "Panel Called on Residency," *Omaha World Herald,* 16 March 1972; "Hart Charges Intimidation by Chambers Supporters," *Omaha World Herald,* 20 March 1972, 2.
128. Trotsky, *Leon Trotsky on Black Nationalism and Self-determination*, 1; Tony Martin, *Race First*, 5–6, 33; Stuckey, *The Ideological Origins of Black Nationalism*, 2–5; Alphonso Pinkney, *Red, Black, and Green: Black Nationalism in the United States* (New York: Cambridge University Press, 1976), ix, x, 129–34, 149–50. The Black Panthers Party's perspective of cultural nationalism was that it was reactionary and lacked a program that challenged African economic exploitation.
129. Alphonso Pinkney, *Red, Black, and Green: Black Nationalism in the United States* (New York: Cambridge University Press, 1976), ix, x, 129–34, 149–50.
130. "Panel Called on Residency." "Hart Charges Intimidation by Chambers Supporters."
131. Ibid.
132. Ibid.

Chapter Four

1. "Caucus Vote to Chambers," *Omaha World Herald,* 10 April 1972.
2. Allen Beermann, "Results of November 7, 1972 General Election," State of Nebraska, 1, Chambers Collection; Chambers, Lincoln, letter to Mayor Eugene Leahy, Omaha, 11 September 1972.
3. Chambers, letter to Leahy.
4. Director Human Relations Roger W. Sayers, Omaha, letter to Chambers, Omaha, 26 March 1971.

5. "Legislative Bill 749: Administrative Review of All Homicides," Floor Debate, 13 January 1978, 06167; Chambers, notes from telephone call apparently from "Pattavina," undated [probably 1970s], Chambers Collection.
6. Chambers, notes from telephone call apparently from "Pattavina," undated [probably 1970s], Chambers Collection.
7. Ibid.
8. Don Walton, "Omaha and Lincoln Drug Probe Sought," *Lincoln Star*, 17 January 1973.
9. "Police Job on Pusher Defended," *Omaha World Herald*, 17 January 1973.
10. Walton, "Omaha and Lincoln Drug Probe Sought"; "Part-Owner of City Hotel Is Policeman," *Omaha World Herald*, 18 January 1973.
11. "Nixon May Declare Cease-fire," *Lincoln Star*, 17 January 1973, 1; Chambers, memo to self, January, 1973, 1, Chambers Collection.
12. "Smoking and Tie Questions Argued," *Lincoln Star*, 9 January 1973.
13. "Candid Carpenter Calls Politics 'Dirty Double-Crossing Racket,'" *McCook Daily Gazette*, 24 July 1975; Don Walton, "Editorial," *Lincoln Star*, 13 January 1975, 4; Berens, *Leaving Your Mark*, 154–56. Also see "Carpenter Praised as Maverick Politician," *Scotts Bluff Star-Herald*, 28 April 1978.
14. Berens, *Leaving Your Mark*, 45–46.
15. "Candid Carpenter Calls Politics 'Dirty Double-Crossing Racket'"; Walton, "Editorial"; Berens, *Leaving Your Mark*, 45–46, 154–56.
16. "Spokesman for a Troubled Minority," *National Geographic*, March 1974, 398.
17. "Senior Goodwin Admits His Haircutting Slower than Danny's Runs," *Omaha World Herald*, 14, November 1979.
18. Ibid.; Nunn and Organ, "Ernie Chambers: In the System But Not of the System," 4.
19. Nunn and Organ, "Ernie Chambers: In the System But Not of the System," 4.
20. Ibid., 2, 4.
21. Ibid.
22. Chambers, Omaha, letter to Assistant Attorney General U.S. Justice Department Civil Rights Division J. Stanley Pottinger, Washington, DC, 16 August 1973, 1.
23. Ibid., 1–2.
24. Larry Parrott, "Board Given Two Weeks for Decision," *Omaha World Herald*, 3 July, 1973; "Chambers Will Seek Veto Override Again," *Omaha World Herald*, 18 January 1974; "Allegation Details Given on 12 Points," *Omaha World Herald*, 3 July 1973.
25. "Omaha School District to Take Integration Order to High Court," *Lincoln Star*, 15 July 1975.
26. Chambers, Omaha, letter to President Gerald Ford, Washington, DC, 19 May 1976.

27. Ibid. Ford submitted his School Desegregation Standards and Assistance Act to Congress on June 24, 1976.
28. J. Stanley Pottinger, Washington, DC, letter to Chambers, Omaha, 15 June 1976; Bobbie Green Kilberg, Washington, DC, letter to Chambers, Omaha, 7 July 1976.
29. Chambers, itinerary and telephone log, 14 September 1988; Darlene Clark Hine, "Reflections on Race and Gender Systems," in Paul A. Cimbala and Robert F. Himmelberg, eds. *Historians and Race: Autobiography and the Writing of History* (Indianapolis: Indiana University Press, 1996), 60–62.
30. Cynthia Grandberry, interview with author, Lincoln, 18 June 2002; Grandberry, note to author, 10 April 2005.
31. Cynthia Grandberry, interview with author, Lincoln, 18 June 2002.
32. Cynthia Grandberry, interview with author, Lincoln, 14 July 2003.
33. Ibid.
34. Ibid.
35. Ibid.
36. Chambers, "Biographical Sketch of Senator," 1993, Chambers Collection; Grandberry, interview with author, 14 July 2003; Grandberry, journal entry, 11 May 1982.
37. Cynthia Grandberry, interview with author, 14 July 2003. See also Johnson, "Ernie the Man." See Omaha Housing Authority letter, 17 May 1971; *Everybody Magazine,* July–August 1970, 27–29, 76; Grandberry, journal entry, 11 May 1982.
38. David Newell, "Adoption," Judiciary Committee Statement of Intent, 5 February 1979, 1; "Adoptions, Legislative Bill 483," Committee on the Judiciary Hearing, 1979, 5. The Chambers family had one girl and three boys; Gayla, Mark, Ernie, and David.
39. "Adoptions, Legislative Bill 483," Committee on the Judiciary Hearing, 1979, 5.
40. "Adoptions, Legislative Bill 483," 16–22.
41. Grandberry, interview by author, 14 July 2003.
42. "Adoptions, Legislative Bill 483," 26.
43. "Clarify Provisions on Criminal Statutes on Abortion: Legislative Bill 316," Floor Debate Nebraska State Legislature, 16 February 1979, 755, 758–60.
44. Ibid., 760.
45. Ibid.
46. Ibid., 761.
47. "Insurance Companies: Legislative Bill 1004," Floor Debate Nebraska State Legislature, 14 April 1980, 10076.
48. "Issue of Abortion, Legislative Bill 316," Committee on the Judiciary Hearing, Nebraska State Legislature, 31 January 1979, 65–66, 70.
49. Ibid., 66.
50. Chambers sponsored passage of a measure that would hold cities liable for

damages to human beings or property that resulted from police violence. Chambers, "The Way It Is Today," 155.
51. Ibid., 155–56.
52. Ibid.
53. Ibid., 156–57.
54. Ibid., 157.
55. "High-Grade Misdemeanors," *Lincoln Star,* 18 June 1970; "Courts," *Lincoln Journal,* 18 June 1970; "Lewis, Sherdell," *Lincoln Journal-Star,* Microfiche Library Archives file, 1970–1975, 1; "Accessory after Fact," *Lincoln Journal,* 19 September 1970.
56. Dick Haws, "Mayor Takes Black Requests Under Advisement," *Lincoln Journal,* 29 September, 1971, 1.
57. "Bombee Arrested," *Lincoln Journal,* 9 May 1975; "Deputy's Shotgun Killed Lewis: Federal Agents Probe Shooting," *Lincoln Journal,* 25 September 1975.
58. "Deputy's Shotgun Killed Lewis: Federal Agents Probe Shooting," *Lincoln Journal,* 25 September 1975.
59. "Deputy's Shotgun Killed Lewis: Federal Agents Probe Shooting;" "Courts," *Lincoln Star,* 26 June 1975; "York High Coach Recalls Lewis," *Lincoln Journal,* 25 September 1975; "Dead Man's Neighbors Are Angry, Fearful," *Lincoln Journal,* 25 September 1975.
60. "Lincolnite Shot by Law Officers," *Lincoln Star,* 25 September 1975; "Dead Man's Neighbors Are Angry, Fearful."
61. "Lincolnite Shot by Law Officers"; Liane Guenther, "Lincoln's Pulse Beating Rapidly," *Lincoln Star,* 26 September 1975.
62. Guenther, "Lincoln's Pulse Beating Rapidly."
63. Ibid.
64. Nate Jenkins, "Protests Prompted by Lincoln Man's Death," *Journal Star,* Reprinted, 20 January 2002; "Police, Eyewitness Descriptions of Fatal Lewis Shooting Differ, "*Lincoln Journal,* 27 September 1975; "FBI Will Hold Report for Ten Days," *Lincoln Star,* 1 October 1975.
65. Chambers, "Shooting of Sherdell Lewis," *Report,* 6 October 1975, x–1.
66. Ibid., 1–2.
67. Ibid., 1, 3.
68. Ibid., 4.
69. Ibid., 4–5.
70. Nancy Hicks, "Sherdell Lewis—Hip, Flashy, Good," *Lincoln Star,* 26 February 1975; "Fund Drive Nets $1,200," *Lincoln Journal,* 23 December 1975; "Slaying Probe Committee May Never Be Appointed," *Lincoln Journal,* 8 October 1975; "Lewis Told to Open the Door," *Lincoln Journal,* 11 October 1975; Nancy Hicks, "Deputy Will Not Be Charged," *Lincoln Star,* 5 October 1975. No charges were filed against Deputy Rod Loos. Loos's fellow officers raised over $1,000 for his legal fees.

71. "Unicameral Debate Legislative Bill 217," Floor Debate, Nebraska State Legislature, 2 January 1974, 4334, 4344–49.
72. Ibid.
73. Ibid.
74. Ibid., 4338.
75. Ibid., 4338–4330.
76. Ibid.
77. Molefi Kete Asante, *Afrocentricity* (Trenton, NJ: Africa World Press), x, 1, 25; James L. Conyers, Jr., ed. *Black American Intellectualism and Culture: A Study of African American Social and Political Thought* (Stamford, CT.: JAI Press, 1999), 85–92.
78. Lateefah Sherry (Hale) Coleman, telephone interview with author, 17 March 2010. The author was a member of BLAC during this period and into the mid-1980s.
79. *Children Under Apartheid* (New York: International Defense and Aid Fund, 1982), 15–17.
80. Ibid.
81. Alphonso Pinkney, 132–34; *Children Under Apartheid*; see also Michael A. Gomez, *Exchanging Our Country Marks* (Chapel Hill: University of North Carolina Press, 1988). For a discussion of African resistance to slavery and oppression, see Peter H. Wood, *Black Majority: Negroes in Colonial South Carolina from 1670 Through the Stono Rebellion* (New York: W. W. Norton & Co, 1996); Eugene D. Genovese, *From Rebellion to Revolution: Afro-American Slave Revolts in the Making of the Modern World* (Baton Rouge: LA: State University Press, 1992); Dugard, *Human Rights and the South African Legal Order*, 133–35, 137, 212–14; "Spear of the Nation."
82. "Spear of the Nation"; Scott Kraft, "Victims in 1976 Soweto Student Uprising Remembered," *Los Angeles Times* June 17, 1991; South African Democracy Education Trust, *The Road to Democracy in South Africa*, Vol. 2 (London: Unisa Press, 2004).
83. Kevin O' Hanlon, "Chambers Suggests South African Blacks Should 'Off' White Minority," *Lincoln Star*, 12 October 1985, 21; Steve Biko, *I Write What I Like: A Selection of His Writing*, Aelred Stubbs, ed. (San Francisco: Harper and Row, 1978), 138–39.
84. Biko, *I Write What I Like*.
85. Alfonza Whitaker, "Neb. Equal Opportunity Commission 234d Biennial Report," (Lincoln, State of Nebraska, 2000), 24–26; "Enrollment Update of Higher Ed. in Nebraska: 1999" (March 2000), Lincoln Coordinating Commission for Postsecondary Education, 2000; Marshall Lux, "Twenty-first Annual Report of the Nebraska Public Counsel" (Lincoln: Office of the Ombudsman, 1991), 1–3. See also, Lux, "Annual Report of the Nebraska Public Counsel,"

numbers 23–24 (1992–1994), 25 (1995), and 27 (1997); Nilene Omodele Adeoti Foxworth, letter to Chambers, 28 April 1984; "Divestment Would Hurt Black South Africans, the Very People It Is Meant to Help" (editorial), *Lincoln Review Quarterly* 5, 3 (Winter 1985): 1–2; "Carpenter Praised as Maverick Politician"; Chambers, interview with author, 25 July 2002.

86. "Legislative Resolution 43," (1979) Legislative Archives, Nebraska State Capitol, Lincoln; "South Africa Divestment, "*Unicameral Update* 2, 67 (April 19–25, 1979): 3; Marilyn McNabb, Senator Steve Fowler's legislative aide, helped to draft Legislative Resolution 43.

87. *Unicameral Update* 3, 13 (April 2, 1980): 3; Nunn and Organ, "Ernie Chambers: In the System But Not of the System," 14–16, Chambers Collection; "Legislative Resolution 43"; *Unicameral Update* 2, 67 (19–25 April 1979): 3.

88. "Legislative Resolution 43"; *Unicameral Update* 2, 67 (19–25 April 1979): 3.

89. "Legislative Resolution 43."

90. "U.S. Maneuvers in Southern Africa," *Sechaba* (April 1984), 1–2; Love, *U.S. Anti-Apartheid Movement*, 13, 15, 21; "Carpenter Praised as Maverick Politician"; Chambers, interview with author, 25 July 2002.

91. Franklin A. Thomas, chair the Study Commission on U.S. Policy Toward Southern Africa, letter to Chambers, New York, 6 May 1980; "Press Release," U.S. Study Commission on U.S. Policy Toward South Africa, New York, 21 May 1981, 3, 6.

92. "U.S. Maneuvers in Southern Africa."

93. "An Ominous Vote in America," *Rand Daily Mail*, Johannesburg, 11 April 1980, 8; "Legislature Condemns Apartheid," *Lincoln Journal*, 31 March 1980.

94. Karen Barker, "States, Cities Fight Apartheid," *Washington Post*, 8 February 1985, A1, A6; Love, *U.S. Anti-Apartheid Movement*, 21.

95. *Unicameral Update* 6, 3 (23 January 1983): 10; *Unicameral Update* 6, 8 (25 February 1983): 5.

96. "Conference on Public Investment and S.A.," *American Committee on Africa Action News* 10 (Fall 1981): 1–4; "Chambers: Racism Here Similar to South Africa's", *Lincoln Journal*, 16 April 1981, 1.

97. "Legislative Resolution 43"; "South Africa Divestment," *Unicameral Update* 2, 67 (19–25 April 1979): 3; Love, *U.S. Anti-Apartheid Movement*, 257–267; Chambers, "Conference on Public Investment and South Africa" (speech, United Nations, 15 April 1981), 1. Love argues that Michigan and Connecticut were the most successful states at imposing sanctions against South Africa, largely because they constructed the debate as a question of morality, with opponents risking being observed as aligned with racists. See also Chambers, "Additional Explanation," journal entry, March 1980. State Senator Steve Fowler was the co-sponsor of LR43. Nebraska's divestment act became law in 1984.

98. Chambers, "Prevention of Execution of ANC Members," itinerary and telephone log, 7 June 1983, Chambers Collection.

99. Chambers, itinerary and telephone log, Susie Prenger, 7 June 1983, Chambers Collection.
100. Ibid.
101. Chambers, itinerary and telephone log, Senator Wesely, 7 July 1983.
102. "Haberman Postcard Draws Angry Reaction by Chambers," *Lincoln Journal*, 21 September 1983.
103. Chambers, itinerary and telephone log, Paul Penny, 27 September 1985.
104. Chambers, "Statement," United Nations Special Committee Against Apartheid, New York City, 15 April 1983.
105. Chambers, itinerary and telephone log, 24 August 1983.

Chapter Five

1. Nunn and Organ, "Ernie Chambers: In the System But Not of the System," 15–16, Chambers Collection; "History Group's Goals: Show Black Contributions," *Journal and Star*, 1 December 1974, 1.
2. "Ernest Chambers: Nebraska's Lone Black Lawmaker," *Odyssey West: Blacks in the Urban West* 4, 2 (April 1985): 22–24, 30.
3. *Unicameral Update* 2, 52 (1979): 4–8; *Unicameral Update* 2, 54 (17–23 January 1979); "First of Session," *Omaha World Herald*, 8 February 1973, 10. Legislative Bill 16 was introduced by Senator Dave Newell, and Legislative Bill 29 was introduced by Chambers.
4. *Unicameral Update* 2, 60 (1–7 March 1979): 5; Chambers sponsored Legislative Bill 262 to repeal the death penalty. See *Unicameral Update* 2, 55 (January 1979): 24–31; and *Unicameral Update* 2, 69 (May 1979): 3–9. Passed by the body, Chambers's bill to repeal the death penalty was vetoed by Governor Charles Thone.
5. Tyson King-Meadows and Thomas F. Schaller, *Devolution and Black State Legislators: Challenges and Choices in the Twenty-First Century* (Albany, NY: State University of New York, 2006); Roger Biles, "Black Mayors: A Historical Assessment," *Journal of Negro History* 77, 3 (Summer 1992): 109–25; "Harold Washington," *Black Americans in Congress*, http://baic.house.gov/member-profiles/profile.html.?int ID=51. See also Florence H. Levinsohn, *Harold Washington: A Political Biography* (Chicago: Chicago Review Press, 1983); "Transforming Ideas into Laws."
6. "Special Edition," 21, 16 *Unicameral Update* (May 1998): 22–39; Will Haygood, *King of the Cats* (New York: Harper Collins, 2006).
7. "Spokesman for a Troubled Minority."
8. "Survey Shows at Least Ten Legislators Favor Omaha Council Districts," *Omaha World Herald*, 26 January 1973, 10; Charles I. Bryant, "Council Districts Would Give Omaha Blacks Voice," *Omaha World Herald*, 25 January 1973. Chambers

introduced Legislative Bill 12, which proposed that Omaha City Council members be elected by district.
9. "Open Meetings Law Change Generates Heavy Opposition," *Omaha World Herald*, 9 January 1973. See "Legislative Bill 219," *Legislative Journal*, 1973; "First of Session".
10. "Open Meetings Law Change Generates Heavy Opposition."
11. "Patrol Chief Asks Chance to Refute Drug Charges," *Omaha World Herald*, 2 September 1976.
12. Chambers, letter to Colleagues, Lincoln, 10 May 1974, 1.
13. Ibid.
14. Ibid.
15. Chambers, "Point of View," *Lincoln Star*, 10 May 1974.
16. Ibid.
17. Ibid.
18. Ibid.
19. Ibid.
20. Ibid.
21. Ibid.
22. "The Chambers Defeat," *Lincoln Star*, 18 January 1975.
23. Ibid.
24. Walton, "Editorial."
25. "Aroused 'Mice' Trap Ernie" (editorial), *Lincoln Star*, 10 January 1975, 3-4.
26. In 1991, Chambers's legislation for district elections for the Douglas County Board of Commissioners passed into law. In 1981, Fred Conley became the first African American elected to the Omaha City Council after passage of the measure.
27. Nunn and Organ, "Ernie Chambers: In the System But Not of the System," 7-8.
28. Ibid.; Chambers, note to author, 25 March 2005.
29. Chambers, note to author, 25 March 2005.
30. Nunn and Organ, "Ernie Chambers: In the System But Not of the System," 7-8, 11.
31. Chambers, note to author, 25 March 2005.
32. Ibid.; Nunn and Organ, "Ernie Chambers: In the System But Not of the System," 7-8, 12-13.
33. George M. Frederickson, "Toward a Social Interpretation of the Development of American Racism," in Nathan I. Huggins, ed., *Key Issues in the Afro-American Experience*, Vol. I (New York: Harcourt Brace Jovanovich, 1971), 241-42, 254.
34. Fred Thomas, "Chambers's Jewish Remarks Upset Some," *Omaha World Herald*, 16 May 1984.
35. "Nebraska Department of Corrections," *Unicameral Update* 4, 1 (2 January 1981): 5-6; "Correctional Facilities," *Unicameral Update* 5, 1 (7 January 1983); *Unicameral Update* 5, 12 (26 March 1982): 1-2.

36. "Treatment of Prisoners," *Unicameral Update* 5, 12 (26 March 1982): 2, 11. Regarding Legislative Bill 921, Chambers co-sponsored a measure to provide for district elections for Douglas County commissioners, which after several failed attempts would eventually pass into law.
37. "Chambers's Prayer Battle Nets Several 'Hate' Letters," *Lincoln Star*, 6 January 1981.
38. Ibid.
39. Ibid.
40. "Chambers's Prayer Battle Nets Several 'Hate' Letters"; "What Ernie Hath Wrought," *Lincoln Journal*, 26 February 1981, 6; Chambers, "Biographical Sketch," 1984, Chambers Collection.
41. "Elect the Attorney General on a Non-partisan Basis: Legislative Bill 875," *Unicameral Update* 9, 1 (10 January 1986): 22.
42. "Douglas Refused to Pick Up Chambers's Gauntlet of Debate," *Lincoln Star*, 9 September 1982.
43. Ibid.; "Debate or No Debates Chambers Can Hardly 'Lose,'" *Lincoln Journal*, 3 September 1982; "Chambers Urges Douglas to Stop Hiding," *Lincoln Star*, 14 September 1982.
44. "Chambers Urges Douglas to Stop Hiding," *Lincoln Star*, 14 September 1982.
45. "Wanted," flyer, 1982, campaign material, Chambers Collection.
46. "Chili Feed," flyer, October 1982, campaign material; "Nomination Committee [list]," September 1982, campaign material. Treasurer Dan Goodwin collected funds at the shop at 3116 North 24th Street in Omaha.
47. "Chambers for Attorney General," flyer, September 1982, campaign material.
48. Chambers, letter to Mike Boyle, 20 October 1981, Chambers Collection.
49. "Chambers Meets with Jimmy Carter and North Freeway," interview by Ben Gray, *Kaleidoscope*, KETV, 2 September 1979, Chambers Collection.
50. Ibid.
51. Chambers, itinerary and telephone log, 11 May 1984.
52. Ibid.
53. "The Chambers Candidacy: A Reason to Vote," *Omaha Star*, 30 September 1982, 1.
54. Ibid.
55. "Chisholm Honoring Omaha," *Omaha Star*, 30 September 1982; "Black Caucus 'Top' New Grand Old Party," *Omaha Star*, 30 September 1982, 1.
56. "North Omaha Soul Dodge 4-H Club Continues Its Community Citizenship Program," *Omaha Star*, 30 September 1982; Erven McSwain, Jr., letter to Pastor and Members C.O.G.I.C. Omaha, 18 October 1982.
57. McSwain, letter to C.O.G.I.C., 18 October 1982.
58. *Unicameral Update* 10, 20 (22 May 1987): 1–3.
59. Vickey Parks, interview by author, Omaha, 19 May 2003.
60. "Elect the Attorney General on a Non-partisan Basis: Legislative Bill 875." Leg-

islative Bill 875 died at end of the session.
61. Parks, interview by author, Omaha, 19 May 2003.
62. Ibid.
63. Chambers, itinerary and telephone log, 30 August, 1983.
64. Chambers, itinerary and telephone log, August 1983; Chambers, note to author, 25 March 2005.
65. Chambers, itinerary and telephone log, "Director of Prison," 29 June 1983; Chambers, itinerary and telephone log, 28 July 1983.
66. In order to secure a cable franchise, Cox Cable agreed to make several public access channels available to community groups. The University of Nebraska at Omaha, religious, and "minority" communities were allocated channels for the broadcast of alternative programming. Eliga Ali organized Channel 22, a public access channel for North Omaha. At one time Chambers and Tariq Al-Amin co-hosted a program on Channel 22. Eventually Chambers started his own call-in show so that his constituents could dialog with him.
67. Rev. Wilkerson M. Harper, Omaha, letter to U.S. President James Carter, Washington, DC, 1981; Calloway and Smith, *Visions of Freedom on the Great Plains*, 153, 157.
68. Buddy Hogan, "Buddy's Byline," *Omaha Star*, 11 September 1980.
69. Manning Marable, *Blackwater: Historical Studies in Race, Class Consciousness, and Revolution* (Niwot, CO: University Press of Colorado, 1993), 93–121.
70. Ibid., 112–13.
71. Ibid., 115.
72. Ibid.; Kenneth O'Reilly and David Gallen, eds., *Black Americans: The FBI Files* (New York: Carroll and Graf Publishers, 1994), 7–9, 17.
73. Marable, *Blackwater: Historical Studies*, 115.
74. Ibid., 117; "Ernie Sticks to His Style for DC Trip," *Lincoln Journal*, 14 August 1979. See also "Chambers and Carter Exchange Racial Views," *Omaha Star*, 23 August 1979.
75. "Chambers and Carter Exchange Racial Views."
76. Ibid.
77. "Ernie Sticks to His Style for DC Trip," *Lincoln Journal*, 14 August 1979.
78. "Chambers Says Young Acted as 'Point Man' for Carter," *Lincoln Star*, 24 August 1979.
79. "Ernie Chambers Was Wrong," *Lincoln Journal*, 26 August 1979.
80. "Rotarians Hear Controversial Senator," *Falls City Journal*, 22 August 1979.
81. Chambers Meets with Jimmy Carter and North Freeway."
82. Ibid.
83. Ibid.
84. Chambers, itinerary and telephone log, 28 January 1984; Chambers, Omaha, letter to *New York Times* writer James Reston, 28 June 1984.
85. Chambers, "Remarks on Jews Taken Out of Context," *Lincoln Star*, 24 May 1984.

86. Ibid.; Minister Louis Farrakhan was born on the 11 of May 1933. Since the mid-1970s he has served as the National Representative and spiritual leader of the Nation of Islam.
87. Ibid.
88. "The Fall of Jesse Jackson," open letter; Chambers, letter to Imam Louis Farrakhan, Omaha to Chicago, 18 July 1984; Chambers, "Meeting Between Black & Jewish Community," interview with Ben Gray, *Kaliedoscope*, KETV, February 1985 (aired), tape series II, 13 June 1986.
89. Chambers, "Meeting Between Black & Jewish Community," interview with Ben Gray, *Kaliedoscope*, KETV, February 1985 (aired), tape series II, 13 June 1986.
90. Ibid.
91. Ibid.
92. Thomas A. Fogarty, "Legislative Leader Elections Leave Bitter, Hostile Feelings," *Journal Star*, 13 January 1985, 2B.
93. Ibid.
94. Ibid.
95. Ibid.
96. Ibid.; "Chambers, Hoagland Seek Chairmanship of Judiciary," *Omaha World Herald*, 8 January 1985.
97. Fogarty, "Legislative Leader Elections Leave Bitter, Hostile Feelings," 2B. "Newsmakers Exercise, Push Away Plate," *Omaha World-Herald*, 11 January 1985.
98. "Legislature Policy Board Has Five New Members," *Omaha World Herald*, 10 January 1985.
99. "Anti-Death Penalty Bill" *Unicameral Update* 2, 60 (1–7 March 1979): 5 (Legislative Bill 262 proposed to repeal the death penalty). See *Unicameral Update* 2, 55 (January 1979): 24–31; *Unicameral Update* 2, 69 (May 1979): 3–9; "LR43," *Unicameral Update* 2, 67 (19–25 April 1979): 3; Chambers, "Racism and White Supremacy Won Over Ability, Seniority, Legislative Archive," January, 1985; Chambers, "Judiciary Committee Chairmanship," journal entry, 9 January 1985, Chambers Collection.
100. Chambers, "Judiciary Committee Chairmanship."
101. Ibid.
102. Chris Beutler, letter to Chambers, 20 November 1984, Lincoln; Chambers, letter to Colleagues, 24 November 1982.
103. Chris Beutler, letter to Chambers, 20 November 1984, Lincoln; Chambers, letter to Colleagues, 24 November 1982.
104. Chambers, Lincoln, letter to Colleagues, Lincoln, 8 June 1976; "Police Practices and the Preservation of Civil Rights," pamphlet (Washington, DC: U.S. Civil Rights Commission, 1980), ii.
105. Chambers, letter to Colleagues, 8 June 1976; "Police Practices and the Preservation of Civil Rights," ii, 1, 3.

106. Kevin O'Hanlon, "Cairo Incident Avoidable, Called 'Close to Murder,'" *Beatrice Daily Sun,* 25 October 1984. Cairo, Nebraska, farmer Arthur Kirk was killed by a State Patrol officer.
107. Ibid.
108. Ibid.
109. Ibid.
110. Samuel Van Pelt, "Report of the Special Investigator to the Governor and to the Chairman of the Judiciary Committee of the Nebraska Legislature," 1 December 1984: 7–8, 80, 123–24; O'Hanlon, "Cairo Incident Avoidable," 26.
111. O'Hanlon, "Cairo Incident Avoidable," 26.
112. Samuel Van Pelt, "Report of the Special Investigator to the Governor and to the Chairman of the Judiciary Committee of the Nebraska Legislature," 1 December 1984: 7–8, 80, 123–24, 253.
113. Chambers to Members of the Legislature, Governor Robert Kerrey, and Col. Elmer Kohmetscher, memorandum, 25 October 1985.
114. Ibid.
115. Chambers, itinerary and telephone log, 9 and 12 August 1983, and 14 November 1983.
116. Chambers, itinerary and telephone log, 18 November 1983.
117. Chambers, itinerary and telephone log, 15, 17, and 22 November 1983.
118. Chambers, Lincoln, note to author, Charlotte, 25 March 2005. See also "Editorial," *Omaha World Herald,* 5 May 1984.
119. Chambers, itinerary and telephone log, 4 May 1984.
120. Ibid.
121. Chambers, itinerary and telephone log, 22 November 1983.

Chapter Six

1. Senator Loran Schmit et al., *Final Report of the Franklin Committee,* Nebraska State Legislature, 1992, 2–8.
2. Ibid., 10.
3. "Homosexual Prostitution Inquiry Ensnares VIP's with Reagan, Bush," *Washington Times,* 29 June 1989.
4. "Legislative Resolution: Authorizes Franklin Committee," *Unicameral Debate,* Nebraska State Legislature, 18 November 1988, 12–22; "Legislative Resolution: Authorizes Franklin Committee," Nebraska State Legislature, 10 January 1989, 12–22.
5. Schmit et al., *Final Report of the Franklin Committee,* 8–14.
6. Ibid., 1, 23–25.
7. Ibid., 27–29.
8. Ibid., 34–36, 47–48.

9., Ibid., 48–51, 57–63.
10., Ibid., 70–74; "Chambers Won't Help Bring in Witnesses," *Lincoln Journal*, 2 March 2, 1990, 10.
11. "Aroused 'Mice' Trap Ernie."
12. Chambers, introducer's statement, 1989, LB 424: 1–2, 39. See also "Introducer's Statement of Intent: LB 588," 22 February 1989.
13. Chambers, "Opening Statement: LB 340," *Unicameral Update* (25 January 1989): 44–46.
14. Ibid., 44–47.
15. Ibid.
16. Ibid.
17. "Campus Speakers Vent Frustration," *Omaha World Herald*, 2 May 1992, 37.
18. Deborah Shanahan, "Riot Rumors Cause Stir, Absences in Omaha Schools," *Omaha World Herald*, 2 May 1992, 37; "Police Procedure," Judiciary Committee Hearing LB 484, 3 March 1975: 27, 30; "Criminal Code: Article 10: LB 83," Floor Debate, 12 April 1977, 02622–02633.
19. "Police Procedure," Judiciary Committee Hearing LB 484, 3 March 1975: 27, 30; "Criminal Code: Article 10: LB 83," Floor Debate, 12 April 1977, 02622–02633; "Parole Board's Recommendation on Rice Is Wrong," *The Shield* (April 1993), 18: 4; "LB 717 Being Pushed by Lies and Name Calling," *The Shield* (June 1993), 15: 6.
20. K. G. Miller, "Homicide: Powell, James," *Omaha Police Division Supplementary Report*, 23 November 1980, 2–3; James Keenan, *Douglas County Coroner's Office Report*, 23 November 1980.
21. James Keenan, *Douglas County Coroner's Office Report*, 23 November 1980.
22. Interdenominational Ministerial Alliance Civic Committee Chair and President Wilkerson Harper and Luke Nichols, Omaha, letter to Mayor Al Veys and Steve Rosenblatt, City Council president, 15 July 1980, Omaha.
23. Ibid.
24. Ibid.
25. Al Veys, mayor, letter to Police Division and Black Ministerial Alliance, 16 July 1980.
26. Ibid.
27. Ibid.
28. Ibid.
29. "Press Release," President Interdenominational Ministerial Alliance, Luke Nichols, Omaha, 3 July 1980.
30. Ibid.; Thomas D. Thalken, U.S. Attorney, letter to Chambers et al., 27 January 1981; Chambers, *Police Abuse of Residents of Hilltop Homes, Report*, 30 November 1981, i.
31. Thalken, letter to Chambers et al., i.
32. Ibid.

33. Ibid.
34. Ibid.
35. Ibid.
36. Chambers, itinerary and telephone log, Robert Wadman, 28 January 1984. For floor debate on police actions in Omaha, see "Police Procedure." See also "Criminal Code: Article 10: LB 83."
37. Chambers, itinerary and phone log, Wadman, 28 January 1984.
38. Ibid.
39. Ibid.
40. Marvin McClarty, Sr., interview by author, 21 May 2003.
41. Ibid.
42. Ibid.
43. Ibid. Native Americans and Hispanic Americans faced similar problems with police department employees.
44. Ibid.
45. Ibid.
46. Ibid.
47. Ibid.
48. Ibid.
49. Tariq Al Amin, interview by author, 20 May 2003.
50. Chambers, itinerary and telephone log, Robert Wadman, 28 January 1984. For floor debate on police actions in Omaha, see "Police Procedure." See also "Criminal Code: Article 10: LB 83." Cindy Gonzalez, "He's Shadowed Buffett for 17 Years," *Omaha World Herald*, 24 April 2011.
51. William Loren Katz, *The Invisible Empire: The Ku Klux Klan Impact on History*. (Washington, DC: Open Hand Publishing, 1986), 41, 135, 141, 149.
52. Ibid., 149.
53. Over 75 groups affiliated with or with similar ideologies to the Klan existed in the late 1970s. An anti-Klan rally at Greensboro, North Carolina, 3 November 1979, ended in the shooting deaths of five protesters. "Hearing Brings Home Danger of Extremism," *Lincoln Star*, 7 December 1985. See also Legislative Bill 772 "Paramilitary Groups, Exhibit J, 1983; "LB 772 Anti-Defamation League," 8, 2 *Law Report*, 1983; Legal Affairs Department Civil Rights Division.
54. Anthony M. Platt, "Between Scorn & Longing: Frazier's Black Bourgeoisie," in James E. Teele, ed. *E. Franklin Frazier and Black Bourgeoisie* (Colombia, MO: University of Missouri Press, 2002), 76. See also E. Franklin Frazier, *Black Bourgeoisie* (New York: Simon and Schuster, 1997), 190–200; E. Franklin Frazier, "Durham Capital of the Black Middle Class," in Alain Locke, ed., *The New Negro* (New York: Touchstone, 1999), 16, 333–40; Johnson, Tekla "Class Divisions Mark the Divide Over LB 1024," *Omaha Star*, June 1, 2006;"Temperance Rally," *Omaha Star* March 1, 2007; "Urban League," *Omaha Star*, March 2005; Fred Conley, letter to Chambers, Omaha, October 17, 1986; "Douglass County

Grand Jury Report," February 1987, *Douglas County State of Nebraska* (Misc. Doc. 3 pg, 0095); Chambers, "Tom Reilly," memo; Chambers, telephone logs for November 29, 1989–January 9, 1990; "Fred Conley, Kellin Resolution," 16 October 1986, Chambers Collection; Mumgaard, Thomas O. "Opinion: on Conley Resolution," Omaha City Law Department (16 October 1986), 1–8; Chambers, "Susan," memo in telephone records (29 November 1989–January 9, 1990); Chambers, "To Mayor Mike Boyle: Regarding the Death of Richard L. Kellin: While in the Custody of Omaha Police," *Report*, 9 June 1986, x, 1.

55. Chambers, "To Mayor Mike Boyle," x, 1.
56. Ibid., 3–4. See also "Editorial," *Omaha World Herald*, 30 May 1986.
57. Chambers, "To Mayor Mike Boyle," 3–4.
58. Ibid., 5.
59. Ibid., 4–10. The first booking or detention officer was Petra Young. Matson gave Kellin a ride in the squad car although an ambulance had arrived; the stretcher and ambulance went unused. The arrest took place at 3361 Erskine Street. Charles Matson and Brenda Windhorst were the arresting officers.
60. Ibid., 11.
61. Ibid., 10.
62. Ibid., 17.
63. Ibid., 45.
64. Ibid.
65. Terry Hyland and Jeff Gauger, "Five Grand Juries Like One Sought by Spire Have Convened in County Since 1941," *Omaha World Herald*, 31 January 1990, 14.
66. Chambers, letter to James A. Ahearn, FBI, 13 June 1986, Omaha.
67. Ibid.
68. "Police Shooting of Richard L. Kellin" and "ADL *Report*," interview by Ben Gray, *Kaleidoscope*, KETV, 13 June 1986.
69. "Police Shooting of Richard L. Kellin" and "ADL *Report*," interview by Ben Gray, *Kaleidoscope*, KETV, 13 June 1986; Hyland and Gauger, "Five Grand Juries Like One Sought by Spire." Additional research should be done about the grassroots organizers who ran the petition-signing protest.
70. "Police Shooting of Richard L. Kellin" and "ADL *Report*," interview by Ben Gray, *Kaleidoscope*, KETV, 13 June 1986.
71. Marvin McClarty, Sr., interview by author, 21 May 2003; "Police Shooting of Richard L. Kellin" and "ADL *Report*."
72. Marvin McClarty, Sr., interview by author, 21 May 2003.
73. Ibid.
74. Tariq Al Amin, interview with author, May 2003. Legislative Bill 676 included provisions to notify Coroner's Office if person dies in police custody. See *Unicameral Update* 10, 20 (22 May 1987): 2–3.
75. McClarty, interview by author, Omaha, 21 May 2003.

76. "Chambers Considers Mayoral Bid in 1981," *Omaha World Herald*, 21 October 1980.
77. "Elections: Discrimination," 44 *United States Law Week*, 13 January 1976, 2303.
78. Ibid. Chambers said that he was never serious about running and that "it was for effect, to try to involve the community in political issues," in Chambers, note to author, 25 March 2005. "City Council Elections by District"; *Unicameral Update* 9, 16 (14 May 1986); *Unicameral Update* 9, 1 (10 January 1986): 22; Chambers, "Biographical Sketch of Senator."
79. "Challengers Brace for Race," *Omaha World Herald*, 2 December 1984.
80. "City Council Elections by District"; Chambers, "Biographical Sketch of Senator."
81. "City Council Elections by District"; Wayne Lowden, letter to Committee on Government, Military, and Veterans Affairs, Omaha to Lincoln, 20 January 1976; Robert L. Patterson, president of Omaha Association of Black Social Workers, letter to Senator Dennis Rasmussen, chair, Government and Military Affairs Committee, Nebraska State Legislature, 30 January 1976.
82. Cynthia Grandberry, interview with author, 14 July 2003. Grandberry brought to Chambers's attention that she earned less in state pension funds than her male counterparts and Chambers responded by initiating legislation to end unequal benefits for male and female state employees. Chambers, "Cindy," poem, Chambers Collection.
83. Van J. Vopat, letter to Chambers, 1 June 1984. The Commonwealth Savings and Loan was declared insolvent on 1 November 1983; Senator Chambers voted in favor of helping out investors. *Unicameral Update* 8, 4 (1 February 1985): 8; Chambers, "Farrakhan Issue Used Against Jackson Candidacy," *Lincoln Star*, 10 July, 1984; Floor Debate LB 363, "Aid to Dependent Children," 9 April 1985: 3011, 3014.
84. Floor Debate LB 363, "Aid to Dependent Children."
85. Ibid., 3011, 3014–15; *Unicameral Update* 4, 4 (30 January 1981). Chambers again introduced increases in Aid to Dependent Children.
86. *Unicameral Update* 4, 4 (30 January 1981).
87. Ibid.
88. See "LB 757 Sports Wagering Act," *Unicameral Update* 10, 3 (January 1987): 5. See also "LB 72 to Establish Provisions for Gambling on Sports Events"; "LB 73: Establish Maximum Fees for Attorney Services"; "LB 669 Change Amount of ADC"; "Sports Wagering Operators to be Licensed," *Unicameral Update* 10, 20 (22 May 1987): 2–3; Chambers, note to author, 25 March 2005.
89. See "LB 757 Sports Wagering Act," *Unicameral Update* 10, 3 (January 1987): 5. See also "LB 72 to Establish Provisions for Gambling on Sports Events"; "LB 73: Establish Maximum Fees for Attorney Services"; "LB 669 Change Amount of ADC"; "Sports Wagering Operators to be Licensed," *Unicameral Update* 10, 20 (22 May 1987): 2–3; Chambers, note to author, 25 March 2005.

90. Chambers, "Farrakhan Issue Used Against Jackson Candidacy."
91. Chambers, itinerary and telephone log, Ed Howard, *Associated Press* reporter, 1 August 1984.
92. "Jesse Jackson Visits," *Unicameral Update* 10, 6 (13 February 1987): 3.
93. Ibid.
94. Michael Kazin, *A Godly Hero: The Life of William Jennings Bryan* (New York: Alfred Knopf, 2006); William Jennings Bryan, "Cross of Gold" (speech), Official Proceedings of the National Democratic Convention, Chicago, 7–11 July 1896, 226–34. William Jennings Bryan ran for president of the United States on the Democratic Party ticket in 1896, 1900, and 1908. He served in the U.S. Congress beginning in 1881, and as secretary of state in 1913.
95. Michael Kazin, *A Godly Hero: The Life of William Jennings Bryan*; Chambers, itinerary and telephone log, Howard; Chambers, note to author, 25 March 2005.
96. Chambers, itinerary and telephone log, "Interviews," 10, 12, 14, 26 October 1988; Chambers, itinerary and telephone log, "Fulani Campaign Press Conference at Wesley House," 15 September 1988; Chambers, itinerary and telephone log, Mike Hardy, 16 September 1988.
97. Pike, Douglas, "Keep Your Eye on the Fulani-Paul Race," *Philadelphia Inquirer*, 20 October, 1988; Fulani Campaign, flyer, 1988, Chambers Collection.
98. Milloy, Courtland, "One Woman's Third-Party Campaign," *Washington Post*, 16 October, 1988.
99. Ibid.
100. Editorial, "Tactics by Chambers Weaken Election System," *Lincoln Star*, 20 September 1988.
101. "New Alliance Party" Platform, c. 1988, Chambers Collection. The New Alliance Party formed in 1979 and was headquartered at 216 W. 102nd Street in New York City. The party claimed 15,000 members in 1988. "Statement by Bob Kerrey," 17 September 1988, Chambers Collection. See also "Statement by Bob Kerrey," 19 September 1988, Chambers Collection.
102. Chambers, itinerary and telephone log, "Speak at Central Park Mall," 8 May 1988.
103. Jim Raglin, letter and draft "Chambers" article, 26 November 1986, 2–4, Chambers Collection.
104. Ronald L. Staskiewicz, *Douglas County Attorney's Report on the Shooting of Officer Gary Schnebel, Officer Kris Jacobson and Kevin Watson Resulting in the Death of Kevin Watson on April 20, 1987*, 4 June 1987, 1.
105. Ibid.; Michael Salisbury, Omaha Police Division, "Crime against Person, *Report* 0169651," 20 April 1987; Erven McSwain Jr., Human Relations Department, letter to Chambers, 7 May 1987, Omaha.

106. Perry W. Hadden, letter to Omaha Mayor Bernie Simon, 30 October 1987, Chambers Collection.
107. Ibid.
108. John P. Newell, "Chambers's Theory Ludicrous," *Omaha World Herald*, 21 May 1987.
109. Ibid.
110. Chambers, "The Watson Case: Chambers Responds to Criticism," *Omaha World Herald*, 4 June 1987.
111. Ibid.
112. Ibid.
113. "Black Rap Honors for Police Officers," *Omaha World Herald*, 20 October 1987.
114. Ibid., Nick Schinker, "Chambers Blasts Wadman for Approving Police Ward," *Omaha World Herald*, 21 October 1987.
115. Nick Schinker, "Chambers Blasts Wadman for Approving Police Ward," *Omaha World Herald*, 21 October 1987.
116. Ibid.
117. Ibid.
118. Ibid. Blood was found on one of the police officers' gun barrel, and on his shirt and shoe, but the blood residue was not tested. "Police Shooting of Kevin Watson," interview with Ben Gray, *Kaleidoscope*, KETV, 15 May 1987.
119. "Police Shooting of Kevin Watson," interview with Ben Gray, *Kaleidoscope*, KETV, 15 May 1987.
120. Cindy Grandberry, interview with author, 15 August 2001; Shanahan, "Riot Rumors Cause Stir"; "Police Procedure"; "Criminal Code: Article 10: LB 83."
121. Chambers, itinerary and telephone log, Scott Fidge, 11 June 1986, Omaha; Calloway and Smith, *Visions of Freedom on the Great Plains*, 153; Erin Schulte, "Chambers Struggles for All," *Daily Nebraskan*, 21 February 1997, 1, 18; Shanahan, "Riot Rumors Cause Stir"; "Campus Speakers Vent Frustration"; "Charles Washington, December 1, 1923–April 28, 1986," funeral program, May 1986, Great Plains Black History Museum Collection of Omaha.
122. Chambers, "Introducer's Statement: LB 465," 2 March 1989, 1–2; "Theatres Wilde for Oscar Wilde," *Omaha World Herald*, 10 July 1997, 40.
123. Mike Reilly, "Bryant's Admission Stirs Controversy," *Omaha World Herald*, 15 February 1991, 12.
124. Scott Bauer, "New Details Emerge in York," *Lincoln Journal Star*, 8 October, 1998, 1B.
125. Ibid.
126. "Authorize Law Practice," *Unicameral* Update 8, 3 (25 January 1985): 15; Chambers, itinerary and telephone log, 4 May 1984; Chambers, itinerary and telephone log, Gene Crump, 11 May 1984; "LB 772: Paramilitary Groups," Committee on Judiciary Hearing, 21 January 1986, 78, 81.

127. "LB 772: Paramilitary Groups," 78, 81, 86, 88–89.
128. Ibid., 78–92.
129. Ibid. 90–92. "Legislative Bill 772," *Unicameral Update* 9, 6 (14 February 1986): 2. When the legislature tried to limit the activities of a paramilitary group, Chambers offered a kill motion because he said that the measure would be used by police to harass citizens.
130. Chambers, "Biographical Sketch of Senator," Chambers Collection. Minniex, Sherryl George, letter to Chambers, 9 June 2002; Chambers, itinerary and telephone log, Mildred Brown, 24 February 1988; Chambers, itinerary and telephone log, Rowena Moore, 28 February 1988; Chambers, itinerary and telephone log, Al Goodwin, 24 February 1988; Chambers, itinerary and telephone log, Preston Love, 13 January 1989; Chambers, itinerary and telephone log, Rodney Wead, 12 January 1989; Raglin, letter and draft "Chambers" article, 26 November 1986, Chambers Collection.
131. Raglin, letter, 2–4.

Chapter Seven

1. Julian Bond, Benjamin Chavis, Jr., David Dinkins, Carol Mosely Braun, Randall Robinson, Chambers, et al., "Statement on the Announcement of Elections and the Call for End of Sanctions on September 22, 1993," The Africa Fund, 23 September 1993, available in the Chambers Collection. See also American Committee on Africa/African Fund Papers, Amistad Research Center, Tulane University, New Orleans (http://www.amistadresearchcenter.org); "Talk of Chairmanship," *Lincoln Star,* 7 January 1991; "Correction: Chambers Chaired," *Lincoln Star,* 8 January 1991. "Nation; The Anguish of Blacks in Blue," *Time* (23 November 1970), retrieved 7 July 2011 at http://www.time.com/time/magazine/; King-Meadows and Schaller, *Devolution and Black State Legislators,* 51–58; Martin Kilson, "The State of Black American Politics," *The Black Commentator* No. 9, 1–3, 10), retrieved 10 August 2010 at http://www.blackcommentator.com/9_nul.html; Haynie, *African American Legislators,* 153–54; Biles, "Black Mayors"; "Harold Washington." See also Levinsohn, *Harold Washington;* Chris T. Owens, "Black Substantive Representation in State Legislatures from 1971–1994," *Social Science Quarterly* 86, 4 (December 2005): 771–91; Manning Marable, *Black Leadership* (New York: Columbia University Press, 1998), 183.
2. Ibid. Jones, "Black Lawmakers in the Quaker State."
3. Owens, "Black Substantive Representation"; "Senators Adopt Rule to Cut Off Filibusters," *Lincoln Journal,* 15 January 1991. Thirty-three legislators or two-thirds of the body would be needed to invoke cloture.
4. "Chambers Bill Would Repeal Death Penalty in Nebraska," *Lincoln Star,* 17 January 1991, 4; Leslie Boellstorff, "Ernie the Unorthodox," *Omaha World Herald,* 26 November 1995.

5. Harold Otey, letter to Chambers, Lincoln, 8 August 1986.
6. Ibid.
7. "Otey's Lawyers Question Stenberg," *Lincoln Journal Star*, 20 August 1994.
8. "Chambers Words About Lindgren Meant to Be Harsh," *Lincoln Journal Star*, 14 July 1991.
9. Ibid.
10. "Chambers Words About Lindgren."
11. "Chambers Files Complaint Against State Assistant Attorney General," *Lincoln Journal Star*, 14 January 1995.
12. Chris Hain, "Death Penalty Supporters, Opponents Rally," *Daily Nebraskan*, August 22, 1994, 7; "Stenberg Questioned," *Omaha World Herald*, 19 August, 1994.
13. "Senator Chambers Failed," *Omaha World Herald*, 8 December 1997.
14. See "Special Edition 1977 Session," *Unicameral Update* 20, 24 (18 July 1997); "Special Edition 1998 Session," *Unicameral Update* (May 1998): 22–39; "Special Edition 1999 Session," *Unicameral Update* 22, 22 (June 1999): 21–38.
15. "I'm Sorry," *Lincoln Journal Star*, 3 December 1997. See also "Pulling the Law's Teeth," *Omaha World Herald*, 14 March 1999.
16. "In the Legislature," *Omaha World Herald*, 8 January 1999, 14.
17. Martha Stoddard, "Execution Moratorium Is Vetoed" *Lincoln Journal Star*, 27 May 1999; "Veto of Governor," *Legislative Journal*, 26 May 1999; "Champion of Justice Award," plaque, 6 November 1999, Chambers Collection.
18. "Chambers, Beermann Disagree about Write-in Running-mate Law," *Lincoln Star*, 28 September 1994.
19. Ibid.
20. Desda Moss, "Men Pledge New Start," *USA Today*, 17 October 1995.
21. "Nazism," *Lincoln Star*, 17 March 1995.
22. Ibid.
23. Ibid.
24. *Disproportionate Confinement of Minority Youth in Nebraska, Report*, Nebraska Commission on Law Enforcement, University of Nebraska–Lincoln Center on Children, Family and the Law, and Voices for Children in Nebraska (July 1993): 30.
25. *Unicameral Update* 18, 21 (26 May 1995): 8.
26. Ibid.
27. Fred Knapp, "New Rule of Debate Would Try to Hush Talkative Legislator," *Lincoln Journal Star*, 11 January 1996.
28. Ibid.
29. "Opening Tonight: Artists and a Senator," *Omaha World Herald*, 8 February 1996.
30. Gabriella Stern, "Chambers to continue his Judiciary Service," *Omaha World Herald*, 8 January 1997.

31. "Opening Tonight: Artists and a Senator"; "Malcolm X Tribute Set by Foundation," *Omaha Star*, 10 May 2007. See Walter Brooks, "Charles Washington Library Reopened," *Omaha Star*, 6 April 2006.
32. Dennis Smith, letter to Chambers, Lincoln, 16 March 1998.
33. *1999 American Community Survey Report*, (Omaha, NE: UNO Center for Public Affairs research, 1999).
34. *Police/Community Relations in Omaha, Nebraska Report*, Omaha Human Relations Board (Aug. 1998), 1–8. Marvin Ammons was shot and killed on October 26, 1997.
35. Ibid., 2.
36. Ibid., 3.
37. Colman McCarthy, "Idealism and Pragmatism in Nebraska," *Washington Post* 15 March 1994.
38. Ibid.
39. Kevin O'Hanlon, *Hastings Tribune*, 4 January 2000.
40. Lynn Marienau, "The Importance of Being Ernest," *Nebraska Municipal Review* (June 2000), 5–6.
41. Ibid.
42. Leslie Reed and Robynn Tysver, "Abortion Ruling May Lead to More Precise Legislation," *Omaha World Herald*, 29 June 2000, 1.
43. Ibid.
44. Leslie Reed, "Chambers Rejects Role by Johanns," *Omaha World Herald*, 8 June, 2001.
45. Nancy Hicks, "Chambers Again a Dominant Force," *Lincoln Journal Star*, 3 June 2001.
46. Ibid.
47. Leslie Reed, "Chambers Rejects Role by Johanns"; Ken Hambleton, "Crowd Pays Tribute to Senator," *Lincoln Journal Star*, 22 June 2001.
48. "Ernie Chambers Appreciation Day," 2, 3 *Stepping Out Newsletter* (June 2001). See also Ken Hambleton, "There's Something Funny about Festivities," *Lincoln Journal Star*, 17 June 2001.
49. Hambleton, "There's Something Funny about Festivities"; John Fulwider, "Fans Line Up to Appreciate Ernie Chambers," StatePaper.com, 22 June 2001, available at http://nebraska.statepaper.com/vnews/display.v/ART/2001/06/22/3b326c070c7fi.
50. Paul Fell, "Opinion," *Journal Star*, 4 January 2002, 5B.
51. "Legislative Bills Introduced by Senator Ernest Chambers: 1971–1993", Chambers Collection. By 1993 Chambers had introduced over 350 bills. "Chambers Amendments," 1983–2001, Chambers Collection; "Sampling of Legislation Sponsored by Senator Ernie Chambers Which Has Become Law," Chamber Collection.
52. Clarence J. Munford, *Race and Reparations: A Black Perspective for the Twenty-first*

Century (Trenton, NJ: Africa World Press, 1996), 75, 95–98, 193–97; Chambers, telephone logs for 29 November 1989–9 January 1990. Until the end of his days in the legislature, Chambers would receive complaints from his constituents about the powers-that-be in Nebraska. Wardell Smith, president of the South Omaha Association, witnessed a police incident and wanted to tell Chambers privately. The senator supported Carl Allison's (aka Eliga Ali's) efforts to get Cox's Consortium agreement for free public access television channels for North and South Omaha. "'Mad Dads' of Omaha Take on Gangs and Drugs," *New York Times,* June 10, 1990; Chambers, letter to John Mackiel, superintendent Omaha Public Schools, 24 October 2006. See also "District Probes Restraint of Girl, 7," *Journal Star,* October 26, 2006; "Two say Excessive Force Used to Hold Pupil, 7," *Omaha World Herald,* 25 October, 2006.

On July 16, 2001, a nineteen-year-old African American youth named Willie Greenlow was shot and killed by Omaha police officers. Police on the scene said that Greenlow had a gun and was firing it. However, Chambers told Mayor Mike Fahey that police gave different versions of what happened, and so did the slain man's mother; see "Cary Admits Making Misstatement," *Omaha World Herald,* 26 July, 2001.) Police slayings of unarmed Spanish-speaking citizens accompanied the growth of Hispanic immigration to Nebraska. In 1994, Francisco Renteria, a non-English speaker, failed to follow the directions of University of Nebraska police officers and sustained injuries during a police assault, from which he died the following day; see "Soto Persists as Optimist" *Lincoln Journal Star,* 18 September, 2004. Abel Barrera-Siguenza was shot to death by Officer Jason M. Messerschmidt in the summer of 2010 after the twenty-two-year-old fired a pellet gun outside a Mexican restaurant; see "Man Fatally Shot" *Omaha World Herald,* 22 February 2010.

One incident where school personnel were accused of physical assault occurred in 2006. Chambers wrote about the allegations in his weekly *Omaha Star* column and discussed the event on his cable television program. Principal Kirk Estee of Sunny Slope Elementary and a staffer were accused of holding a seven-year-old African American girl face down on the carpet and twisting her arms behind her back; see Chambers, interview with author, 8 June 2004.

Chambers filed a lawsuit against "God" in Douglas County Court in September 2007. The senator said that he was making the point to his colleagues that the Constitution allows all lawsuits, and that their practice of prohibiting some types of suits, which they deemed frivolous, was unconstitutional. Chambers's intent was to demonstrate the freedom that all citizens have to file lawsuits. For more information, see "State Senator Ernie Chambers Sues God," KETV, 17 September 2007 available at http://www.ketv.com/news/14133442/detail.html; Erin Grace and Maggie O'Brien, "Winner's Work Is Cut Out for Him," *Omaha World Herald,* 27 April 2009.

53. Author, journal entries, 14 January 2002 and 8 July 2002.
54. "Legislative Bill 51" Floor Debate, 27 February 2001, 1677–1690.
55. Ibid.
56. Ibid.
57. Ibid.
58. Ibid.
59. Ibid.
60. Chambers, letter to Jon Bruning, Attorney General, 10 May 2003.
61. Chambers, "Racists Target Bonds," *Omaha World Herald*, 9 August 2007.
62. Author, journal entry, 14 January 2002.
63. Coalition Against Injustice, "*Information Letter,*" August 2000, Chambers Collection.
64. "Juvenile Arrests," *Omaha Police Department Annual Report* (2001), 1–2. See also "Adult Arrests," *Omaha Police Department Annual Report Annual Report* (2001), 1–2.
65. Author, journal entry, 8 July 2002. *Unicameral Update* 24, 23 (2001): 9.
66. Author, journal entry, April 2002.
67. Ibid.
68. Ibid.
69. "Anguished, Personal Remembrance of Mollie Rae," *Omaha Star*, 14 May 2002.
70. Ibid.
71. "Third Special Session," *Unicameral Update* 25, 18 (November 2002): 2–3; Chambers, memo to author, 22 June 2011; Director of Research for the Nebraska State Legislature Nancy Cyr, interview with author, 7 July 2011; *Legislative Journal*, Nebraska State Legislature, 7 April 1982 (LB 787, pp. 1788), and 18 April 1988 (LB 1266, p. 1990); "Third Special Session," *Legislative Journal*, 22 November 2002 (LB 1, p. 84); "A Review: Ninety-Seventh Legislative Second Session," Nebraska Legislative Research Office, 2002.
72. Kevin O'Hanlon, "Did Chambers Win by Losing on Bill?" *Lincoln Journal Star*, 23 November 2002.
73. Ibid.
74. Ibid.
75. "Peacemaker of the Year," *Nebraska Report* (March 2002): 3–5.
76. Lela Knox Shanks, "Senator Chambers Survey," 27 May 2003; Leola J. Bullock, "Senator Chambers Survey," 17 May 2003.
77. Shanks, "Senator Chambers Survey".
78. Marshall Lux, "Senator Chambers Survey," 19 May 2003. Bob Kerrey, Ben Nelson, and Mike Johanns were all governors of the state of Nebraska during the last years of the twentieth or early years of the twenty-first centuries.
79. Chambers, interview with author, 25 July 2002.
80. Author, journal entries, 14 January 2002 and 21 July 2002.
81. Chambers, "Appeal to County Attorney Jim Jansen to File Charges Against Jerad

Kruse," *Omaha Star*, 23 July 2002, 1–5. In 2000, Chambers started writing a regular column in the African American weekly, the *Omaha Star*.
82. Ibid.
83. Ibid.
84. Chambers, "Omaha World Herald's Double Standard," *Omaha Star*, 23 October 2003.
85. Ibid. See also Dana Taylor, "Omaha Police Officer Tariq Al-Amin Reinstated," *Omaha Star*, 4 March 2004; Anthony Flott, "Tom Warren from the Chiefs to Chief," *University of Nebraska News and Events*, retrieved 3 August 2009 from http://www.unomaha.edu/news/features/warren_t.php; Todd Cooper, "Omaha Police Chief's Staffing Plan Stopped by Judge," *Omaha World Herald*, 14 February 2007; Equinox137, "Omaha Police," blog, 15 February 2007, available at http://forums.officer.com/forums/archive/index.Php./t-61352.htm.
86. Chambers, "In Memory of Preston Love—The Maestro," *Omaha Star*, 5 October 2006, reprinted from *Omaha Star*, 19 February 2004. Preston Love was born April 26, 1921, and died February 12, 2004, of lung cancer. For more on Love's legacy, see his autobiography, *A Thousand Honey Creeks Later: My Life in Music from Basie to Motown and Beyond* (Hanover, NH: Wesleyan University Press, 1997).
87. Sara Catania, "The Importance of Being Ernie," *Mother Jones* (January–February 2006): 13.
88. "Tolerance vs. Hate," *Journal Star*, 18 July 2004; Chambers, "Winston Churchill Advises Iraq on Resisting Enemy Invaders," *Omaha Star*, 3 April 2003.
89. Catania, "The Importance of Being Ernie," 13–15.
90. Ibid.; Chambers, memo to author, June 22, 2011.
91. Catania, "The Importance of Being Ernie," 13–15.
92. "Special Report: Hall of Fame," *Lincoln Journal Star*, 30 December 2005; "Ernie Chambers Court Groundbreaking Ceremony," program, 26 October 2005.
93. Dana Taylor, "Omaha Locals Honored During King Celebration," *The Omaha Star*, 20 January 2005.
94. "Twenty-Eighth Convention," Freedom from Religion Foundation, program, 11–13 November 2005, 1–2, Chambers Collection.
95. Jo Anne Young, "Chambers: Thanks But No Thanks for Award," *Lincoln Journal Star*, 8 August 2007.
96. "Law to Segregate Omaha Schools Divides Nebraska," *New York Times*, 20 April 2006.
97. See Tekla Ali Johnson et al., "African American Administration of Predominately Black Schools: Segregation or Emancipation in Omaha, Nebraska," in *Africana Cultures and Policy Studies*, Zachary Williams, ed. (New York: Palgrave Macmillan, 2009).
98. "Law to Segregate Omaha Schools Divides Nebraska."
99. Ibid.; Catania, "The Importance of Being Ernie, 15.

100. Chambers, "Teaching Chinese to Black Students Prudent or Irrational?" *Omaha Star*, 15 June 2006.
101. "Law to Segregate Omaha Schools Divides Nebraska."
102. Matthew C. Stelly, "Police Home Invasions on the Rise," *Omaha Star*, 20 July 2004; "Remains in Park Belong to Amber Harris: Hummel Park Body Is that of Missing 12-Year-Old," KETV, 19 May 2006, retrieved at http://www.ketv.com/r/9208830/detail.html; "Amber Harris' Funeral Today," *Omaha World Herald*, 4 August 2006. See also any issue of the *Omaha Star*, December 2006–May 2006; Author, journal entry, 17 July 2001.
103. Stelly, "Police Home Invasions on the Rise"; "Behind Omaha Shootings: 73 Gangs Now Claim City as Home Turf," *Omaha World Herald*, 18 July 2010; Munford, *Race and Reparations*, 326; Chambers, "Private Prisons: Profit Not Penology," *Omaha Star*, 28 June 2001; "The Editor Speaks—Wake Up Black Omahans" *Omaha Star*, 14 June 2007; Chambers, telephone logs for 29 November 1989–January 9, 1990; Platt, *Between Scorn & Longing*. See also Frazier, *Black Bourgeoisie*.
104. McCarthy, "Idealism and Pragmatism in Nebraska."
105. Chambers, letter to members of the Nebraska Supreme Court, Lincoln, 29 April, 2007.
106. Ibid.
107. Catania, "The Importance of Being Ernie, 15; Chambers, memo to author, 22 June 2011.
108. "Wrath of Contrarian Chambers Can Strike Fear," *Omaha World Herald*, 3 June 2007. For first use of Chambers's pseudonym "King Cobra," see "Chambers Again a Dominant Force" *Lincoln Journal Star*, 3 June, 2001.
109. "Wrath of Contrarian Chambers Can Strike Fear".
110. Lela Knox Shanks, "Dedication of Nebraska Judiciary to Senator Chambers," 12 November 2008.
111. Paul Hammel, "Chambers Leaves the Capitol as a Respected Masterful Agitator," *Omaha World Herald*, retrieved 6 January 2009 at http//www.omaha.com/print_friendly.Php?_mod=story.1/8/2009.
112. Ibid.

Afterword

1. "Learning Community Starts Work," *Omaha World Herald*, 9 January 2009. The section of the law to reorganize OPS that divided the school district into three smaller districts was repealed.
2. Joanne Young, "Capitol Flag Rises on 101st Legislature," *Lincoln Journal Star*, 8 January 2009.

Index

Abbott, James, 31
abortion, 108–9, 189, 197
Adams, John, Jr., 13
Adams, John, Sr., 12–13, 70
Adams, Michael B., 70–72, 86, 95
Adams, Ralph, 13
affirmative action, 135, 144, 146
Africa, John, 187
African Americans, 4–24, 27–28, 31, 33, 36–38, 42, 117, 122–24, 186
African American Patrolman's League, 186
African Methodist Episcopal Church, 77
African National Congress, 42–46, 115, 235n23
African People's Union (APU), 115, 121, 124
Africans, 115–16, 118–25, 186
Afrikaans (language), 117
Afrikaner government (South Africa), 117
Afro-American Collegiate Society, 58
Aid to Dependent Children (stipend), 99, 173
Al Amin, Tariq (Terry Thompson), 144, 164, 167, 170, 186, 201, 210, 253n66

Ali, Eliga, 253n66, 265n52
Ali, Muhammad, 25
Althouse, George, 68, 69–73, 76, 77, 81
Amen, Paul, 154
American War for Independence, 94
Ammons, Marvin, 195
Andersen, Richard R., 49
Andersen, Harold, 163
Andersen, Richard R. (Chief of Police), 49, 196
anti-abortion, 109, 189
anti-Apartheid Movement, , 115, 117–18, 121–25, 127, 185
anti-colonial, 55
anti-religious, 17
anti-Vietnam protesters, 25
Apartheid, 5, 43, 46, 115–24, 127, 149, 151, 185, 197
Armstrong, Louis, xviii, 15
Army Reserves, 16, 26
Ashberi, Shomari (Mark Jones), 115
atheism, 213
Augustana Lutheran Church, 23–24

Baer, Alan, 157, 158
Bakers' Supermarket, 179

Bantustans, 116
Baraka, Amiri (Leroi Jones), 94, 115
Barlow, William, 210
Barry, Marion (Mayor), 140, 186
Basie, Count, xviii, 15, 211
Bazaar, Mona, 49–50, 86
Beermann, Allen, 97, 192
Belgrave, Oran, 195, 230n41
Beutler, Chris, 150–51
Bibins, George, 209–10
Bi-Congressional District Conference, 16
Biko, Stephen, 117–18
Bill of Rights, U.S., 90
black
    bourgeoisie, 166
    capitalism, 145
    electoral politics, 4, 148
    middle class, 135
    Nebraskans, 67
    power. *See* Black Power Movement
Black Association for Nationalism Through Unity (BANTU), 46–47
Black Liberators for Action on Campus (BLAC), 115, 121, 124
Black Nationalist Movement, 115
Black Nationalists, 24, 55, 59, 65, 76, 94, 115, 145–46, 174, 219 (see also under nationalism)
Black Panther Party (BPP), xix, 4, 19, 38–39, 47–72, 53–54, 57, 60–61, 72, 85, 89, 198, 206, 234n126, 244n128
    newspaper, 53
black political machine, 74
Black Power Movement, 3–4, 23–28, 31–35, 37–39, 41, 46, 61, 68, 76, 145, 185, 231n71
Black Rainbow Art Gallery, 195
Black Republican Party, 140
Bloom, Bill, 44
Blue Lion Center (Omaha), 144

Blues and Jazz Fest, 202
B'nai B'rith Anti-Defamation League, 85
Bolden, Eddie, 38, 39, 54
Bonacci, Paul, 157, 158
Bond, Julian, 185
Boner, Troy, 157, 158
Boosalis, Helen (Mayor), 112, 113
Boozer, Bob, 23, 75, 180
Boyle, Mike (Mayor), 139, 163, 167–68, 172, 180
Bradley, Eunice, 104–5
Brashear, Kermit, 192, 208
Briese, Paul, 163
Brightman, Ed, 39
Brooks, Catherine, 191
Broom, Robert V., 95
Brotherhood of the Midwest Guardians, 44, 165, 171, 178, 201
Brown-Gilbert, Mildred, 18, 200, 213, 217
Brown v. Board of Education, 14
Brown, Frank, 201, 206, 209
Brown, H. Rap, 21, 46
Brown, J. Kirk, 190–91
Brown, William (Will), xvii-xviii, 13, 227n1
Bryan, William Jennings, 174, 212, 260n94
Bryant, Paul, 181
Buffalo Chip (newsletter), 39, 234n130
Bullock, Leola, 16, 29, 139, 198, 208
Burden, Elizabeth, 115
Burns, Jimmy Wayne, 161
Byndon, Ajamal, 148, 176, 205

Cairo, Nebraska, 153
Calley, William, 90
Calloway, Bertha, 18, 19, 114, 127
Calloway, James, 20
capitalism, 37, 134, 176
Caradori, Gary, 157–58

Carey, Thomas D., Esquire, 22, 30
Carmichael, Stokely (Kwame Toure), 21, 22
Carpenter, Terry, 53, 69, 79, 81–82, 88, 90–91, 97, 99, 100, 118, 120, 133, 176
Carter, Jimmy (U.S. President), 144, 146–47
Carter, Lucy, 19
Carter's Restaurant (Omaha), 19
Cavanaugh, Jim, 207
Cavanaugh, John, 100, 133
Cecil, Robert E., 39, 89
Chambers for Attorney General Campaign, 139–40, 198
Chambers, Ernest W. "Ernie", 8, 61, 85
   as "Dean of the Legislature", 6, 27, 131, 185, 187
   as "Defender of the Downtrodden", xx, 134, 159
   Douglas County Courthouse, speaks at, 179, 206
   "Ernie Chambers Court" (housing complex), 213
   federal government, surveillance on, 27–33
   and "Five Year Plan to Increase Faculty Diversity", 195
   and "The Fourth of July Barbecue, Bugs and Bondage," 201
   as "King Cobra", 218
   legislative primaries, 72
   Malcolm X rally, speaks at, 38
   on Native American rights, 159
   as "Ombudsman", 12, 101, 119, 136, 190, 209
   opinion page writings of, 15, 198
   and Peacemaker of the Year Award, 208
   symposium on violence, speaks at, 36
   and "The Way It Is Today", 109

Chambers family, 8, 228n1
   Chambers, Alyce (sister), 8
   Chambers, David (son), 8
   Chambers, Eddie (brother), 85
   Chambers, Ernie, Jr. (son), 8
   Chambers, Gayla (daughter), 77, 232n88, 246n38
   Chambers, Gilbert (brother), 8
   Chambers, Jacklyn "Jackie" née Lee (wife), 26
   Chambers, JoAnn (sister), 8
   Chambers, Lillian née Swift (mother), 8
   Chambers, Malcolm (father), 8
   Chambers, Mark (son), 8
   Chambers, Nettye (sister), 8
   Chambers, Robert (brother), 8
Channel 22 (North Omaha public access), 207, 253n66
Charles, Doreen, 115
Chavis, Benjamin, Jr., 185
Chicago Police Department, 186
Childers, Elijah, Jr., 111, 113
Chisholm, Shirley, 140
Christian Methodist Episcopal Church, 77
Christian Patriots, 182
Christianity, 28, 33, 165, 209, 233n110
Citizens Coordinating Committee for Civil Liberties, 10, 45, 77
Citron, Peter, 157
Civil Rights Division of the Department of Justice, 102
Civil Rights Era, 3, 180
Civil Rights Movement, 23, 28, 46, 68, 78, 121
civil service, fair hiring, 28, 129
Civil Service Commission Bureau of Personnel Investigations, 28
Civilian Review Board, 186
Clair Memorial United Methodist Church, 19

Clark, B. Akporode (Ambassador), 124
Clark, Dan, 165
Clark, Dick (U.S. Senator), 117–18
Clark, Tim, 202
Clarke, Harold, 190, 206
Cleaver, Eldridge, 39
Clemons, Michael, 73
Coalition Against Apartheid, 124
Coca-Cola bottling plant (Omaha), 10, 19
Colautti case, 108
Coleman, Sherry *née* Hale (Lateefah), 115
colonialism, 17, 33, 42, 46, 54–55, 116
Commonwealth Savings and Loan, 153–54, 155, 172, 259n83
Communist Party, 61
Community, The, xvi, 5, 11–12, 14–15, 20, 23, 26–27, 31, 33, 35, 42–45, 48–57, 60–61, 65, 67, 70, 72–80, 83–88, 94–95, 113–14, 139
ConAgra, 173
Conference on Public Investment and South Africa, 124
Congress of Racial Equality (CORE), 10, 208
Congressional Black Caucus, 140
Congressional Committee for Un-American Activities, 42
Conley Resolution, 167
Conley, Fred, 144, 163, 167, 173, 180–81
consent decree, 102, 165
Constitution, U.S, 15, 25, 27, 30, 37, 63, 90
Constructive Engagement (federal policy), 121
Cornhusker State, 93, 103
Council for Community Justice, 87
Council on African Affairs, 42
Council, Brenda, 179, 213, 221
Counter Intelligence Program (COINTELPRO), 61
Creighton University, xix, 10, 14, 16, 18, 42, 61, 75, 109, 211

Medical Center, 76, 211
School of Law, 26, 114, 131
Criminal Code of Nebraska, 160
Criminal Section, United States Civil Rights Division, 160
Cropper, Walter (Judge), 51
Crump, Gene, 140
Cudaback, Jim, 194
Curtis, Al (Sergeant), 112
Curtis, Carl T., 97

Dacus, Robert, 63
Daily Nebraskan, The, 180
Danner Community Service Award, 88
Danner Williams, Marian. *See* Williams, Marian Danner
Danner, Edward (State Senator), 16, 22, 55, 61, 65, 69, 81–88
Davis Insurance, 86, 202
Davis, Angela Y., 61, 146, 206
Davis, Dick, 202
Davis, Ossie, 84
Davis, Rick, 23, 86
De Porres Club, xviii, 10, 18–19
death penalty, 90, 99, 128–29, 136, 151, 189–92, 197–99, 207–8, 218, 250n4, 254n99
moratorium on, 198
protests against, 254n99
DeCamp, John, 81, 108, 242n84
Delany, Martin R., 94, 117
Democratic National Convention, 25
Democratic Party, xix, 25, 82–83, 145, 148, 174–75, 188, 201, 214–19
Dillard, George, 144, 149, 178, 180
Dinkins, David, 185, 186
Direct Action Committee, 16
diasporic Africans, 11, 46, 166
discrimination, xvi, 10, 17, 25, 27, 28, 41, 59, 65, 68, 72, 74, 85, 102–3, 109, 119–20, 122, 130, 131, 134–35, 149, 151, 165, 171, 180, 193, 199, 203, 239n14

divestment, 118
DNA, use in criminal investigations, 212
Dodd, Bernice Stephens, 200
Douglas County (Nebraska), xvii, xviii, 13, 22, 48, 51, 161, 166–67, 179, 183, 197, 206, 209, 211
    attorney, 197
    board, 197
    commissioner, 183
    coroner, 161, 167
    corrections, 206
    courthouse, 198
    district court, 198
    register of deeds, 198
Douglas, Paul, 138–39, 140, 141, 153–54, 197
Douglass, Frederick, 21, 117
Dr. King Humanitarian Award, 213
Dreamland Hall (Omaha), 10
DuBois, W.E.B., 42
Dundee Sun, 35–36
Dworak, James J. (Mayor), 17, 18, 66

Ebony, 21, 24
Echo Hawk, Walter, 159
Economic Empowerment Committee, 205
Eighth Circuit Court of Appeals, U.S., 103
El Hajj Malik El Shabazz (Malcolm X), 3, 21, 45, 76, 123, 127, 195
Eleventh Legislative District (Omaha), xv, 55–56, 70, 78, 129, 196, 221, 238n89, 242n84
Eppley Airfield, 10
Eppley Boys Club, 70
Ernie Chambers Information Center, 142
Eure, Dorothy, 16, 180
Euro-Americans, 32–33, 93, 109, 134–35, 183

European trusteeships, 42
Evers, Medgar, 29
Everybody Magazine, 23, 61, 70
Exon, James J., 80

Fair Employment Practice Act, 119
Farrakhan, Louis, 148, 193, 254n86
Federal Bureau of Investigation (FBI), 23, 26–30, 33, 36–39, 47, 56, 59–61, 99, 111, 146, 156, 162–63, 169–70, 181
Federal Highway Administration, 140
Federal Works Program, 88
Fletcher, Arthur A., 76–77
Florence Boulevard (Omaha), 215
Florence Pinkston's School of Music, 11
For Civil Liberties Club, 10, 45, 77
Ford, Gerald, 103
Forty-Eighth Legislative District, 133
Foster, Sonny, 180
Fowler, Steve (U.S. Senator), 121, 127, 249n97
Foxall, Pitmon, 24, 56
Franklin Committee, 155, 157–59
Franklin Credit Union, 155–158
Franklin School, 102
Freedom From Religion Foundation, 213
Freedom Incorporated, 74
Friend, Joe, 56, 163
Friends of Ernie Chambers Campaign, 88
Fulani, Lenora, 175

Garrison, George, 171
Geiger, Bernie, 114
Geneva Conventions, 90
German Consul General, 193
ghetto, xv, 7, 14, 17, 20, 25, 33, 50, 66, 78, 109, 114
Gibson, Bob, 23, 212, 214n32
Goldberg, Michael A., 204
Goldwater, Barry, 17

Goode, Wilson, 187
Goodwin, Al, 163, 180
Goodwin, Dan, 16, 30, 44, 51–53, 75, 87, 88, 89, 95, 101, 138, 139, 141, 252n46
Government, Military, and Veterans Affairs Committee, 128, 130, 133, 136, 185
Governor's Emergency Fund, 69
Graf, Nanette, 75
grand jury, 62, 98, 112, 157–59, 161, 166–67, 170, 210
Grandberry, Cynthia, 103, 168, 172, 192, 221,
Gray, Ben, 142, 147–48, 163, 169, 179, 201, 213–14
Great Plains Black Museum, 19
Greater Omaha Community Action, 33, 70, 72
Greek Town (South Omaha), 13

Haberman, Rex, 124
Hamer, Fannie Lou, 25, 82
Harper, Wilkerson, 161
Harris, Amber Marie, 215
Hart, James, Jr., 95, 162
Henderson, Gerald, 113
Henry, Patrick, 21
Herzog, David, 56
Hicks, Nancy, 113
Hicks, Phyllis, 217
Hill, Elijah, 167
Hilltop Homes Housing Project, 163
HIV/AIDS, 180
Hoagland, Peter, 150
Hogan, Buddy, 145, 148, 149, 163, 169, 171, 178–80, 200, 201
Holiness Church, 19
Holland, Denny, 18–19
Hoover, J. Edgar, 28, 59
Hopkins, Anna, 111
Horace Mann School, 54, 62

House, Raleigh, 38–39
Human Rights Movement, 36, 44
humanism, 44
Humanist of the Year Award, 213

independent (political affiliation), 4, 82, 101, 138, 140–141, 150, 174–75
Indian Hill (South Omaha), 13
Interdenominational Ministerial Alliance, 161
International Association of Chiefs of Police, 54
International Conventions on Human Rights, 90
integration, xvii, xviii, 4, 20, 45, 103
Islam. *See* Nation of Isalm

Jackson, Jesse, 135, 144, 148–49, 173–75
Jackson, Kenneth (Hadari Sababu), 115
Jacobson, Kris, 176, 178
Jaha (Deresa Oliver Hall), 115
Jansen, Jim, 209
Jesse Jackson for President Campaign, 144, 148
Jet (magazine), 75
Jewell Building (Omaha), 10
Jewell, Cecilia, 10
Jewell, James, 10
Jewish community, 32, 57, 147–49, 159, 182
jitney services, 11
Johannesburg, South Africa, 63, 117
Johanns, Mike, 192, 197–98, 209
Johnson, Lerlean, 205–6
Johnson, Lyndon Baines, 25, 59
Johnson, Nettye (Chambers), 8, 70
Jones, Charles E., 73, 187
Jones, Kelsey, 180
Jones, Mark (Shomari Ashberi), 115
Joubert, John J., 192

Kaleidoscope (television program), 147, 149, 169, 179, 213
Keefe, Dennis, 131
Keenan, James, 167–68
Kelley, Barbara, 111–12
Kelley, J.R., 20
Kellin, Richard, 166–71
Kellom School, 102
Kennedy Onassis, Jacqueline, 195
Kerner Commission on Civil Disorders, 20
Kerner Commission Report, 201
Kerner, Otto, 20
Kerrey, Robert, 143, 153, 154
KETV Channel Seven, 85, 147, 163, 169, 179. See also *Kaleidoscope*
Keyes, Orval, 146
Kiewit, Peter, 20, 70
Kilberg, Bobbie Green, 103
Kimsey, Gary, 68,
King, Coretta Scott, 135
King, Danny, 157–58
King, Larry, 158, 163
King, Martin Luther, Jr., 24, 28, 38, 46, 213
King, Rodney, 179
Kirk, Arthur L., 152–53
Knowles, Donald, 51, 168
Knutzen, Owen, 103
Kountze Park. *See* Malcolm X Memorial Park
KRCB Radio, 52
Krumme, Charles, 34
Ku Klux Klan (KKK), 8, 165, 182, 211–12, 257n53

Labedz, Bernice, 108, 155
Lahners, Ronald, 111
Lancaster County Sheriff, 111
Landis, David, 194
Lateefah (Sherry Hale Coleman), 115
latinos, 175, 216

Lauck, Gary "Gerhard," 193
Leahy, Eugene, 22, 30, 50–52, 53, 97, 98
Legal Aid Society, 95
Legislature, Nebraska. *See* Nebraska Unicameral
Legislative Bill 1046 (to reorganize Omaha Public School District), xxi, 213
Lewis, Arvid Sherdell, 110, 112–13, 131
Libertarian Party, 175
Life Magazine, 23–24
Lincoln, Nebraska, 8, 10, 16, 20, 29, 38, 58, 67–69, 73, 81, 83–84, 95, 101, 110–115, 118–19, 124, 131–32, 136–39, 142–43, 153, 155–56, 158, 181, 191, 193, 196–98, 209, 212
Lincoln Action Program, 110, 113
Lincoln Committee to Elect Ernie Chambers for State Attorney General, 139
Lincoln Interfaith Council, 193
Lincoln Police Department, 111–12, 139, 156
Lincoln Journal, 79, 92, 138, 172, 197–98, 212
Lincoln Star, 14, 91, 133, 138, 185
Lindgren, Sharon, 190
Lispcomb, Ennice, 68
Little Black Sambo, 28
Loder, James, 48
Loos, Rodney, 111, 112, 247n70
Lothrup Elementary School, 33–35, 62, 102
Love, Preston, Jr., 201
Love, Preston, Sr., 15, 201, 211
Lutheran Film Associates, 23
Lux, Marshall, 19
lynching, xvii, xviii, 8, 13, 43, 227n1, 229n24

Mad Dads, 144, 200
Mahoney, Eugene T. "Gene", 79

Malcolm X (El Hajj Malik El Shabazz), xv, xvii, 3–4, 21–22, 28–38, 45–46, 50, 55, 76, 78, 84, 89, 123, 127, 195, 212
Malcolm X Memorial Park (Omaha), 38
Mandela, Nelson, 122, 185
Manire, Jennifer, 181
Marable, Manning, 145
Markoe, Father John, 10, 16, 19
Marsh, Frank, 91, 145
marxism, xix, 134
Masonic lodges, 20
Matson, Charles, 166, 168
Matula, Floyd, 47
Maxey, Albert, 181
Mayo, C.B., 11
McCarthyism, 42
McClarty, Marvin, Sr., 24, 44, 54, 56, 58, 73, 86, 144, 163–65, 170–71, 201
McManus, Jane, 190
McNair, Rudolph, 180
McSwain, Erven, Jr., 141, 163, 177
McVoy, Lawrence W.M., 16
Metoyer, Raymond, 18, 86
Metropolitan Entertainment and Convention Authority (MECA), 217
Middle America, 38, 183, 219
Middle West, 188, 207
Midwest, 5, 8, 29, 38, 44, 74, 92, 117, 121, 165, 171, 174, 178, 187, 199, 201
The Militant, 46
Million Man March, 193
Minard, Larry, 56, 57
Miss Black Nebraska Pageant, 19
Mississippi Democratic Party, 25, 83
Mississippi Freedom Democratic Party, 25, 83
Missouri River, 20, 80, 202
Missouri State Legislature, 74
Mogocrane, Simon, 123
Mondale, Walter, 135, 174
Moore, Rowena, 97

Morgan, P.J., 174
Morrison, Frank, 43, 66
Morton Park swimming pool, 19
Moses, Wilson Jeremiah, 37
Mosely Braun, Carol, 185
Mosoli, Jerry, 123
Motaung, Marcus, 123
Mother Jones, 212
Mothers for Adequate Welfare, 95
Mothibamele, J.L.T., 125
Moul, Maxine, 190
Mt. Moriah Baptist Church, 19
Movement, The. *See* Civil Rights Movement
Muhammad Speaks (newspaper), 7
Mumgaard, Thomas O., 167
Mutual of Omaha, 45, 120
Myers, Lawrence R., 86, 180

Naledi High School, 117
Nation of Islam, xix, 4, 7, 25, 26, 148, 193, 254n86
National Anti-defamation League, 148
National Association for the Advancement of Colored People (NAACP)
  NAACP Junior, 26
  NAACP Lincoln, Nebraska, 29, 139, 193, 198, 208
  NAACP Omaha, Nebraska, xxi, 10–11, 16, 25–26, 145, 169, 171, 178, 200–01, 206, 215
National Association of Criminal Defense Lawyers, 192
National Black Caucus of State Legislators, 188
National Black Political Convention, 115
National Coalition to Abolish the Death Penalty, 192
National Commission on Civil Disorders, 20
National Conference on Racial Problems in New York, 33

National Educational Television, 24
National Geographic, 101
National Guard, 16, 21, 32, 42, 47
National Park Service, 159
National Urban League, 10
nationalism, 94, 151, 244n128
Black Nationalism, xix, 37, 56, 93–94, 227n4, 237n65,
Native Americans, 151, 159–60, 175, 192
Naylor, Kirk, Jr., 131, 156
Nazis, 32, 182
Near Northside, xviii, xix, xxii, 5, 9, 16, 22, 55, 66. *See also* North Omaha
Near Northside Police Community Relations Council, 16, 22
Nebraska (state of), 4–5, 58, 92, 97, 121, 123, 125, 137, 217
Nebraska and Congressional District Legislation Conference Committee, 16
Nebraska Association of Trial Attorneys, 132
Nebraska Attorney General, 156, 157, 159
Nebraska Black Political Caucus, 97
Nebraska Civil Rights Code, 65
Nebraska Conference on Race and Religion, 17
Nebraska Department of Corrections, 136
Nebraska Department of Roads, 119
Nebraska Equal Opportunity Commission, 68, 86, 119
Nebraska National Guard, 47
Nebraska Press Association, 183
Nebraska School for the Deaf, 174
Nebraska State Bar Association, 131, 171, 182
Nebraska state capitol, 29, 80, 83, 100, 158, 159, 160, 191, 203, 211–12, 218–19
Nebraska State Historical Society, 159, 160,
Nebraska State Patrol, 99, 131, 152, 157, 161
Nebraska State Penitentiary, 75, 216
Nebraska State Trooper, 216
Nebraska Statehouse, 186, 202
Nebraska Supreme Court, 154, 159, 218
Nebraska Unicameral, xvi, 5, 56, 65, 67, 69–71, 78–79, 82, 86, 88–90, 92–93, 95, 104, 110, 113, 117–18, 123, 128–30, 133–34, 136–37, 140, 150–51, 160, 167, 171, 173, 175, 182–83, 185, 188, 193, 197, 204, 207, 211–12, 215, 218–19, 221
   Executive Board, 136, 150
   Judiciary Committee, 107, 128, 131–32, 136, 139, 149–51, 153, 165, 180, 182, 194, 218–19
   Labor Committee, 68
   Legislative Clerk's Office, 78, 83
   Legislative Research Office, 130
   legislative resolutions, 5, 131, 182
   Public Works Committee, 88
   Washington Conference Committee, 16
Nebraska Urban League, 86, 95
Nebraska Wesleyan University, 88
Nebraskans Against the Death Penalty, 207
Nebraskans for Justice, 106
Nebraskans for Peace, 123, 208
Negro Historical Society of Nebraska, 114
Nelson, Ben, 189, 193
Neo-Nazi Movement, 193
Neo-Nazi Party, 182
Nesbitt, Eugene, 24, 47
Nevels, Fred, 20
Nevels, Marvel, 111
New Alliance Party, 175–76, 182
New York City, 33, 124, 129, 148, 175, 186
New York Times, xxi
Newby, Linda, 180

INDEX—277

Newman United Methodist Church, 139
Nichols, Luke, 161–62
Nightwatch (CBS television program), 142
Nixon, Richard, 60, 82, 97, 99, 148
Nkrumah, Kwame, 42, 117
Norris, George, 254
North Omaha (North O., Near Northside), xv, xviii, xix, 5–6, 8–15, 17–20, 22–24, 31, 34, 36, 42–44, 46–50, 54–55, 57, 65–69, 71, 73–74, 77, 84–86, 93, 98, 100–102, 104, 114, 117, 121, 124, 127, 129, 139–42, 144–45, 149, 155, 158, 161, 164–67, 172–73, 176–77, 179–82, 185, 188, 193, 195, 199, 200–201, 205–6, 210–11, 215–16, 218, 221
North Omahans, community of, 11, 13, 15, 22, 74, 86, 126, 140, 182, 195, 200

Oberg, Marvin, 18
O'Connor, Sandra Day, 197
O'Donnell, Patrick, 205
Odyssey West Magazine, 127
Office of Public Counsel (Ombudsman), 119
Oliver Hall, Deresa (Jaha), 115,
Olson, Paul, 208
Omaha, Nebraska, 3, 10, 53, 63, 104,
    24th Street, 10, 18, 22, 29, 43, 50, 52, 101, 142, 162, 176
    30th Street, 12, 17, 23, 52
    Ames Avenue, 12, 17, 139, 179
    Chamber of Commerce, 66, 95
    City Auditorium, 45, 48
    City Council, 28, 37, 44, 134, 140, 171–172, 181, 183, 201, 209, 214
    City of, xxi, 49, 66, 69, 85, 114, 120, 134, 144, 167, 178, 206, 213
    Community Foundation, 202
    Cuming Street, 11, 80
    Housing Authority, 85, 131, 142, 213
    Human Relations Board, 17, 44, 68, 195
    Human Rights Board, 85
    Lake Street, 73, 139, 144
    legal department, City of Omaha, 167
    Personnel Board, City of Omaha, 49, 67
    police administration, 152
    police court, 75
    police union (AFL-CIO), 60, 93, 161, 178
    public library, 195
    public safety department, 35
    public safety director, 35–36, 78, 141, 162–64
    public schools, 14, 85, 102
    police department (OPD), 23, 29, 44, 54, 56, 72, 109, 161, 178, 196
    race riot in (1919), 13
    school board, 12, 37, 74, 85, 87, 91, 102–03, 134, 180, 183, 199
    school district, 81, 114
"Omaha, City of Fascism" (essay), 53
Omaha Conditions Survey, 195
Omaha Human Relations Board, 17, 195
Omaha Metropolitan Utilities District, 164
Omaha National Bank, 20
Omaha Opportunities Industrialization Center, 87
Omaha Police Department Internal Affairs Division, 169
Omaha Public Schools Learning Community Council, 213, 221
Omaha Real Estate Board, 20
Omaha Star, 15, 18, 35, 75, 77, 114, 140, 145, 180, 200–201, 207, 209, 211, 213, 215, 217, 264n52
Omaha World Herald, 17, 41, 47, 65,

69–70, 76–77, 84–85, 90, 150, 157, 163, 168, 177, 179,
Organ, Claude H., 18, 35, 67, 76
Organ, Gregory M., 101
Osborne, Tom, 143
Otey, Harold Lamont, 190–92, 198
Owen, Alisha, 157
Owens, Talmadge, 162

Palestinian Liberation, 147
Pan African Congress, 117
Parks, Charles, 214
Parks, Vickey, 141, 170
Pattavina, Al, 78, 98, 164
Patterson, James, 144
Patton, Herb, 18
Paul, Ron, 175
Payne, Jessie, 113
Peace and Freedom Party, 39
Peak, Duane, 57
Peak, Frank, 39
Peak, William, 39
Pearson, Drew, 32
Penny, Paul, 124, 205
Penny, Quinzola, 205
Pepin, Al, 210
Persian Gulf War, 195
Person, Earle G., 84, 86
Phillips, Wilbur L., 18, 22
Pinkett, H.J., 11
Podhaisky, Frank, 22, 23
Poindexter, Ed, 39, 55, 57, 59, 206
police, xvii, 4, 9, 13, 16–17, 20, 22, 23–25, 29–33, 35, 37, 38, 66, 68–69, 72–73, 75, 78–79, 84, 86–87, 98–99, 101, 109–14, 116–18, 123, 130–32, 135, 139, 142, 144, 151–52, 156, 158, 176–79, 181–82, 195–96, 199–200, 206, 209–12, 215–16, 257n43, 258n74, 261n118, 264n52
  brutality, xix, 7, 21, 24–26, 36, 42–63, 68, 73, 92–93, 98, 110–14, 117, 152, 160–71, 186–87, 193, 201, 234n126, 247n50, 262n129
  community relations with, 16–17, 22, 24, 35, 177, 195
Police Practices and the Preservation of Civil Rights (pamphlet), 152
political action committees, 188
Polk, Donna, 113
Polk, Felix, 20
Posse Comitatus, 153, 182
Pottinger, J. Stanley, 102
Powell, James, 161
Pratt, Jason, 210
President's Commission on Civil Disorders, 20–21, 32–33, 38
Preston Love Music Scholarship, 221
Prince Hall Masons, 70
Project Excellence, 90
Proud, Richard, 91
Public Health and Welfare Committee, 133
"Public Pulse" (*Omaha World Herald*), 17, 191, 205

Quinn Chapel African Methodist Episcopal Church, 38

racism, 24, 26, 30, 38–39, 42, 45, 55, 60, 67–68, 70, 72, 75–76, 78–82, 84, 102, 109, 115–19, 123, 125, 130, 134–35, 143, 147–48, 149–50, 152, 170–71, 174, 179, 181, 185–86, 204–5, 208, 217, 219
Rae, Mollie, 207
Raglin, Jim, 183
Raikes, Ron, xxi, 213
Rainbow Coalition, 148
Rand Daily Mail, 122
Randolph, Cleveland, 110
Rasmussen, Dennis, 132–33
Reagan, Ronald, 121, 122, 140–141, 156, 187

Realities Magazine, 59, 62
Reeves, Randolph, 192
Republic of South Africa, 121, 125
Republican National Committee, 140
Republican Party, 4, 140, 155, 188
Resolution 43 (South African Resolution), 5, 121–23, 127
Reynolds, Everett, 29, 201, 206
Rice, David (Mondo we Langa), 33, 39, 55, 56, 72, 206
Riley, Lonetta, 104
Riverfront Development Project, 97–98
Robeson, Paul, 42
Robinson, John, 111
Robinson, Randall, 117–18, 185
Robinson, Renault, 186
Robinson, Smokey, 211
Rodgers, Johnny, 180
Roosevelt, Franklin D., 9
Rosenblatt, Steve, 161
Rountree, Carney, 86
Roe v. Wade, 108
Rowe, Virginia, 191
Rucker, Albert, 210
Rucker, C.H., 11

Sababu, Hadari (Kenneth Jackson), 115
Saint Benedict Church, 19, 201
St. John's African Methodist Episcopal (AME), xv, 19, 70, 77
Strategic Arms Limitation Treaty II (SALT II), 146
Saratoga School, 103
Sayers, Gayle, 23
Sayers, Roger W., 55, 95, 180
Schiermann, Jacob, 111
Schimek, DiAnna, 217
Schmit, Loran, 155–58, 173
Schnebel, Gary, 176, 178
School District Reorganization Bill (LB 1024), xxi, 214
Schultz, George, 123
Schwartzkopf, Sam, 110
Scottsbluff, 99, 119
Seale, Bobby, 53
Sears, Todd, 195
Sechaba (newspaper), 122
Secret Service, 148
Secretary of State, 97, 123, 192
segregation, xviii, 10, 14, 16, 18–20, 42–43, 61, 72, 75, 78, 99, 103, 110, 113, 116, 135
Senate Subcommittee on Africa, 118
Seventh Circuit Court of Appeals, 171
Seventh Day Adventist, 19
sexism, 107, 109, 124, 190
Shanks, Lela Knox, 139, 198, 208, 219
Shield, The, 161
Shipman Brothers Road Building Co., 11
Simon, Bernie, 177
Sims, Patricia, 139
Sixty Minutes (television program), 142
Skinner, Eugene, 86
Smith, Rudy, 16
Social Settlement House, 10
socialism, 37, 134
Sones Real Estate, 19
Sorensen, A.V. (Mayor), 7, 17, 26, 35, 38, 43–45, 67, 70, 162
Soto, José, 193
South Africa, xix, 5, 42–43, 46, 63, 115–18, 120–25, 149–51, 185, 197, 219
South African Black Consciousness Movement, 117
South African Government, 116, 120, 123
South African Resolution. *See* Resolution 43
South Omaha, 10–11, 13, 16, 66, 264n52
South Omaha Stockyards, xvi, 11
Southern Christian Leadership Conference, 37
Soweto Township, 117
Special Agent in Charge at Omaha, 30, 60, 181

Special Forces Unit of the Nebraska State Patrol, 152
Spencer Street Barbershop, 16, 23, 29, 30, 36, 44, 47, 52, 54, 75, 89, 101
Spire, Bob, 180
Spitznogle, Carol "Dolly," 112
Squire, Robert M., 159
St. Martin De Porres Center, 10, 18–19, 124, 176 (*See also* De Porres Club)
Standard, John, 75
Standifer, Stella, 163
Starkweather, Charles, 189
State of Nebraska Investment Council, 121
State of North Omaha, 176
Staton, Eddie, 144, 200
Stelly, Matthew, 163, 215–16
Stenberg, Don, 190
Stevenson, Howard, 48, 51
Stone Soul Picnic, 19
Stoops, Raymond, 30
Strong, Vivian, 48, 50–51, 53–54, 57–58, 63, 73
Stuckey, Sterling, 94
Study Commission on United States Policy Toward Southern Africa, 122
Study of the Nebraska Legal System, 131
Sullivan Principles, 122

Tambo, Oliver, 46, 117
Tarpley, McKinley, 20
Taylor, Marshall, 200
teachers, 10, 12, 14, 18, 25, 27, 34–35
Technical High School (Omaha), 14, 46–47, 101–03,
Theoharis, Jeanne, 3
Theopholis X, 7–8
Thomas, Ruth, 49
Thompson, Terry (Tariq Al Amin), 144, 164, 167
Thone, Charles, 97, 128, 151
Thornton, Alvin, 175
Thurston County, Nebraska, 153

Time for Burning, A (documentary film), 23
TransAfrica, 115, 118
Troia, Joseph, 211
two-party system, 219

Unicameral. *See* Nebraska Unicameral
Union Local Number Forty-Seven, 66
Union Pacific Railroad, xvi, 179,
United Methodist Church, 19, 45, 139, 144, 169
United Methodist Church Community Center Wesley House, 72, 95, 97, 144, 169, 177, 200
United Nations, 46, 115, 122, 149
United Nations Conference on Public Investment and South Africa, 124
United Nations Security Council, 115
United Nations Special Committee Against Apartheid, 124
United States, xvii, 4, 33, 38–39, 41–43, 45–46, 55, 62, 73, 93, 115–18, 122, 125, 127, 130, 145, 149, 160, 188
University of Alabama, 48
University of Nebraska at Omaha, xvi, 15, 29, 57–58, 94, 101, 115, 119, 123, 142, 174, 193, 195, 253n66
  Black Studies Department, 174
  Board of Regents, 94
  Medical Center, 57, 120
University of Nebraska Foundation, 208
University of Nebraska—Lincoln (UNL), 69, 110, 115, 124, 139, 142, 180, 182
Unmarked Human Burial Sites and Skeletal Remains Protection Act, 159
Urban Action Association, 49
Urban Housing Foundation, 95
Urban League (National), 10, 25, 68, 77, 95, 229n29,

Nebraska Urban League, 86, 95, 144, 178
Omaha Urban League, 10, 18, 66, 166
urban renewal, 4, 45
Urbom, Warren K. (Judge), 137, 143, 191
U.S. Army, xvi, 16, 26–28, 41
U.S. Attorney for District of Nebraska, 162
U.S. Attorney General, 28, 61, 157
U.S. Bureau of the Census, 195
U.S. Civil Rights Commission, 152
U.S. Congress, xvi, 25, 60, 213
U.S. Constitution, 15, 25, 27, 37, 90, 151, 154, 160, 170, 197, 212, 264n52
   Fifth Amendment, 62
   First Amendment, 210, 213
   Second Amendment, 182
U.S. Department of Health, Education, and Welfare Civil Rights Office, 85
U.S. Department of Housing and Urban Development, 67, 213
U.S. Department of Justice, 92, 102, 112, 162
U.S. Department of Labor, 77
U.S. District Court, 137, 190
U.S. House of Representatives, 82, 97, 129, 186
U.S. Justice Department, Midwest Region, 92
U.S. Military, 60
U.S. Post Office, 26, 28, 34
U.S. Senate, 45, 84, 97, 100, 175, 219
U.S. State Department, 123

U.S. Supreme Court, 14, 103, 108, 137–38, 197, 207

Van Pelt, Samuel, 153, 158
Varner, Durwood, 94
Veys, Al, 161
Vietnam War, 38–39, 89, 160
Von Malsen-Tiborch, Gabriele, 193
Voting Rights Act of 1965, 73

Wadman, Robert, 158, 167
Wahl, Jan, 139
Wallace, George, 31, 48
Wallwey, Elmer, 91
Walton, Don, 91, 133
Warner, Jerome, 79, 90, 100, 155
Warren, Thomas, 210, 215
Washington, Carl, 92
Washington, Charlie B., 15, 45, 75, 77, 86, 179–80, 195
Washington, Harold, 186
Washington, Marguerita, 213, 217,
Washington Post, 32, 196, 218
Washington Times, 156
Watkins, Bruce, 73
Watson, Kevin, 176–77
Watson, LaDonna, 178
Watts riot, 21, 49
Wead, Rodney, 95, 144, 169, 200
Wesley House, 72, 95, 97, 144, 169, 177, 200. *See also* United Methodist Church Community Center Wesley House
Wesley United Methodist Church, 19
Wesley, Don, 124

West Omaha Unitarian Church, 31
Westpoint (Mississippi), 8, 228
Wherry, Daniel, 111
white power, xix, 36, 49, 68, 71, 73, 101, 134, 152, 172, 200
White, Milton, 94
whites, 9, 13–14, 17–18, 20, 25–26, 28, 31–32, 34, 38, 41–44, 49, 55, 57–60, 65, 68, 71–72, 75–76, 78, 82, 84, 93, 95, 98, 101, 103, 115–17, 120 133, 135, 140, 144–45, 174, 177, 182, 206, 216, 218
Wilde, Oscar, 180
Wilder, Douglas, 129
Williams, Marian Danner, 71
Williams, Robert E., 191–92
Wilson, Alyce, 68
Wilson, Tommie, 201
Women's Rights Movement, 108, 135
Woodard, Komozi, 3
Woods Harris, Carole, 209
Woodson Center, 10–11, 68
Woodstock, 90
working class, xxii, 5, 6, 115, 133, 135, 148, 166, 173, 186, 188, 216, 217–18
World War II, 160
WOWTV, 19
write-in campaigns, 100, 175, 192

York, Nebraska, 87, 136, 181
Young Democrats, 174
Young, Andrew, 37, 146, 187
Young, Coleman, 186
Youngdahl, William, 23–24

Zionist, 149

About the Author

Tekla Agbala Ali Johnson, born in North Omaha, Nebraska, is assistant professor of history at Salem College in Winston-Salem, North Carolina.